Digital Images and Human Vision

INFORMATION AND LIBRARY SERVICES
UNIVERSITY OF WESTMINSTER
HARROW LRC CENTRE
WATFORD ROAD
NORTHWICK PARK
HARROW HA1 3TP

edited by Andrew B. Watson

Digital Images and Human Vision

A Bradford Book
The MIT Press
Cambridge, Massachusetts
London, England

© 1993 Massachusetts Institute of Technology
All rights reserved. No part of this book may be reproduced in any form
by any electronic or mechanical means (including photocopying, recording, or
information storage and retrieval) without permission in writing from the
publisher.

This book was set in Palatino by Asco Trade Typesetting Ltd., Hong Kong
and was printed and bound in the United States of America.

Library of Congress Cataloging-in-Publication Data

Digital images and human vision / edited by Andrew B. Watson.
    p.   cm.
  "A Bradford book."
  Includes bibliographical references and index.
  ISBN 0-262-23171-9
    1. Image processing—Digital techniques.   2. Coding theory.
3. Data compression (Telecommunications) 4. Vision. I. Watson,
Andrew B.
TA1637.D54   1993
621.36'7—dc20   93-19697
                                  CIP

Contents

Contributors

Albert J. Ahumada, Jr.
NASA Ames Research Center
Moffett Field, California

Erhardt Barth
Department of Telecommunications Engineering
Technical University
Munich, Germany

V. Michael Bove, Jr.
MIT Media Lab
Cambridge, Massachusetts

Gershon Buchsbaum
Department of Bioengineering
University of Pennsylvania
Philadelphia, Pennsylvania

Philippe M. Cassereau
3DO, Inc.
Palo Alto, California

Pamela C. Cosman
Electrical Engineering Department
Stanford University
Stanford, California

Scott Daly
Electronic Imaging Research Laboratories
Eastman Kodak Company
Rochester, New York

Michael P. Eckert
NASA Ames Research Center
Moffett Field, California

Bernd Girod
The Academy of Media Arts
Cologne, Germany

William E. Glenn
Department of Electrical Engineering
Florida Atlantic University
Boca Raton, Florida

Robert M. Gray
Electrical Engineering Department
Stanford University
Stanford, California

Paul J. Hearty
Advanced Television Evaluation Laboratory
Communication Research Center of Canada
Kanata, Ontario, Canada

Bradley Horowitz
MIT Media Lab
Cambridge, Massachusetts

Stanley A. Klein
School of Optometry
University of California, Berkeley
Berkeley, California

Jeffrey Lubin
David Sarnoff Research Center
Princeton, New Jersey

Cynthia H. Null
NASA Ames Research Center
Moffett Field, California

Karen L. Oehler
Electrical Engineering Department
Stanford University
Stanford, California

Alex Pentland
MIT Media Lab
Cambridge, Massachusetts

Todd R. Reed
Department of Electrical Engineering and
Computer Science
University of California, Davis
Davis, California

Andrew B. Watson
NASA Ames Research Center
Moffett Field, California

Bernhard Wegmann
Department of Telecommunication Engineering
Technical University
Munich, Germany

Christof Zetzsche
Department of Telecommunication Engineering
Technical University
Munich, Germany

Preface

We live in a visual age. The first revolution in popular culture and knowledge, enabled by the mass production of the printed word, has been superseded by a second revolution fueled by the broadcast electronic image. Although analog television and printed pictures have carried the first battles of this revolution, a second wave of this revolution is now upon us. The advent of *digital* image technology will allow the visual image to penetrate still further into our information environment. The inexorable advance of technology for the processing and display of electronic imagery has in recent years offered up the possibility of radically new means of communicating visual information. These new means range from commercial high-definition television (HDTV) to packet video, picturephone systems, teleconferencing, multimedia, high-density optical digital discs, so-called personal digital assistants, and advanced image communication systems for space, aeronautics, military, industrial, and commercial applications.

Bandwidth, memory, and computational resources are limiting factors for all these systems and in every instance directly affect their cost, quality, and practicality. A major goal must be to increase efficiency, which may be loosely defined as the ratio of image quality to costs in bandwidth, memory, and computation. Because the human eye is the final arbiter of image quality, it is essential to understand the human visual system in order to understand the ingredients of image quality. It is for this reason that there has been a growing appreciation of the need for vision science to be applied to the problem of image communications.

This book brings together a number of important ideas and perspectives on this issue. It does not presume to be exhaustive or to be the final word on this rapidly changing subject; but it does attempt to address some questions of the following sort:

• What are the key aspects of human visual sensitivity relevant to image communications?

- What are the leading problems in image communications on which vision science might bear?
- What mathematical models of human vision might be useful in the design of image communications systems?
- What are reliable and efficient methods of evaluating visual quality?
- Are there unexploited aspects of human vision than can provide substantial improvements in coding efficiency?

The contributions to this volume have been organized into three sections. The first section provides an introduction to some of the principles of image coding by examining several important coding methods. The chapters in the second section discuss in detail some visual factors that are relevant to image coding. The third section considers the problem of evaluating the quality of a coded image, using both experimental methods and computer models based on human vision.

This book is intended to educate, antagonize, and intrigue. It is addressed to those who are in a position to enhance the quality of the future generation of electronic image communication systems: electrical engineers, computer scientists, imaging scientists, experts in digital signal processing and image processing, and vision scientists. I hope that the reader will find herein something that will be of use.

The papers in this text were first presented at a workshop organized by the Committee on Vision of the National Research Council. The authors and editor express their thanks and appreciation to the committee for its interest in and support of this exciting research area in the visual sciences. I also thank Louis Silverstein of VCD Sciences, Inc. for his vital role in the genesis of both the workshop and this text.

Part I

Image Coding and Compression

The communication of visual information by electronic means requires that light be transformed into electrical signals. Furthermore, a two-, three-, or possibly four-dimensional light distribution must be transformed into a one-dimensional electrical signal. These transformations may be regarded as a coding process. In this book we focus almost exclusively on digital electrical signals, which allows us to abstract the conceptual and mathematical problem of image coding from the physical details of wires and voltages.

The most conventional method of digital representation of an image is in terms of a rectangular array of pixels, each representing the intensity (or color) of the image at a point. But from a mathematical point of view, this array is merely a collection of numbers that may be transformed in a wide variety of information-preserving ways. For example, one might represent the image in terms of the discrete Fourier transform (DFT) of the rectangle of pixels.

Selection of a representational scheme depends on many factors, but two general features are particularly important. The first is what we may call *convenience*: the ease of performing any image manipulations that are contemplated. For example, cutting, pasting, and painting are generally more difficult in a DFT representation than in a pixel representation. On the other hand, progressive transmission, edge enhancement, and image compression may be more easily achieved in the DFT representation. The second important feature is *efficiency*: the number of bits required to represent a particular image. Because images typically consume enormous amounts of memory, this feature has assumed a dominant role in coding decisions in many applications.

Efficiency of image representation is closely related to the notion of image compression. If an image represented in one form can be converted to another form that requires fewer bits, then we say that the image has been *compressed*. The most efficient representation is the one that is most compressed. If the transformation from one form to another is invertible, then the compression is said to be *lossless*. Lossless compression is possible because of redundancies in certain representations. For example, in a pixel representation of photographic images, nearby pixels tend to be highly correlated. Although they are important, current lossless compression techniques usually provide only modest amounts of compression, perhaps a factor of 2, in photographic images.

Further reduction in the size of image files is possible using *lossy* techniques. These transformations are not invertible. They are useful only because the human eye is insensitive to certain elements of images, so the loss of some image information can be tolerated. All the techniques discussed in this text are lossy. Because lossy techniques depend on human visual sensitivity for their success, it is interesting to examine some of these techniques to discover how they exploit the limitations of visual sensitivity, and the nature of visual coding.

I noted above some advantages of pixel-based and frequency-based image representations. It is interesting that many leading techniques use representations that are a compromise between these two extremes. Chapter 1 discusses a number of these so-called local frequency representations. Chapter 2 describes a particularly important class of local frequency representations: the wavelet transforms. These are of interest in part because the human visual brain appears to use a waveletlike code (Daugman, 1989; Watson, 1987; Watson, 1990; Watson and Ahumada, 1989). Wavelet codes and their relatives are also intriguing because they allow construction of *scalable* codes in which the resolution can be easily varied to suit different purposes (Watson, 1990). This is an instance of code convenience. Chapter 3 provides a look at one effort to implement an efficient and convenient scalable code for digital video.

Many prominent compression methods consist of a linear image transform followed by quantization of transform coefficients and lossless coding of the result. These are called *transform* codes. A rather different approach is *vector quantization*, in which each block of an image is replaced by one of a small set of possible substitutes. The substitutes form a *codebook*, which is derived by examination of some set of images. Gray, Cosman, and Oehler describe this powerful and general technique in chapter 4 and suggest some ways in which perceptual factors can be introduced into the process.

Fractals, because they generate such extraordinary complexity from simple rules, have been suggested as a technique for image compression. Published demonstrations of their value do not yet exist, but chapter 5 shows a way in which the fractal principle of self-similarity over scales may be exploited within the context of transform coding and vector quantization.

References

Daugman, J. G. (1989). Entropy reduction and decorrelation in visual coding by oriented neural receptive fields. *IEEE Transactions on Biomedical Engineering 36*(1), 107–114.

Watson, A. B. (1987). Efficiency of an image code based on human vision. *Journal of the Optical Society of America A 4*(12), 2401–2417.

Watson, A. B. (1990). Perceptual-components architecture for digital video. *Journal of the Optical Society of America A 7*(10), 1943–1954.

Watson, A. B. and Ahumada, A. J., Jr. (1989) A hexagonal orthogonal oriented pyramid as a model of image representation in visual cortex. *IEEE Transactions on Biomedical Engineering 36*(1), 97–106.

Local Frequency Representations for Image Sequence Processing and Coding

Todd R. Reed

Localization is an important process in visual perception, and it can be appreciated in an intuitive, nonrigorous sense based on daily experience. That we routinely assign locations to objects and surfaces in our field of view makes it clear that some type of spatial localization takes place in the visual system. That we also distinguish between various characteristics of objects and surfaces, such as the smoothness or roughness of surface texture, implies that there is localization in some type of feature domain, as well. Our assignment of these characteristics to specific objects and surfaces (regions in our field of view) implies that the process is joint, localizing simultaneously in the spatial and feature domains. We might refer to the representation of information underlying this process as a spatial/feature representation.

The determination of the exact nature of the features involved in visual perception is a classic problem. The ease with which surface characteristics and frequency content can be correlated, and the success of frequency analysis in modeling certain aspects of the visual system, make the use of some type of frequency decomposition attractive. This leads us to consider spatial/spatial-frequency representations, both for visual modeling and for the design of visual information systems.

A very large (essentially infinite) number of decompositions could be developed and plausibly referred to as spatial/spatial-frequency representations. The precise way in which the representation is local, and the degree to which this localization is relevant to vision and/or the design of systems for visual communication, provide one criterion for the selection of a specific representation. Unfortunately, as discussed below (and in greater detail in the literature, e.g., Stork and Wilson, 1990), there is not currently widespread agreement on which measures of localization are the most visually relevant. Furthermore, even given a measure, the formulation of a representation that is optimal with respect to that measure may not be straightforward.

However, the need for joint representations of various kinds has long been recognized in other fields. In some cases, these representations have been derived in completely different spaces (such as the position/momentum space in quantum mechanics), but they can be adapted to spatial/spatial-frequency analysis without great difficulty. As a result, many classic works in physics and communications (e.g., Wigner, 1932; Gabor, 1946) have enjoyed renewed interest.

Because these representations were developed for applications other than vision, it may well be that they are suboptimal either as models of visual perception or in vision-oriented applications. Nonetheless, we shall see that this general class of techniques shows promise for the analysis and design of image sequence processing and coding systems designed for human viewing, and we shall discuss the relevance of some specific joint representations to human vision.

Examples of Local Frequency Representations

In this section we consider three spatial/spatial-frequency representations that have been introduced in fields other than vision science: the finite-support Fourier transform, the Gabor representation, and the Wigner distribution. In addition to being classic techniques for the analysis of nonstationary phenomena, these methods illustrate a number of important issues relating to local representations in general.

The Finite-Support Fourier Transform

The short-time one-dimensional Fourier transform has long been used in the analysis of time-varying signals (e.g., Allen and Rabiner, 1977). The two-dimensional extension of this idea yields the finite-support Fourier transform

$$F_{x,y}(u, v) = \int_{-\infty}^{\infty} \int_{-\infty}^{\infty} f_{xy}(x', y')e^{-j(ux'+vy')}\,dx'\,dy', \qquad (1.1)$$

where

$$f_{xy}(x', y') = f(x', y')h(x - x', y - y'),$$

$f(x', y')$ is the original image, and $h(x - x', y - y')$ is a window centered at (x, y). The properties of the transform are heavily dependent on the properties of this window.

The finite-support Fourier transform has been used in a number of image-processing and computer vision applications. Examples include its use by Bajcsy and Lieberman (1976) for the extraction of texture features and by Pentland (1984) for the estimation of fractal dimension.

The Gabor Representation

The Gabor representation was first introduced for the one-dimensional case (Gabor, 1946). The functions upon which the representation is based are each formed by a product of a Gaussian window (centered at a particular point in time) and a complex exponential (frequency modulation term). It has been shown that under certain conditions a complete basis can be formed using these functions, which results in an invertible transform. This transform is not, however, orthogonal. The most obvious consequence of this is that the transform coefficients cannot be calculated by simply computing the inner products of the basis functions and the signal of interest (or, equivalently, by convolving with the basis functions and subsampling).

An image can be represented as the weighted sum of two-dimensional Gabor functions of the form

$$g(x, y) = \hat{g}(x, y)e^{j[u_0(x-x_0)+v_0(y-y_0)]}, \qquad (1.2)$$

where

$$\hat{g}(x, y) = \frac{1}{2\pi\sigma_x\sigma_y} e^{-\{[(x-x_0)/\sigma_x]^2 + [(y-y_0)/\sigma_y]^2\}/2}$$

is a two-dimensional Gaussian function, σ_x and σ_y determine the scale of the Gaussian along the respective axes, (x_0, y_0) is the center of the function in the spatial domain, and (u_0, v_0) is the center of support in the frequency domain. The Fourier transform of this class of functions is

$$G(u, v) = e^{-\frac{1}{2}(\sigma_x^2(u-u_0)^2 + \sigma_y^2(v-v_0)^2)}e^{j(x_0(u-u_0)+y_0(v-v_0))}. \qquad (1.3)$$

Because these functions are oriented (anisotropic), the resulting representation is four-dimensional.

If we denote by D the distance between the spatial centers of a basis formed by these functions, and the distance between their centers of support in the frequency domain as W, then the basis is complete if $W \cdot D = 2\pi$ (Porat and Zeevi, 1988). Because the constraint is on the product of these values, the selection of the sampling density in one domain determines the density in the other.

For example, a dense sampling in space can be selected at the expense of a sparse sampling in spatial frequency.

Daugman (1985) has shown that these functions achieve the lower limits of uncertainty imposed by the inequalities

$$\Delta x \cdot \Delta u \geq \frac{1}{2} \tag{1.4}$$

and

$$\Delta y \cdot \Delta v \geq \frac{1}{2} \tag{1.5}$$

Δx, Δy, Δu, and Δv are the effective widths of the functions in the spatial (x, y) and spatial-frequency (u, v) domains:

$$(\Delta x)^2 = \frac{\int_{-\infty}^{\infty} \int_{-\infty}^{\infty} (x - x_0)^2 g(x, y) g^*(x, y) \, dx \, dy}{\int_{-\infty}^{\infty} \int_{-\infty}^{\infty} g(x, y) g^*(x, y) \, dx \, dy}, \tag{1.6}$$

$$(\Delta u)^2 = \frac{\int_{-\infty}^{\infty} \int_{-\infty}^{\infty} (u - u_0)^2 G(u, v) G^*(u, v) \, du \, dv}{\int_{-\infty}^{\infty} \int_{-\infty}^{\infty} G(u, v) G^*(u, v) \, du \, dv}, \tag{1.7}$$

$$(\Delta y)^2 = \frac{\int_{-\infty}^{\infty} \int_{-\infty}^{\infty} (y - y_0)^2 g(x, y) g^*(x, y) \, dx \, dy}{\int_{-\infty}^{\infty} \int_{-\infty}^{\infty} g(x, y) g^*(x, y) \, dx \, dy}, \tag{1.8}$$

and

$$(\Delta v)^2 = \frac{\int_{-\infty}^{\infty} \int_{-\infty}^{\infty} (v - v_0)^2 G(u, v) G^*(u, v) \, du \, dv}{\int_{-\infty}^{\infty} \int_{-\infty}^{\infty} G(u, v) G^*(u, v) \, du \, dv}. \tag{1.9}$$

As in the completeness constraint discussed above, the uncertainty equalities constrain the products of the effective widths in the two domains. As a result, for example, basis functions that are highly localized in space (with small values of Δx and Δy) can be selected at the expense of a low degree of selectivity in the spatial-frequency domain (large Δu and Δv). This is accomplished by selecting appropriate values of σ_x and σ_y (which do not affect the completeness of the basis).

Through the selection of sampling densities (W or D) and the scale of Gaussian used in the basis (σ_x and σ_y), then, the spatial locality of the representation can be traded against its spatial-frequency selectivity.

As noted by Clark et al. (1987), and earlier by Kulikowski et al. (1982), the Gabor functions can be written in the form

$$g(x, y) = g_c(x, y) + j g_s(x, y), \tag{1.10}$$

where

$$g_c(x, y) = \hat{g}(x, y) \cos(u_0 x)$$

and

$$g_s(x, y) = \hat{g}(x, y) \sin(u_0 x),$$

where for simplicity we have set x_0, y_0, and v_0 to 0. It can be seen that $g_c(x, y)$ and $g_s(x, y)$ differ only by a shift in phase of $\pi/2$.

Pollen and Ronner (1981) have observed that at least some simple cells in the visual cortex of the cat are arranged in pairs, with the members of each pair having the same orientation and spatial frequency tuning but with phase responses differing by approximately $\pi/2$. That the respective members of each pair are in quadrature phase has been cited as supporting evidence that the cell pairs correspond to the real and imaginary parts of complex Gabor receptive fields. It has also been demonstrated (Marčelja, 1980; Daugman, 1985; Webster and DeValois, 1985; Field and Tolhurst, 1986; Jones and Palmer, 1987) that the Gabor functions agree reasonably well with receptive-field profiles measured for simple cells in the cat striate cortex.

Gabor filters (filters with Gabor functions as impulse responses) have been employed in many applications recently, notably in the area of texture segmentation. One of the earlier uses in this area was by Clark et al. (1987). More recently, the correlation between human performance in texture segmentation tasks and that predicted using Gabor-based models has been studied (Sutter et al., 1989; Malik and Perona, 1990; Landy and Bergen, 1991; Graham et al. 1992). Texture discrimination based on Gabor phase has been investigated by du Buf (1990) and du Buf and Heitkamper (1991).

The Wigner Distribution

The Wigner distribution, shown here in its original one-dimensional form,

$$W_f(x, \omega) = \int_{-\infty}^{\infty} f\left(x + \frac{\alpha}{2}\right) f^*\left(x - \frac{\alpha}{2}\right) \cdot e^{-j\omega\alpha} \, d\alpha, \tag{1.11}$$

was introduced in 1932 to characterize the quantum-mechanical duality between the position and the momentum of a particle (Wigner, 1932). The Wigner distribution was later suggested by J. Ville (1948) for signal analysis. The one-dimensional Wigner distribution has been applied in a number of areas, including speech analysis (Bartelt et al., 1980) and optics (Bastiaans, 1978, 1979).

Extending the preceding definition to two dimensions, we define the two-dimensional Wigner distribution as

$$W_f(x, y, u, v) = \int_{-\infty}^{\infty} \int_{-\infty}^{\infty} f\left(x + \frac{\alpha}{2}, y + \frac{\beta}{2}\right)$$
$$\times f^*\left(x - \frac{\alpha}{2}, y - \frac{\beta}{2}\right) \cdot e^{-j(\alpha u + \beta v)} \, d\alpha \, d\beta,$$

(1.12)

where the asterisk denotes complex conjugation. The Wigner distribution is similarly defined in terms of the Fourier transform of $f(x, y)$ as

$$W_f(x, y, u, v) = \frac{1}{4\pi^2} \int_{-\infty}^{\infty} \int_{-\infty}^{\infty} F\left(u + \frac{\eta}{2}, v + \frac{\xi}{2}\right)$$
$$\times F^*\left(u - \frac{\eta}{2}, v - \frac{\xi}{2}\right) \cdot e^{j(\eta x + \xi y)} \, d\eta \, d\xi.$$

(1.13)

It should be noted that the Wigner distribution is real valued and therefore lacks the explicit phase component present in, for example, the Fourier transform. Nonetheless, the image can be recovered (to within a constant factor) from its Wigner distribution. This indicates that phase information is implicitly present in this representation. The use of this distribution for two-dimensional and three-dimensional image processing, and as a potential model of visual perception, was first advanced by Jacobson and Wechsler (1982, 1984, 1987).

The Wigner distribution itself is not, in general, computable, and various discrete approximations exist. These approximations are sometimes referred to as pseudo-Wigner distributions. An example of such an approximation, used by Reed and Wechsler (1990, 1991) in a number of texture segmentation and perceptual grouping experiments, is shown in equation 1.14:

$$PW(m, n, p, q)$$
$$= 4 \sum_{k=-N_2+1}^{N_2-1} \sum_{l=-N_1+1}^{N_1-1} h_{N_1, N_2}(k, l)$$
$$\cdot \sum_{r=-M_2+1}^{M_2-1} \sum_{s=-M_1+1}^{M_1-1} g_{M_1, M_2}(r, s)$$
$$\cdot f(m + r + k, n + s + l)$$
$$\cdot f^*(m + r - k, n + s - l)e^{-j(2\pi kp/P + 2\pi lq/Q)},$$

(1.14)

where $p = 0, \pm 1, \ldots, \pm(N_2 - 1)$, $q = 0, \pm 1, \ldots,$

$\pm(N_1 - 1)$, $P = 2N_2 - 1$, $Q = 2N_1 - 1$, m and n are integers, and the functions $h_{N_1, N_2}(k, l)$ and $g_{M_1, M_2}(r, s)$ are window functions.

It is interesting to note that the spectrogram, the Gabor power representation (the squared magnitudes of the finite-support Fourier transform and Gabor representation, respectively) and the Wigner distribution are all members of the more general Cohen class of distributions (Cohen, 1966). Furthermore, it can be shown that the spectrogram and Gabor power representation are smoothed versions of the Wigner distribution. For a comprehensive review of these ideas applied to time-frequency analysis, see Cohen (1989). Some recent work in the design of smoothing kernels for time-frequency distributions can be found in Jeong (1992).

That the Gabor representation is widely considered to have optimal joint resolution but that its squared modulus (which would be expected to have the same resolution characteristics as the complex representation) can be expressed as a smoothed Wigner distribution illustrates that the evaluation of resolution is not a straightforward process and bears further examination.

Joint Resolution

A key issue in comparing joint spatial/spatial-frequency representations is the resolution that can be attained (simultaneously) in the two domains. The uncertainty principle dictates that arbitrarily high resolution cannot be achieved in both domains. Joint resolution can range from singular functions in one domain (with infinite extent in the other domain) to the reverse (e.g., the pixel representation at one extreme, the Fourier transform at the other). The impact of this principle has been considered for image-processing applications by Wilson and Granlund (1984).

Despite the importance of resolution in evaluating these representations, there is not widespread agreement on the most appropriate resolution measure. As mentioned previously, it has been found that the class of Gabor filters achieve the lower limit of uncertainty as measured by the product of effective widths in the spatial and spectral domains. In this case the uncertainty is measured separately along each dimension of the joint spatial/spatial-frequency representation. This approach is most suitable when the signal of interest is separable, which is in general not the case. Furthermore, it is applied to the individual components of the decomposition (the individual basis functions) rather than to the decomposition itself. In an attempt to address these issues, Jacobson and Wechsler (1988) have proposed the use of a joint entropy-based measure (derived in the joint Cartesian ($s \times sf$) domain rather than over each dimension separately), previously introduced by Leipnik (1959, 1960).

What the most visually relevant measure (or measures) of joint resolution might be is also an open question. As discussed by Stork and Wilson (1990), there are potentially a very large number of definitions of resolution, only some of which are satisfying from the standpoint of visual perception. The idea of visual relevance itself may vary with the application. It could mean that the measure is the same one for which the human visual system is optimal (if indeed such a measure exists). More to the point for image coding, however, is the criterion that leads to the most efficient representation, providing the best perceived image quality for the least amount of information. The two views of relevance may or may not lead to the same measure.

Although the most appropriate definition of joint resolution may not always be obvious, it is clear that it is an important characteristic. Its effect in image and image sequence coding is considered in the following section.

Application to Image and Image Sequence Coding

Three primary mechanisms are utilized in the design of image and image sequence compression systems (a generic form of which is shown in figure 1.1). The first is the local correlation between pixels in the image or sequence. This property of image data is widely recognized and used. The second is the bounded frequency response of the human visual system, as characterized by its contrast sensitivity function (CSF). This effect, too, is widely used, particularly in the formulation of quantization rules in transform and subband coders. The third is visual masking, in which visual sensitivity is reduced in the vicinity of edges. This property of the visual system, although well known, is not as effectively utilized in most existing coding techniques.

The joint resolution of the representation that forms the basis of the coder affects directly its ability to exploit these mechanisms. To take advantage of local spatial correlation, the representation itself must be spatially local. If the CSF is to be used, for example, to coarsely quantize high-frequency transform coefficients, then the basis functions of the transform must be sufficiently localized in the spatial-frequency domain so that the effects of the quantization are not seen at lower frequencies, where the visual system is more sensitive. Finally, if advantage is to be taken of the effect of visual masking, then errors (which are typically induced by edges) must be constrained to the neighborhoods of the edges. This requires spatial localization as in the exploitation of local correlation, but of a greater degree. The effect of masking decreases rapidly with distance from the edge, (Hentea and Algazi, 1984) so errors must be held to within a few pixels of the edge.

To illustrate these points, we shall consider the case of image coding based on the discrete cosine transform. Although this transform is not itself local, in coding applications it is typically applied over subblocks of the image. As we shall see, the result is a transform very similar in nature to the finite-support Fourier transform. We can therefore discuss this "finite-support discrete cosine transform" within the general framework of spatial/spatial-frequency representations.

Discrete Cosine Transform Based Coding

The discrete cosine transform (DCT), shown below, is widely used in transform coding, due to its good energy compaction properties (that is, the concentration of energy in a relatively few coefficients in the transform domain) and ease of implementation.

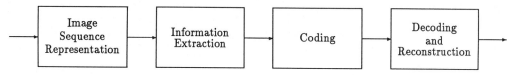

Figure 1.1
A generic image sequence coding system.

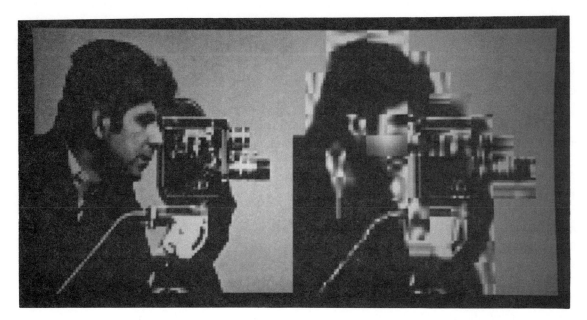

Figure 1.2
The original (left) and compressed and reconstructed images (right), using baseline JPEG compression and a quality factor of 1 (31:1 compression).

$$F(u, v) = \frac{4c(u, v)}{N^2} \sum_{m=0}^{N-1} \sum_{n=0}^{N-1} f(m, n) \cos \frac{(2m + 1)u\pi}{2N}$$

$$\cdot \cos \frac{(2n + 1)v\pi}{2N}$$

$$u, v = 0, 1, \ldots, N - 1,$$

where

$$c(u, v) = \begin{cases} \frac{1}{2} & \text{for } u = v = 0 \\ 1 & \text{otherwise.} \end{cases}$$

Under the assumption that the input image can be modeled as a first-order Markov process, the energy compaction performance of the DCT approaches that of the Karhunen-Loève transform, while having basis functions that are image independent. These basis functions are not, however, spatially localized. Since exploitation of local correlation in images is one of the main mechanisms for compression, the DCT is typically calculated over subblocks of the image, thereby imposing some degree of locality. The result is a finite-support DCT (analogous to the finite-support Fourier transform) with a rectangular window function.

Within each block, joint resolution is at the extreme of singular functions in the frequency domain and extends infinitely (to the boundary of the block) in the spatial domain. This greatly simplifies the utilization of the effect of the CSF, since high-frequency coefficients can be coarsely quantized with no "leakage" to lower frequencies. However, the lack of spatial locality implies that errors due to an event anywhere within the block are propagated without attenuation throughout the block. Consequently, errors due to edges are spread over the block (not localized to the vicinity of the edge), so that visual masking is not well exploited. In addition, this can cause block boundaries to become visible at relatively modest compression ratios.

These effects are illustrated in figures 1.2 through 1.4, where we have applied the baseline JPEG compression method (which is DCT based) (Pennebaker and Mitchell, 1993) at various compression ratios. The original image is 256 × 256 pixels in size. A 100 × 100 pixel portion of the image has been magnified for display. In each case the original image is on the left, the compressed and reconstructed image on the right. In figure 1.2, the lowest quality level (a quality factor of 1) has been used, resulting in a compression ratio of about 31:1. This clearly shows the locations of the blocks in the image. In figure 1.3 we have increased the quality factor to the more useful value of 32, for a compression ratio of about 5:1. The overall image quality is relatively good; however, in the presence of high-contrast edges the spread of errors throughout the associated blocks can be seen. This effect is still noticeable at the relatively high quality factor of 50 (figure 1.4), with

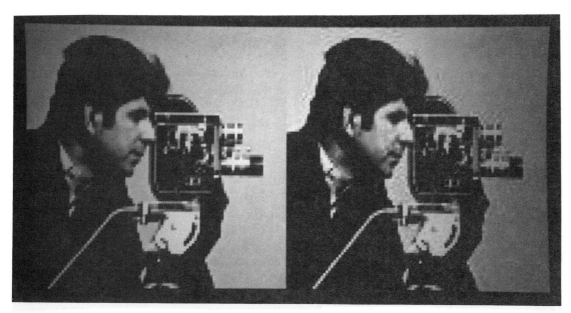

Figure 1.3
The original and reconstructed images for a quality factor of 32 (5:1 compression).

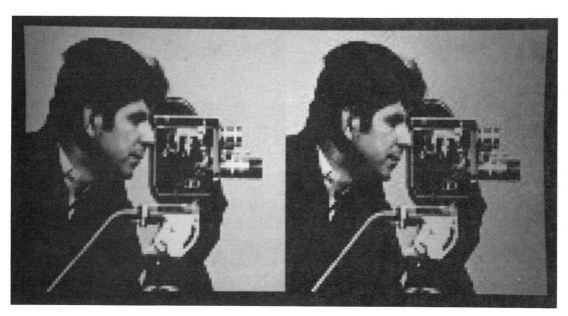

Figure 1.4
The original and reconstructed images for a quality factor of 50 (4:1 compression).

a compression ratio of slightly less than 4:1. It should be emphasized, of course, that the viewing conditions implied by the magnification of the respective subimages are equivalent to fairly close inspection of the associated image. At greater viewing distances the effect is correspondingly less noticeable.

Future Directions

We have seen in the previous example that the joint resolution of the representation upon which a coding method is based can have a strong effect on the performance of the method. From this example it is clear that a balance must be struck between resolution in the spatial and spatial-frequency domains. The precise nature of this balance, and how it is best quantified, remain to be determined.

A balance between resolution in the two domains, leading to a high joint resolution (by at least one measure), is one of the factors that makes the Gabor functions interesting for the representation of images, particularly for coding. Although the perceptual relevance of the measure of localization is debatable, these functions are nonetheless highly localized in both space and spatial frequency. They form a complete basis, making perfect reconstruction of the image possible, when necessary. Although the basis is nonorthogonal, the computation of the Gabor decomposition is substantially simpler than, for example, the various approximations to the Wigner distribution. That these functions agree, at least in general, with measured receptive field profiles is also interesting.

Preliminary results (Ebrahimi et al., 1990a, 1990b) indicate that the Gabor functions are indeed useful for coding, at least for cases where high compression ratios (e.g., over 200:1 for image sequences) and modest image quality are required (such as in the 64 kbit/sec transmission of image sequences). As expected, the resulting images do not exhibit the blocking artifacts demonstrated in the preceding examples, due to the inherent spatial locality of the Gabor functions. The use of these functions for high-quality image and sequence compression and the degree to which masking and the characteristics of the CSF can be exploited using a Gabor decomposition are topics of current research.

An additional area for future investigation is the treatment of motion in image sequences using local frequency representations. In the preceding discussion, we considered the coding of images and sequences as a frame-by-frame process. For applications in which complex sequences must be compressed substantially yet reproduced with high quality, motion must be explicitly taken into account.

Two possible approaches are motion-compensated prediction (e.g., as proposed in CCITT Recommendation H.261 or the upcoming MPEG I standard) and the processing of the image sequence as a three-dimensional (spatiotemporal) volume of data. The first approach is relatively simple, is widely used, and has the substantial practical advantage that it can be implemented without storing several frames. The second approach, although more complicated from the standpoint of implementation, has some interesting features.

First, processing the image sequence as spatiotemporal data allows the characteristics of motion in the frequency domain to be exploited. Watson and Ahumada (1983) have shown that an image undergoing uniform translational motion occupies a tilted plane in the spatiotemporal-frequency domain. In essence, this can be considered as the compression of the three-dimensional volume of data into a two-dimensional plane. This is one motivation for the use of various three-dimensional spatiotemporal-frequency (stf) decomposition methods in image sequence coding (e.g., Karlsson and Vetterli, 1988). The use of stf decompositions also provides a more convenient framework than motion compensation for the incorporation of models of spatiotemporal perception. An example of such a system that is particularly notable for its extensive use of models of human perception has been proposed by Watson (1990).

The case of uniformly translational motion is of course a special one, and as motion becomes more complex, the clustering in the stf domain decreases. However, if an image sequence is examined over a suitably local region in space and time, locally translational motion becomes a reasonable approximation. As the region examined becomes more local, the clustering of energy in the vicinity of a plane in the stf domain can be expected to increase, approaching the ideal case in the limit. This feature is exploited to some extent in stf decompositions when the spatiotemporal extent of their filters is small. Because they can provide a large degree of spatiotemporal locality and spatiotemporal-frequency selectivity simultaneously (within the bounds of uncertainty), spatiotemporal/spatiotemporal-frequency (st/stf) representations (the extension of local frequency representations to include time) should prove particularly useful. Their use retains the advantage of stf decompositions as well, in that perceptual models can be used in a more straightforward fashion than in the case of motion compensation. Finally, by explicitly enforcing localization in the temporal dimension, st/stf representations should also allow improved exploitation of temporal masking, a phenomenon not widely utilized in present systems.

Conclusions

Local frequency representations are an interesting and powerful framework for the analysis, processing, and coding of images and image sequences. By integrating both spatial (or spatiotemporal) locality and spatial-frequency (or spatiotemporal-frequency) selectivity, they provide a means to account for phenomena in both domains. Furthermore, through the proper choice of basis functions (in the case of linear representations), the integration of perceptual models can be accomplished in a relatively convenient manner. Because of their ability to exploit local image correlation while localizing edge-induced coding error without blocking artifacts and while maintaining locality in the spatial-frequency or spatiotemporal-frequency domain, representations with high joint resolution are promising candidates for use in future coding systems.

References

Allen, J. B., and Rabiner, L. R. (1977). A unified approach to short-time Fourier analysis and synthesis. *Proceedings of the IEEE* 65(11):1558–1564.

Bajcsy, R., and Lieberman, L. (1976). Texture gradient as a depth cue. *Computer Graphics and Image Processing* 5:52–67.

Bartelt, H. O., Brenner, K. H., and Lohmann, A. W. (1980). The Wigner distribution function and its optical production. *Optics Communications* 32(1):32–38.

Bastiaans, M. J. (1978). The Wigner distribution function applied to optical signals and systems. *Optics Communications* 25(1):26–30.

Bastiaans, M. J. (1979). Wigner distribution function and its application to first-order optics. *Journal of the Optical Society of America* 69(12):1710–1716.

Clark, M., Bovik, A. C., and Geisler, W. S. (1987). Texture segmentation using a class of narrow-band filters. *Proceedings of International Conference on Acoustics, Speech and Signal Processing* 14.6.1– 14.6.4.

Cohen, L. (1966). Generalized phase-space distribution functions. *Journal of Mathematical Physics* 7(5):781–786.

Cohen, L. (1989). Time-frequency distributions: A review. *Proceedings of the IEEE* 77(7):941–981.

Daugman, J. G. (1985). Uncertainty relation for resolution in space, spatial frequency, and orientation optimized by two-dimensional visual cortical filters. *Journal of the Optical Society of America A* 2(7):1160–1169.

du Buf, J. M. H. (1990). Gabor phase in texture discrimination. *Signal Processing* 21:221–240.

du Buf, J. M. H., and Heitkamper, P. (1991). Texture features based on Gabor phase. *Signal Processing* 23:227–244.

Ebrahimi, T., Reed, T. R., and Kunt, M. (1990a). Sequence coding by Gabor decomposition. In *Signal Processing V: Theories and Applications, Proceedings of EUSIPCO-90*, ed. J. Torres, E. Masgrau, and M. Lagunas, 769–772, Barcelona, Spain. Elsevier Science Publishers B.V. (North-Holland).

Ebrahimi, T., Reed, T. R., and Kunt, M. (1990b). Video coding using a pyramidal Gabor expansion. In *Proceedings of Visual Communications and Image Processing '90*, 489–502, Lausanne, Switzerland.

Field, D. J., and Tolhurst, D. J. (1986). The structure and symmetry of simple-cell receptive-field profiles in the cat's visual cortex. *Proceedings of the Royal Society of London* 228(1253):379–400.

Gabor, D. (1946). Theory of communication. *Proceedings of the Institute of Electrical Engineers* 93(26):429–457.

Graham, N., Beck, J., and Sutter, A. (1992). Nonlinear processes in spatial-frequency channel models of perceived texture segregation: Effects of sign and amount of contrast. *Vision Research* 32(4):719–743.

Hentea, T. A., and Algazi, V. R. (1984). Perceptual models and the filtering of high-contrast achromatic images. *IEEE Transactions on Systems, Man, and Cybernetics*, SMC-14(2):230–246.

Jacobson, L., and Wechsler, H. (1982). A paradigm for invariant object recognition of brightness, optical flow and binocular disparity images. *Pattern Recognition Letters* 1:61–68.

Jacobson, L., and Wechsler, H. (1984). A theory for invariant object recognition in the frontoparallel plane. *IEEE Transactions on Pattern Analysis and Machine Intelligence* 6(3):325–331.

Jacobson, L., and Wechsler, H. (1987). Derivation of optical flow using a spatiotemporal-frequency approach. *Computer Vision, Graphics, and Image Processing* 38:29–65.

Jacobson, L., and Wechsler, H. (1988). Joint spatial/spatial-frequency representation. *Signal Processing* 14(1):37–68.

Jeong, J., and Williams, W. J. (1992). Kernel design for reduced interference distributions. *IEEE Transactions on Signal Processing* 40(2):402–412.

Jones, J. P., and Palmer, L. A. (1987). An evaluation of the two-dimensional Gabor filter model of simple receptive fields in cat striate cortex. *Journal of Neurophysiology* 58(6):1233–1258.

Karlsson, G., and Vetterli, M. (1988). Three-dimensional sub-band coding of video. In *Proceedings of the IEEE International Conference on Acoustics, Speech, and Signal Processing*, 1100–1103, New York.

Kulikowski, J. J., Marcelja, S., and Bishop, P. O. (1982). Theory of spatial position and spatial frequency relations in the receptive fields of simple cells in the visual cortex. *Biological Cybernetics*, 43:187–198.

Landy, M. S., and Bergen, J. R. (1991). Texture segregation and orientation gradient. *Vision Research*, 31(4):679–691.

Leipnik, R. (1959). Entropy and the uncertainty principle. *Information and Control* 2:64–79.

Leipnik, R. (1960). The extended entropy uncertainty principle. *Information and Control* 3:18–25.

Malik, J., and Perona, P. (1990). Preattentive texture descrimination with early vision mechanisms. *Journal of the Optical Society of America A* 7(5):923–932.

Marčelja, S. (1980). Mathematical description of the responses of simple cortical cells. *Journal of the Optical Society of America*, 70(11):1297–1300.

Pennebaker, W. B., and Mitchell, J. L. (1993) *JPEG Still Image Data Compression Standard* Van Nostrand Reinhold, New York.

Pentland, A. P. (1984). Fractal-based description of natural scenes. *IEEE Transactions on Pattern Analysis and Machine Intelligence*, 6(6):661–674.

Pollen, D. A., and Ronner, S. F. (1981). Phase relationships between adjacent simple cells in the visual cortex. *Science* 212:1409–1411.

Porat, M., and Zeevi, Y. Y. (1988). The generalized Gabor scheme of image representation in biological and machine vision. *IEEE Transactions on Pattern Analysis and Machine Intelligence* 10(4):452–468.

Reed, T. R., and Wechsler, H. (1990). Segmentation of textured images and Gestalt organization using spatial/spatial-frequency representations. *IEEE Transactions on Pattern Analysis and Machine Intelligence* 12(1):1–12.

Reed, T. R., and Wechsler, H. (1991). Spatial/spatial-frequency representations for image segmentation and grouping. *Image and Vision Computing* 9(3):175–193.

Stork, D. G., and Wilson, H. R. (1990). Do Gabor functions provide appropriate descriptions of visual cortical receptive fields? *Journal of the Optical Society of America A* 7(8):1362–1373.

Sutter, A., Beck, J., and Graham, N. (1989). Contrast and spatial variables in texture segregation: Testing a simple spatial-frequency channels model. *Perception and Psychophysics* 46(4):312–332.

Ville, J. (1948). Théorie et applications de la notion de signal analytique. *Cable et Transmission* 2(1):61–74.

Watson, A. B. (1990). Perceptual-components architecture for digital video. *Journal of the Optical Society of America A* 7(10):1943–1954.

Watson, A. B., and Ahumada, A. J. (1983). A look at motion in the frequency domain. In *SIGGRAPH/SIGART Interdisciplinary Workshop MOTION: Representation and Perception*, 1–10, Toronto, Canada.

Webster, M. A., and De Valois, R. L. (1985). Relationship between spatial-frequency and orientation tuning of striate-cortex cells. *Journal of the Optical Society of America* 2(7):1124–1132.

Wigner, E. (1932). On the quantum correction for thermodynamic equilibrium. *Physical Review* 40:749–759.

Wilson, R., and Granlund, G. H. (1984). The uncertainty principle in image processing. *IEEE Transactions on Pattern Analysis and Machine Intelligence* 6(6):758–767.

2

Wavelet-based Image Coding

Philippe M. Cassereau

The wavelet transform of an image is a multiresolution and multiscale representation of that image. The resolution of an image is related to the bandwidth or frequency content of the signal. As the resolution increases, the amount of detail visible in the image increases. For an image that is a digitally sampled representation of an analog image, the resolution of the signal is represented by the number of samples in the image only if the signal is critically sampled (sampled at its Nyquist rate). The scale of an image is related to the size or length of the signal. At large scales, the signal is contracted. At small scales, the signal is dilated. In practice, the scale of a digital image is represented by the number of samples of the image in one dimension. For example, doubling the vertical and horizontal scales of an image results in a quarter-size duplicate of the original. If the signal is oversampled, increasing the scale (i.e., down-sampling) may not change the resolution. For the wavelet transform of a critically sampled signal, scale and resolution are inversely proportional.

Multiscale, multiresolution image representations have received considerable attention in the area of computer vision [16] and image coding. Because the human visual system appears to be multiresolution in nature, these techniques seem to make sense from a perceptual point of view [13]. Multiresolution techniques for image coding have mostly been of two different types: subband coding [8], [19], [24], and pyramid coding [1], [4], [17]. Wavelet theory was developed for multiresolution signal representation [12], [13]. The discovery of compactly supported wavelets [5] related wavelet theory with the signal-processing theory of multirate finite impulse response (FIR), filters and perfect reconstruction filter banks [18], [20], [21], [22].

We present the fundamental aspects of the theory of dyadic wavelets. We describe how the discrete case of the wavelet transform can be computed using a perfect reconstruction filter bank. Finally, we present the application of a two-dimensional wavelet transform to the coding of images. In this case, wavelet image coding is a special case of subband coding [2], [26]. In this chapter we illustrate this method of image compression.

The Continuous Wavelet Transform

We present here only the fundamentals of dyadic wavelet theory. For a more detailed study, [5], [12], and [13] are very good references. We also restrict ourselves to the study of multiplier 2 (or dyadic) wavelets. Higher multiplier wavelet systems do exist and fall within the more general theory of multirate filter banks. We also consider here only one-dimensional filters. Multidimensional wavelet systems also exist [19].

A set of real coefficients $\{a_k\}$ is a set of scaling function coefficients if the following constraints are satisfied:

$$\sum_k a_k = 2, \tag{2.1}$$

$$\sum_k a_k a_{k+2l} = 2\delta(l). \tag{2.2}$$

Constraint (2.2) means that

$$\sum_k a_k^2 = 2$$

and

$$\sum_k a_k a_{k+2l} = 0,$$

for any integer shift l not equal to zero. This constraint guarantees orthogonality.

Given a set of scaling coefficients $\{a_k\}$, the scaling function $\varphi(x)$ is defined implicitly as follows:

$$\varphi(x) = \sum_k a_k \varphi(2x - k). \tag{2.3}$$

The function $\varphi(2x)$ is the function $\varphi(x)$ scaled by 2, contracted by a factor of 2. Equation (2.3) means that a scaling function is one that can be represented by a linear combination of itself, translated and contracted by 2. Many such functions exist. The simplest scaling function is $\varphi(x) = 1$ for $0 \leq x < 1$, and $\varphi(x) = 0$ otherwise. It is clear that

$$\varphi(x) = \varphi(2x) \quad \text{for } 0 \leq x < \tfrac{1}{2},$$

$$\varphi(x) = \varphi(2x - 1) \quad \text{for } \tfrac{1}{2} \leq x < 1. \tag{2.4}$$

Thus, $\varphi(x) = \varphi(2x) + \varphi(2x - 1)$, and $a_0 = a_1 = 1$; all other a_k's are equal to zero. Note that constraints (2.1) and (2.2) are also satisfied.

The wavelet function $\psi(x)$ is explicitly defined as a linear combination of the translated and scaled scaling function $\varphi(x)$:

$$\psi(x) = \sum_k (-1)^k a_{k+1} \varphi(2x + k). \tag{2.5}$$

In equation 2.4, $\psi(x) = \varphi(2x) - \varphi(2x - 1)$. In other words,

$$\psi(x) = 1 \quad \text{for } 0 \leq x < \tfrac{1}{2},$$
$$\psi(x) = -1 \quad \text{for } \tfrac{1}{2} \leq x < 1. \tag{2.6}$$

The preceding example is known as the Haar wavelet.

Define $\psi_{jk}(x) = 2^{j/2}\psi(2^j x - k)$, for integers j, k. The set $\{\psi_{jk}(x)\}$ is the set of translated and scaled wavelet functions $\psi(x)$. Under the scaling coefficients constraints (2.1) and (2.2), one can demonstrate that $\{\psi_{jk}\}$ is an orthonormal basis of $L^2(R)$, [5] and [12]. Therefore, if $f(x)$ is a square integrable function, $f(x)$ can be uniquely expressed in terms of the functions $\psi_{jk}(x)$:

$$f(x) = \sum_j \sum_k c_{jk} \psi_{jk}(x), \tag{2.7}$$

where the coefficients c_{jk} are computed as follows:

$$c_{jk} = \int_{-\infty}^{\infty} f(x) 2^{j/2} \psi(2^j x - k) \, dx = \int_{-\infty}^{\infty} f(x) \psi_{jk}(x) \, dx. \tag{2.8}$$

The c_{jk}'s for integers j, k are the wavelet coefficients of $f(x)$.

Define $\varphi_l(x) = \varphi(x - l)$, for integer l. The set $\{\varphi_l(x)\}$ is the set of translated scaling functions $\varphi(x)$. One can show that $\{\varphi_l, \psi_{jk}\}$ for integers l, k and positive integer j is an orthonormal basis of $L^2(R)$. Therefore, any function $f(x)$ of $L^2(R)$ can be uniquely written:

$$f(x) = \sum_l c_l \varphi(x - l) + \sum_{j \geq 0} \sum_k c_{jk} 2^{j/2} \psi(2^j x - k), \tag{2.9}$$

where

$$c_l = \int_{-\infty}^{\infty} f(x) \varphi(x - l) \, dx = \int_{-\infty}^{\infty} f(x) \varphi_l(x) \, dx. \tag{2.10}$$

The c_l's are the scaling coefficients of $f(x)$. Typically, the c_l's are the low-pass terms, and the c_{jk}'s are the high-pass terms. The scaling coefficients capture the sum of the projections of $f(x)$ onto the $\psi_{jk}(x)$'s for $j < 0$.

The Discrete Wavelet Transform

A class of wavelets particularly useful for image coding is *compactly supported wavelets*. A wavelet function (and its corresponding scaling function) has compact support if only a finite number of the scaling coefficients a_k's are nonzero. Most of the original work on compactly supported wavelets was done by I. Daubechies [5]. Suppose that there are $2N$ nonzero scaling coefficients a_k's. Figures 2.1 and 2.2 are the plots of, respectively, the scaling function $\varphi(x)$ and the wavelet function $\psi(x)$ for the $N = 3$ Daubechies wavelet (D6). Consider a discrete signal x_i and assume x_i is sampled at a sampling rate of 2^J. To relate the wavelet transform of x_i to the continuous wavelet transform (2.9), we assume that the samples x_i are the scaling coefficients of the continuous signal $x(t)$ at the scale J (i.e., sampling rate). Therefore, we have

$$x_i = \varphi_{J,i} = \int_{-\infty}^{+\infty} x(t) 2^{J/2} \varphi(2^J t - i)\, dt \qquad (2.11)$$

and

$$x(t) = \sum_i x_i 2^{J/2} \varphi(2^J t - i). \qquad (2.12)$$

In other words, the scaling coefficients at scale J are assumed to give an exact representation of $x(t)$. The wavelet coefficients at scale J are equal to zero. The scaling and wavelet coefficients can then be computed for the scale $J - 1$:

$$\varphi_{J-1,i} = \int_{-\infty}^{+\infty} x(t) 2^{(J-1)/2} \varphi(2^{J-1} t - i)\, dt \qquad (2.13)$$

and

$$\psi_{J-1,i} = \int_{-\infty}^{+\infty} x(t) 2^{(J-1)/2} \psi(2^{J-1} t - i)\, dt. \qquad (2.14)$$

By combining equations 2.13 and 2.14 with equation 2.12 and the dilation equations 2.3 and 2.5, we get

$$\varphi_{J-1,i} = \frac{1}{\sqrt{2}} \sum_k a_k x_{2i+k} \qquad (2.15)$$

and

$$\psi_{J-1,i} = \frac{1}{\sqrt{2}} \sum_k (-1)^k a_{2N-1-k} x_{2i+k}. \qquad (2.16)$$

The function represented by the scaling coefficients $\varphi_{J-1,i}$ is only then projected onto the scaling and wavelet functions at scale $J - 2$. This cascading process is repeated until the scale is 0. The scaling coefficient is then the DC term of the signal if the signal has only 2^J non-zero samples. This represents the coefficient c_l in equation 2.9. The wavelet coefficients for the scales $J - 1$ to 0 represent the $c_{j,k}$'s in equation 2.9. Equations 2.15 and 2.16 explain how the discrete wavelet transform is computed and how it relates to the continuous wavelet transform. The scaling and wavelet coefficients are the outputs of two FIR digital filters followed by down-sampling by 2: 2.15, and 2.16. The scaling coefficients are the outputs of a low-pass FIR

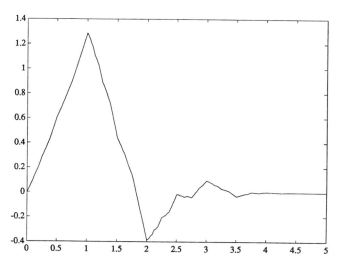

Figure 2.1
D6 scaling function $\varphi(x)$.

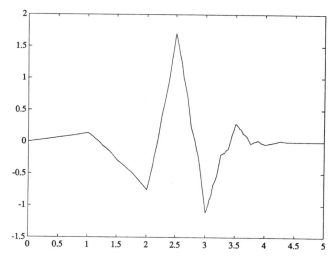

Figure 2.2
D6 wavelet function $\psi(x)$.

filter whose coefficients are the scaling coefficients a_k's. The wavelet coefficients are the outputs of a high-pass FIR filter that is a conjugate quadrature mirror filter (QMF) of the scaling coefficients' low-pass filter. Therefore, the scaling and wavelet coefficients at a given scale are computed by passing the input sample through a perfect reconstruction filter bank composed of a conjugate quadrature mirror FIR filter pair (H_1, H_2), followed by down-sampling by 2. The decomposed signal can be synthesized by (1) up-sampling by 2 the scaling and wavelet coefficients; (2) passing the scaling coefficients through the time-reversed low-pass filter H_1; (3) passing the wavelet coefficients through the time-reversed high-pass filter H_2; and, (4) adding the outputs of each filter. These analysis and synthesis processes are illustrated in figure 2.3.

The complete discrete wavelet decomposition is obtained by cascading the outputs of the low-pass filter into the same filter bank, as illustrated in figure 2.4. The outputs of each filter are critically sampled. The decomposition results in a fine-to-coarse representation of the input signal. The scaling coefficients at a given scale are a low-pass-filtered and contracted version of the scaling coefficients at the previous scale. The wavelet coefficients at a given scale represent the difference detail information needed to reconstruct the signal at the previous finer scale. The wavelet decomposition can be interpreted as a logarithmic binary tree decomposition. It is also a subband decomposition with octave band splitting.

Wavelet filters that are really useful for image compression are called *regular wavelet filters*. There always exists a $2N$ wavelet coefficient system with $N - 1$ vanishing moments [5]. In other words, the scaling coefficients a_k's satisfy the following constraint:

$$\sum_{k=0}^{2N-1} (-1)^k a_k k^n = 0 \quad \text{for } n = 0, \ldots, N - 1. \quad (2.17)$$

In terms of the FIR filters H_1 and H_2, equation (2.17) means that $H_1(z)$ has an N-order zero at $z = -1$, and $H_2(z)$ has an N-order zero at $z = 1$. For example, the Haar wavelet that corresponds to $N = 1$ has no vanishing moment (actually, it has a zero-order vanishing moment). In the case of $N = 3$, the 6-tap Daubechies wavelet filter

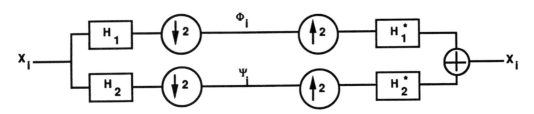

Figure 2.3
Analysis and synthesis stages.

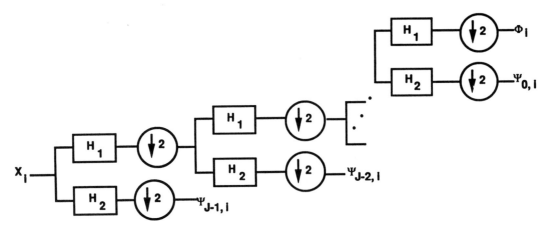

Figure 2.4
Filter bank for the computation of the discrete wavelet transform.

(D6) has two vanishing moments: linear and quadratic. The properties of the vanishing moments can be interpreted in two different ways. The high regularity of the wavelet filter means that when the low-pass filter is cascaded with subsampling by 2 between each stage, the resulting output signal is a smooth interpolation of the original. For the D6 wavelet, a signal that can be represented by piecewise second-order polynomials will have only nonzero φ terms. All the wavelet coefficients are equal to zero. The scaling coefficients alone are needed to reconstruct the original signal exactly. Since most natural images can be approximated by local quadratic expansions, most of the signal energy is preserved in the scaling coefficients. The wavelet coefficients, or output of the high-frequency bands, will typically contain little energy. For an image this means that most of the energy is concentrated in very few scaling coefficients. This energy compaction feature is very important for transform efficiency in image coding applications.

A Two-Dimensional Wavelet Transform

The theory of wavelets can be extended from one to multiple dimensions. Many two-dimensional wavelet systems exist. We consider here a very simple extension of the one-dimensional wavelet transform to a two-dimensional form. This two-dimensional transform is useful for image coding and easy to implement. The two-dimensional wavelet transform we use is a separable transform. In other words, the two-dimensional transform can be computed by taking two one-dimensional transforms: the first one along one dimension, the second transform along the other dimension. Given the one-dimensional scaling and wavelet functions $\varphi(x)$ and $\psi(x)$, there is one separable two-dimensional scaling function $\varphi(x)\varphi(y)$, and there are three separable two-dimensional wavelet functions $\varphi(x)\psi(y)$, $\psi(x)\varphi(y)$, and $\psi(x)\psi(y)$. The scaling function captures the low-frequency information. The wavelet functions capture the high-frequency information for various orientations. Figures 2.5–2.8 show the two-dimensional plots of the scaling and wavelet functions for the separable D6 transform. In practice, if a digital image is sampled on a rectangular grid, the two-dimensional wavelet transform of that image is computed using the same FIR filter bank as the one used to compute the one-dimensional transform. Each image row first goes through

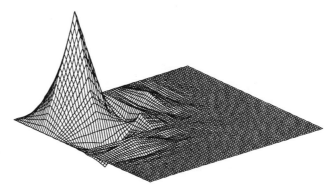

Figure 2.5
Scaling function $\varphi(x)\varphi(y)$.

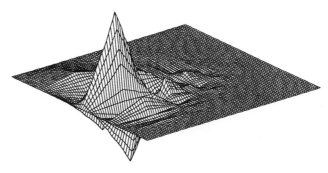

Figure 2.6
Wavelet function $\varphi(x)\psi(y)$.

the scaling and wavelet filters, then is down-sampled by 2. The resulting image is shown in figure 2.9. The horizontal resolution is halved, and the horizontal scale is doubled. The output of the wavelet filter captures the high-frequency information (edges and textures) with horizontal orientation. After one level of row transform, each resulting column goes through an identical process. The resulting image is shown in figure 2.10. The image is then divided into four subimages. The $\varphi\varphi$ subimage is the low-pass image, at half the vertical and horizontal resolutions. The $\varphi\psi$, $\psi\varphi$, and $\psi\psi$ subimages are the high-pass images, critically subsampled. They capture the fine detail information, edges and textures, with horizontal, vertical, and diagonal orientations. After the first level of decomposition is completed, the same decomposition is repeated in the $\varphi\varphi$ subimage, and so on. This cascaded decomposition of the $\varphi\varphi$ subimages is stopped after several levels of decomposition when the coarsest $\varphi\varphi$ subimage is small enough for the coding application considered. The two-dimensional wavelet transform of an image is, therefore, a pyramid fine-to-coarse decomposition. The $\varphi\varphi$ subimage

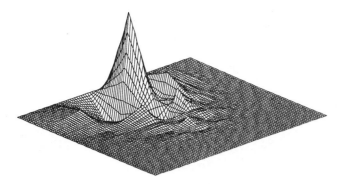

Figure 2.7
Wavelet function $\psi(x)\varphi(y)$.

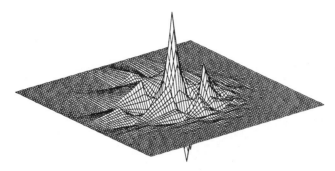

Figure 2.8
Wavelet function $\psi(x)\psi(y)$.

Figure 2.9
One-level horizontal wavelet decomposition.

Figure 2.10
One-level horizontal and vertical wavelet decomposition.

at the top of the pyramid is a very coarse contracted replica of the original. To reconstruct a $\varphi\varphi$ subimage from one scale to the next finer scale, each row and column of scaling and wavelet coefficients go through the synthesis stage described for the one-dimensional transform. The resulting $\varphi\varphi$ subimage has twice the vertical and horizontal resolution. The two-dimensional inverse wavelet transform is a coarse-to-fine recomposition from the top of the pyramid all the way down to the full original image resolution. At each level of recomposition, another layer of detail is added to the image. In summary, the described two-dimensional wavelet transform yields a multiscale, multiresolution image representation. At each scale, the detail information is the output of three wavelet filters, respectively tuned to horizontal, vertical, and diagonal orientations. Also, at each scale, spatial localization of edges is preserved.

Application of the Wavelet Transform to Image Coding

The application of the wavelet transform to image coding is straightforward: It is just a special case of subband coding [1], [8], [22], [24], [26]. Like most image transform

Lena Original (512 x 512 x 24 bit)

Wavelet Compression @ 25 : 1

Wavelet Compression @ 35 : 1

Wavelet Compression @ 50 : 1

Figure 2.11
(Top left) Original (512 × 512 × 24 bit). (Top right) Wavelet coded at 25:1. (Bottom left) Wavelet coded at 35:1. (Bottom right) Wavelet coded at 50:1. In both original and coded images, only luminance component is shown.

coding algorithms, wavelet image coding is composed of three steps: transformation (decomposition), quantization, and entropy coding. At the decoder these three steps are inverted in reverse order. After the multiresolution decomposition of an image is computed, quantization is the lossy processing. Each subimage at each scale of the wavelet decomposition is a different band, and each band is quantized with a different quantizer. With the exception of the coarsest $\varphi\varphi$ subimage, we have found that the Laplacian distribution is a fairly good model for the statistical distribution of the wavelet transform coefficients. The variance of each band is computed, and an optimum rate

is computed to minimize the distortion (mean-squared error) at a given bit rate, using the rate-distortion curve for a Laplacian-distributed random variable and assuming statistical independence between the coefficients of different bands. From the bit rate, a bin width is computed for each independent uniform scalar quantizer for each band. This quantization scheme is simple and well understood [7], [10]. Techniques such as lattice and vector quantization can also be used with the wavelet transform [2], [7]. In the coding examples given in this chapter the quantization is optimized in terms of the mean squared error only. No psychovisual modeling has been used thus far. The final stage of the encoding process is a lossless entropy coding scheme. One scheme is run-length coding combined with Huffman coding with row or column scanning of each band. Alternatively, arithmetic coding can also be used in the given examples.

Original (1212 x 888 x 24 bit)

Wavelet Compression @ 101 1

Figure 2.12
(Left) Original (1212 × 888 × 24 bit). (Right) Wavelet coded at
100:1. In both original and coded images, only luminance
component is shown.

Figures 2.11 and 2.12 show examples of images compressed with the wavelet transform coding algorithm. Most noticeably, blocking effects are absent even at large compression ratios. Contrary to the DCT, the wavelet transform is a global image transform whose basis functions overlap at each scale. Due to the small number of coefficients in the wavelet filters, Gibbs ringing effects do not propagate far from edges, creating only a halolike effect. When the compression ratio is increased, the finer details are lost first, and the overall image content (large-scale information) is preserved. The artifacts created by wavelet image coding are of a noisy type. At high compression ratios, fine details in textures are lost, and fine

edge aliasing can appear. At fine scales, edge aliasing is the most noticeable artifact in wavelet coding. When the high-pass terms are severely quantized, the aliasing of the scaling coefficients is no longer perfectly canceled.

Conclusions

The wavelet transform decomposes visual information by scale (or resolution) and orientation. The decomposed visual information remains spatially localized at each scale. Because of the multiresolution nature of the transform, wavelet coding can exploit properties of the human visual system. Because of the pyramid nature of the wavelet transform, wavelet image coding is a naturally hierarchical and layered coding scheme. Consequently, it is easily scalable, which means that various resolution images can be reconstructed from the same coded image file or bit stream. Finally, the computational complexity of the wavelet transform is $O(n)$, where n is the number of data points. Therefore, the transform can easily be implemented in hardware. The wavelet transform is parallelizable or pipelineable and can thus be efficiently laid out onto very-large-scale integrated circuits. For all these reasons the wavelet transform is an attractive alternative to other transforms for efficient image compression and coding.

Acknowledgment

I wish sincerely to thank Johnathan Devine, Christina Gorecki, and Peter Heller, who helped me produce this paper. The pictures are courtesy of USC. A part of this work was supported by DARPA contract F19620-89-C-0125.

References

[1] Adelson, E., Simoncelli, E., & Hingorani, R. (1987). Orthogonal pyramid transforms for image coding. *SPIE Visual Communication and Image Processing II* 845:50–58.

[2] Antonini, M., Barlaud, M., Mathieu, P. & Daubechies, I. (1990). Image coding using vector quantization in the wavelet transform domain. *Proceedings of IEEE ICASSP '90*, 2297–2300.

[3] Baaziz, N. & Labit, C. (1990). Laplacian pyramid vs. wavelet decomposition for image sequence coding. *Proceedings of IEEE ICASSP*.

[4] Burt, P. & Adelson, E. (1983). The Laplacian pyramid as a compact image code. *IEEE Transactions on Communication* 31:532–540.

[5] Daubechies, I. (1988). Orthonormal bases of compactly supported wavelets. *Communication on Pure and Applied Mathematics* 41:909–996.

[6] Gabor, D. (1946). Theory of communication. *Journal of the IEE* 93:429–457.

[7] Gersho, A. & Gray, R. (1991). *Quantization*. Norwell, Mass.: Kluwer Academic Publishers.

[8] Gharavi, H. (1990). Subband coding of video signals. In J. Woods (Ed.), *Subband Image Coding*. Norwell, Mass.: Kluwer Academic Publishers.

[9] Jain, A. (1989). *Fundamentals of Image Processing*. Englewood Cliffs, N.J.: Prentice-Hall.

[10] Jayant, N. & Noll, P. (1984). *Digital Coding of Waveforms*. Englewood Cliffs, N.J.: Prentice-Hall.

[11] Karlsson, G. & Vetterli, M. (1988). Three dimensional sub-band coding of video. *Proceedings of IEEE ICASSP* 1100–1103.

[12] Mallat, S. (1989). A theory for multiresolution signal decomposition: The wavelet representation. *IEEE Transactions on Pattern Analysis and Machine Intelligence* 11:674–693.

[13] Mallat, S. (1989). Multifrequency channel decompositions of images and wavelet models. *IEEE Transactions on Acoustics, Speech, and Signal Processing* 37:2091–2110.

[14] Netravali, A. & Haskell, B. (1988). *Digital Pictures: Representation and Compression*. New York: Plenum Press.

[15] Safranek, R. & Johnston, J. (1989). A perceptually tuned subband image coder with image-dependent quantization and post-quantization data compression. *Proceedings of IEEE ICASSP* 1945–1948.

[16] Rosenfeld, R., ed. (1980). *Multiresolution Techniques in Computer Vision*. New York: Springer-Verlag.

[17] Uz, K., Vetterli, M. & LeGall, D. (1991). Interpolative multiresolution coding of advanced television with compatible subchannels. *IEEE Transactions on Circuits and Systems for Video Technology* 1:86–99.

[18] Vaidyanathan, P. (1987). Quadrature mirror filter banks, M-band extensions and perfect reconstruction techniques. *IEEE Acoustics, Speech, and Signal Processing Magazine*, 4:4–20.

[19] Vetterli, M. (1984). Multi-dimensional sub-band coding: some theory and algorithms. *Signal Processing* 6:97–112.

[20] Vetterli, M. & LeGall, D. (1989). Perfect reconstruction FIR filter banks: Some properties and factorizations. *IEEE Transactions on Acoustics, Speech, and Signal Processing* 37:1057–1071.

[21] Vetterli, M., Kovacevic, J. & LeGall, D. (1990). Perfect reconstruction filter banks for HDTV representation and coding. *Image Communication* 2:349–364.

[22] Vetterli, M. (1990). Multirate filter banks for subband coding. In J. Woods (Ed.), *Subband Image Coding*, Norwell, Mass.: Kluwer Academic Publishers.

[23] Westerink, P., Biemond, J. & Boekee, D. (1988). An optimal bit allocation algorithm for subband coding. *Proceedings of ICASSP '88* 757–760.

[24] Woods, J. & O'Neil, S. (1986). Sub-band coding of images. *IEEE Transactions on Acoustics, Speech, and Signal Processing* 34:1278–1288.

[25] Woods, J. & Naveen, T. (1989). Subband encoding of video sequences. *Proceedings of the SPIE Conference on Visual Communications and Image Processing* 724–732.

[26] Zettler, W., Huffman, J. & Linden, D. (1990). Application of compactly supported wavelets to image compression. *SPIE Image Processing Algorithms and Techniques* 1244:150–160.

3

Scalable (Extensible, Interoperable) Digital Video Representations

V. Michael Bove, Jr.

Digital coding and distribution of image sequences is now beginning to move out of the laboratory and into both business and consumer applications, and the amount of research and development of suitable representations for these images increases daily. However, many of those involved with the technologies and applications for digital video seem to think that the impact and benefits of a digital representation lie only in the areas of compression (or, conversely, resolution: fitting a better image into an existing channel as in high-definition television) and robustness to noise.

I suggest instead that the most important and lasting change that will result from the introduction of digital video will come from the realization that the bit stream representing the images is in fact data of a sort that may be subjected to computation and that at both the origin and display ends of the system the signal is being processed by what are fundamentally computing devices. A properly designed representation for the video can take advantage of the flexibility engendered by this computation.

This viewpoint leads to the conclusion that many current digital video standardization activities are emphasizing requirements of secondary importance. Higher definition is perhaps the least important aspect of advanced television, which if properly designed could solve the current international incompatibility problems and facilitate a broader variety of delivery mechanisms. Simple compression ratio is certainly less important in compression standards for multimedia than supporting a broad range of origination possibilities, channel or storage capacities, and decoder costs and complexities.

Within a few years processor architectures will permit video signals and stills to incorporate instructions for a programmable decoder, and standardization discussions will be much different from those at present. But even before we reach that time, we can identify a number of features that will increase interconnection options, add

Scalable, Interoperable Video Coding Model

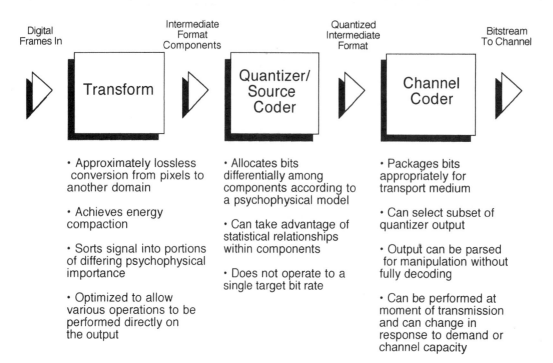

Digital Frames In · Intermediate Format Components · Quantized Intermediate Format · Bitstream To Channel

Transform
- Approximately lossless conversion from pixels to another domain
- Achieves energy compaction
- Sorts signal into portions of differing psychophysical importance
- Optimized to allow various operations to be performed directly on the output

Quantizer/ Source Coder
- Allocates bits differentially among components according to a psychophysical model
- Can take advantage of statistical relationships within components
- Does not operate to a single target bit rate

Channel Coder
- Packages bits appropriately for transport medium
- Can select subset of quantizer output
- Output can be parsed for manipulation without fully decoding
- Can be performed at moment of transmission and can change in response to demand or channel capacity

Figure 3.1
A scalable video coding algorithm must package the data in such a way that a subset of the data may be identified and decoded.

degrees of freedom in system design, and resolve many of the current incompatibilities among different video sources and displays. These features can be condensed into definitions of the first three words of the chapter title:

- *Scalability:* The bit stream can be parsed and decoded in part or in full to produce images at differing quality levels (to accommodate different channel capacities or decoder capabilities).

- *Extensibility:* The representation easily extends to accommodate higher-resolution imagery and higher-bandwidth channels as they become available.

- *Interoperability:* The numerical parameters of source and display (resolution, frame rate) need not match.

Figure 3.1 illustrates a simple model for understanding the requirements of a scalable video coder. In this model the images are first converted from frames and pixels to some other domain via a lossless transformation that will both achieve energy compaction and sort the signal in

such a way that later lossy compression can be fitted to a psychovisual model of the viewer. Typically the lossy compression takes advantage of the human visual system's sensitivities to various frequencies and orientations in horizontal/vertical/temporal frequency space and its spatiotemporal sensitivity to luminance and chrominance components by making the quantization error equally visible (or, ideally, invisible) throughout. Watson has called image coding that mimics the early stages of the human visual system a "perceptual-components architecture" [21], although it is not necessary strictly to follow the understood operation of low-level vision to take advantage of psychophysical phenomena in a scalable coder. A thorough review and bibliography of the relevant psychophysical research may be found in Watson's paper and in [14]; much research remains to be done in mapping these phenomena to various spatiotemporal transforms and quantizers in an analytical (rather than empirical) fashion. In a scalable system the lossy compression is performed by a quantizer whose goal is not to meet a single target bit rate but rather to allocate bits in such a way that either the transmitting device or the receiver can further reduce the bit rate by disregarding some of the data (presumably

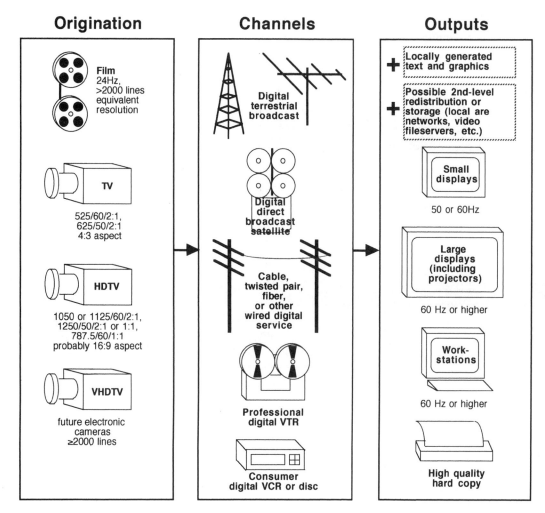

Origination | **Channels** | **Outputs**

Film
24Hz,
>2000 lines
equivalent
resolution

TV

525/60/2:1,
625/50/2:1
4:3 aspect

HDTV

1050 or 1125/60/2:1,
1250/50/2:1 or 1:1,
787.5/60/1:1
probably 16:9 aspect

VHDTV

future electronic
cameras
≥2000 lines

Digital
terrestrial
broadcast

Digital
direct
broadcast
satellite

Cable,
twisted pair,
fiber,
or other
wired digital
service

Professional
digital VTR

Consumer
digital VCR or disc

+ Locally generated
text and graphics

+ Possible 2nd-level
redistribution or
storage (local are
networks, video
fileservers, etc.)

Small
displays

50 or 60Hz

Large
displays
(including
projectors)

60 Hz or higher

Work-
stations

60 Hz or higher

High quality
hard copy

Figure 3.2
Open Architecture Television system decouples the numerical
parameters of origination, channel, and output of video images (from
[1]). Numerical parameters associated with origination are given as
lines/frame rate/interlace.

also following the viewer's sensitivity to the components)
and still produce images of reasonable quality. The quantization step is followed by a channel coder that packages
some or all of the quantizer output to match the capacity
of the transport or storage medium.

In the remainder of this chapter I briefly explore the
implications of considering moving images as scalable,
extensible, interoperable data with examples drawn from
recent research within the Entertainment and Information Systems Group of the MIT Media Laboratory and
elsewhere.

Experiments with Video Representation

Open Architecture Television

Scalable open architecture television [1] is a body of work that
has been under investigation for several years. Its goals
are in large part summarized by figures 3.2 and 3.3. Fundamentally, open architecture seeks to remove discussion of
video transmission and display from the domain of numerical parameters like resolution and frame rate and instead
examines the entire television system, employing image
representations that maximize the interconnection options.
The requirement is a digital image representation that is
scalable in resolution, so that the number of lines on the
display is determined strictly by the receiving hardware
and is not coupled to the number of lines employed by the

Figure 3.3
Open Architecture Television permits signals originating at three different frame rates and resolutions to be displayed simultaneously on a screen operating at yet a fourth frame rate (from [1]).

production equipment. It should be possible to view an NTSC-originated signal on an 1125- or 2000-line raster, and a 525- or 625-line receiver should be able to display a signal originating with a higher definition. Likewise, the signal representation is scalable temporally, so that the frame rate of production and display are decoupled. Bandwidth scalability means that the bit streams coming from different transport or storage media can "look the same" to receiving equipment. Thus consumer recording devices can store the bit stream directly without decoding it and can permit capacity versus quality trade-offs similar to those available on current analog VHS videocassette recorders.

The open architecture concept is not tied to any particular image representation, although we have used one for proof of principle: a separable quadrature mirror filter (QMF) subband decomposition by octaves is applied horizontally and vertically (as first suggested by Vetterli [20]; see also [22]), and the temporal direction is divided into uniform 10- or 12-Hz subbands (as proposed by Schreiber [15]; earlier applications of temporal subband coding are described in [4] and [9]). The overall spatiotemporal frequency volume of a three-dimensional decomposition is illustrated in figure 3.4. Various sources will fill subvolumes

of this volume depending on the resolution and rate of the origination, and displays will pick out subsets of the bit stream representing subvolumes corresponding to the display circumstances. The structure of a subband decoder assures that a display operating at higher resolution than the source (i.e., picking out a subvolume in which some of the subbands contain zero energy) will inherently interpolate as required. The temporal decomposition and reconstruction are illustrated in figures 3.5 and 3.6. Via this process we have shown that sources of 24, 50, and 60 H may be decoded for display at common frame rates such as 50, 60, and 72 H. To reduce motion blur in rapidly moving regions of the image, we have extended this process to include motion compensation (figure 3.7) [11]. In the motion-compensated version of our temporal processing, all sources are interpolated to a very high frame rate, which is itself decomposed to fill all subbands. This method provides improved image quality at the cost of added encoding complexity and bandwidth.

Scalable compression involves scalar or vector quantization with allocation of bits among the spatiotemporal components, modified so that the channel coder or decoder can further reduce the bit rate by ignoring all or some of the bits allocated to individual components, presumably following the psychovisual phenomena cited above (figures 3.8, and 3.9). It is readily apparent that the subband hierarchy is extensible to accommodate higher-resolution future cameras and displays.

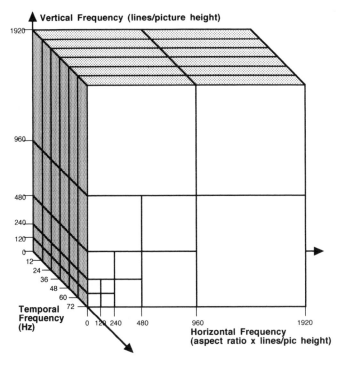

Figure 3.4
Spatiotemporal volume of a three-dimensional separable subband decomposition, where division is by octaves spatially and by uniform 12-Hz subbands temporally. Various sources from the first column of figure 2 will fill differing portions of this volume.

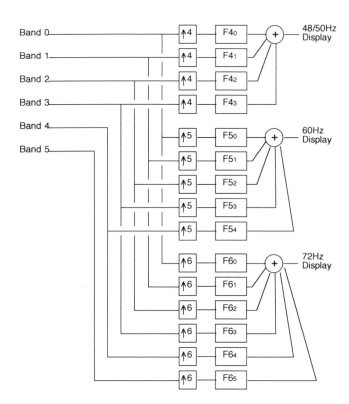

Figure 3.6
Linear temporal reconstruction for various display rates, each of which has a different synthesis filter bank (labeled F) associated with it.

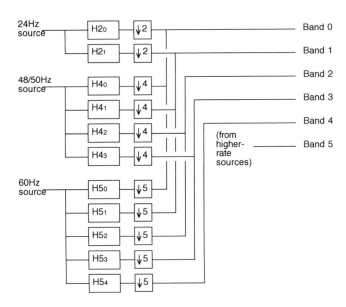

Figure 3.5
Linear temporal decomposition into 12-Hz subbands accommodates 24-Hz film, 50-Hz European television (here mapped into 48 Hz), and 60-Hz North American television. Here the H's represent analysis filters, where each rate source has a different filter bank.

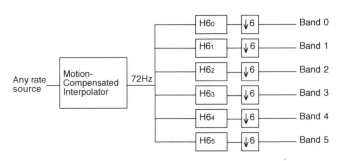

Figure 3.7
Motion-compensated temporal decomposition improves the reconstructed images when the display frame rate is higher than that of the source and gives more flexibility in the input frame rate. This encoding method uses the same reconstruction method as the linear version.

Figure 3.8
This frame, monochrome for clarity, was taken from a 525-line color sequence spatiotemporally subband-coded, quantized, and Huffman variable-length-coded. With all subbands included, this bit stream (which contains more information than needed for visual losslessness, even for viewing as stills) requires approximately 30 Mbits/s, or slightly under a 6:1 compression rate.

Figure 3.9
This frame results from scalable reconstruction of the preceding, here including only subbands comprising 11 percent of that bit stream, or just over 3 Mbits/s (from [1]). Note the effect of removing combinations of high spatial and temporal frequency, which is much more apparent in this image viewed as a still than in a moving sequence.

Scalable Motion Compensation

The requirement for multiple framestores imposed by temporal finite impulse response filtering may make motion compensation a more attractive method for handling the temporal dimension in many applications. A hybrid coder for subband images would involve deriving a motion-vector field for use in predicting a frame from the preceding one, subtracting the resulting predicted frame from the actual frame at that point, and performing a spatial subband decomposition on the error signal [5]. Proper operation of a differential coder of this sort requires that the encoder keep track of the decoder's state so that the encoder and decoder assume the same prediction [8]. Such a method is unscalable and makes it difficult to produce a consistently good image at reduced size or with reduced bandwidth, since disregarding any of the transmitted error information breaks the prediction loop and may result in noticeable degradation. If the subbands could be motion-compensated individually, putting each into a separate motion-compensation loop, each subband of a predicted frame would be predicted from only the corresponding subband in the previous frame. By breaking the interdependency among the predictions, applying a block-matching algorithm directly to the subbands would eliminate the problem of lack of scalability of motion compensation. Unfortunately for this simple approach, subband decomposition is a space-variant process, and the effect of decimation is that translational motion in an image produces phase changes rather than simple translations in the resulting subbands. Scalable motion compensation has been shown to be possible; here the subbands are individually coded with vectors derived from the full image, allowing bands to be decoded independently [18]. The phase problem is solved by up-interpolating the sampled subband (to remove the effects of the decimation), applying the motion compensation, and then resampling it. The basic algorithmic structure is similar to that of a pel-recursive motion-compensated subband coder earlier proposed by Woods and Naveen, although scalable decoding was not their stated design goal [23]. Experiments on several 525-line image sequences at bit rates in the range of 4 to 9 M bits/sec have shown that the cost of scalable over nonscalable motion compensation is 1 dB or less of signal-to-noise ratio, but more investigation

Figure 3.10
Quadrature-mirror-filter subband decomposition produces visible aliasing when high-pass bands are not included in a scalable reconstruction (effect particularly noticeable on high-contrast diagonal edges). Here the top two octaves of the pyramid were zeroed out.

remains to be done of the quality/complexity/scalability trade-offs involved [19].

Alias Minimization

Some of the frequency-domain transformations used in image compression may create difficulty when the images are to be decoded scalably. As an example, quadrature mirror filters often used in subband coding are designed to cancel the aliasing that otherwise would result from maximally decimating the output of imperfect (overlapping) bandpass filters. However, in the case where lack of channel bandwidth or decoder capacity necessitates disregarding the high subband, the result of decoding the remainder of the signal is not just a low-passed version of the image but instead contains aliasing that in many cases is annoyingly visible. We have found that a slight modification to the low-band synthesis filter (which entails no additional decoder complexity) greatly minimizes this aliasing component and provides visibly improved images. Essentially we use an approximate model for the spectrum of the image and regard the uncanceled aliasing as noise, making it possible to derive a Wiener filter for interpolating a low-pass image from just the low subband [16] (see figures 3.10 and 3.11). A similar problem for a uniform-bandwidth subband decomposition is treated by Kawashima et al. in [10], although without any modeling of the original signal. This sort of optimization of existing methods

Figure 3.11
As in the preceding illustration, the top two octaves of a QMF subband pyramid were not included in reconstruction, but the QMF interpolation filter was replaced by a Wiener filter of the same length to minimize the aliasing (see [16]).

is perhaps just a stopgap approach until signal transformations can be developed that are amenable to significant compression and inherently avoid aliasing problems when decoded scalably.

Scalable Multidimensional Quantizers

In a separable spatial or spatiotemporal subband representation for an image sequence, using a scalar quantizer for the subbands and running a variable-length coder over them individually enables fine bandwidth control by requantizing the bands at the moment of transmission (effectively reducing the number of bits sent per subband). However, when a multidimensional, or vector, quantizer is applied to groups of adjacent samples within each subband (see for example [4]), the scalability afforded—retaining or discarding an entire given band—may be too coarse for some applications or may result in objectionably visible degradations. To allow finer bandwidth control and dynamic spatiotemporal allocation of quantization error, we have explored modifications to vector and lattice quantizing algorithms that enable any number of the most significant bits of the codebook indices to be transmitted [17]. Related research and analysis has been conducted by Mahesh and Pearlman [12]. Normally, a k-dimensional tree implementation of a vector quantizer makes each leaf, or quantized vector, be the centroid of the multidimensional region associated with it; with scalability we have imposed a new requirement that the nodes at any level of the tree—representing the quantized vectors for only the most significant several bits of the indices—be a subset of the full codebook. Such a criterion will no longer yield a mathematically optimal codebook, although the price paid (additional quantizer distortion) for the added scalability has been shown to be relatively small.

Model-Based Coding

A compact video representation that possesses the desirable properties enumerated above has existed for many years under the guise of computer-graphics languages. Efficient rendering of images from these descriptions is a much better understood problem than the creation of such descriptions to represent reality. Called either model-based coding or analysis-synthesis coding, the process of representing a real scene as a three-dimensional description tion has seen a great deal of research in applications

to videoconferencing images [6]. The Media Laboratory continues to investigate hybrids of traditional waveform coding and structural representations of images through techniques such as range-sensing cameras and three-dimensional motion estimation [3], synthetic structural data [7], and isolating moving objects from a known background [13].

Model-based representations of scenes will perhaps never totally replace waveform-based coding of images, but in the longer term, the large amount of compression and useful scene modifications possible from the former will doubtless make structural processing part of many applications for Image communications.

Hardware Development

Because of our desires to conduct more extensive digital video processing experiments than can easily be performed

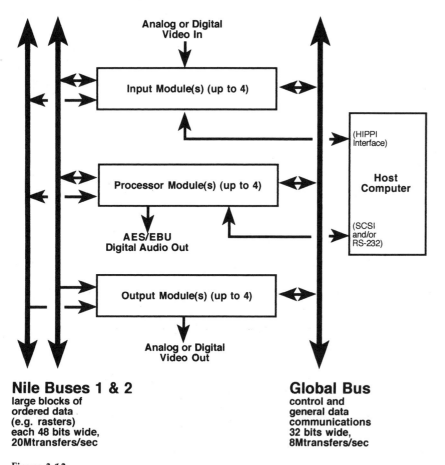

Figure 3.12
Cheops is a modular system for the real-time processing of image sequences.

on general-purpose computers, to explore the design of advanced interactive information displays, and to demonstrate that our video coding approach may be implemented with practical amounts of hardware, we have undertaken the development of a compact, bus-oriented processing platform called Cheops [2]. Cheops is modular, divided into video digitizing modules, processor modules, and display drivers (figure 3.12) and is designed to evolve as computational requirements change and as digital processing technology advances. Up to four of each of these modules may exist in a system, interconnected by two logically separate data channels: the Nile Bus (of which there are two copies) and the Global Bus. The Nile Bus is dedicated to very rapid transfer of ordered data arrays between input/output and processor modules. Nile Bus transfers into and out of the processor module pass through a color space converter, decoupling the color components

used in the processing from those used for input and output. The Global Bus is a general-purpose computer bus that is used for supervisory communication and flexible transfer of smaller blocks of data.

The philosophy behind the design of the Cheops processor module is to abstract a basic set of computationally intensive operations required for real-time performance of a variety of desired applications. These operations are then embodied in specialized hardware provided with a very high throughput memory interface. A general-purpose central processing unit is provided for sequencing and controlling the flow of data among the different functional units, implementing the portions of algorithms for which a specialized processor is not available, and performing higher-level tasks such as resource management and user interface. The current-generation "P2" module (figure 3.13) centers on a crosspoint switch through which

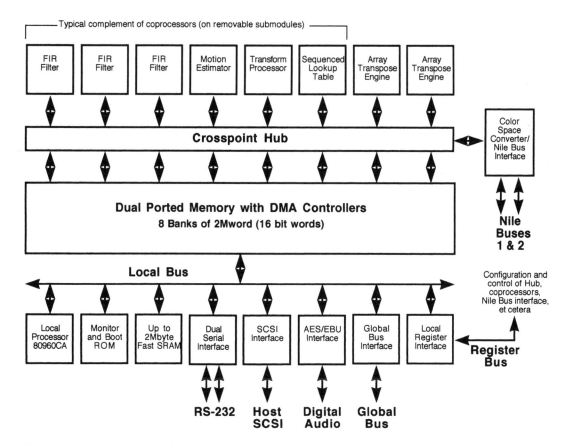

Figure 3.13
The current Cheops processor module contains a reconfigurable set of specialized processors whose dataflow and configuration are under the control of a general-purpose central processing unit.

eight stream processors (on removable submodules for easy reconfigurability) access banks of memory with high-speed multidimensional direct-memory-access (DMA) controllers and perform operations such as finite impulse response (FIR) convolution, correlation, block transforms, and matrix algebra. The configuration illustrated provides sufficient processing power to apply a three-dimensional subband algorithm in real time to at least two 640×480 pixel interlaced color image sequences or one progressive image sequence. Full subband coding of HDTV image sequences will likely require two or more processor boards. Display modules are capable of driving screens at a variety of resolutions from 640×480 pixel resolution 60Hz interlaced up to 2048×2048 60Hz progressively scanned.

Because this system is intended to be an experimental platform rather than an implementation of a single algorithm, it is designed to provide a flexible and reconfigurable set of hardware and software tools for the processing of moving images, both for computationally intensive waveform coding operations and for low-level machine vision operations to be used in model-based coding experiments. To make using the system easier, resource management software has been developed that permits an algorithm to be described as a simple doubly linked list of source and destination buffers and processing tasks. The resource manager is a background process that maintains an inventory of available processing resources and accepts requests for these resources and the Nile Buses from application programs. Actual execution of the requests on the manager's queue is dependent on the availability of the desired hardware, the completion of all prerequisite processing, and user-specified schedule times (e.g., for maintaining the update rate of the video display). Centralized management of the stream processing and transfer resources for all user programs permits the most efficient processor utilization.

Conclusion

Scalability and interoperability in many cases come at some price in either encoding complexity or compression efficiency, but the advantages are sufficiently compelling that future experimentation on digital representations for moving images should emphasize minimizing this trade-off rather than increasing sheer efficiency at the expense of flexibility. The goal of this research is not so much to develop a single image representation for all applications as to examine various methods in light of the system requirements outlined and to improve them as necessary to allow degrees of freedom more in line with current needs and desirable future features.

Acknowledgments

The author wishes to thank many co-workers who have contributed their ideas and time to the research described in this article, particularly William Schreiber, Edward Adelson, Andrew Lippman, Walter Bender, John Watlington, Henry Holtzman, Patrick McLean, Lin Liu, Abha Singh, Irene Shen, Joseph Stampleman, Kenji Tsunashima, William Butera, and Pasquale Romano. These projects have been supported by the Television of Tomorrow and Movies of the Future research consortia and by DARPA/ISTO under contract DAAD 05-90-C-0333.

References

[1] Bove, V. M. Jr., & Lippman, A. B. (1992). Scalable open architecture television. *SMPTE Journal* 101(1):2–5.

[2] Bove, V. M. Jr., & Watlington, J. A. (1991). Cheops: a modular processor for scalable video coding. *SPIE* 1605:886–893. Bellingham, Wash.: Society of Photo-Optical Instrumentation Engineers.

[3] Bove, V. M. Jr., (1989). Synthetic movies derived from multidimensional image sensors. Ph.D. diss. MIT, Cambridge.

[4] Butera, W. J. (1988). Multiscale coding of images. Master's thesis, MIT, Cambridge.

[5] Gharavi, H. (1991). Subband coding algorithms for video applications: Videophone to HDTV-conferencing. *IEEE Transactions on Circuits and Systems for Video Technology* 1:174–183.

[6] Harashima, H., Aizawa, K. & Saito, T. (1989). Model-based analysis-synthesis coding of videotelephone images: Conception and basic study of intelligent image coding. *Transactions of the IEICE* E72(5): 452–459.

[7] Holtzman, H. N. (1991). Three-dimensional representations of video using knowledge-based representations. Master's thesis, MIT, Cambridge.

[8] Jayant, N. S. & Noll, P. (1984). *Digital Coding of Waveforms.* Englewood Cliffs, N.J.: Prentice-Hall, 252–257.

[9] Karlsson, G. & Vetterli, M. (1988). Three-dimensional subband coding of video. *Proceedings of ICASSP* 88, 1100–1103. New York: IEEE.

[10] Kawashima, M. & and Tominaga, H. (1991). Method to convert image resolution using M-band extended QMF banks. *SPIE* 1605: 107–111. Bellingham, Wash. Society of Photo-Optical Instrumentation Engineers.

[11] Liu, L. L. (1990). Digital intermediate format for video frame rate conversion. Master's thesis, MIT, Cambridge.

[12] Mahesh, B. & Pearlman, W. A. (1991) Multiple-rate structured vector quantization of image pyramids. *Journal of Visual Communication and Image Representation* 2(2): 103–111.

[13] McLean, P. C. (1991). Structured video coding. Master's thesis, MIT, Cambridge.

[14] Schreiber, W. F. (1984). Psychophysics and the improvement of television image quality. *SMPTE Journal* 93(8): 717–725.

[15] Schreiber, W. F., et al. (1989). Channel-compatible 6-MHz HDTV distribution systems. *SMPTE Journal* 98(1): 5–13.

[16] Shen, I. J. & Bove, V. M. Jr., (1992). Minimization of aliasing artifacts during partial subband reconstruction with Wiener filters. *SPIE* 1657: 14–23. Bellingham, Wash.: Society of Photo-Optical Instrumentation Engineers.

[17] Singh, A. & Bove, V. M. Jr., (1992). Multidimensional quantizers for scalable video. *IEEE Journal on Selected Areas in Communications*, forthcoming.

[18] Stampleman, J. B. (1992). Scalable video compression. Master's thesis, MIT, Cambridge.

[19] Tsunashima, K., Stampleman, J. B. & Bove, V. M. Jr., (1992). A scalable motion-compensated subband image coder. *IEEE Transactions on Communications*, forthcoming.

[20] Vetterli, M. (1984). Multidimensional subband coding: Some theory and algorithms. *Signal Processing* 6: 97–112.

[21] Watson, A. B. (1990). Perceptual-components architecture for digital video. *J. Optical Soc. America A* 7(10): 1943–1954.

[22] Woods, J. W. & O'Neil, S. D. (1986). Subband coding of images. *IEEE Transactions on Acoustics, Speech, and Signal Processing ASSP*-34(5): 1278–1288.

[23] Woods, J. W. & Naveen, T. (1989). Subband encoding of video sequences. *SPIE* 1199: 724–732. Bellingham, Wash.: Society of Photo-Optical Instrumentation Engineers.

4

Incorporating Visual Factors into Vector Quantizers for Image Compression

Robert M. Gray, Pamela C. Cosman, and Karen L. Oehler

Image compression maps an original image into a bit stream suitable for communication over or storage in a digital medium, so that the number of bits required to represent the coded image is smaller than that required for the original image. Ideally one would like the coded image to require as few bits as possible so as to minimize the storage space or communication time. In some applications one may also require that the original image be perfectly recoverable from the coded form. Unfortunately, this latter goal is often not possible. For example, if the original image is an analog photograph, then it is impossible to recreate it exactly from a digital representation regardless of how many bits are used. As one might expect, using enough bits in a digital representation should result in a coded image that is perceptually indistinguishable from the original. "Enough bits," however, can be too many to fit into available storage or to communicate over an available link in reasonable time. Furthermore, information might still be missing that could conceivably be important, even though the untrained eye might not detect its absence. The definition of fidelity or quality or usefulness of a reproduction is therefore strongly dependent on the application. A mathematically tractable measure of quality such as squared error may be used to help a computer optimize a code. A more complicated perceptually derived subjective test might be used to validate the code designed for a particular application.

The development of compression systems optimized for a particular application has proceeded along a variety of parallel paths. Early systems used prediction or linear transformation techniques to reduce "redundancy" in signals, leading to more efficient simple quantization of the resulting linearly transformed signal components. Shannon showed how digital information such as quantized images (or inherently digital images) could be compressed in an invertible fashion provided enough bits were available [35]. The lossy compression techniques typified by quantization were early combined with the lossless techniques introduced by Shannon by simply cascading them to provide an overall compression system. Such a system typically consisted of linear operations, followed by quantization of the transformed or predicted data using several quantizers with differing bit rates, followed by an invertible code. This traditional approach has worked well and still dominates in practice.

Along with invertible coding, Shannon also introduced what he called "source coding with a fidelity criterion" [36]. This referred to the mapping of blocks or vectors produced by a signal into binary codewords to form a coded representation that was optimum in the sense of minimizing the average of some mathematically defined distortion measure between the original signal and the digital reproduction. Such coding schemes for vectors have become known as block quantizers or vector quantizers.

We begin with a description of the general image compression problem from a Shannon point of view. Several specific coding techniques are briefly described and compared. We emphasize codes that are in the spirit of Shannon in the sense that they are designed specifically to be optimized with respect to a fidelity criterion subject to constraints on code structure. This is accomplished by clustering algorithms based on training sets of data, thereby avoiding the use of mathematical models, such as Gaussian or Markov, for real data. In statistical terms the design is nonparametric. We consider several ways in which knowledge of human visual factors can be incorporated into the design of such compression systems.

Because overall complexity gets rapidly out of hand if the code structure is unconstrained, we place structural constraints on the code (as do traditional methods). To simplify implementation while preserving fidelity, we consider codes with a tree structure. Along with the use of empirical distributions in design, this approach has its origins in statistics, especially in classification and regression [2].

Both clustering and classification trees have long been used for image enhancement and classification. It is natural to suspect that enhancement and classification can be combined with quantization to improve the quality of compressed images or to render the images more suitable for a specific application such as medical diagnosis. We consider several such applications.

As our goal is a general overview of fundamentals and variations, not much time is spent on detail. The interested reader is referred to [1] and [10] for a thorough study of the fundamentals of vector quantization and an extensive bibliography and to the cited papers for further details of specific examples.

Image Compression

The basic goal of image compression is to convent an original image into a compressed image with a binary coding having R bits per pixel (bpp) so that the reproduction has the best possible fidelity. Image compression aims at attaining the best possible quality for the available storage or communication capacity.

Compression can be useful in a variety of ways including conserving storage space, reducing data rate, permitting progressive transmission, and reducing the complexity of digital signal processing (DSP). The last attribute will be explored at some length here. Compression can also perform various image-processing operations such as edge detection, halftoning, or low-level classification. Unlike other types of data compression, image compression occurs almost always in the context of human viewing, so perceptual factors are key to determining quality. Before seeing how perceptual factors may be integrated into compression systems, we first review the basic types of compression and the principles and techniques of vector quantization.

There are two basic types of compression:

• *Lossless compression* or noiseless coding, data compaction, entropy coding, or invertible coding, where the original image can be perfectly recovered from the digital representation; thus factors of human perception play no role in developing or validating the algorithms. Lossless compression is applicable only for already digital images and requires variable-rate coding techniques: A varying number of bits are needed for different pixels or pixel patterns. Basically, long codewords are used for unlikely inputs, short for likely. The codes are explicitly designed to make the average number of bits per input pixel is as small as possible. The most popular lossless coding techniques are Huffman, adaptive Huffman, run-length, Ziv-Lempel, and arithmetic codes [15, 9, 44, 45, 40, 23, 32, 38, 10]. Typical compression ratios for lossless codes on still-frame 8-bit gray-scale images run from expansion (poor) to 4:1 compression (unusually good).

It is widely believed that lossless coding is necessary in many applications; hence a great deal of effort has been spent fine-tuning these algorithms and developing hardware for their implementation. The need for perfect reproduction is obvious in some applications such as the compression of computer programs and arbitrary binary files but is less clear in other applications. The ultimate limits to lossless compression are determined by the Shannon source entropy (kth order entropy if k-dimensional vectors are coded). Loss is *inevitable* if the bit rate R is smaller than the entropy of the source.

• *Lossy compression*, where the original pixel intensities cannot be perfectly recovered, for example, simple quantization or A/D conversion. A possible goal is to minimize an average distortion such as average squared error for a given bit rate. Typical compression ratios range from 4:1 to 32:1 for still-frame 8-bit gray-scale images using common techniques, and much better compression is reported for some more recent techniques.

Even in cases where lossless codes are required for legal reasons or simply to be safe, lossy coding may be useful for progressive transmission in an eventually lossless system (such as in telebrowsing or quick-look systems).

Lossy compression systems can be clustered into several basic overlapping types, including scalar quantization (PCM) with entropy coding [17], predictive coding with scalar quantizers (predictive DPCM) [17], transform and subband coding [41, 6, 24, 42] (including the popular discrete cosine transform), "second-generation" codes [18], multiresolution codes [4], and vector quantization (VQ) [1, 24, 10]. In the abstract, VQ is simply Shannon's model for source coding. The idea is to compress a group of pixels jointly, instead of one at a time. In its most general form, vector quantization includes any block-structured compression technique (such as DCT-based transform coding). By operating directly on vectors, however, quantizers can be designed specifically to minimize average distortion given an assumed code structure. Choosing distortion measures that are sensitive to visually important features permits visual factors to be explicitly included in the optimization algorithms used to design the codes.

Vector quantization has several other potential advantages:

• Fractional bit allocations for the vector coordinates are possible, because vectors are used instead of scalars.

• Clustering techniques can be incorporated into code design to provide good quality.

• Tree-structured codes can be used to give efficient implementations.

• Tree-structured codes have a natural progressive transmission or successive approximation structure.

• The codes can incorporate simple enhancement and classification because extensions of clustering and classification tree design methods are used to design codes. Both techniques have long been used for enhancement and classification.

• Vector quantization permits optimal (without asymptotic approximations) bit allocation and interpolation/estimation.

• Vector quantizers have fast software decompression based on table lookup and little, if any, computation.

• Vector quantization can be incorporated into other techniques, such as transform coding (the coefficients or the possible bit allocation vectors can be vector quantized).

Vector Quantization

A VQ for image compression is depicted in figure 4.1. The image is parsed into a sequence of groups of pixels, often

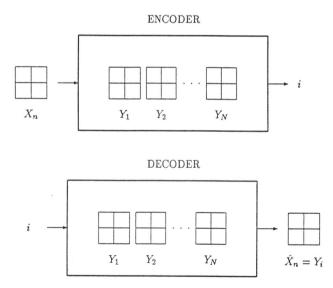

Figure 4.1
Vector quantizer.

2×2 squares as shown in the figure, but larger squares and rectangles are commonly used. Later we consider nonrectangular vectors that potentially can lessen the artifacts perceived by the human visual system. The encoder views an input vector X_n at time n and produces a channel codeword i, which is a binary R-tuple if the code has R bits per vector and the system has fixed rate. If the indices i have variable dimension, permitting more bits to be used on active vectors, then R is the average length of the binary vectors. The decoder is a table lookup: On receiving a channel codeword i, the decoder outputs a stored codeword or template Y_i, that is, a word in memory indexed by the channel codeword. Given a codebook containing all possible codewords, the decoder is completely described. The basic Shannon source code model provides an encoder that is optimal for a given codebook if the goal is to minimize an average distortion. If we assume $d(X, \hat{X}) \geq 0$ measures the distortion or cost of reproducing an input vector X as a reproduction $\hat{X}$, and if we further assume that the overall distortion (or lack of fidelity) of the system is measured by an average distortion, then the optimal encoder for a given codebook selects the vector Y_i if

$$d(X_n, Y_i) \leq d(X_n, Y_j), \quad \text{for all } j, \tag{4.1}$$

that is, the encoder operates in a nearest neighbor or minimum distortion fashion. For the moment the code is not assumed to have any structure, that is, it can be an arbitrary collection of codewords, and the encoder finds the best one by exhaustive search. Such unconstrained codes are called *full search* codes.

If the codebook of reproductions is fixed for all input vectors, then the VQ operates in a memoryless fashion on each input vector; that is, each vector is encoded independently of previous inputs and outputs of the encoder. In general an encoder can have memory if the codebook applied to the input vectors is varied according to past actions. Predictive and finite-state vector quantizers are examples of VQ with memory.

The choice of distortion measure permits us to quantify the performance of a VQ in a manner that can be computed, used in analysis, and used in design optimization. The theory focuses on average distortion in the sense of a probabilistic average or expectation. Practice emphasizes the time average or sample average distortion

$$D = \frac{1}{L} \sum_{n=1}^{L} d(X_n, \hat{X}_n) \tag{4.2}$$

for large L. This expression is frequently normalized and a logarithm taken in order to form a signal-to-noise ratio (SNR) or peak signal-to-noise ratio (PSNR). With well-defined stationary and ergodic random-process models instead of real signals, the sample average and expectation are effectively equal.

We confine our interest to the class of input-weighted squared error distortion measures of the quadratic form

$$d(X, \hat{X}) = (X - \hat{X})^T B_X (X - \hat{X}), \tag{4.3}$$

where B_X is a positive definite symmetric matrix [12]. The most common B_X is the identity matrix, which yields a simple squared error. In many of our examples we consider more general weightings that have the potential advantage of counting the distortion to be more or less according to how important the input vector is judged to be. For example, B_X can adjust the distortion according to how the input X is classified (e.g., as being active, textured, bright, dim, important, unimportant). All the basic VQ design methods work for such input-weighted quadratic distortion measures. Of particular interest is the case where $B_X = w_X I$, yielding

$$d(X, \hat{X}) = w_X (X - \hat{X})^T (X - \hat{X}), \tag{4.4}$$

where w_X is a scalar function of the input vector X. Examples of w_X include the energy or intensity of the vector (to weight bright areas more), a numerical value proportional to how textured a vector appears, and a weighting depending on the membership of X in some user-defined class. Knowledge of the human visual system can be easily incorporated into a design of this type by relating the w_X to the perceptual importance of the input vector X.

Although a tractable distortion measure is needed for optimizing the design, other explicit or implicit measures of distortion may be required to validate the worth of a compression system. For example, in medical imaging it may be far more important to verify that diagnostic accuracy remains as good or better with compressed images than it is to compare SNRs [22].

A final important attribute of a VQ is its implementation complexity; because this is not easy to quantify, we restrict our discussion to comparisons among the various code structures.

Code Design

Of the many approaches to vector quantizer design some commonly seen ones are random codebook population, lattice codes, annealing algorithms, and clustering techniques such as the Lloyd (Forgey, Isodata, k-means) algorithm or the pairwise nearest neighbor algorithm [39, 8]. The Lloyd algorithm is the approach emphasized here. One of the simplest clustering techniques, it iteratively improves a codebook by alternately optimizing the encoder for the decoder (using a minimum distortion or nearest neighbor mapping) and the decoder for the encoder (replacing the old codebook or collection of templates with by generalized "centroids"). For squared error distortion, centroids are the Euclidean mean of the input vectors yielding a given channel binary codeword. They are well defined but slightly more complicated for the general input-weighted squared error distortion [12]. Code design is an iterative procedure usually based on a training set of typical data rather than on mathematical models of the data. For example, in medical imaging applications one might train on several images of the modality and organ scanned for a particular application. The Lloyd algorithm has been described in detail in a variety of places (see, e.g., [11], [1], [10]).

Structured VQ

Shannon theory states that VQ can perform arbitrarily close to the theoretical optimal performance for a given rate if the vectors have a sufficiently large dimension. Unfortunately, however, code complexity grows exponentially with vector dimension. The practical solution to this "curse of dimensionality" is to constrain the code structure. This may result in codes that are not mathematically optimal but that can have significantly reduced implementation complexity. Lower complexity in turn means that larger vectors can be used, which can provide better performance than unconstrained full-search VQ for any given bit rate. The most common constrained memoryless code structures are lattice-based codes, classified VQ [26], tree-structured VQ, multistep VQ, product codes, and transform VQ. The most common constrained recursive code structures are predictive VQ (vector DPCM) and finite state VQ. This chapter focuses on tree-structured VQ (TSVQ); details of the other algorithms can be found in [10].

Tree-structured Vector Quantization

The key idea in tree-structured VQ (TSVQ) is to perform a tree search on a codebook designed for such a search rather than to perform a full search of an unstructured codebook. Figure 4.2 depicts two simple binary trees.

In both cases the codeword is selected by a sequence of binary decisions. The search begins at the root node, where the encoder compares the input vector to two possible candidate reproductions and picks the one with minimum distortion. This is a full search of a binary codebook. If the input-weighted squared error of equation 4.4 is used, the selection is equivalent to a maximum correlation test or a hyperplane test. The encoder advances to the selected node. If the node is not a terminal node or leaf of the tree, the encoder continues and chooses the best available node of the new pair presented. The encoder produces binary symbols to represent its sequence of decisions. For example, a 0 indicates the left child is selected, and a 1 indicates the right child. The binary codeword is then a path map through the tree to the terminal node, which is labeled with the final codeword. The two trees in the figure differ in that the one on the right is *balanced*, and all binary-channel codewords have the same length R. This tree yields a fixed-length or fixed-rate code. The other tree is *unbalanced* and has binary channel codewords of different lengths. Here the instantaneous bit rate, the number of bits per input vector or pixel, changes, but the average is constrained. As with a lossless code, this gives the code the freedom to allocate more bits to active areas where they are needed, and fewer bits to uninteresting areas such as background. The goal in lossy compression is to choose long or short codewords so as to minimize average distortion for a given bit rate, not to match probable or improbable vectors, as in lossless coding.

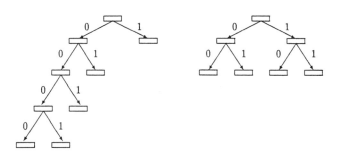

Figure 4.2
Unbalanced and balanced trees.

The search complexity of a balanced tree is linear in bit rate instead of exponential, at the cost of a roughly doubled memory size. For unbalanced trees the search complexity remains linear in the average bit rate, but the memory can be considerably larger unless constrained.

A potentially great advantage of the tree structure is that if it is properly designed, each successive decision will further refine the reproduction, at least in an average sense. Such a code will have a built-in successive approximation or progressive character. As more bits describing a given vector arrive, the quality of the reproduction improves. This progressive structure also means that the rate can be adjusted according to available communication capacity. If the available rate is cut, one codes less deeply into the tree, and vice versa. The same tree is used regardless of the allowed rate, and the quality is as good as possible for the allowed rate. How is a tree-structured code designed to have these properties? This is accomplished by combining clustering with ideas from classification and regression tree design [2]. Classification trees are effectively a sequence of questions or tests on an input in order to classify it. The general philosophy of classification tree design is a gardening metaphor: First *grow* a tree and then *prune* it.

Growing Trees

The root node can be considered to be labeled with the optimum rate 0 codeword, which is the centroid of the learning set or distribution. We split the node into two new child nodes. The split can involve simply perturbing the root node label slightly and using the root node label and its perturbation as the two new child labels or, more cleverly, forming two new labels along the axis produced by a principal components analysis [43]. We then run a clustering algorithm on the pair to produce a good 1-bit codebook as level 1 of the tree. Two quite different options are then available:

Split All Terminal Nodes

Given a tree, one way to extend it is simultaneously to split all current terminal nodes, which at the moment amount to two nodes, and then cluster. Thus, for each current terminal node, all the learning set (or the conditional probability) surviving to that node will be used in the clustering algorithm to design a good 1-bit code that forms the given node's children. When the clustering algorithm converges for all the split nodes, we shall have a new tree with twice as many nodes. Because we began this step with a balanced tree with two nodes in the first level, we now have a balanced tree with four nodes in the second level. We can continue in this fashion. We split all terminal nodes, simultaneously run the clustering algorithm for all the new nodes, and obtain a new balanced tree.

Balanced trees have two clear drawbacks:

• As the tree grows, some nodes may become quite sparse in training vectors (or low in conditional probability), hence the resulting clusters cannot be trusted. Some nodes may even be devoid of training vectors and will be a waste of bits.

• Since all binary codewords have the same length, there will likely be too many bits to represent inactive vectors and too few to represent active vectors.

Split One Node at a Time

An alternative design paradigm is to split nodes one at a time rather than an entire level at a time. After the level-1 codebook has converged, we choose one of the two nodes to split and run a clustering algorithm on that node alone to obtain a new, unbalanced tree. We then repeat the process, splitting one node at a time until the tree reaches the desired average rate. How do we choose which node to split? There are two common answers, neither of which is optimal. The first is to split the *worst* node, the one with the largest contribution to the average distortion. This technique was introduced by Makhoul, Roucos, and Gish [19] and will be referred to as *worst-node splitting*. Alternative definitions of "worst" are possible. For example, we might split the node with the largest conditional average distortion rather than the largest partial distortion (the difference being whether or not the node distortion is normalized by the node probability).

The second approach is optimal in an incremental or greedy fashion. Splitting a node will cause an increase in average rate, ΔR, and a decrease in average distortion, ΔD. We choose to split the node that maximizes the magnitude slope $|\Delta D / \Delta R|$, thereby getting the largest possible decrease in average distortion per increase in average bit rate [30]. This turns out to be a natural extension of a fundamental design technique for classification and regression tree design as exemplified in the CART™ algorithm of [2].

Pruning

Whether the tree is balanced or unbalanced, the growing algorithm greedily optimizes for the current split only and does not anticipate the impact of the current split on future splits. Furthermore, even the unbalanced tree can result in sparsely populated or improbable nodes that cannot be fully trusted to typify long-run behavior. A solution to both these problems is to take a grown tree and prune it back using a similar strategy of trading-off rate with distortion [5, 14, 31, 29]. Pruning by removing a node and all its descendents will reduce the average bit rate, but it will increase the average distortion. The idea is to minimize the increase of average distortion per decrease in bit rate, that is, to minimize the magnitude slope $|\Delta D / \Delta R|$. Now, however, we can consider the effect of removing entire branches rather than individual nodes. This permits us to find the optimal subtrees of an initial tree in the sense of providing the best rate-distortion trade-off. The key property that makes such pruning work is that the optimal subtrees of decreasing rate are nested, that is, the optimal TSVQs formed by pruning an initial tree form embedded codes. In particular, this means that these codes have the successive approximation character: The distortion decreases on average as the bit rate increases. Figure 4.3 depicts a sequence of pruned subtrees.

To summarize its good points: unbalanced TSVQ

• Yields lower distortion than fixed-rate full-search VQ for a given *average* rate.

• Has a simple encoder: It is a sequence of binary decisions.

• Has a simple design algorithm: grow and prune.

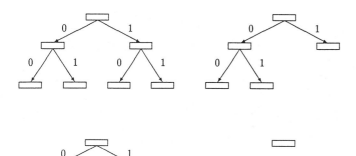

Figure 4.3
Pruned subtrees.

• Has a natural successive approximation (progressive) property.

• Is well matched to variable-rate environments such as storage or packet communications.

• Provides as a byproduct an automatic segmentation into active and inactive regions by bit rate.

• Can have its tree tailored by an input-dependent importance weighting, permitting the incorporation of enhancement and classification into the tree.

The final attribute will be explored shortly. Having listed the good points of TSVQ, we should admit the principal bad points. In some applications we need to maintain a fixed-rate communications link, and the buffering required to send a variable-rate bit stream over a fixed-rate link is not justified. We might still desire the TSVQ advantages of fast encoding/fast table-lookup decoding and good performance. A simple solution due to [19] for an unbalanced TSVQ is simply to relabel the nodes using fixed-size binary words. This relabeling preserves the fast search and table-lookup decoder but loses some rate-distortion performance. More importantly, in some applications it loses the successive approximation property.

The second drawback of TSVQ is that the total codebook size can become quite large, even though the average rate is constrained to be small. This problem can be lessened by trading-off average distortion against a linear combination of rate and the number of nodes in the tree so that the latter is included in the cost of the tree.

Human Perception and Vector Quantization

To explicitly consider human perceptual effects in a VQ system, we begin with a basic example of memoryless VQ applied to the often-cited USC image database at a relatively low rate in order to point out some of the artifacts introduced by compression. A TSVQ was designed using 10 images from this set, not including the Lenna image. The vector used was a 16-dimensional 4×4 square. The resulting PSNR ($10 \log_{10} 255^2 / D$) on the test Lenna image was 30.63 dB. The image compressed from 8 bpp to 0.5 bpp is shown in figure 4.4. The bit rate is low enough to show some of the common problems with VQ. The blocking effect resulting from square vector shapes is clearly visible, especially in the sawtooth or staircase arti-

Figure 4.4
Memoryless TSVQ: Lenna at 0.5005 bpp.

facts in the edges of the arm and nose and in the gentle shading transitions in the shoulder and band of the hat that appear edgelike, an effect known as contouring. One goal of compression algorithm design is to diminish these perceptual artifacts introduced by the coding without increasing the bit rate. There are a variety of ways to accomplish this, some of which explicitly take advantage of properties of human vision. Some of these techniques are sketched; other recent techniques are detailed later in the chapter.

VQ Based on a Model of the Human Visual System

A variation on the techniques of transform coding and subband filters exploits knowledge of the human visual spatial-frequency response. In a sense the input vectors are mapped into "model space" by two-dimensional filtering of the image that attenuates or amplifies spectral components according to a human visual model [37] of perceptually unimportant or important frequency bands. This approach was used by Budge et al. [3] to obtain significantly better perceived quality at fractional bit rates than were acheived by the same memoryless full-search VQ on the original image. The cost of the improvement was the

additional two-dimensional filtering of the entire image required before and after quantization.

A variation on this theme was considered by Safranek and Johnson [33, 34] for subband coding with scalar quantization. They developed a measure of the perceptual sensitivity to noise, mean intensity, and local variation in each spatial-frequency band using simple subjective tests. This measure provided an importance weighting to squared errors in the various frequency bands that in turn led to an adjustment of bit rates of the scalar quantizers in each band to provide roughly equal subjective distortion across the bands. Although their sensitivity measurements were based on the effects of additive random noise and not signal-dependent quantization noise, the system achieved significant improvement of perceived quality.

Both these approaches share a common philosophy: Use more bits to code components of the image that are more visible and fewer bits to code components that are visible. The quantization noise should be "hidden" where the eye is not sensitive to noise. Another approach toward this end will be considered shortly.

A further variation on this theme was developed by Ramamoorthy and Jayant [25], who used perceptual information to provide transparent quality in a low-rate image-compression system that used a finite-state vector quantizer when it provided a good fit to the signal and switched to a scalar quantization system when the VQ did not work within a prescribed threshold. The scalar system took advantage of the spatial-frequency sensitivity of the eye as previously described, but it also took advantage of nonlinear saturation effects to further reduce the bit rate.

Classified VQ

Ramamurthi and Gersho's classified vector quantizer [26] can be viewed as incorporating visual properties because it explicitly classifies edges and orientations and background and uses more bits and a smarter code to compress the perceptually more important edge information.

Frequency-dependent Distortion Measures

Instead of transforming the input by filtering and then using a squared-error distortion measure, one can use a distortion measure that effectively computes a weighted squared-error distortion in the transform domain. This allows one to use distortion measures such as those introduced by Mannos and Sakrison [20] that appear to correspond well to subjective distortion. Unfortunately, however, these distortion measures can be quite difficult to compute, as they require logarithms and odd powers of the transforms of the image and reproduction.

A variety of other recent perceptually based techniques, including input-weighted distortion measures, dynamic range adjustments, and alternative vector shapes, are considered in later sections.

Diagnostic Accuracy

An indirect use of human visual factors to influence compression system design is to validate a compression system by studying its effects when the compressed images are substituted for the original images and used by experts in a specific application. The goal of such studies is to show that a specific compression system either does or does not affect decisions made by experts on the images in a statistically significant manner. An example of such an experiment is an ongoing study designed to quantify the diagnostic accuracy of compressed images using predictive TSVQ [22]. Three Stanford radiologists evaluated chest CT images with two common radiologic findings: pulmonary nodules and mediastinal adenopathy. Forty-eight images with either lung nodules or abnormal nodes, or no clinical abnormalities were viewed in randomized experiments at various levels of compression. Diagnoses were made in a typical fashion and the results were analyzed for the effects of compression on sensitivity (the probability of correctly detecting a lesion) and predictive value positive (the probability that a detected lesion is in fact a lesion). Although detailed statistical analyses are currently in progress, preliminary results indicate that predictive value positive is largely unaffected by compression down to the lowest bit rates considered (approximately 0.5 bpp from an 11-bpp original) and that sensitivity is fairly constant down to rates near 1 bpp. Human vision is a key part of such experiments, because the study seeks to determine what sort of visual artifacts introduced by compression are more likely to lead to diagnostic errors.

Histogram-Equalized VQ

Historically, several signal-processing techniques have been developed that provide images that are perceived as

being better than the original, at least for some applications. Although human perception may play only an incidental role in their design, it is subjective quality as perceived by humans that validates the usefulness of an algorithm. In some cases it is possible to apply such signal processing to the VQ codewords off-line to form an alternative codebook that the user can select to provide an enhanced reproduction with no further computation. An example of such a technique is *histogram equalization*, a method for making visible a wider dynamic range in images, showing features that might previously have been hidden in the dark or washed out by the light areas.

Histogram equalization remaps each pixel to an intensity proportional to its rank among surrounding pixels [16]. By transforming each pixel according to the inverse of a cumulative distribution function, the histogram or empirical distribution of the pixel intensities can be altered. If the cumulative distribution function is the empirical distribution of the image, the result is to form a more uniform distribution of pixel intensities, effectively widening the perceived dynamic range of the image. A histogram equalized in units of image intensity will not also be equalized in the corresponding log scale of image density, and one can debate whether to use a scale corresponding to physical luminance on the monitor or to signal amplitude or to perceived brightness. In the following example we are primarily concerned with illustrating the application of such a dynamic range adjustment to the codebook rather than with the merits of any particular type of dynamic range adjustment.

In global histogram equalization one calculates the intensity histogram for the entire image and then remaps each pixel's intensity proportional to its rank among all the pixel intensities. Instead of performing the decoding and equalizing operations sequentially, one can perform them simultaneously by equalizing the decoder's codebook off-line [7]. Thus the decoder's reconstruction of the image and the histogram equalization are performed in the same time required by the decompression alone. For example, one can construct a global histogram containing all pixels in the training images, and each pixel of each codeword can be equalized using this global histogram. Thus each pixel of each terminal node will be remapped to a new intensity that is proportional to its rank in the global histogram. These new codewords can be stored at the decoder along with the original codewords. The resulting system is diagramed in figure 4.5. The encoder

Encoder

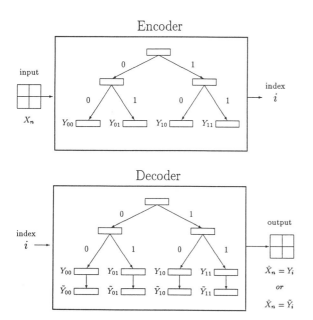

Decoder

Figure 4.5
VQ with equalized and unequalized codebooks.

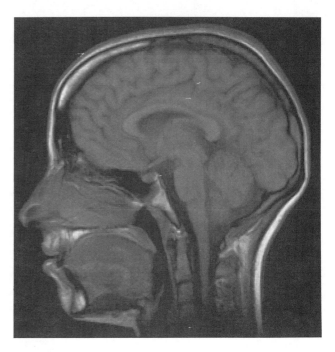

Figure 4.6
Original image.

is unchanged. The decoder takes the same set of indices and puts them through the same tree, but upon reaching a terminal node of the tree, the decoder now has the option of outputting either Y_i, the compressed reproduction, or $\tilde{Y}_i$, the compressed and histogram-equalized reproduction. The radiologist thus has the option of looking at either the equalized or the unequalized series of compressed scans and either way requires the same amount of time to reconstruct the image. The idea of using VQ to perform image processing was first suggested by Read et al. at Brigham Young University [27, 28].

To demonstrate the technique, an unbalanced TSVQ was grown to an average depth of 2 bpp based on a training sequence of 5 magnetic resonance (MR) mid-sagittal brain scans blocked into 2×2 vectors. The tree was pruned back to 1.7 bpp, and the resulting codebook equalized according to the global histogram of the learning set. Figure 4.6 shows the original test image at 8 bpp. Application of the code to this image yields the histogram-equalized compressed image at 1.7 bpp along with the unequalized compressed image in figure 4.7. The image quality of the equalized compressed image is very high, and its contrast is enhanced, for example, the invaginations of the cortex are more obvious, and the vertebrae are more clearly differentiated from the interstitial spaces. The quality of this enhancement is essentially indistinguishable from the case in which the decoding and equalization are done *sequentially*, despite the fact that sequential operations allow one to use the histogram of the decoded image rather than the histogram of the training images.

Input-weighted Distortion

A class of distortion measures that can incorporate visual properties yet are relatively easy to use and compute and that do not require full-frame transforms for implementation is the class considered in equation 4.4, the input-weighted squared-error distortion. The distortion measure is used in ordinary TSVQ in three distinct ways, namely,

1. In the minimum distortion selection rule;

2. In the computation of a centroid corresponding to a binary channel codeword;

3. In the splitting criterion in a greedily grown TSVQ.

The last attribute means that by weighting a distortion measure according to input behavior, the tree can be forced to throw more bits at important inputs. The advantage is that the tree splitting is done entirely off-line. The centroid computation is also performed off-line and can use the weighted distortion measure, but this does not

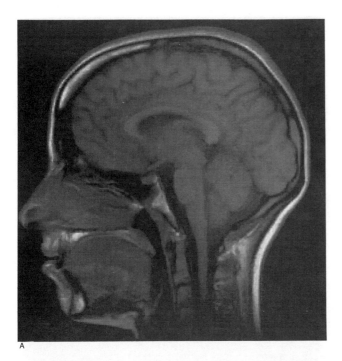

A

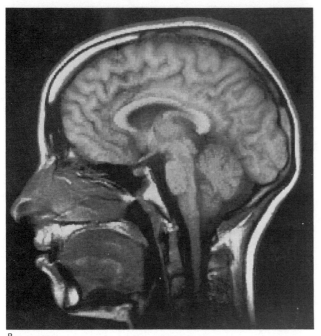

B

Figure 4.7
Compressed images at 1.7 bpp: regular (A) and equalized (B).

always help (and sometimes hurts perceptually). The minimum distortion is selected without the weighting, since the weighting depends only on the input and hence does not affect codeword choice. (This would not necessarily be the case if the weighting were a more general positive-definite matrix B_x instead of a scalar w_x.)

We consider three examples of weighted distortion measures: weighting proportional to image intensity, weighting dependent on automatic texture classification, and weighting determined by hand labeling a training set for important features.

Intensity Weighting

A classification based on intensity, in which bright training vectors are weighted more heavily than dark ones, is appropriate for MR brain scans because the bright parts of the image typically correspond to what is medically most important in the image. Certainly the dark background of the image is of no importance, and a high distortion can be tolerated there. The training sequence consisting of eight MR brain scans at 8 bpp was blocked into 2×2 pixel blocks, and each vector was assigned a weight proportional to its Euclidean norm, that is, the square root of its energy:

$$w_x = \left[\frac{1}{20} \sqrt{\sum_{i=1}^{4} x_i^2} \right]. \tag{4.5}$$

Using the weighted distortion measure for splitting, a tree was grown to 2 bpp, pruned back to 0.75 bpp, and evaluated on images not in the training sequence. The same training sequence without weights assigned was used to grow an unweighted unbalanced tree according to the original greedy growing algorithm. The original test image of figure 4.6 was used. An example of the compressed images at 0.75 bpp produced by the two different trees is given in figure 4.8. The image made from the weighted tree looks better in the bright regions (e.g., the cortex and cerebellum), which generally correspond to the diagnostically important part of these images.

Texture Weighting

Due to pattern masking, the human visual system is generally less sensitive to noise in highly active or textured regions of an image. The greedy growing algorithm can be used to accomplish such a redistribution of quantization noise into regions of more texture by using a texture-

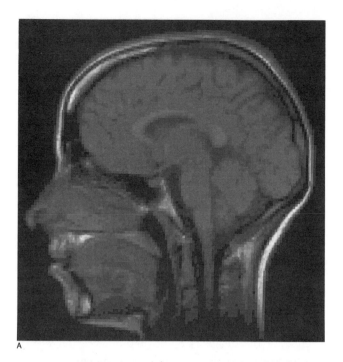

A

Figure 4.9
Unweighted distortion measure.

based classification scheme. It is not appropriate to use MR scans for this purpose, because the most highly textured part of the image is the cortex, which is often the most important medically. Hence noise should not be placed in textured regions of MR scans. Instead we considered the USC database images for this application. The training sequence consisted of six USC database images, blocked into 4 × 4 vectors. The weights were assigned to the training vectors as follows: For each 4 × 4 block, 24 possible pairs of adjacent pixels were examined to see if the difference between them exceeded some threshold. Highly textured vectors, which have many pairs exceeding the threshold, were assigned low weights. Highly homogeneous vectors were assigned large weights.

A tree was grown to 2 bpp using the weighted distortion for the splitting criterion and then was pruned back to 0.54 bpp. Examples of compressed test images at approximately 0.54 bpp produced by a normal unweighted tree and by the weighted tree are shown in figures 4.9 and 4.10.

The compressed image from the weighted tree has less distortion in the cloud regions, where distortion is most noticeable, and more in the areas of trees, where the high texture masks the noise. Nontextured regions misclassified as textured have clearly inferior quality; hence the

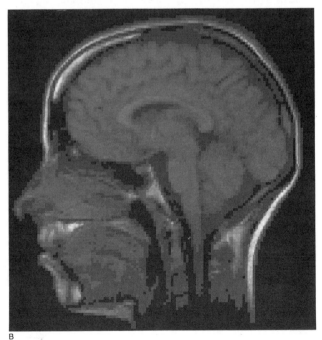

B

Figure 4.8
Compressed images at 0.75 bpp: regular (A) and weighted distortion measure (B).

Figure 4.10
Weighted distortion measure.

Figure 4.11
Original aerial image.

performance of the technique is quite sensitive to the classifier.

Hand-labeled Classification

In this section the emphasis is on classification rather than compression. By combining VQ and low-level classification, one can automatically classify certain simple features in an image as part of the compression process. Such a combination can be used to highlight regions in the reconstructed image belonging to a specific class to draw attention to certain features. The classification of the training set is performed by a person labeling by hand those features that are to be recognized in subsequent images. In our example, aerial photographs are hand-labeled as regions of artificial and natural objects. This a priori knowledge is used when designing the TSVQ codebook so that both small average distortion and accurate implicit classification are achieved.

A new idea [21] is to perform the classification simultaneously with the image encoding. Hence one tree-structured search is sufficient to both encode a particular subblock and classify it into one of the previously determined categories. Stored with each codeword in the codebook is a class label representing the best class prediction for image subblocks that will be represented by that particular codeword. Thus once the encoder selects the most appropriate codeword, the preliminary classification of the subblock at hand is simply a matter of memory lookup; no other computations are required. In effect, we are getting this classification knowledge "for free."

The training set consisted of five images provided by ESL, Inc. The images were 512×512 pixels of 8-bit gray scale consisting of aerial photography of the San Francisco Bay area. Each 16×16 pixel subblock in the training set was assigned to be either artificial or natural based on the perceptions of a human observer. Although the codebook construction and image encoding were carried out using 4×4 pixel subblocks as vectors, the training vectors were classified into 16×16 subblocks to simplify the task of the human classifier (even using the 16×16 subblocks, over 5000 decisions had to be made.) Using a training set classified with finer resolution might improve classification ability. The original test image to be compressed and classified is shown in figure 4.11.

The best predictive class for a given codeword in a VQ codebook was determined by a majority vote of the a priori class assignments of the training vectors represented by that codeword.

Gray et al.: Incorporating Visual Factors into Vector Quantizers

Table 4.1
PSNR and Classification Ability Using TSVQ Codebooks

	Criterion		
	1	2	3
Test PSNR (dB)	23.4	22.8	22.7
Test classification ability	0.71	0.74	0.75

Codebooks were generated using three different splitting criteria:

Criterion 1 Ignore the classification information and split the node with the largest $\lambda_1 = |\Delta D/\Delta R|$, where ΔD is the change in squared error resulting from the split, and ΔR is the change in average rate. This design yields an ordinary greedily grown VQ for comparison.

Criterion 2 Split the node that has the greatest percentage of misclassified training vectors, that is, split the node that is worst in the sense of having the largest value of

$$\lambda_2 = \frac{\text{(Number of misclassified vectors in node)}}{\text{(Total number of vectors in node)}}. \quad (4.6)$$

Here the encoder nearest-neighbor mapping and the centroid reproduction levels are chosen to minimize squared error, but the tree is grown to reduce classification error.

Criterion 3 Split the node that is worst in the sense of having the greatest number of misclassified training vectors.

Each splitting criterion was used to construct a TSVQ codebook at an average bit rate of 0.5 bpp. A test image outside the training sequence was encoded with the resulting codebooks. Compression and classification ability results are given in table 4.1. Classification ability is defined as the percentage of vectors classified correctly by the encoder compared with the classification standard created by the human observer. In general, the first splitting criterion provided the lowest mean-squared error in the encoded images at the expense of reduced classification ability. The latter splitting methods provided poorer compression ability (the encoded images were more blocky in appearance) but better classification ability, at least for the test image. Choosing the splitting criterion involves a trade-off between compression and classification quality; some splits serve one purpose better than the other.

Ideally, the compressed images are viewed on a color monitor so that classification information can be indicated by color superimposed on the gray-scale reconstructed

Figure 4.12
Image compressed to 0.46 bpp by compression/classification encoder.

image. Such a contrast makes the natural and artificial features of the image easier for a human viewer to differentiate. Because the simultaneous display of the compression and classification results is difficult in a gray-scale format, the results of the compression and classification are shown separately here. Experimental data are shown for images encoded and classified with a codebook grown using criterion 2. Figure 4.12 shows the image after compression at 0.46 bpp. Figure 4.13 shows the subblocks in the compressed image that the encoder classified as natural; the artificial subblocks are replaced by solid white subblocks. The classification ability was modest; at 0.5 bpp the best classification encoder still had 25 percent misclassification error on the training set. However, this large error was partly due to the quality of the hand-labeled training set. The hand-labeling was affected by the human observer's resolution and consistency limitations.

Tiling Shapes

Virtually all published applications of vector quantization to image compression use square or rectangular vectors. Such blocks are a natural and convenient means of tiling an image, that is, of covering the image with nonover-

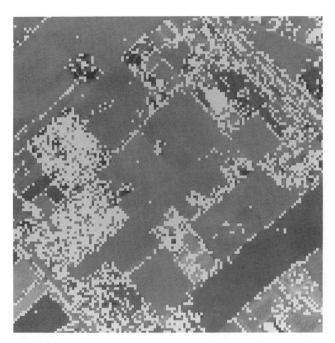

Figure 4.13
Natural subblocks using compression/classification encoder. Artificial subblocks are replaced by solid white subblocks.

Figure 4.14
Test image with 17-dimensional sharp tile.

Figure 4.15
Test image with 23-dimensional hexagonal tile.

lapping replicates of a single pattern or tile. This produces the visual artifacts of blockiness, sawtooth patterns, and contouring. Alternative shapes might reduce these unwanted visual artifacts. Tiles with edges tending to be more diagonal than vertical or horizontal might take advantage of the *oblique effect* of human vision: the fact that human visual acuity is greater in the vertical and horizontal directions; therefore humans are less sensitive to diagonal edges than to horizontal or vertical ones. Tiles that interlock pixels instead of having straight edges may lead to less abrupt changes by the innate filtering of high-frequency artifacts by the eye. We shall indeed see that a suitable choice of tile shape can effectively remove the contouring effect and can smooth the sawtooth patterns.

A wide variety of tiles may be found in [13]. We have chosen two of the better ones to illustrate the potential gains: the 17-dimensional sharp tile (figure 4.14) and the 23-dimensional hexagonal tile (figure 4.15). The shading transitions are much improved in the alternative tiles, and the sawtooth nature of edges is subdued but not eliminated. A speckling artifact not present with the square tile is introduced, but it is perceptually minimized with the hexagonal tile. Because tiles of these shapes cannot com-

Gray et al.: Incorporating Visual Factors into Vector Quantizers

pletely cover the square test images, a small number of pixels at the borders are left unencoded.

Dimension 17 Sharp Tile

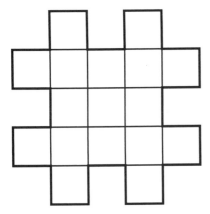

The interlocking pixels around the border were intended to reduce the blockiness of the usual square tile. The PSNR was 30.20 dB at 0.4937 bpp.

Dimension 23 Hexagonal Tile

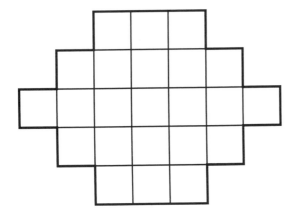

Here the idea was to make the edges lie along the diagonals, making use of the "oblique effect" of vision. The PSNR was 30.59 dB at 0.4855 bpp.

Concluding Comments

Our goal has been to survey the fundamental ideas underlying image compression from the point of view of vector quantization and to sketch ways in which design algorithms based on clustering and classification trees can be modified to take advantage of properties of the human visual system. We have provided examples of some of these methods: combining histogram equalization with compression, using input-weighted distortion measures to better code important behavior, and using nonrectangular vectors to reduce visual artifacts of low-rate coded images. Some of these techniques are recent in origin and the results are preliminary, but they suggest that quantifiable visual factors can be incorporated into the optimization algorithms used to design vector quantizers for image compression. The combination of compression with classification also suggests that further advantage can be taken of the inherent enhancing and classifying capabilities of clustering and classification trees to yield compression algorithms that enhance or highlight important features that are selectable by human experts or automatic algorithms.

Acknowledgments

The research reported here was partially supported by the National Institutes of Health, the National Science Foundation, and ESL, Inc. The authors gratefully acknowledge the helpful cooperation and contributions to this research of Professors Eve Riskin and Richard Olshen and of Sang-Ju Park, Jack May, and Amanda Heaton.

References

[1] H. Abut, ed. (1990). *Vector Quantization*. IEEE Reprint Collection. Piscataway, N.J.: IEEE Press.

[2] L. Breiman, J. H. Friedman, R. A. Olshen, and C. J. Stone (1984). *Classification and Regression Trees*. Belmont, Calif.: Wadsworth.

[3] S. E. Budge, T. J. Stockham, Jr., D. M. Chabries, and R. W. Christiansen (1988). Vector quantization of color digital images within a human visual model. In *Proceedings of the International Conference on Acoustics, Speech, and Signal Processing* 816–819.

[4] P. J. Burt and E. H. Adelson (1983). The Laplacian pyramid as a compact image code. *IEEE Transactions on Communications* COM-31: 552–540.

[5] P. A. Chou, T. Lookabaugh, and R. M. Gray (1989). Optimal pruning with applications to tree-structured source coding and modeling. *IEEE Transactions on Information Theory* IT-35: 299–315.

[6] R. J. Clarke (1985). *Transform Coding of Images*. Orlando, Fla.: Academic Press.

[7] P. C. Cosman, E. A. Riskin, and R. M. Gray. Combining vector quantization and histogram equalization (1991). In J. A. Storer and J. H. Reif, eds., *Proceedings Data Compression Conference*, 113–118, Snowbird, Utah: IEEE Computer Society Press.

[8] W. H. Equitz (1989). A new vector quantization clustering algorithm. *IEEE Transaction on Acoustics, Speech and Signal Processing* (October): 1568–1575.

[9] R. G. Gallager (1978). Variations on a theme by Huffman. *IEEE Transactions on Information Theory* IT-24: 668–674.

[10] A. Gersho and R. M. Gray (1992). *Vector Quantization and Signal Compression*. Boston: Kluwer Academic Publishers.

[11] R. M. Gray (1984). Vector quantization. *IEEE ASSP Magazine* 1(2): 4–29.

[12] R. M. Gray and E. Karnin (1982). Multiple local optima in vector quantizers. *IEEE Transactions on Information Theory* IT-28: 256–261.

[13] R. M. Gray, S. J. Park, and B. Andrews (1991). Tiling shapes for image vector quantization. In *Proceedings Third International Conference on Advances in Communication and Control Systems*, Victoria, B.C., October.

[14] R. M. Gray and E. A. Riskin (1988). Variable rate pruned tree-structured vector quantizers for medical image coding. In *Proceedings 1988 ComCon (Advances in Communication and Control)*, Baton Rouge, La., October.

[15] D. A. Huffman (1977). A method for the construction of minimum redundancy codes. *Proceedings of the IRE* 40: 1098–1101.

[16] R. Hummel (1977). Image enhancement by histogram transformation. *Computer Graphics and Image Processing* 6: 184–195.

[17] N. S. Jayant and P. Noll (1984). *Digital Coding of Waveforms*. Englewood Cliffs, N.J.: Prentice-Hall.

[18] M. Kunt, M. Bénard, and R. Leonardi (1987). Recent results in high compression image coding. *IEEE Transactions on Circuits and Systems* CAS-34(11): 1306–1336.

[19] J. Makhoul, S. Roucos, and H. Gish (1985). Vector quantization in speech coding. *Proceedings of the IEEE* 73(11): 1551–1587.

[20] J. L. Mannos and D. J. Sakrison (1974). The effects of a visual fidelity criterion of the encoding of images. *IEEE Transactions on Information Theory* IT-20: 525–536.

[21] K. L. Oehler, P. C. Cosman, R. M. Gray, and J. May (1991). Classification using vector quantization. In *Conference Record of the Twenty-Fifth Asilomar Conference on Signals, Systems and Computers*, Pacific Grove, Calif. November.

[22] R. A. Olshen, P. C. Cosman, C. Tseng, C. Davidson, L. Moses, R. M. Gray, and C. Bergin (1991). Evaluating compressed medical images. In *Proceedings Third International Conference on Advances in Communication and Control Systems*, Victoria, B.C., October.

[23] R. Pasco (1976). *Source coding algorithms for fast data compression*. Ph. D. diss., Stanford University.

[24] M. Rabbani and P. W. Jones (1991). *Digital Image Compression Techniques*. Vol. TT7 of *Tutorial Texts in Optical Engineering*. Bellingham, Wash.: SPIE Optical Engineering Press.

[25] V. Ramamoorthy and N. S. Jayant (1988). High quality image coding with a model-testing vector quantizer and a human visual system model. In *Proceedings of the International Conference on Acoustics, Speech, and Signal Processing*, 1164–1167, New York.

[26] B. Ramamurthi and A. Gersho (1986). Classified vector quantization of images. *IEEE Transactions on Communications* COM-34: 1105–1115.

[27] C. J. Read, D. V. Arnold, D. M. Chabries, P. L. Jackson, and R. W. Christiansen (1988). Synthetic aperture radar image formation from compressed data using a new computation technique. *IEEE Aerospace and Electronic Systems Magazine* 3(10): 3–10.

[28] C. J. Read, D. M. Chabries, R. W. Christiansen, and J. K. Flanagan (1989). A method for computing the DFT of vector quantized data. In *Proceedings of the International Conference on Acoustics, Speech, and Signal Processing* 1015–1018.

[29] E. A. Riskin (1990). *Variable Rate Vector Quantization of Images*. Ph. D. diss., Stanford University.

[30] E. A. Riskin and R. M. Gray (1991). A greedy tree growing algorithm for the design of variable rate vector quantizers. *IEEE Transactions on Signal Processing* 39: 2500–2514.

[31] E. A. Riskin, T. Lookabaugh, P. A. Chou, and R. M. Gray (1990). Variable rate vector quantization for medical image compression. *IEEE Transactions on Medical Imaging* 9: 290–298.

[32] J. Rissanen (1976). Generalized Kraft inequality and arithmetic coding. *IBM Journal of Research and Development* 20: 198–203.

[33] R. J. Safranek and J. D. Johnston (1989). A perceptually tuned sub-band image coder with image dependent quantization and post-quantization data compression. In *Proceedings of the International Conference on Acoustics, Speech, and Signal Processing* 1945–1948, Glasgow, UK.

[34] R. J. Safranek, J. D. Johnston, and R. E. Rosenholtz (1990). A perceptually tuned sub-band image coder. In *Proceedings of the SPIE, The International Society for Optical Engineering* 284–293. IEEE: Santa Clara.

[35] C. E. Shannon (1948). A mathematical theory of communication. *Bell Systems Technical Journal* 27: 379–423, 623–656.

[36] C. E. Shannon (1959). Coding theorems for a discrete source with a fidelity criterion. In *IRE National Convention Record*, pt. 4, 142–163.

[37] T. G. Stockham, Jr. (1972). Image processing in the context of a visual model. *Proceedings of the IEEE* 60: 828–842.

[38] J. Storer (1988). *Data Compression*. Rockville, Md.: Computer Science Press.

[39] J. Ward (1963). Hierarchical grouping to optimize an objective function. *J. Amer. Stat. Assoc.* 37: 236–244.

[40] T. A. Welch (1984). A technique for high-performance data compression. *Computer* 8–18.

[41] P. A. Wintz (1972). Transform picture coding. In *Proceedings of the IEEE* 60:809–820.

[42] John W. Woods, ed. (1991). *Subband Image Coding.* Boston: Kluwer Academic Publishers.

[43] X. Wu and K. Zhang (1991). A better tree-structured vector quantizer. In J. A. Storer and J. E. Reif, eds., *Proceedings Data Compression Conference* 392–401, Snowbird, Utah.: IEEE Computer Society Press.

[44] J. Ziv and A. Lempel (1977). A universal algorithm for sequential data compression. *IEEE Transactions on Information Theory* IT-23:337–343.

[45] J. Ziv and A. Lempel (1978). Compression of individual sequences via variable-rate coding. *IEEE Transactions on Information Theory* IT-24:530–536.

5

A Practical Approach to Fractal-based Image Compression

Alex Pentland and Bradley Horowitz

Fractal geometry was introduced by Mandelbrot [7] in the late seventies and has had important consequences in a number of domains. In image processing and synthesis, fractals have been important because they can describe and generate natural-looking images with (potentially) infinite detail using only a small number of simple rules and parameters. The simplicity of these rules led the computer graphics community immediately to adopt fractals as their primary stochastic modeling tool.

In the image processing and compression community, fractals have generated a great deal of interest because of the prospect of solving the inverse problem, that of automatically recovering simple rules that describe complex imagery. Pentland [8] was perhaps the first to apply fractals to image processing, using estimates of fractal parameters to perform texture segmentation and shape extraction. More recently, Barnsley and Sloan [2] have proposed using iterated function systems (IFS) to achieve compression of some images, while Walach and Karnin [14] have proposed a "yardstick" technique to achieve a fractal encoding of images.

Most common fractals exhibit a type of statistical self-similarity, that is, a fixed pattern of relationships exists between the fractal's values at different scales of examination. Brownian fractals, for instance, exhibit a self-affine correlation structure. Consequently, we may characterize these fractal signals by discovering the pattern of relationships that exists within and between the different scales.

As an example, let us examine the appearance of some different-scale subbands of a typical image. Figure 5.1 shows a three-level Laplacian pyramid computed from an image, a decomposition of the signal into roughly octave-wide subbands. This transform was introduced by Burt and Adelson [3] and uses separable Gaussian linear filters to recursively bandsplit the image, generating a pyramid-like data structure that provides a relatively compact, multiscale representation of an image. Even a cursory examination of these subbands reveals that there is great similarity among the various scales. In large part this is

Figure 5.1
Three-level Laplacian pyramid of the image *face*.

due to the self-similarity of edges. A perfect edge appears the same at all scales and hence appears in the same location in each subband.

The image model that we have adopted is a generalization of the behavior of edges in subbands and characterizes images as a simple type of recursively defined, nonlinear fractal. In particular, in our model (1) all subbands of the same orientation consist of unions of the same primitive elements (e.g., edge fragments, textures), and (2) for all subbands of the same orientation there is a fixed, one-to-many function that maps that subband's elements to the elements of the next-higher-frequency subband. In the case of perfect edges the subband-to-subband mapping is simply the identity operation; however, in most cases the mapping is not only one-to-many but also non-deterministic. Our model defines a simple type of iterative fractal that when applied recursively can generate a wide class of imagery.

The main idea behind our approach to image compression is to characterize the set of mappings that exist between subbands and to use this knowledge to achieve greater compression ratios. By using a standard vector quantization approach (see chapter 4) we are able to characterize the patterns that exist within subbands, and by using a simple histogramming approach we are able statis-

tically to characterize the mapping between subbands. Using these characterizations we are then able to remove redundancies that exist between and within subbands.

Our work is similar in spirit to image extrapolation or interpolation techniques that attempt to predict high-frequency detail (or subbands) from lower-frequency content (or subbands). Extrapolation research, however, has focused almost exclusively on the use of linear and quasi-linear filters [10], whereas our approach is based on the observation that the conditional probabilities that relate different image subbands are inherently nonlinear and multimodal. Our work is also similar to the iterated function systems research of Barnsley [2]. In our approach, however, we limit ourselves to a much smaller class of iterated functions, thus simplifying the search for the correct set of iterative mappings.

A Testbed System

In this chapter we explain and demonstrate our fractal technique by applying it to a subband coding system using a wavelet decomposition (also referred to as a quadrature mirror filter (QMF) pyramid) and vector quantization (VQ). Several properties of the wavelet transform make it especially suitable for VQ. In particular, each oriented subband generated by the decomposition exhibits internal structure: The horizontal, vertical, and diagonal subbands show horizontal, vertical, and diagonal structure, respectively, due to the frequency response of the filter. It is important to remember, however, that our technique may potentially be adapted to any subband coding system.

The testbed system we describe is intended to be a simple, general-purpose image-compression facility rather than being optimized for low bit rates. In particular, because the system employed here is intended for near-real-time encoding/decoding, it avoids complex bit allocation schemes. Typical bit rates for this system are 0.57 bits per pixel (bpp) for a 30-dB SNR (approximately 35-dB peak SNR) using 256×256 8-bit gray-level imagery. The wavelet transform (QMF pyramid) employed is based on the 9-tap filter developed in our laboratory by Adelson, Simoncelli, and Hingorani [1].

The Wavelet Transform

Perhaps the earliest study using the QMF pyramid for image compression was by Adelson and Simoncelli [1],

Figure 5.2
(a) Original *face* image and (b) its wavelet (QMF) decomposition.

whereas Vetterli was the first to use quadrature mirror filters for image compression [13]. However, other researchers, such as Mallat [6], Gharavi and Tabatabai [5], and Tran et al. [12], also suggested use of the wavelet transform at about the same time.

A wavelet transform typically consists of a set of spatially localized orthonormal linear filters that split an image into oriented spatial-frequency bands. An important property of the wavelet transform (QMF pyramid) is that it can be constructed by recursive application of a base filter to successive low-pass subbands, requiring only $O(n)$ operations, where n is the number of image pixels.

The result of this transform is a set of subbands that are localized in scale (spatial frequency), orientation, and space. An example of such a transform is shown in figure 5.2; for additional detail see Simoncelli and Adelson [9].

Vector Quantization

This transform may be efficiently encoded by standard vector quantization techniques (see chapter 4). Vector quantizers map an input signal onto a set of finite reproduction vectors known as the *codebook*. In image compression each input signal is a two-dimensional $k \times l$ image patch. Once the codebook is constructed, pattern matching occurs between the input vector and the codebook entries. Ordering schemes, such as uniform lattices and K-dimensional trees, have been suggested to prune search times in the coding and generation processes.

Our implementation uses the Equitz nearest neighbor (ENN) algorithm to approximate a minimum distortion quantizer over the set of training vectors. The algorithm iterates by replacing the two "nearest neighbor" vectors in the codebook with a vector that optimally encodes their constituency. Codebook distance is measured using mean squared error, and vectors are weighted by the number of samples that depend on them. Typically the ENN algorithm iterates over the entire set of training vectors until it converges to a solution; we have chosen to incrementally build the codebook and constrain its maximum size to 256 entries. This greatly reduces the combinatorics of codebook generation while only slightly affecting the quality of the resulting codebook.

Figures 5.3 (a), (b), and (c) show the oriented subbands resulting from filtering with a separable 9-tap QMF filter. The magnitudes of the DFTs of each of the subbands are shown in figure 5.3(d), (e), and (f). These images have been

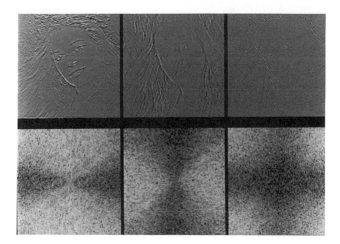

Figure 5.3
Horizontal, vertical, and diagonal subbands produced by QMF filtering image 2, and their respective DFTs. (High-magnitude coefficients are shown darker.)

contrast stretched to enhance visibility; thus the relative magnitudes between the images should be ignored. As can be seen, each of the subbands is highly structured and so lends itself to a VQ block classification technique. The differences in structure among the different orientation subbands also suggests that we use independent codebooks for each [10]. In our testbed implementation we give the subbands zero mean and unit variance before computing the VQ tables.

Entropy Coding

Because the information content among subbands varies widely, we investigated methods that adaptively allocate bandwidth based on the entropy in a subband. These methods depend on the information content in the images and also on the characteristics of the human visual system. A standard heuristic for determining information content is image variance. In VQ, variable bandwidth is implemented by using variable-length codebooks. The nature of the transform and coding/decoding procedure can also be used to discard redundant information. For instance, QMF filters are "leaky" with respect to orientation; the diagonally oriented energy leaks into the horizontal and vertical subbands of the same frequency, and vice versa. This overlap between subbands, combined with the relatively poor response of the human visual system to diagonal orientation, diminishes the perceptual importance of the high-frequency diagonal subbands [11].

Although entropy coding is a standard technique (and indeed is a large motivation behind pyramid coding in general), we have used fixed-length codebooks, since the multiscale fractal prediction technique is more easily implemented and demonstrated in this context. Entropy coding can be integrated into our system by using a multistage VQ scheme. In this approach, codebooks are represented in a hierarchical tree structure. This allows for easy traversal between levels (bit rates), and statistical correlations between subbands need be expressed only at the root of each tree.

Fractal-based Encoding

The output of the VQ stage is a set of codes for each of the horizontal, vertical, and diagonal subbands within each of the scales (pyramid levels) included in the wavelet transform. The codes for a lower-frequency subband will contain one-fourth the number of entries contained by the next-higher-frequency subband. The goal of our fractal-based encoding scheme is to first estimate the conditional probabilities between the codes of various subbands and then use these statistical relationships in a predictive coding algorithm.

In the pyramid subband structure shown in figure 5.2b, a $k \times I$ patch in one subband corresponds spatially to four $k \times I$ patches in the next-higher-frequency subband. Similarly, a single entry in that subband's coded representation corresponds to four entries in the coded representation of the next-higher-frequency subband. Determining the conditional probabilities between these codes is thus quite simple. As images are coded, the mappings between the VQ codes for each subband and the next-higher-frequency subband are tallied to obtain a histogram of the frequency of each of the mappings. Separate histograms are required for each of the four lower-to-higher frequency mappings. These histograms are called the *prediction lookup tables*.

Once this frequency histogram is constructed, the conditional probabilities between the various subband codings can be analyzed to determine an optimal lossless (with respect to the VQ coding) encoding scheme. In this scheme each VQ-coded entry of each band is recoded by comparing it with the codes most frequently associated with the VQ code at the corresponding location in the next-lower-frequency band. Typically the higher-frequency band's VQ code is one of the $2^n - 1$ codes found most frequently in the prediction lookup table associated with the lower-frequency band's VQ code. The VQ code for the higher-frequency band can then be recoded by use of an n-bit index into that prediction lookup table.

Thus each VQ code in the higher-frequency band is recoded by the following token:

n prediction index bits

m-bit VQ index (for prediction failures)

The prediction index indicates which of the $2^n - 1$ most frequent entries in the prediction lookup table is the correct lower-to-higher frequency mapping. In the event that the correct code for the higher-frequency subband is not one of the $2^n - 1$ most frequent predictions, the 2^nth index is reserved to indicate that the next token is a standard VQ codebook index. An optimal value for n is determined by minimizing

$$\frac{\text{bits}}{\text{token}} = P_n n + (1 - P_n)(n + m) = n + (1 - P_n)m, \quad (5.1)$$

where n is the number of bits used to index into the prediction lookup table, P_n is the percentage of low-to-higher frequency mappings accounted for by the most frequent $2^n - 1$ mappings, and m is the number of bits used to encode a full codebook index in case of a prediction failure. The optimal n is determined by analyzing the prediction lookup tables.

In our system the prediction index tokens and the VQ tokens resulting from the recoding are separately passed through standard Huffman and run-length encoders, thus forming the code that is finally transmitted. The lengths of these final codes, rather than entropy estimates, are the basis for all the bit rates quoted in this chapter.

Examples

Table 5.1 shows how the percentage of recodings, and the resulting bit rate, varies as a function of the number of bits n used to encode the lower-to-higher frequency mapping. These statistics were calculated using the testbed wavelet-and-VQ system described in the previous section and are averages over a set of 10 standard 256 × 256 8-bit gray-scale images. A three-level wavelet transform (QMF

Table 5.1
Bit Rate as a Function of Predictions over Training Set

Predictions	Bits	Percentage Encoded			Bit Rate
		Horizontal	Vertical	Diagonal	
0	0	0.0	0.0	0.0	0.57
1	1	33.96	34.65	28.61	0.47
3	2	57.75	61.40	52.91	0.43
7	3	78.98	82.01	75.13	0.36
15	4	93.53	96.06	91.81	0.35
31	5	99.88	99.98	98.94	0.38

pyramid) was used, and the vector quantizer used a vector size of 4 × 4 pixels. Separate codebooks were used for each orientation within the pyramid, and all coding occurred at the fixed rate of 8 bits per vector to simplify and facilitate determining the statistical relationship between subbands.

As the table shows, our fractal coding scheme produces up to a mean improvement of 1.5 times the testbed's original 0.57 bpp average coding rate. Because the fractal scheme is lossless with respect to the original VQ coding, the mean 30-dB SNR (35-dB peak SNR) is maintained even at a mean bit rate of 0.35 bpp. It is important to remember that our fractal coding scheme can potentially be combined with any subband coder.

Figure 5.4(a) shows the original *girl* image, at 256 × 256 pixel and 8-bit gray-level resolution. This image was coded by the testbed system at 0.57 bpp with 28.9-dB SNR (34.9-dB peak SNR). By combining our fractal coding scheme (using five prediction index bits) with the testbed coding system, we achieved a typical bit rate of 0.35 bpp. Since the technique is lossless with respect to the original VQ coding, the image shows no additional degradation as a function of bit rate. Figure 4(b) shows the reconstructed image at 0.31 bpp with 28.9-dB SNR (34.9 dB peak SNR).

Lossy Fractal Coding

The fractal coding scheme described gives lossless compression with respect to the original VQ coding. The same approach can readily be adapted to lossy coding by simply removing the "catch" entries. That is, rather than reserving the 2^nth entry of the prediction index as an indicator that a standard VQ codebook entry follows, we can instead transmit the prediction codebook index that is closest to the correct VQ entry. In our experiments, using 10 standard 256 × 256 8-bit gray-scale imagery, this approach has resulted in a threefold mean increase in coding

Figure 5.4
(a) Original 256 × 256, 8-bit *girl* image; (b) reconstructed image, 0.31 bpp at 28.9-dB SNR (34.9-dB peak SNR).

Figure 5.5
(a) Original 256 × 256, 8-bit *girl* image; (b) reconstructed image, 0.125 bpp at 26.8-dB SNR (31.9-dB peak SNR).

efficiency as compared with the original testbed coding system. Typical results are bit rates of approximately 0.125 bpp with approximately 28-dB SNR (approximately 33-dB peak SNR).

An example of this type of fractal coding is shown in figure 5.5. Figure 5.5(a) shows the original image, and figure 5.5(b) shows the lossy fractal coding at 0.125 bpp with 26.8-dB SNR (31.9-dB peak SNR).

Conclusion

We have described a fractal coding technique based on a very simple type of iterative fractal. In our algorithm a wavelet transform (QMF pyramid) is used to decompose an image into bands containing information from different scales (spatial frequencies) and orientations. The conditional probabilities between these different-scale bands are then determined and used as the basis for a predictive coding scheme.

We have found that the wavelet transform's various scale and orientation bands have a great deal of redundant, self-similar structure. This observation lends support to the assertion that most images conform to our fractal model of image structure. The resulting predictive coder is easily integrated into existing subband coding schemes and produces an average 1.5-fold gain in coding efficiency with no loss in image quality and up to a fourfold gain with slight loss in image quality. Coding and decoding are implemented by small table lookups, making the scheme practical for real-time applications.

Acknowledgment

This research was supported by Aberdeen Proving Ground and DARPA under contract DAA05-90-C-0333.

References

[1] Adelson, E., Simoncelli, E., and Hingorani, R. (1987) Orthogonal pyramid transforms for image coding. In *Proceedings of SPIE*, October 1987.

[2] Barnsley, M. (1988) *Fractals Everywhere*. New York: Academic Press.

[3] Bergen, J. R, Burt, P. J., Adelson, E. H., Anderson, C. H., and Ogden, J. M. (1984). Pyramid methods in image processing *RCA Engineer* 29(6):33−41.

[4] Burt, P. J., and Adelson, E. H., (1983). The laplacian pyramid as a compact image code. *IEEE Transactions on Communications* COM-31(4): 532−540.

[5] Gharavi, H., and Tabatabai, A., (1987). Application of quadrature mirror filters to the coding of monochrome and color images. In *Proceedings ICASSP* 1−32, 8,4.

[6] Mallat, S. G. (1987). A theory for multiresolution signal decomposition: The wavelet representation. *IEEE Transactions on Pattern Analysis and Machine Intelligence* 11(7):674−693.

[7] Mandelbrot, B. (1982). *The Fractal Geometry of Nature*. San Francisco: W. H. Freeman and Co.

[8] Pentland, A. P. (1984). Fractal-based description of natural scenes. *IEEE Transactions on Pattern Analysis and Machine Intelligence* 6(6):661−674.

[9] Simoncelli, E. P. and Adelson, E. (1990). Nonseparable extensions of quadrature mirror filters to multiple dimensions. *Proceedings of the IEEE* 78(4):652−664.

[10] Romano, P. (1989). *Vector Quantization for Spatiotemporal Sub-band Coding*. Master's thesis, MIT, Cambridge.

[11] Seno, T., and Girod, B. (1990). Vector quantization for entropy coding of image subbands. *MIT Vision and Modeling Group Technical Note no. 139*. May, 1990.

[12] Tran, A., Liu, K., Tzou, K., and Vogel, E. (1987). An efficient pyramid image coding system. In *Proceedings ICASSP* 18.6.1−18.6.4.

[13] Vetterli, M. (1984). Multi-dimensional sub-band coding: some theory and algorithms. *Signal Processing* 6(2):97−112.

[14] Karnin, E., and Walach, E., (1986). A fractal-based approach to image compression. *IEEE Transactions on ASSP*.

Part II

Perceptual Aspects of Image Coding

Lossy image coding is useful only because the human visual system is insensitive to certain image components. This suggests that visual system concepts should be prominent in the design of image codes and compression algorithms. There are two ways in which aspects of human vision may be exploited in image coding and compression. The conservative way is to adapt existing coding schemes to visual sensitivity. An example of this approach is described in the chapter by Gray, Cosman, and Oehler in the previous section, in which perceptually appropriate distortion criteria are used to design vector quantization codebooks. Another example is the use of the human contrast sensitivity function to design a quantization matrix for discrete cosine transform compression (Ahumada and Peterson, 1992; Daly, 1990; Peterson, 1992). A more radical approach is to design a code that mimics the code used by the visual brain (Watson, 1987; Watson, 1990; Watson and Ahumada, 1987). The logic of the radical approach is that it will automatically discard those elements of the image to which the human observer is blind.

When a compressed image cannot be distinguished visually from the original, the compression is said to be "perceptually lossless" (Watson, 1989). In chapter 6 Glenn reviews a number of the spatial and temporal aspects of visual sensitivity that may be exploited to achieve perceptually lossless compression. In a similar vein, Klein in chapter 7 examines the question of how many bits are required for a "perceptually lossless" pixel code and also considers visual aspects of the discrete cosine transform.

The fact that human spatial acuity is reduced for images in motion has long been proposed as an opportunity for significant compression of motion video. This proposal is critically analyzed by Eckert and Buchsbaum in chapter 8. Although color provides a powerful subjective effect, it requires remarkably few bits to encode. The reasons for this are examined by Buchsbaum in chapter 9. The final chapter in this section, by Zetzsche, Barth, and Wegmann, attempts to explain the fundamental basis and limits of perceptually lossless coding, considering both the properties of the eye and the statistics of natural images.

References

Ahumada, A. J., Jr. and Peterson, H. A. (1992). Luminance-model-based DCT quantization for color image compression. In B. E. Rogowitz, J. P. Allebach and S. A. Klein (Ed.), *Human Vision, Visual Processing, and Digital Display III, Proc. SPIE* 1666, paper 32.

Daly, S. (1990). Application of a noise-adaptive contrast sensitivity function to image data compression. *Optical Engineering* 29(8):977–987.

Peterson, H. A. (1992). DCT basis function visibility in RGB space. In J. Morreale (Ed.), *Society for Information Display Digest of Technical Papers*. Playa del Rey, Calif. Society for Information Display.

Watson, A. B. (1987). Efficiency of an image code based on human vision. *Journal of the Optical Society of America A* 4(12):2401–2417.

Watson, A. B. (1989). Receptive fields and visual representations. *SPIE Proceedings* 1077:190–197.

Watson, A. B. (1990). Perceptual-components architecture for digital video. *Journal of the Optical Society of America A* 7(10):1943–1954.

Watson, A. B. and Ahumada, A. J., Jr. (1987). *An orthogonal oriented quadrature hexagonal image pyramid*. NASA technical memorandum 100054.

6

Digital Image Compression Based on Visual Perception

William E. Glenn

Visually lossless digital compression is tested by viewing a standard digital image compared with a reconstructed compressed image at normal viewing distance. If the viewers cannot detect a difference, then the ratio of the bit rates of standard and compressed images can legitimately be called its compression ratio.

Visually lossless compression can be performed only by leaving out information that would normally be transmitted in a standard image. The only information that can be left out without visible degradation is either information that can be predicted about the image or information that the human visual system cannot see.

First we must define the standard image against which the reconstructed compressed image is compared. As a reference format let us assume the standard format that most television engineers use as a source for moving images. In the following discussions we will assume as reference an RGB image in interlaced scan format with 8-bit encoding of a gamma-corrected image ($\gamma = 1/2.2$) with a noise level lower than the least significant bit viewed at a distance such that the limiting test chart resolution on the viewer's retina is 22 c/deg.

As defined here, the term visually lossless *compression* will be used only if the reconstructed image looks like the original as defined above, when the two images they are compared in a two-alternative forced-choice test, and the preference for one image over the other is not statistically significant.

For compression of digital signals used in program production, another criterion determines the information that can be omitted. Postproduction operations frequently leave out information (such as digital gamma correction of the gray scale). They also need more information than is required for transmission (such as for color key operations). An original recording must have "head room" to allow for losses in postproduction and subsequent signal processing (including further compression). The reconstructed compressed image should show no difference from the original after postproduction. The compressed and uncompressed image should both survive color key and other operations equally well.

Compression Based on Image Predictability

Entropy encoding (such as Huffman coding) and some aspects of systems like differential pulse code modulation (DPCM) are based on a statistical prediction of properties of an image. These systems are often referred to as *lossless* because the original image can be reconstructed exactly. Only information that cannot be predicted is transmitted. However, if the transmission system has a fixed bit rate, it will not work for scenes where the unpredictable information exceeds the bit rate.

Although entropy encoding can produce lossless compression, it does not result in high compression ratios on all scenes. White noise, or a scene that looks much like white noise (a Christmas scene with lots of falling snow), cannot be compressed using entropy encoding, since it is totally unpredictable both spatially and temporally. Typically a white-noise signal will require an increase in the bit rate over standard transmission using entropy coding.[1]

Compression Based on Visual Perception

Any information contained in a standard reference image that the visual system cannot see can be left out and still meet the criterion for visually lossless compression as defined in the introduction. This is frequently referred to as *lossy* compression, since measuring instruments other than humans can detect a difference between the original and the reconstructed image. Such compression is frequently referred to as *visually lossless*.

In visually lossless compression the strategy is to keep all differences between the original image and the reconstructed image below the threshold of perception. For example, if we organize the information content of an image in terms of spatial frequencies, temporal frequencies, and amplitudes of luminance and isoluminant color, these data represent a rather complex "information space." Large portions of this space are invisible but consume a large portion of the bit rate presently used for image transmission. This portion of the allocation can be left out without visible image degradation.

In the visible portions of information space, one type of information can be replaced by another that is equally visible but indistinguishable from the original. For example: A continuum of color spectra can be replicated by three fixed primaries; a continuous gray scale can be represented by a set of fixed intensities; a continuum of spatial frequencies can be represented by a set of fixed spatial frequencies; and a continuum of temporal frequencies or velocities can be represented by a set of fixed frequencies or velocities. As long as the differences between the fixed components are indistinguishable, this process saves bits, that is, it takes fewer bits to use three primary colors rather than five, 8 bits for gamma-corrected gray scale rather than 10, and so forth. Transform coding does the same for spatial frequency and temporal frequency: Information can be removed that results in imperceptible inaccuracies in the image.

A large fraction of the compression with discrete cosine transform (DCT) or wavelet transform systems and systems using three-dimensional subband coding take advantage of these effects. As the bit rate is reduced, the measured difference between the original image and the reconstructed image increases. However, if the system is designed so that the difference is always below the threshold of perception because of its spatial-frequency distribution or because of raised visual thresholds due to masking effects, it can still be visually lossless. Other errors in the reconstructed image that cannot be distinguished from the original image are also not perceived. Taking advantage of the limits of perception has the advantage that it will work on all scenes in a fixed-bit-rate channel.

Effects Used in Visually Lossless Compression

Psychophysical measurements of perception provide a guide for determining the threshold of perception of various components of an image. All information below this threshold can be removed from the image without detection of the loss. A measurement that is frequently used is the contrast sensitivity threshold. This value is determined from experiments in which a low-contrast sinusoidal stripe pattern is presented to the observer. The contrast sensitivity threshold (the contrast below which the grating becomes invisible) is plotted against spatial frequency. This grating may be either static (DC) or alternating in counterphase at different temporal frequencies. The contrast sensitivity threshold is expressed as $I_{max} - I_{min}/I_{max} + I_{min}$, where I is intensity.

The measurements shown in figure 6.1 were taken at about 60 ft-lamberts screen brightness, a typical value for normal television viewing conditions.

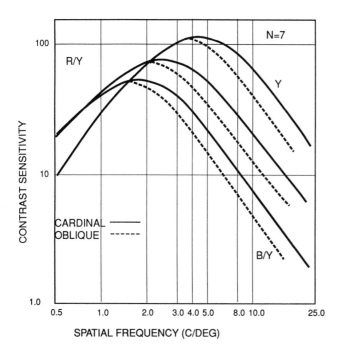

Figure 6.1
Contrast sensitivity threshold functions for static luminance gratings (Y) and isoluminance chromaticity gratings (R/Y,B/Y) averaged over seven observers.

In the case of color contrast sensitivity threshold measurements, an isoluminant color grating is used. This grating varies sinusoidally in saturation between complementary colors. Because the grating is isoluminant, it is expressed as a ratio of one of the primary colors to luminance (such as R/Y or B/Y). The contrast sensitivity threshold numbers that are presented in the plots represent the $I_{max} - I_{min}/I_{max} + I_{min}$ of one of the primary colors with the complementary color turned off.

In the data given here only contrast sensitivity thresholds are presented. Psychophysical measurements have been made of suprathreshold isosensitivity curves. These are generally flatter in their response as the contrast increases.[2] However, in designing compression systems, one is more concerned with information below the threshold of perception that can be left out. Suprathreshold response can affect the gray scale or color saturation transfer characteristic that is optimum to minimize the number of bits needed in a given spatial frequency band. However, in compression systems after information has been left out of camera-generated images, the contrast is low for the errors between the original and reconstructed image. One is mostly concerned with keeping these errors below the contrast sensitivity threshold.

Use of the Contrast Sensitivity Threshold Function

Figure 6.1 shows the contrast required at the threshold of perception plotted against spatial frequency for luminance, isoluminant color, and for both cardinally oriented (horizontal and vertical 0 deg and 90 deg) and obliquely oriented (45 deg and 135 deg) gratings. These are the original curves that were presented in normalized form in reference 3. All patterns of lower contrast than this plot cannot be detected. From these plots one can conclude the following:

1. Errors in image reconstruction that are below this contrast sensitivity threshold cannot be detected.

2. At high spatial frequencies for equal threshold detectability the spatial frequency of R/Y is about half that of Y, and B/Y is about one-quarter that of Y.

3. For equal threshold detectability the spatial frequency of obliquely oriented gratings is about 0.7 that of cardinally oriented gratings.

4. Because visual acuity falls off at high spatial frequencies for both luminance and color, fewer bits are needed for gray scale at these frequencies. Consequently, fewer suprathreshold levels are needed than at lower spatial frequencies.

The choice of the coefficient truncation thresholds in transform coding takes advantage of (1), (2), and (3). The number of bits needed above threshold depends on (4), which can be determined by evaluating suprathreshold data (not shown here) combined with the modulation transfer function of the image source.

Isoluminant color signals can use far fewer pixels both vertically and horizontally than are used for luminance. Therefore, most systems (even NTSC) take advantage of (b) but seldom by the proper amount.

Diagonal sampling as is used by MUSE and many other systems takes advantage of (3) by making the angular distribution of resolution match that of the visual system. The zigzag scan truncation procedure used in DCT coefficients achieves the same result with cardinal sampling.

Printers have been using diagonal sampling in halftone images for years. Wendland has reported a significant improvement in sharpness (on a quality scale) by the use of diagonal sampling in television images.[5,6] We wanted to get a quantitative comparison of the relative number of pixels required to produce a diagonally sampled image with the same perceived sharpness as a cardinally sampled image. In this experiment, color fixed images were sampled both cardinally and diagonally. Images were presented in random pairs to six subjects. The diagonally sampled image had a fixed number of samples, whereas the cardinally sampled image varied in pixel spacing. The pixels were generated by clusters of smaller pixels. The images were pre- and postfiltered with Gaussian filters that were appropriate for the pixel spacing. The viewing distance was chosen to make the limiting resolution of the diagonally sampled image at 20 cycles/degree on the subjects' retina. The subjects were asked to tell which image looked sharper. For the pair that the choice between the images was 50:50, the number of pixels in the cardinally sampled image was 1.4 times the number of pixels in the diagonally sampled image.

Many systems have been designed that simply leave out half the pixels of a cardinally sampled image to produce a diagonal pattern. This reduces the number of pixels by a factor of about 2 but, according to our experiment, will result in visible loss in sharpness. However, the 1.4 saving in number of pixels for the same perceived sharpness is a significant difference.

Reducing the number of bits in the high spatial frequency coefficients of transform systems or the number of bits designating adjacent pixel differences as in DPCM takes advantage of (d).

Use of the Dynamic Contrast Sensitivity Threshold Function

Figure 6.2, which is reprinted from reference 7, shows the dynamic contrast thresholds of luminance and color at different temporal frequencies. From these curves we can conclude that:

1. Low-resolution luminance increases in contrast sensitivity threshold at low temporal frequencies and then falls off above about 10 Hz.

2. High-resolution luminance and all isoluminant color gratings fall off in threshold contrast sensitivity response at temporal frequencies above about 2 Hz.

Systems that use three-dimensional subband coding take advantage of (1) and (2) by sending detail luminance and isoluminant color at a slower rate than low-resolution

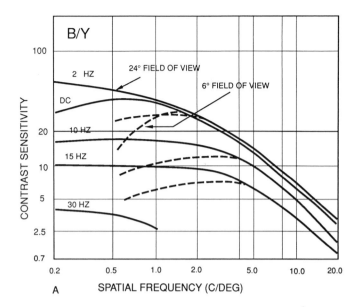

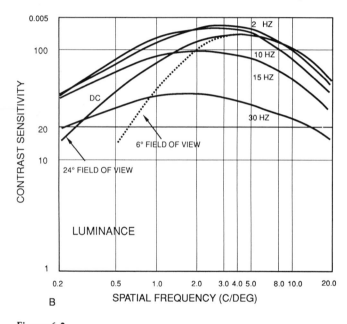

Figure 6.2
Dynamic contrast sensitivity function for DC and counterphase flicker at 2, 10, 15, and 30 Hz for R/Y and B/Y (A) and Y (B).

luminance. In these systems the temporal response decreases as the spatial frequency response increases. This factor is incorporated either directly or indirectly in many systems for moving images. Nyquist subsampling as used in MUSE or systems that depend on "interframe redundancy" frequently results in images that exploit this property of vision. In these systems, motion detection is used to take all the information from the lower-resolution current field in the presence of motion and all the information from the low temporal frequency but higher-resolution frame where there is no change. As a result, high spatial frequencies are displayed slowly, and low spatial frequencies are displayed rapidly if there is a change in the image.

Interlace is actually a crude form of three-dimensional subband coding as is much of the processing in MUSE. Three-dimensional subband coding of a progressively scanned image results in about the same bandwidth as interlace without incurring many of the objectionable artifacts produced by interlace. However, there is no difference in the number of bits required if we compare the two on an equal basis. An interlaced system with camera-generated images has a vertical Kell factor of about 0.62, whereas a progressively scanned camera can have a Kell factor of about 0.92. The interlaced system therefore has two-thirds the resolution of the progressively scanned image. A 30 frame per second (fps) interlaced image has half the bandwidth of a 60 fps progressively scanned image. Consequently, it would take three-fourths the bandwidth to get the same resolution (by increasing the number of lines). In a three-dimensional subband coded image from a progressively scanned camera, if the top octave of vertical resolution is updated at 30 Hz (the same frame rate as the interlaced image), the resulting bandwidth will be three-fourths that of the 60 fps progressively scanned image. In both cases horizontal resolution is updated at 60 fps to compare "apples with apples."

Three-dimensional subband coding can produce greater savings in bit rate than the comparison cited by matching the spatiotemporal response of the visual system more closely.

Very few systems take advantage of (2) by sending color at a low temporal rate. The most important reason is that most systems use color difference signals rather than isoluminant color signals. Color difference signals have a large component of low-resolution luminance to which the visual system has a high temporal response.

Motion artifacts will be visible in saturated colored objects with this technique unless isoluminant color signals are used (R/Y and B/Y).

The Use of Spatial, Temporal, and Orientation Tuning Properties of Visual Processing

Analysis of the processing used by the visual system shows that at threshold, spatial-frequency "tuning" channels are used by the visual system to analyze spatial frequency. As reported by Ginsburg, these channels analyze an image with about an octave bandwidth in spatial frequency over the entire visible range.[8] Temporal tuning channels have also been reported in the vision research literature with temporal bandwidths of about two octaves.[9,10,11,12] The spatial channels are also tuned for angle of orientation with an angular resolution of about ± 20 deg,[13] and the temporal channels are tuned for direction of motion.[14]

Although these observations were generally made using threshold-of-detection methods, they seem to be valid at the low-contrast conditions that generally apply for errors generated as bits are removed in transform coding and at the high spatial and temporal frequencies derived from a camera.

From these observations we can conclude that:

1. Low-contrast spatial frequencies within a range of something less than an octave over a range of orientations of about ± 20 deg are indistinguishable from one other.

2. Low-contrast temporal frequencies over a range of frequencies of about two octaves and velocities and directions of motion over a certain range are indistinguishable from one other.

From (1) we can conclude that the low-contrast information in an image can be represented by a series of discrete spatial frequencies with discrete orientations. The sampling process both spatially and temporally restricts the spatial and temporal frequencies that can be represented by the sum of a set of discrete frequencies. In transform coding like DCT, these frequencies are assigned amplitude coefficients. Both DCT and wavelet transform contain the same amount of information in the transform as in the original sampled image for exact reconstruction. However, when information is removed from the transform, the errors are indistinguishable from the original information because of 1 or 2. In practice these systems frequently have considerable errors in the angular distribution and spatial frequency of the information after the number of bits in the coefficients is reduced, with little visible image degradation. Wavelet transform systems and subband coding systems using factor-of-2 scaling come closer to matching the octave band tuning of the visual system for low-contrast information. In a practical system the difference between DCT and wavelet transform in compression ratio for equivalent performance has not been well established. One of the main advantages of transform coding is that by processing the image in a way somewhat similar to that used by the visual system, the accuracy of encoding the information can more closely match that needed by the visual system.

In theory one must use a sharp cutoff prefilter before sampling an image and a sharp cutoff postfilter, both with their cutoff just below the Nyquist limit. This process eliminates alias frequencies that result from the sampling process. As demonstrated by Windland, eliminating these frequencies eliminates the obvious zigzags that occur when a line is slightly inclined with respect to the sampling pattern.[5] Experimentally, many researchers have observed that a little aliasing is good and actually improves the perceived sharpness of the image.

Use of the proper spatial frequency response for pre- and postfiltering can also take advantage of (1). Some allowable "alias" frequencies are indistinguishable from the correct frequency near the Nyquist limit. A spatial frequency just above the Nyquist limit will produce an alias frequency just below (and vice versa). As long as these low-contrast frequencies are within one "tuning band" of visual processing, they are perceived as the same. This fact can consequently be used to lower the number of pixels slightly for a given perceived sharpness. In our experiments we used a spatial prefilter with a sharp cutoff half an octave above the Nyquist limit followed by a sharp cutoff postfilter at the Nyquist limit. This setup was compared with a Gaussian pre- and postfilter (which most systems use) at the Nyquist limit. For equal perceived sharpness in a two-alternative forced-choice comparison, the number of pixels in the image with the higher cutoff prefilter was decreased by a factor of about 2.

From (2) we can conclude that a moving portion of an image can be represented by interpolating the position using a series of discrete motion vectors applied to the positions of less frequently sampled images. In these systems all objects within a small area are displaced at the same velocity as the average velocity. Objects that move at differing velocities within that area have low-contrast velocity errors in the reconstruction that go undetected because of (2).

A subjective example of (2) is the temporal alias visible in wagon wheels in the movies. Temporal aliasing frequently produces velocity errors in the spokes of the wagon wheels that rotate in the right direction but within about a factor of 2 of the right velocity. Nobody notices these artifacts. Only when the spokes of the wheels stop or rotate backward due to aliasing does the artifact becomes obvious. Motion-vector position interpolation does an accurate job of correcting the velocity of a pan or the motion of large rigid objects where the observer's eye can track the motion. However, the accuracy that is required and the effects of tracking moving objects with the eye's oculomotor system have not been completely studied to date. Many systems, including MUSE and MPEG, use motion vectors to interpolate the positions of moving objects as described above. They have significant velocity errors when two objects with differing velocities are in the same area defined by the motion vector.

The Use of Masking Effects to Further Reduce Bit Rate

In a pattern-masking experiment we presented viewers with a fixed sinusiodal grating of 0.25 contrast superimposed on a pattern that varied in spatial frequency from 0.5 to 12.5 c/deg and varied in contrast from 0.25 to 0.001. The subject was asked to trace the curve where the threshold of perception of the test grating occurred. The data shown are the average response of five subjects.

Figure 6.3 shows the threshold of perception in the presence of a masking grating with 25 percent contrast. This effect depends on orientation. Masking is much greater for gratings that are oriented in the same direction rather than it perpendicular to the test grating. In our measurements the differences between the unmasked threshold and the threshold with a perpendicular mask were within the experimental error of measurement and were not statistically significant. Thresholds with the mask in the same direction and orthogonal to the test grating are shown. Thresholds are shown for luminance gratings masked either by a luminance grating mask or by an isoluminant color grating mask. Our masking data for luminance on luminance masking agree well with previous measurements.[15,16,17]

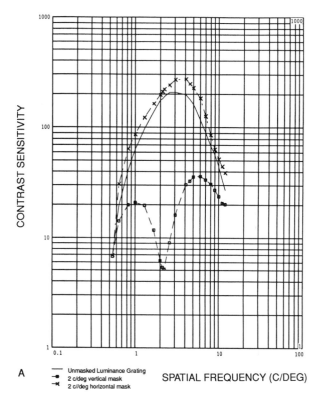

A

- Unmasked Luminance Grating
- 2 c/deg vertical mask
- 2 c//deg horizontal mask

SPATIAL FREQUENCY (C/DEG)

Figure 6.3(A)
Threshold contrast sensitivity of a vertically oriented test grating
with a superimposed 0.25 contrast red/cyan isoluminant mask.

The contrast sensitivity threshold in luminance is masked
very strongly by the presence of either a luminance or
isoluminant chromaticity grating oriented in the same
direction and within $\pm\frac{1}{2}$ octave of the same spatial frequency. Masking is much lower for the mask perpendicular to the test stimulus. These data are consistent with the
octave tuning theory of visual processing in reference 8
and the angular dependence of masking effects reported
in reference 13. Data described previously show that a
temporal transient increases perception threshold significantly in high spatial frequencies for about 80 ms.[18]

From these data we conclude that:

1. The presence of a high-amplitude luminance or color
grating significantly raises the threshold of perception
within about $\pm\frac{1}{2}$ octave of the grating for the same
orientation. The masking effect depends on angle and
is reduced if the orientation is orthogonal. The angular
dependence is described in reference 4.

These results are also consistent with the microelectrode
studies on macaque monkey striate cortex cells reported

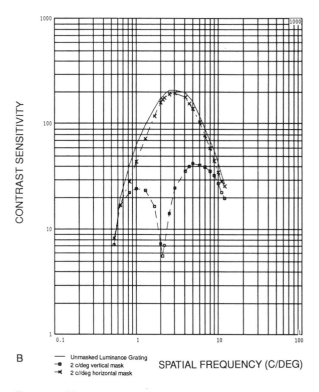

B

- Unmasked Luminance Grating
- 2 c/deg vertical mask
- 2 c//deg horizontal mask

SPATIAL FREQUENCY (C/DEG)

Figure 6.3(B)
Threshold contrast sensitivity of a vertically oriented test grating
with a superimposed 0.25 contrast blue/yellow isoluminant mask.

in reference 13. In these studies a cell would respond to
any grating within about $\pm\frac{1}{2}$ octave of spatial frequency
and within about ± 22 deg of angular orientation. It is not
surprising that pattern masking has the same relationship.
It is surprising that an isoluminant chromaticity grating
can be almost equally effective.

DCT systems that use a "priority" system of encoding
the highest amplitude gratings first, take advantage of
this effect to some extent. In these systems high-amplitude
coefficients are transmitted, whereas lower-amplitude coefficients nearby in spatial frequency are not transmitted
(set to zero). Since the lower-amplitude spatial frequencies
are masked, their omission goes undetected. Wavelet
transforms and subband coding, due to their octave pass
bands, tend to inherently include this effect as the quantization levels are restricted. However, for the angular dependence of masking effects to match that reported in
reference 4, two-dimensional filters rather than two cascaded one-dimensional filters must be used. None of the
proposed systems to date takes advantage of color on
luminance masking.

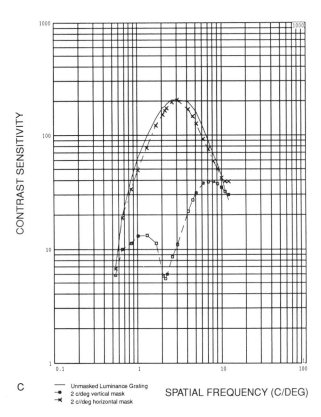

C
— Unmasked Luminance Grating
•— 2 c/deg vertical mask
✕— 2 c//deg horizontal mask

SPATIAL FREQUENCY (C/DEG)

Figure 6.3(C)
Threshold contrast sensitivity of a vertically oriented test grating with a superimposed 0.25 contrast luminance mask.

2. The presence of a temporal change in the image makes low-amplitude detail and color less visible. This effect as well as the differences in the temporal response of high and low spatial frequencies is used in three-dimensional subband coding systems.

Summary

Perceptually lossless compression can achieve significant compression ratios by eliminating information that the visual system cannot see. Some additional compression can always be achieved with entropy coding based on the predictable limits of spatial and temporal response of the television camera. For higher compression ratios, using entropy encoding, which is used in fixed-bit-rate systems, will "crash" or produce visible artifacts that will appear more frequently as the bit rate is reduced.

For visually lossless compression, table 6.1 shows the effects that can be used that are based on measured thresholds of perception. Also included is a slight improvement

Table 6.1
Effects Used for Compression (even if the scene is white noise)

	Estimated Compression Ratio
Use progressive scan with three-dimensional subband coding of luminance rather than interlaced scan	1.0
Take advantage of transient masking in luminance and color in three-dimensional subband coding	1.4
Do not encode high-amplitude high spatial frequencies due to low MTF of camera	1.3
Take advantage of low-contrast sensitivity of vision in high spatial frequencies to increase truncation thresholds and reduce number of bits of gray scale	1.7
Use lower resolution isoluminant color signals for color at a lower temporal frequency	2.7
Take advantage of the oblique effect (diagonal sampling or reduced diagonal coefficients for DCT)	1.4
Use optimum pre- and postspatial filtering	2
Use optimum pre- and posttemporal filtering	?
Take advantage of pattern-on-pattern masking in luminance to raise truncation levels in transform coefficients	?
Take advantage of color-on-luminance pattern masking to raise truncation levels in transform coefficients	?
Represent images by discrete spatial frequencies and discrete orientations	1.5
Represent motion by discrete vectors in velocity and direction applied to temporally sampled images	1.5
	Total > 53

that can be achieved in both lossy and lossless systems by not encoding the high-amplitude high spatial frequencies that never exist in a real system. The "graceful" high spatial frequency roll-off produces the subjectively best looking image in a real system. If the roll-off does not occur, the image has objectionable ringing or jagged edges. The table also includes an estimate of the reduction in bit rate that can be achieved for each effect. The product of all of these effects is about 53. Because all these effects are not totally independent, the compression ratio using all of them together would be somewhat less. However, there are a few effects with unknown improvement that were not included in the product. Some improvement can also be achieved by combining entropy coding techniques with the techniques listed in the table. Consequently, one might expect visually lossless compression to be possible with a compression ratio somewhere between 50 and 100.

A compression ratio of 50 to 100 would be attained by omitting 98 to 99 percent of the original bits for a moving color image and still having an image that is indistinguishable from the original by a human observer. This would be an incredible achievement.

Acknowledgments

The author wishes to acknowledge his appreciation to the late Dr. Karen Glenn for her contributions to the understanding of visual perception and to Fouad Guediri, Barry Rynk, and Jerrilyn Engelbrecht for obtaining and analyzing the psychophysical data in this project. This project was sponsored primarily by the NASA Television Development Division, Robert Shafer, Director, under contract NASW-4557.

References

[1] Rabbani, Majid, and Paul W. Jones (1991). Digital image compression techniques. *SPIE*. vol. TT 7.

[2] Georgeson, M. A. & G. D. Sullivan. (1975). Contrast constancy: Deblurring in human vision by spatial frequency channels. *J. Physiol.* (London) 252:627–656.

[3] Glenn, W. E., K. G. Glenn, and C. J. Bastian (1985). Imaging system design based on psychophysical data. *SID* 26:1.

[4] Glenn, W. E., (1991). Digital image compression based on visual perception and scene properties. *SMPTE Journal* 40:1–18.

[5] Wendland, B. (1983). Extended definition television with high picture guality. *SMPTE Journal* 92:1028–1035.

[6] Wendland, B., and H. Shroeder (1984). On picture quality of some signal processing techniques. *SMPTE Journal* 93:915–922.

[7] Glenn, W. E., and K. G. Glenn (1989). Signal processing for compatible HDTV. *SMPTE Journal* 57:812–816.

[8] Ginsburg, A. P. (1978). Visual information processing based on spatial filters constrained by biological data. *Air Force Aerospace Medical Research Lab Tech Report 1978:* AMRL-TR-78–129.

[9] Billock, V. A., and T. H. Harding (1991). The number and tuning of channels responsible for the independent detection of temporal modulation. *ARVO, Investigative Ophthalmology & Visual Science, Annual Meeting Abstracts* 32(4):840, Sarasota, Fla.

[10] Hess, R. F., and G. T. Plant (1985). Temporal frequency discrimination in human vision: Evidence for an addition mechanism in the low spatial and high temporal frequency region. *Vision Research* 25(10):1493–1500.

[11] Tolhurst, D. J. (1975). Sustained and transient channels in human vision. *Vision Research* 15:1151–1155.

[12] Watson, A. B., and J. G. Robson (1981). Discrimination at threshold: Labelled detectors in human vision. *Vision Research* 21:1115–1122.

[13] De Valois, R. L., Albrecht, and Thorell (1982). *Vision Research* 22:545–559.

[14] Tolhurst, D. J. (1973). Separate channels for the analysis of the shape and the movement of a moving visual stimulus. *J. Phys.* 231:385–402.

[15] Campbell F. W., and J. J. Kulikowski. (1966) Orientational selectivity of the human visual system. *J. Physiol.* (London), 187:437–445.

[16] Phillips G. C., and H. R. Wilson (1984). Orientation bandwidths of spatial mechanisms measured by masking. *J. Opt. Soc. Am.* A1(2):226–232.

[17] Blakemore, C., and F. W. Campbell (1969). On the existence of neurones in the human visual system selectively sensitive to the orientation and size of retinal images. *J. Physiol.* 203:237–260.

[18] Glenn W. E., and K. G. Glenn (1989). The design of systems that display moving images based on spatiotemporal vision data. *J. Imaging Technology* 15(2).

7

Image Quality and Image Compression: A Psychophysicist's Viewpoint

Stanley A. Klein

The inspiration for writing this chapter came from the difficulty that I had when I first attempted to connect my area of expertise, visual psychophysics, to the applied work in image quality and image coding being done by engineers. There often seemed to be a gap between my understanding of human vision and the version being used in the engineering community. This chapter was written to try to help close that gap. Applied researchers and basic researchers can be of great help to one another once they understand each other's needs, interests, and capabilities. Not the least of the rewards will be the satisfaction of seeing practical benefits from investigations of the underlying mechanisms of human vision.

There are important questions concerning image quality and image compression for which further data on the human visual system are needed. Since the pace of events in the image compression field is faster than we vision scientists are used to, an extra effort is needed to speed up the dialogue between engineers and vision researchers. This book attempts to further this effort.

As part of the goal of developing connections between vision researchers and display engineers, this chapter examines several topics on the relationship between human vision and image quality and asks which areas need more study:

- What images should be used for judging image quality and image compression?

- What is a good metric for measuring image quality?

- How does one explain the discrepancy in bits/min^2 needed for lossless compression: Image coders often claim 1 bits/min^2 is sufficient (Rabbani and Jones, 1991; Netravali and Haskell, 1988), whereas I claim that 20 bits/min^2 are needed.

- How can the effects of the human visual system and the effects of image redundancy be separated?

• How can the vision community contribute in setting quantization levels for the JPEG-DCT compression standard?

• How does the nonlinear gamma of the display affect image quality?

• Can spatial masking be used to gain more compression than what is allowed by JPEG?

The "Perfect" Image: A Worst-Case Approach

My approach to image quality differs from that of others mainly because I am adopting a stricter criterion. In image processing one starts with image 1 and ends up with image 2. One then judges whether image 2 is of higher, equal, or lower quality than image 1. This chapter is not concerned with image enhancement, so the first alternative, of ending up with an image of higher quality, is not considered. Our concern is whether the image has been perceptually degraded by being processed. The amount of degradation will depend on the quality of the original image. Suppose, for example, that image 2 is a blurred version of image 1. If image 1 were already blurred, the additional blur might not be visible. However, if the original image were sharp, the added blur could be easily detected. So we must ask, What should be the quality of the starting image? Usually, in the image-processing field one starts with a digitized image that has already been processed. This approach has the problem that the starting image is of uncertain quality. The present approach, however, starts with the original, predigitized, analog, continuous, real-world image. An image that is perceptually indiscriminable from this original is called a *perfect* image, since the original image was "as good as could be." Thus this chapter considers a worst-case analysis of image quality and image compression. This approach has the consequence that we find more bits/min^2 are needed than is claimed by other researchers in this field.[1] One could claim that this worst-case approach is too demanding and not relevant to the typical images that are presently being processed. Our answer is that our analysis is relevant to the most demanding displays and compression schemes of the present (i.e., medical imaging) and to those of the twenty-first century, when present hardware limitations will be overcome. Our goal is to find the maximum amount of information that needs to be preserved in an image for

it to be truly lossless. With this approach, future technical achievements will not undo the conclusions of this chapter. Present studies on image compression that start with degraded images will become obsolete when future image technologies shrink the size of a pixel and provide for more bits of gray level. Our approach will be unaffected by those advances.

Sampling the Image to Minimize Aliasing

Because our original image is *continuous* we must consider what is the best way to digitize it. This step is often skipped if one starts from a digitized image. Consider, for simplicity, the task of creating a digital image of a thin line that has a slope of negative 0.1 (it drops by 1 pixel every 10th pixel). How should the line be sampled? The simplest sampling scheme would be the following: For each point on the line, turn on the pixel closest to that point. This method has the drawback that visible "jaggies" will be present. The vernier acuity threshold for seeing jaggies is about five times smaller (4–6 sec) than the resolution threshold (20–30 sec). Therefore, to avoid supersmall pixels one must use gray levels to smoothly shift the line position between pixels. A popular smoothing technique is to interpolate by convolving the image with a sinc function ($\sin(x)/x$). This function is used because in the Fourier domain it is flat up to the Nyquist frequency and is zero thereafter. This seems like a reasonable choice, since it leaves the visible portion of the image (below the Nyquist frequency) untouched and totally eliminates the higher (invisible) frequencies that can cause aliasing problems. The left side of table 7.1 shows the effect of the sinc function on the tilted line. The pixels closest to the line have been underlined for clarity. The big problem with the sinc function is that negative luminance may be needed. If a background luminance is present it is possible to obtain luminance values below the background. However, for a bright line on a zero luminance background (a common stimulus in vision studies) the required negative luminances are impossible to obtain. Sinc function interpolation is therefore not generally possible. The linear interpolation scheme (using triangular interpolation) shown in the right panel of the table 7.1 can always be achieved, albeit at the expense of nonperfect Fourier properties; there is some attenuation of visible frequencies below the Nyquist limit and some nonvanishing frequencies above the Nyquist limit. The linear scheme also has the advantage of simplic-

Table 7.1
Two Sampling Schemes for Representing a Thin Line with a Slope of −0.1

Sinc interpolation											
0	.02	.04	.06	.07	.07	.07	.05	.04	.02	0	−.02
0	−.03	−.06	−.08	−.09	−.09	−.08	−.07	−.05	−.03	0	−.02
0	.05	.09	.11	.13	.13	.12	.10	.07	.03	0	−.03
0	−.09	−.16	−.2	−.22	−.21	−.19	−.15	−.10	−.05	0	.05
1	.98	.94	.86	.76	.64	.50	.37	.23	.11	0	−.09
0	.11	.23	.37	.50	.64	.76	.86	.94	.98	1	.98
0	−.05	−.10	−.15	−.19	−.21	−.22	−.20	−.16	−.09	0	.11
0	.03	.07	.10	.12	.13	.13	.11	.09	.05	0	−.05
0	−.03	−.05	−.07	−.08	−.09	−.09	−.08	−.06	−.03	0	.03

Linear interpolation												
0	0	0	0	0	0	0	0	0	0	0	0	
0	0	0	0	0	0	0	0	0	0	0	0	
1	.9	.8	.7	.6	.5	.4	.3	.2	.1	0	0	
0	.1	.2	.3	.4	.5	.6	.7	.8	.9	1	.9	
0	0	0	0	0	0	0	0	0	0	0	.1	
0	0	0	0	0	0	0	0	0	0	0	0	

ity, and it is the method of choice in this paper. Linear interpolation has the consequence that there will be positions where the line is somewhat blurred (at positions where the line is represented by a pair of pixels), as discussed in later sections.

Multidimensional Image Quality

Two Surprises for Newcomers to the Field

Two surprises greet vision researchers who become involved with issues of image quality and image compression. The first surprise is that most of the images being processed and judged by the applied vision community are complex images of natural scenes. This choice of images, although understandable given the pragmatic end goals of image compression, should not be used exclusively. Natural images are much harder to analyze than the simple lines, edges, and repetitive gratings that are characteristic of most basic vision research. It is even difficult to define the local contrast of a complex image. Simple stimuli should be used as well as the present complex ones so that a precise understanding can be gained about the operation of the compression and image-quality algorithms.

The second surprise is that a one-dimensional image-quality metric is commonly used (Barten, 1989; Roufs and Boschman, 1990; Hultgren, 1990). We argue that image quality is multidimensional and more than one number is needed for its specification (see chapters 11 and 12).

These first two surprises are linked: If one uses complex images, it is difficult to tease apart the multiple components of image quality. As we discuss next, in addition to using complex images, one needs to use special simpler stimuli to assess particular dimensions of image quality.

Evaluating Multidimensional Image Quality

As we stated earlier, greater clarity could be brought to image-quality research and consequently to image compression if the multiple aspects of image quality could be judged separately. One way to achieve this goal is to devise a battery of images such that each image will be associated with one of the image-quality factors of interest. Finding this battery will not be easy—for one reason because the dimensionality of image quality is not at all well defined. However, just because it is ill defined does not mean that research on the topic should stop. In this section we make suggestions regarding what might be independent image-quality factors. Although they do not have a sound theoretical or experimental foundation, we feel that they must be discussed, and theory development and experiments should be encouraged, to improve image-quality assessment.

For any given image-quality factor, a research program is needed to determine *two* thresholds: a threshold for the visibility of the factor and a threshold to assess the degree to which that factor is bothersome. For example, a small amount of blur may be visible, but not bothersome, whereas a jaggie may be bothersome as soon as it is visible. The difference between these two measures is the difference between image fidelity and image quality. Good fidelity means that the displayed image is hard to discriminate from the starting image, where the starting image may be a sampled version of the real-world original. Psychophysicists like to measure fidelity, since one can measure a threshold in d' units, where d' is a psychophysical measure of the number of just-noticeable differences between the two images. Image quality is much harder to define and measure than fidelity, since quality includes the weightings whereby some fidelity dimensions are less bothersome than others and also whether the starting image was degraded. The rest of this section discusses fidelity rather than quality.

The candidate images for assessing fidelity that are discussed in this section do not provide a complete or independent list of possible images. They are suggested in an attempt to prod us all in the direction of using stimuli that can be easily analyzed and quantified. Only static images are considered in the present chapter (except for an experiment discussed in a later section that involves a moving grating).

Image fidelity can be degraded by either the software or the hardware. By software we mean items such as the compression algorithm used and the extent of quantization. By hardware we mean items such as nonlinear interactions between adjacent phosphors due to limitations in the electronics of the display. There are also degradations due to interactions between hardware and software. In the following examples of the dimensions of fidelity we ignore whether the loss of fidelity is due to a hardware or to a software problem. In either case a diagnostic battery of tests would be useful. The elimination of the hardware contribution to fidelity loss is easy to achieve: Simply compare the images before and after compression using the same hardware. For the present we are mainly concerned with discovering that there is a loss in fidelity, from whatever source, and being able to quantify that loss in a multidimensional space.

One must keep in mind that the use of special stimuli such as is being suggested here may produce a worst-case test. As we discussed earlier, this worst-case approach must be treated judiciously. Just because an algorithm fails on a worst-case image does not necessarily mean that it is a bad algorithm for general real-world images. The use of special images must be tempered with knowledge of the following: (a) How often does that image characteristic occur in the real world? (b) Even though there may be a fidelity loss for a particular image, is there also a quality loss? (Maybe the fidelity loss isn't annoying, so there is no loss in judged quality.) The advantages of using special images rather than real-world images are that (a) it is easier to apply vision models to simple stimuli in order to predict discrimination thresholds, and (b) one can isolate specific fidelity dimensions.

A Ramp to Test for Sufficient Gray-Scale Bits and for Blocking Artifacts

One fidelity dimension is the appearance of luminance steps on a uniform field. Images of the sky often show this degradation of smoothness. Smoothness can be lost in several ways: (l) The number of gray levels used in the final image may be insufficient. (2) There may be glitches in the digital-to-analog converter. (3) If quantization was too severe, there may be blocking artifacts due to the square blocks of the JPEG image-compression algorithm.[2]

A shallow ramp is good for testing the smoothness of the compression scheme. Several ramps are needed to cover a wide range of luminances and yet not have the ramp luminance change so rapidly as to hide the step artifact. One of the ramps should be at the very lowest end of the luminance scale. As we discuss in a later section, the low-luminance regime is most sensitive to quantization errors. In addition, a relatively steep ramp should also be used to test for blocking artifacts of the DCT algorithm. The steep ramp should produce substantial errors in the middle and high spatial frequency components, for which the quantization error can be large. The ramps should be in the vertical, horizontal, and diagonal directions to test for possible asymmetries in the quantization tables or display hardware.

A Large Thin-Line Circle to Test for Jaggies and Blurring

We discussed the need for a prior low-pass filtering of the image to avoid the jagged appearance of thin lines or edges that are slightly tilted from the raster direction. A large *thin* semicircle consists of a line with all orientations, so it should be a good stimulus to assess whether the prefiltering or the compression scheme was inadequate. By *large* we mean a semicircle with as large a radius as possible. For an image that is 640 pixels across, a radius of about 300 pixels would be possible without hitting the edge of the display. With a radius of 300 pixels the "sag" of a 50-pixel segment is only 1 pixel.[3] By having long straight segments it should be possible to notice any jaggies. Silverstein, Krantz, Gomer, Yeh, and Monty (1990) used circles and lines at different angles for their image-quality studies. Their largest circle had a diameter of 1.5 deg. We feel that for an adequate test the circle should be at least three times as large. Our example of a 640-pixel circle would be more than 5 deg across using 0.5-min pixels. With smaller circles the "straight" sections may be too short to allow the jaggies to be easily visible. A concentric set of closely spaced rings would also be a good stimulus, since moiré effects would exaggerate any defects.

This stimulus should also provide a test to determine whether the pixel size is small enough. The right half of table 7.1 shows that a tilted line is sometimes 1 and sometimes 2 pixels thick. If the pixel size is too big, then the line will appear blurred in regions where the line is 2 pixels wide. The large radius of the circle aids the detection of blur, since the extent of the blurred region is proportional to the radius. The ability of the visual system to detect small amounts of blur (Levi and Klein, 1990a) places an upper limit of 0.35 min on the pixel size (see Section 4.1 for further details). A test image sensitive to resolution loss is therefore essential for assessing image quality.

Alternating Pixels to Test Linearity of the Image at High Frequencies

Linearity of the display is assumed by most image-processing algorithms. This proposed test provides a sensitive measure of linearity (albeit of only three points of the lookup table). On one-half of the display are lines in the direction of the raster alternating between two luminance levels. On the other half is a uniform field whose luminance is intended to lie halfway between the alternating levels. The observer observes the screen from a large enough distance so that the alternating pixels look uniform. If the luminance of the two halves appears to differ, then one may conclude that there is a problem with the lookup table that is being used to correct for the nonlinear luminance behavior of the display. This is too contrived to be a good test for image fidelity after compression, since compression algorithms with severe quantization of high spatial frequencies *should* do poorly on this test.

A much more intriguing problem occurs if one replaces the uniform field by alternating lines that are perpendicular to the direction of the raster. The two intended luminance levels are chosen to be the same on both sides. The limited signal bandwidth together with the accelerating connection between voltage and luminance (the display gamma) causes the mean luminance to be lower on the side where each raster sweep has alternating luminances. This problem cannot be resolved by improving the bandwidth of the display, since the higher bandwidth will simply encourage computer makers to use smaller pixels, thereby bringing back the problem. Some preliminary steps toward understanding this nonlinearity were taken by Mulligan and Stone (1989).

A Set of Square-Wave Spokes to Test Aliasing and Resolution

A high-resolution radial square-wave pattern (like a dartboard) is ideal for testing resolution and aliasing. If either of the prefiltering operations discussed in table 7.1 (extended to two dimensions) is implemented, then aliasing artifacts should be greatly reduced. The advantage of the spoke pattern is that it samples all orientations. The resolution limit can be judged by noting the point at which the spokes become blurred. A dartboard is not a particularly sensitive stimulus to use for measuring resolution, so one may desire to include additional resolution targets. These patterns have been around for a long time and should be included in any assessment of fidelity.

A Bisection Stimulus to Detect Small Luminance Changes near High Contrasts

A bisection stimulus (three parallel bright lines along the direction of the raster, separated by 1.4 min, on a dark background) is especially sensitive to degradation by compression algorithms for reasons to be discussed. The observer in a bisection task makes a judgment about whether the middle line is high or low relative to the midpoint of the outside lines. Bisection thresholds are exceedingly low. Our thresholds of less than 1 sec if arc (Klein and Levi, 1985) with a 5-line bisection task are listed in the *Guiness Book of World Records* (McFarlan, 1991) in the category of *Highest Visual Acuity*. Bisection stimuli in the small separation regime are especially troublesome for image compression because a subtle luminance judgment must be made in close proximity to a strong luminance edge between the bisection stimulus and the dark background. Small quantization steps at relatively high spatial frequencies are needed to maintain visible information. If the DCT block boundary falls in the middle of this stimulus, it is quite difficult to maintain all the perceptually visible information unless the quantization steps are very small.

Tiny Snellen Letters and Complex Natural Images
as a Double-Check

Complex stimuli should continue to be used. Complex stimuli such as Snellen letters (the standardized letters used in eye charts) and natural scenes have the advantage that these are the types of stimuli that are used in many practical applications. Text is especially useful to include in test images, since the human visual system may be quite sensitive to seeing distortions in familiar letters. Letters are of high contrast and are therefore able to produce nonlinearities. It is surprising that text isn't a more common test target. Complex stimuli (natural scenes) have the disadvantage that they consist of multiple factors whose contributions to image fidelity are difficult to tease apart. However, they should be used so that the results using the newly proposed stimuli can be compared with all the past work in image fidelity and image compression.

In addition to using a battery of simple images one can also use a battery of responses. Klein (1985) showed that double-judgment psychophysics can provide rich data not only about the underlying dimensions of the stimulus but also about the observer's strategies and fluctuations of attention. One could use the stimuli discussed in this section and, for example, ask the observer to make a double judgment about the visibility of jaggies and also about the visibility of blur.

Fidelity Metrics

After an image has been processed (say, it has been compressed and decompressed) one would like to know whether image fidelity has suffered. There is a psychophysical and a computational approach to this problem. In the psychophysical approach to image fidelity one asks observers whether the processed image is discriminable from the original. In the computational approach an image fidelity metric is developed that presumably correlates well with psychophysical judgments. Most popular is the mean square error (MSE) metric for calculating the difference between the final and the original images. Many authors have attempted to improve the MSE metric (Pratt, 1978; Natrevali and Haskell, 1988; Klein, Silverstein, and Carney, 1992, see also chapter 15) by including properties of the human observer. Hultgren's excellent review (1990) clarifies the interconnections among several of these objective metrics. He shows that these objective metrics are closely related to the subjective sensation of image sharpness. He emphasizes that a common feature of successful image-quality metrics is that they involve a weighted sum over log frequency (a $1/f$ weighting) rather than linear frequency.[4] (We have a little quibble about whether these $1/f$ metrics should be called sharpness metrics, since the use of log frequency deemphasizes high spatial frequencies. A sharpness metric should emphasize the higher spatial frequencies.) The MSE measures of fidelity cannot be expected to work too well, because they do not use the oriented filters, the gain controls, and the nonlinearities of human visual processing. Watson (1987) and Daly (1992a and chapter 14) among others have proposed filter-based image-fidelity metrics that can be applied to real-world scenes. Improvements continue to be made on these models (Klein, 1992), and within a few years we hope that a decent model of human vision will have been developed.

A problem with both the psychophysical and the computational methods is that multiple aspects of image quality are lumped together into a single number. There are many specific types of image degradation, including blurring, jaggies, luminance steps, blocking, aliasing, and nonlinear luminance distortions, that would be useful to classify. Knowing what *types* of errors a particular image-processing algorithm produces is more useful for improving the algorithm than simply knowing that the algorithm produces general degradation. Model makers should be encouraged to develop their models so that the model gives multiple outputs about a number of fidelity dimensions instead of a single output giving an estimate of overall fidelity.

How Many Bits/Min² Are Required of a Perfect Display?

This section examines the specifications for a perfect display. *Perfect* means that the displayed image is indistinguishable from the original "gold standard" (predigitized) image, which has a *continuum* of gray levels and a *continuum* of sample points. We ask, How many bits/min² must the display be capable of producing to present a perceptually lossless image? We use units of bits/min² rather than bits/pixel or bits/cm² to gain independence of pixel size and observer distance (see note 1).

The next three subsections are especially interesting because in each section there is a surprise. First we argue that the display must be spatially sampled above the human eye's Nyquist frequency (surprising because many people think that the Nyquist sampling rate is sufficient). Second, we describe an experiment leading to the conclusion that 15 bits of address are needed (surprising because it is generally thought that fewer than 11 bits are sufficient). Last, we argue for the counterintuitive result that an optimal lookup table should have more addresses (15 bits worth) than stored values (12 bits).

The Need for 9 Pixels/Min²

Three pixels/min are needed because of the 0.35-min resolution threshold for high-contrast stimuli (Levi and Klein, 1990b). The resolution threshold means that two thin lines separated by 0.35 min can *just* be discriminated from a single line of twice the contrast. This implied sampling density of 180 samples/deg (3 samples/min) is greater than the 120 samples/deg expected from the Nyquist frequency of 60 c/deg (this frequency is chosen because the human contrast sensitivity function does not pass any information above 60 c/deg). The need to sample above the Nyquist frequency may seem surprising. We now give two arguments that demonstrate the need for supra-Nyquist sampling.

One might think that it should be possible to simply eliminate all spatial frequencies above 60 c/deg, since those frequencies are invisible. The process of truncating the high frequencies is equivalent to convolving the image with a sinc function $(\sin(x)/x)$. However, table 7.1 shows that sinc function interpolation does not always work, because for many high-contrast stimuli the sinc filter produces regions where negative luminances are needed [see table 7.1(a)]. The alternative of using linear interpolation [table 7.1(b)] produces some blurring of the image (attenuation of frequencies below 60 c/deg), so one is forced to use a small-enough pixel size to keep the blurring low.

A second argument for supra-Nyquist sampling involves the visibility of a 60-c/deg rectangular profile grating with a contrast of say, 165 percent. In this section, contrast means the contrast of the Fourier fundamental. For these very high spatial frequencies the higher harmonics are not visible, so the grating visibility is based on the contrast of the fundamental. A contrast of 165 percent can be obtained by having one bright pixel alternating with two dark pixels, assuming each pixel has a *uniform* distri-

bution.[5] The Michelson contrast of the fundamental of a rectangular grating where the dark region has zero luminance is given by $2 \sin(\pi x)/(\pi x)$ (obtained by taking the Fourier transform of a rectangle wave grating), where x is the fractional duty cycle.[6] For the present example of a 33 percent duty cycle, $x = \frac{1}{3}$. To obtain a fundamental contrast of 165 percent, 3 pixels per cycle (3 pixels/min) are needed, corresponding to sampling at 180 samples/deg for the 60-c/deg grating with the phase of the samples aligned with the peak of the grating. Because we are assuming that each pixel has a uniform profile, the case of 3 pixels/min means that the display must be viewed from a larger distance than would be the case for 2 pixels/min. Image intensities can't get blacker than black, so the desired 165 percent image contrast must be produced by decreasing the duty cycle rather than by generating a pure sinusoid whose contrast is greater than 100 percent. The *retinal* image does not face the same problem of requiring supra-Nyquist sampling because the retinal image is severely blurred by the optics of the eye. Thus, a cone spacing of 2 cones/min is adequate to sample the low-contrast retinal image.

One might be tempted to carry this argument further and say that to achieve an image fundamental contrast of 195 percent ($= 2 \sin(\pi x)/(\pi x)$ with a duty cycle of $x = \frac{1}{8}$) one would need a duty cycle of 1 pixel on and 7 pixels off, corresponding to 8 pixels/min. However, it is not easy in a psychophysical experiment to distinguish object contrasts of 195 percent and 165 percent, because the difference is less than 20 percent. So in practice a duty cycle of $\frac{1}{3}$ should be sufficient to achieve contrasts near the ceiling. In any case, our main argument for supra-Nyquist sampling (pixel spacing of less than 0.5 min) was not based on the visibility of 60-c/deg gratings, but rather on the 2-line resolution threshold being less than 0.5 min.

An Experiment to Measure the Number of Discriminable Gray Levels

How many discriminable gray levels should a typical monitor be capable of producing? A reasonable upper luminance for most displays is about 200 cd/m². A reasonable lower limit, based on how black the display might be in a dimly lit room, is about 1 cd/m². A recent experiment showed that it is possible to detect a grating whose change in luminance is as small as 0.006 cd/m². We measured the contrast discrimination threshold of a 2-c/deg sinusoidal grating drifting at 5 Hz at a mean luminance of 1 cd/m². This luminance level was generated by using goggles with 2 ND (neutral density) filters to produce a 100-fold reduction in luminance of the display, whose mean luminance was 100 cd/m². We could discriminate (with a signal-to-noise ratio of $d' = 1$) between two gratings whose contrasts were 1.5 percent and 1.9 percent. Thus the detection threshold was 0.4 percent. The detection threshold of 0.4 percent is quite good considering the low mean luminance. When we performed this same experiment at 100 cd/m², the detection threshold was 0.04 percent! Stromeyer and Chaparro (1992) have reported similar thresholds. The contrast of the moving pedestal was chosen to place the test conditions at the bottom of the "dipper" function to make use of the contrast facilitation effect (Nachmias and Sansbury, 1974; Stromeyer and Klein, 1974).[7] If a square wave rather than a sine wave is used, the contrast becomes $\pi/4$* 0.4 percent = 0.314 percent. This corresponds to a luminance increment of 1 cd/m²* 0.314 percent *2 = 0.00628 cd/m². The factor of 2 is introduced because the luminance change from the peak to the trough of a square wave is twice the Michelson contrast of the square wave. The total number of equally spaced steps going from 1 to 200 cd/m² is 199/0.00628 $\approx$ 31,700 (15 bits).

The Need for Nonsquare Lookup Tables

What constraints must be placed on the display lookup table to achieve optimal fidelity? The answer to this question came as a surprise to us, so it is worth bringing to the attention of others concerned with applying knowledge of human vision to areas such as improving the capabilities of displays.

The need for specifying the image with large numbers of gray levels can be seen from the following problem. One of our display systems has a *nonsquare* lookup table (LUT) with 12 bits of addresses, each storing a 14-bit value that controls a 14-bit digital-to-analog converter (DAC). We call a LUT with the number of output bits (the LUT values) differing from the number of input bits (the LUT addresses) a nonsquare LUT. We had assumed that this system with its 14-bit DAC should be capable of displaying whatever luminances we wanted, but as Klein and Carney (1991b) showed, we were wrong. To fully appreciate our argument the reader should consult the original article. Here we give just an overview of the

results. With 12 bits to cover from 1 to 200 cd/m² each step is about 199/2^{12}, or approximately 0.05 cd/m². However, as we discussed in the preceding section, we found that on a 1 cd/m² background, luminance increments smaller than 0.006 cd/m² were visible, a factor of almost 10 smaller than what could be provided by our lookup table with its 12 bits of image information! Thus about 15 bits are needed to specify the intended luminance. Our LUT was designed backward. Instead of 12 bits for input and 14 bits for output, we need 15 bits for input (the intended luminance values, which become the LUT addresses) and only 12 bits of output. The reduced need for output bits is because of the accelerating gamma of the display scope:

$$L - L_0 = \alpha(V - V_0)^\gamma, \tag{7.1}$$

where L and V are the luminance and voltage; α, V_0, and L_0 are constants, and the γ is approximately 2.2. The accelerating display gamma is well matched to the compressive nonlinearity of the visual system. At low luminances the display luminance is a very shallow function of input voltage, so it is quite easy to achieve increments of 0.006 cd/m² even with the "coarse" steps of a 12-bit DAC. Klein and Carney (1991b) present a detailed discussion of how the number of bits needed for representing the image (LUT address) is controlled by the contrast sensitivity of the human visual system at the lowest luminances, whereas the number of bits of the DAC (LUT values) is controlled by the contrast sensitivity at the highest luminances.

The Total Number of Bits/Min²

Using values of 9 pixels/min² and 15 bits/pixel, one arrives at a total of 135 bits/min². This is the number of bits/min² that are needed to generate all images that can be discriminated by human vision. The factors entering this calculation are the resolution threshold of 0.35 min and the luminance discrimination threshold of 0.0063 cd/m² out of a 199 cd/m² range. We also assume (as is almost universally the case) that the input to the lookup table (the addresses) is uniformly spaced. One further, most important, assumption is being made in arriving at 135 bits/min²: the separability of the spatial resolution and the gray-level resolution. It is the separability assumption that allows us to multiply 9 times 15 to arrive at 135. This assumption is valid for a display monitor where no image processing (dithering, halftoning) is allowed. One can get dramatic savings of bits/min^2 by abandoning separability, because for high spatial frequencies far fewer gray levels are needed than for low spatial frequencies. This is one feature of image compression, the next topic.

Image Compression and the JPEG-DCT Standard

There now exists an image compression standard that was developed by JPEG (Joint Photographic Experts Group). The JPEG standard is based on the discrete cosine transform (DCT). An excellent discussion of the standard is given by Rabbani and Jones (1991). One sign that the standard is being well received is the proliferation of JPEG-based image-compression packages for personal computers. Of all the schemes that the JPEG committee considered for the compression standard, the DCT is probably the closest to the world of vision research for two reasons. (1) It is closely related to the contrast sensitivity function, as we show in the forthcoming calculation of information capacity. (2) JPEG's use of independent, repeating blocks of pixels is similar to the cortical hypercolumns of human vision (Hubel and Wiesel, 1974; Levi, Klein, and Aitsebaomo, 1985). In both cases, within one of these blocks there is considerable masking and interaction between adjacent features. We call this the *filter* regime (Levi, Klein, and Aitsebaomo, 1985). Past this distance, stimuli are relatively independent. We call this the *local sign* regime (Levi and Klein, 1990a). We argue that within a hypercolumn the separations of features are represented by the activity of size-tuned filters of different sizes (similar to Fourier amplitudes), and between hypercolumns they are represented by the relative positions of hypercolumns. Thus we are claiming that the DCT representation is remarkably similar to the representation actually used by the visual system.

Calculating the Number of Bits/Min^2

Klein (1990) showed how to calculate the amount of information in bits/min^2 visible to the human visual system. A brief summary of this calculation is presented here. The images to be considered here are chosen to have a pixel size of 0.5 min to maintain sharp image fidelity. This is less than half the size that is typically used and about 1.5 times the size (0.35 min) that is needed to be able to represent the sharpest lines and edges (see Klein, 1990, for

consideration of a 0.35-min pixel). Our use of a 0.5 min pixel means we are calculating the number of bits/min^2 that is needed for an almost worst-case image. With a 0.5-min pixel size and a DCT standard block size of 8 pixels, each 4-min block has eight horizontal DCT coefficients with frequencies of 0, 7.5, 15, 22.5, 30, 37.5, 45, and 52.5 c/deg. This analysis can be extended to two dimensions, in which case higher frequencies are present according to the Pythagorean sum of the horizontal and vertical frequencies.

Table 7.2 tabulates the number of bits needed at each frequency. The horizontal and vertical components of spatial frequency are indicated along the left and the top of the table. Consider, for example, the cell with horizontal and vertical spatial frequencies of 7.5 c/deg. The Pythagorean sum gives a spatial frequency of $f = 7.5 \times 2^{0.5} = 10.61$ c/deg. The contrast sensitivity at this frequency is $CSF(f) = 205$. This estimate is based on a CSF similar to that used by Klein and Levi (1985):

$$CSF(f) = 250\, f^{0.5} \exp(-0.13f). \tag{7.2}$$

The high-frequency falloff is 1 db per c/deg; the peak sensitivity is 300 at a spatial frequency of 4 c/deg. This choice of peak sensitivity is somewhat conservative (a factor of 2 lower than that of Levi and Klein, 1985). The number of discriminable contrast levels is given by twice the number of jnd's from a contrast of 0 to the maximum contrast. The factor of 2 is because the contrast can be

Table 7.2

A Table of the Number of Bits Needed for each DCT Coefficient within a 4 × 4 min block

	0	7.5	15.	22.5	30.	37.5	45.	52.5	(60.)
0	11.	6.90	6.72	6.47	6.14	5.69	5.03	3.95	(2.16)
7.5	6.90	6.84	6.67	6.42	6.09	5.64	4.96	3.85	(2.03)
15.	6.72	6.67	6.52	6.28	5.94	5.47	4.74	3.53	(1.61)
22.5	6.47	6.42	6.28	6.04	5.69	5.16	4.33	2.94	(.91)
30.	6.14	6.09	5.94	5.69	5.29	4.66	3.64	2.03	
37.5	5.69	5.64	5.47	5.16	4.66	3.85	2.56	.76	
45.	5.03	4.96	4.74	4.33	3.64	2.56	1.05		
52.5	3.95	3.85	3.53	2.94	2.00	.76			
(60.)	(2.16)	(2.03)	(1.61)	(.91)					

The horizontal and vertical spatial-frequency components are shown on the left and the top. For a pixel size of 0.5 min the spatial frequencies range from 0 to 52.5 c/deg in steps of 7.5 c/deg. For a pixel size of 0.333 min (still with a 4 × 4 min block) the spatial frequencies range from 0 to 82.5 c/deg also in steps of 7.5 c/deg. Because spatial frequencies of 67.5 c/deg and above are not visible, they are not shown. The extra components that are associated with the 0.333-min sampling are shown in parentheses.

either negative or positive. The number of jnd's is equal to the signal detection d' value (Klein and Levi, 1985). Using the transducer function discussed by Klein & Levi (1985), d' is given by

$$d' = \frac{\ln(1 + c_{\max}^2/5)}{\ln(1 + 1/5)}, \qquad (7.3)$$

where $c_{\max}$ is the maximum contrast in threshold units. The denominator of equation 7.3 has been chosen to give $d' = 1$ when $c_{\max} = 1$. This transducer function is quadratic at low contrast and has a 10 percent Weber fraction at high contrast (see Klein, 1990). Because the maximum contrast is 200 percent (Klein, 1990), $c_{\max} = 2$ CSF, since CSF is the reciprocal of the contrast threshold. For our example of $f = 10.61$ c/deg a contrast of 200 percent corresponds to $2 \times 205 = 410$ contrast threshold units (820 contrast threshold units if both polarities are included). The number of discriminable levels (from Equation 7.3) becomes

$$\text{number of levels} = 2d' = \frac{2\ln(1 + (2\,\text{CSF}(f)^2/5)}{\ln(6/5)}. \quad (7.4)$$

For our example, the number of discriminable levels is 114.3. This latter number is lower than the maximum number of contrast threshold units (820) because Equation 7.4 takes into account Weber's law whereby at high contrasts the contrast jnd increases. The number of bits needed to encode these levels within one DCT block is

$$\text{number of bits/block} = \log_2(\text{number of levels})$$
$$= \log_2(114.3) = 6.84. \qquad (7.5)$$

This is the explanation for the value 6.84 that is found in table 7.2 for $f_x = f_y = 7.5$.

In figure 7.1 the DC component is assumed to require 11 bits rather than the 15 discussed earlier because here we are counting the number of jnds, so that at high luminance the jnd is larger than at low luminance.

The open squares in figure 7.1 show the number of bits for each coefficient within one block as a function of the spatial frequency of the coefficient. The third point from the left is the datum that we have just calculated. Of greater interest is the total number of bits cumulated over all frequencies. This is shown in figure 7.1 as the filled diamonds. Being displayed is the cumulative number of bits/min². The number of bits/min² is obtained by dividing the number of bits/block by 16, since there are 16 min² in

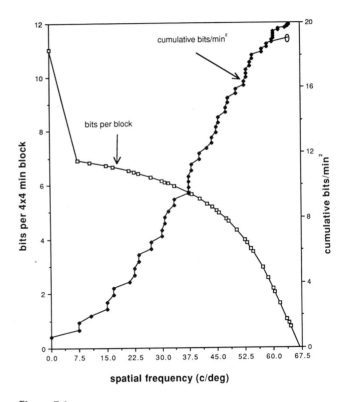

spatial frequency (c/deg)

Figure 7.1

A plot of the number of bits of information usable by the visual system. The open squares give the number of bits per block required for each DCT coefficient in a 4 × 4 min block. These values are taken from table 7.2. The filled diamonds are the cumulative bits/min². They are calculated by summing the contributions from each coefficient. In order to convert to min² the bits/block is divided by 16 min²/block. For example, the DC value is 11/16 = 0.69. At 7.5 c/deg there are two contributions, from $(f_x, f_y) = (7.5, 0)$ and $= (0, 7.5)$. Each contribution is 6.9/16 = 0.43. Thus up through 7.5 c/deg the number of bits required is 0.69 + 0.43 + 0.43 = 1.55 bits/min². The circle at the upper right corner of the plot is the cumulative number of bits/min² for the case of a 4 × 4 min block with 0.5-min pixels. This value is slightly lower than the filled diamonds that represent a 4 × 4 min block with 0.333-min pixels.

one 4×4 DCT block. The coefficient at $f = 10.61$ contributes $6.84/16 = 0.427$ bits. The coefficient at 7.5 c/deg contributes 0.431 bits twice since there are two 7.5 c/deg components, one on the horizontal axis and one on the vertical axis (see table 7.2).

There are a total of 19.1 bits/min² based on a 4×4 min DCT block with 0.5-min pixels. If we had used a 4×4 min block with 0.333 min pixels (a 12×12 block rather than the 8×8 block specified by JPEG) then a few extra coefficients would contribute and the total number of bits would be 19.9. These extra coefficients are those in which either the horizontal or vertical spatial frequency is 60 c/deg (indicated by parentheses in table 7.2). The data plotted in Figure 7.1 are for the 0.333-min pixel case. The total number of bits for the 0.5-min case is indicated by a circle near the upper right corner of the figure.

One of the most important messages conveyed by Figure 7.1 is that about $\frac{2}{3}$ of the total number of bits come from spatial frequencies above 25 c/deg. These high spatial frequencies are rarely considered, since the usual investigations of image compression start with images in which the pixel size is greater than 1 min. So it is not surprising that most calculations of the number of bits/min² arrive at smaller values than the present calculation.

This calculation of about 20 bits/min² is much smaller than the 135 bits/min² that was calculated earlier. This discrepancy is because in arriving at the 135 bits/min² requirement for displays we made a separability assumption such that the number gray levels was independent of spatial considerations (the human CSF was ignored). Thus 135 bits/min² was calculated as the product of 15 bits/pixel and 9 pixels/min². The lower value of 20 bits/min², which is a measure of the information density that human vision is capable of taking in, did not assume separability. Both the CSF (Equation 7.2) and the contrast discrimination function (included in Equation 7.3) are taken into account.

This section examined how knowledge of human visual processing can be used to calculate the information available to a human observer. Further details are discussed by Klein, Silverstein, and Carney (1992). That article explores in mathematical detail several topics on the connection between characteristics of human vision, image compression and image fidelity including (1) why the discrete cosine basis functions have a better shape (including a gentle envelope at high spatial frequencies) for achieving compression and for evaluating fidelity than the discrete

Fourier basis functions; (2) a discussion of a "killer dot" image that causes problems for compression algorithms, since it is quite visible before compression but disappears after compression; (3) a discussion of the mean-square-error metric including variants to make it closer to a human vision metric; (4) a discussion of the visibility of DCT basis functions including a calculation of their Fourier transform, and (5) a discussion of the number of bits/min² for different pixel sizes.

Uniform Quantization Versus Weber Quantization

In calculating the number of bits required for each coefficient we used the transducer function given by Equation 7.4. The logarithm in this formula for d' was based on the Weber's law relationship whereby at high contrasts the contrast jnd is approximately proportional to the contrast (actually it is proportional to contrast raised to the 0.7 power). A common application of visual system constraints to image compression (e.g., Peterson, Rajala, and Delp, 1989) is to use Weber's law as a means for having coarser quantization at high contrasts than at low contrasts. Many display engineers and vision scientists were therefore surprised that the JPEG standard allows only uniform quantization with no flexibility that would allow the user to choose Weber's quantization.[8] Was this an error on the part of JPEG? This section argues that the JPEG decision was not in error. Neither was the decision based simply on a desire to make the DCT algorithm faster (uniform quantization is very rapid). Rather, it had a good basis in what we know about facilitation and masking in visual performance.

The contrast facilitation found by Stromeyer and Klein (1974) and Nachmias and Sansbury (1974) decreases the savings that can be expected from Weber's law quantization. Although near the peak of the CSF the difference in bits/min² between uniform quantization and a Weber's law–based quantization is substantial (11.01 versus 6.90 bits/min² at 7.5 c/deg), at higher frequencies the savings due to Weber's law are limited. Consider, for example, the 22.5 c/deg component. The CSF is 63.6, which means that the detection threshold is $1/63.6 = 1.572\%$. Because of the facilitation effect, contrast steps of about half the detection threshold ($1.572\%/2 = 0.786\%$) would be discriminable at the optimal pedestal contrast. The total number of levels needed to cover the range from from -200% to $+200\%$ (see Klein 1990 for why 200% is used rather than 100%) would thus be $400/0.786 = 509$. The 509 steps require $\log_2(509) = 8.99$ bits. The use of Weber's law (the procedure outlined earlier) reduces this value to 6.47 bits (table 7.2), or about a 30 percent reduction in bits. At a higher spatial frequency of 45 c/deg these values become 5.27 and 5.03, which correspond to a savings of less than 5 percent due to Weber versus uniform quantization. The reduced savings is because at higher spatial frequencies the detection threshold is larger and there isn't much of a range, after the facilitation regime, for the Weber masking to raise thresholds. As seen in table 7.2, the main contribution to the total number of bits/min^2 come from spatial frequencies above 25 c/deg, so a quantization scheme based on Weber's law will not produce dramatic reductions in the number of bits/min^2 as compared to the uniform quantization of the JPEG standard. Girod (1989) provided further evidence that the savings of bits that can be expected from spatial masking (and also temporal masking) is small.

Uniform quantization is preferable over Weber quantization because of nonlinear masking. Consider the task of discriminating between the following pair of 8 pixel stimuli: (26 25 25 25 25 25 25 255) and (25 25 25 25 25 25 25 255). The task involves the discrimination of levels 25 and 26 in the presence of a masking stimulus of intensity 255 that is separated by 7 pixels (3.5 min). This discrimination should be easy for the human observer, since a 4 percent luminance change (1 part in 25) should be above threshold. Preservation of information about the low-contrast step requires the preservation of small differences in DCT coefficients that are highly stimulated because of the distant 255 luminance level (see Klein, 1990, for details). If Weber's law had been used, then the DCT coefficients would be coarsely quantized because of their high level of stimulation, and the discriminability of levels 25 and 26 would have been lost. Uniform quantization is needed to avoid these effects of nonlocal masking.

Viewprints: An Alternative to DCT and Wavelet Compression?

A Problem with DCT and Wavelet Compression

We have not yet discussed a prime alternative to the DCT, namely, the wavelet transforms. The two are quite similar. Wavelets provide a complete expansion that use filters at all scales, whereas the DCT expansion uses filters only within a 8×8 pixel block. An advantage of wavelets is that they avoid the blocking artifacts associated with the DCT blocks. They also reduce errors typical of Fourier-based methods, such as the Gibbs phenomenon (Zettler, Huffman, and Linden, 1990).[9] The wavelet transform has several disadvantages: (1) It doesn't lend itself as well as the DCT with block matching to the task of compressing image sequences. (2) The DCT-basis functions at the highest spatial frequencies have narrower tuning than do the wavelets and can thus be more severely quantized. (3) The low-frequency wavelets are very large spatially and thus are susceptible to the effects of nonlocal masking. This could be a problem, since the low frequencies control the local luminance that in turn controls the contrast gain of the human visual system. Errors in average local luminance could therefore distort the perception of higher spatial frequencies.

The DCT and the wavelet schemes have a drawback whereby slight shifts of the image can produce large changes in the transform coefficients. This can cause a problem for motion compression where the scene is stationary except for a slight camera jiggle. A very small shift of the camera can produce dramatic changes in all the high spatial frequency components. These changes could be troublesome for transmitting changing images where one desires to send only information that is truly changing. Exciting recent work shows promise that some amount of translation, rotation, and scale invariance can be incorporated into a wavelet transform (Simoncelli, Freeman, Adelson, and Heeger, 1992). In this section we discuss the viewprint representation that was developed with the same goal of including some amount of translation invariance.

The Viewprint Model: Getting Rid of Absolute Phase

The viewprint model is the name given by Klein & Levi (1985) to the model they used for accounting for the bisection data discussed earlier. The same representation was used by Stromeyer and Klein (1975) to do probability summation over both space and spatial frequency. A viewprint is similar to the wavelet transform in that it represents the output of a bank of filters, all of the same shape, but of different sizes and positions. A viewprint is generated by first producing two wavelet transforms (here we use the word *wavelet* loosely, without its beautiful completeness properties). The first wavelet transform could use even-symmetric wavelets, and the second transform would use odd-symmetric wavelets that are the Hilbert transform of the first wavelet's receptive field. The Cauchy functions (Klein and Levi, 1985) form a convenient set of wavelet bases, since the Hilbert pairs have a very simple analytic form (the Fourier transform of both is $f^n \exp(-f/f_0)$). The viewprint value is given by plugging the Pythagorean sum of the two wavelet transforms into equation 7.3 to obtain a d' value (signal-to-noise ratio). The point of taking the Pythagorean sum is to eliminate the local phase. This representation is the visual analogue of the "voiceprint" or "sonogram" for analyzing speech and bird song, and of the 5-line, treble, and bass clef notation used by musicians (Klein, 1992). In these representations, time is the abscissa, and temporal frequency is the ordinate. In the spatial domain the ordinate represents relative position (the size or spatial frequency of objects), and the abscissa is absolute position. The human visual system is very sensitive to relative position (spatial frequency) but not sensitive to small displacements of entire objects (absolute phase). The Pythagorean sum has also been called the *energy representation*. Ross, Morrone and Burr (1989) use the energy representation to explain the perception of Mach bands. One problem with the viewprint representation is that it has lost the distinction about whether a feature is black or white. Thus we have appended to the viewprint "1 bit" of phase (Klein and Levi, 1985): the sign of the original symmetrical wavelet transform. We believe that 1-bit phase is like color and is not maintained at the highest spatial frequencies. Although there are circumstances in which it is possible to reconstruct the image from 1 bit of phase information (Pillai and Elliott, 1990), the transition points must be known with greater accuracy than is feasible for the visual system. The scale-space zero-crossing theories of Witkin (1985) and Yuille and Poggio (1983) are also relevant to our "1-bit-phase" map rather than the energy map of the full viewprint. Very little research has been devoted to the energy representation.

The advantage of the viewprint representation over the wavelet or DCT representation is that it changes more slowly across the image. The characteristic oscillation of the wavelet is governed by the mean spatial frequency of the wavelet. The characteristic oscillation of the viewprint is governed by the envelope of the wavelet. Thus the viewprint is does not change much after a small shift of eye position (or digitizer position).

A dramatic feature that stands out in the viewprint representation is the rapid changes in activity near the null points. It is this rapid change that makes it possible to achieve the very low hyperacuity thresholds that we reported (Klein and Levi, 1985). To determine the spatial frequency of the null points accurately, we believe the viewprint must be sampled more finely in the spatial frequency direction than what is required for the wavelet transform. This overcompleteness may be a problem for compression, but the advantages may compensate.

At present, the viewprint scheme is not a viable candidate as a representation for image compression because there has been so little research on it. Further details on the advantages and problems of the viewprint representation are given by Klein (1992). There is much that must be learned: how to invert the viewprint representation, what sampling grain is adequate, what filters are optimal, how accurately must the null points be located, how to extend the viewprint representation from one dimension to two. The robustness of this representation to small translations seems sufficiently promising that further research should be encouraged.

What Are the Best (and Worst) Wavelet Functions?

In choosing a filter shape for the viewprint or for wavelet compression the goal is to use a receptive field that is local in both space and in spatial frequency. Spatial localization is needed to avoid nonlocal masking whereby a separated high-contrast edge interferes with a local low-contrast feature. Localization in spatial frequency is needed to aid the quantization savings; if the high-pass wavelets had broad bandwidth, then their low-frequency content would aid the visibility of the wavelet, thereby reducing the amount of compression. As we pointed out earlier, the main contributions to the number of bits/min^2 come from frequencies above 25 c/deg, so most attention must be paid to compressing the high spatial frequencies. In the viewprint model, spatial frequency tuning is needed, since many of the cues needed for hyperacuity discriminations are jointly localized in both space and spatial frequency. Broadly tuned mechanisms would be masked by irrelevant stimulus components.

There has been a recent controversy about what filter shape minimizes the joint uncertainty U in space and spatial frequency that is given by

$$U^2 = \langle x^2 \rangle \langle f^2 \rangle. \tag{7.6}$$

It is well known that the Gaussian is the unique function that is the global minimum of Equation 7.6. Gabor (1946) and Stork and Wilson (1990) used the calculus of variations and claimed that the Hermite polynomials times Gaussians are local minima. Their claim is not quite correct. The Hermite functions turn out to be saddle points. If we constrain the filters to be a Gaussian times an nth order polynomial, then it turns out that the nth order Hermite function *maximizes* the uncertainty (Klein and Beutter, 1992). Thus Gabor found the worst possible functions rather than the best. He correctly found an extremum using the calculus of variations, but he didn't realize that the extremum was a maximum rather than a minimum! The message here is to not use Hermite functions for the filters in either image compression or in vision modeling.

Suggestions for Compression

The establishment of the JPEG-DCT image-compression standard provides an excellent framework for communication between vision researchers and display engineers. We offer three suggestions that can aid the communication.

Two numbers are needed. Separate vision constraints from redundancy constraints

There are two steps in compression algorithms at which the number of bits/min^2 is reduced: (1) Irrelevancy removal (discarding image content that is not visible to the eye). This is the quantization step based on the poor visibility of high spatial frequencies. (2) Redundancy removal (taking advantage of the statistical correlation between image samples). Natural images tend to have an approximately $1/f$ spectrum similar to the Fourier transform of an edge (not surprising, since natural images often consist of objects of different luminances separated by edges). The $1/f$ spectrum means there is not much energy at high spatial frequencies, so "entropy coding" can have a strong effect in reducing the number of bits needed to encode an image.

Researchers in human vision are mainly interested in the first of the two steps, since the second is a property of the image rather than a property of the observer. We recommend that everyone doing image compression research should *separately* report the reduction in bits/min^2 from each of these two factors. It would be most useful to know both the quantization savings and the image redundancy savings for a variety of images, for different choices

of compression rules. The number of bits/min^2 due to human vision assumptions made about the CSF can be calculated as in figure 7.1 or as given in more detail by Klein (1990) and Klein, Silverstein, and Carney (1992). The number of bits/min^2 due to redundancy reduction can be calculated by first calculating the average number of bits/min^2 achieved by the full compression algorithm and then subtracting the contribution from the first step.

Do not underestimate the number of quantization levels

In the quantization step one must be careful not to underestimate the number of contrast levels that are needed. We have already discussed the need to take facilitation into account when deciding on the quantization interval. Facilitation occurs not only within one DCT coefficient but also between coefficients. Stromeyer and Klein (1974) showed that a suprathreshold fundamental (say at 7.5 c/deg) could facilitate the third harmonic (at 22.5 c/deg). Thus the sharpness of a square-wave grating can be discriminated *before* the third harmonic of the square wave can be detected, contrary to the earlier findings of Campbell and Robson (1968). These interactions between well-separated spatial frequencies may seem to violate the independence of channels that is often assumed in channel models; however, Stromeyer and Klein (1974) showed that in fact the results fit well with independent medium bandwidth channels.

A second factor that should not be ignored when quantizing the DCT coefficients is to remember that the contrasts range between -200% and $+200\%$. It would be a natural mistake to have contrasts range between -100% and $+100\%$. Klein (1990) provided details on the need for the extended contrast range. Although this discussion has focussed on the DCT, it applies to other compression schemes as well.

Use simpler images to assess the multiple dimensions of image quality

Probably the most important recommendation that I can think of is to modify the pictures that are being used. In the section that addressed the general question of what images should be used for assessing image quality, a strong case was made that to disentangle the multiple dimensions of image quality a battery of simple images should be used in addition to the presently used images of natural scenes. Each of the new images should be chosen to isolate a particular factor of image quality. This recommendation is especially relevant to image compression, since the quantization step destroys information about the image. To accurately determine the consequence of losing information one must develop techniques that are more sensitive than those presently used. Once separate factors are isolated, the compression algorithms can be improved to eliminate the specific problems.

Acknowledgments

This research was supported by a grant from the Air Force Office of Sponsored Research, AFOSR 89-0238. Portions of this chapter were presented previously (Klein, 1990; Klein and Carney, 1991a). I wish to thank Andrew Watson and two reviewers for their detailed and helpful suggestions.

Notes

1. Throughout this chapter image information is specified in units of bits/min^2 rather than bits/pixel or bits/mm^2. Only if one uses bits/min^2 can the role of the human observer be used, since the human eye takes in angular information. For example, visual sensitivity is specified in terms of spatial frequency (c/deg), which is an angular unit. If the image information was specified in bits/mm^2, no limits on the information could be set, since the observer might want to get very close to the screen and use a magnifying glass to see a tiny displayed object. The display engineer, who would like to specify information in terms of bits/mm^2, must translate our angular units of minutes into spatial units of millimeters by assuming a viewing distance. This chapter sticks with angular units to keep visual information independent of viewing distance.

2. In case some readers aren't familiar with the JPEG algorithm, it breaks up the image into 8 × 8 pixel blocks, applies the DCT (discrete cosine transform, similar to a Fourier transform), and then quantizes the DCT coefficients according to something like the contrast sensitivity function so that high spatial frequencies are coarsely quantized. The resulting coefficients (many of which will be zero after quantization) can be transmitted quite efficiently using schemes called *entropy coding*.

3. Sag is the distance between an arc of a circle and the chord spanning the arc at the midpoint of the arc. The formula for sag is approximately: sag $= a^2/8R$, where a is the chordlength of the arc, and R is the radius of the arc. For the example cited, $a = 50$ and $R = 300$, so sag $= 50^2/8 \times 300 \cong 1$.

4. Note that at this point we are going back to discussing "quality" rather than "fidelity," because that is what was being measured in the older studies.

5. This argument for supra-Nyquist sampling was based on the assumption that the luminance profile within each pixel is uniformly spread out across the pixel. If each pixel's profile was much sharper, then this argument for supra-Nyquist sampling would lose its power, since the contrast of the fundamental would be close to 200 percent independent of the number of black pixels between each white pixel.

6. Michelson contrast of a sinusoidal grating is defined as the amplitude of the grating (the change in luminance from the mean luminance to the peak or trough luminance) divided by the mean luminance.

7. The facilitation effect refers to the finding that the visibility of a test stimulus is enhanced when the test is added to a suprathreshold stimulus called a *pedestal*. For small pedestal strengths the test threshold is lower than the zero pedestal threshold. For large pedestal strengths Weber's law masking elevates the thresholds. This dipper shape is called the *dipper function* (Legge and Foley, 1980).

8. Uniform quantization means having the same ΔL luminance discriminability at all luminances for the DC DCT component and the same Δc contrast discriminability at all contrasts for the DC components.

9. I suspect the smooth envelope of the DCT basis functions at high spatial frequencies also minimizes the Gibbs phenomenon for DCT compression.

References

Barten, P. G. J. (1989). The square root integral (SQRI): A new metric to describe the effect of various display parameters on perceived image quality. *Human Vision, Visual Processing*, and *Digital Display*, ed. Bernice E. Rogowitz. *Proceedings of the SPIE* 1077:73−82.

Campbell, F. W. & Robson, J. G. (1968). Application of Fourier analysis to the visibility of gratings. *Journal of Physiology* (London) 197:551−566.

Daly, S. (1992). The visible differences predictor: An algorithm for the assessment of image fidelity. *Human Vision, Visual Processing, and Digital Display III*, ed. Bernice E. Rogowitz, Jan P. Allebach, and Stanley A. Klein. *Proceedings of the SPIE* 1666.

Gabor, D. (1946). Theory of communication. *Journal of the Institute of Electrical Engineering* 93:429−457.

Girod, B. (1989). The information theoretical significance of spatial and temporal masking in video signals. *Human Vision, Visual Processing, and Digital Display*, ed. Bernice E. Rogowitz. *Proceedings of the SPIE* 1077:178−187.

Hubel, D. H. & Wiesel, T. N. (1974). Uniformity of monkey striate cortex: A parallel relationship between field size, scatter, and magnification factor. *Journal of Comparative Neurology* 158:295−306.

Hultgren, B. O. (1990). Subjective quality factor revisited. *Human Vision and Electronic Imaging: Models, Methods, and Applications*, ed. Bernice E. Rogowitz and Jan P. Allebach. *Proceedings of the SPIE* 1249:12−23.

Klein, S. A. (1985). Double judgment psychophysics: Problems and solutions. *Journal of the Optical Society of America A* 2:1568−1585.

Klein, S. A. & Levi, D. M. (1985). Hyperacuity thresholds of one second: Theoretical predictions and empirical validation. *Journal of the Optical Society of America A* 2:1170–1190.

Klein, S. A. (1990). High resolution and image compression using the discrete cosine transform. *Human Vision and Electronic Imaging: Models, Methods, and Applications,* ed. Bernice E. Rogowitz and Jan P. Allebach. *Proceedings of the SPIE* 1249:135–146.

Klein, S. A. & Carney, T. (1991a). "Perfect" displays and "perfect" image compression in space and time. *Human Vision, Visual Processing, and Digital Display II,* ed. Bernice E. Rogowitz and Jan P. Allebach. *Proceedings of the SPIE* 1453:190–205.

Klein, S. A. & Carney, T. (1991b). How the number of required gray levels depends on the gamma of the display. *Society for Information Display 91 Digest* 22:623–626.

Klein, S. A. (1992). Spatial vision models: Problems and successes. In L. Harris and M. Jenkin (Eds.) *Spatial Vision in Humans and Robots,* (3–26). Cambridge University Press.

Klein, S. A. & Beutter, B. (1992). Minimizing and maximizing the joint space-spatial frequency uncertainty of Gabor-like functions: Comment. *Journal of the Optical Society of America A* 9:337–340.

Klein, S. A., Silverstein, D. A. & Carney, T. (1992). Relevance of human vision to JPEG-DCT compression. *Human Vision, Visual Processing, and Digital Display III,* ed. Bernice E. Rogowitz, Jan P. Allebach, and Stanley A. Klein. *Proceedings of the SPIE* 1666.

Legge, G. E. & Foley, J. M. (1980). Contrast masking in human vision. *Journal of the Optical Society of America* 70:1458–1471.

Levi, D. M., Klein S. A. & Aitsebaomo, P. A. (1985). Vernier acuity, crowding, and cortical magnification. *Vision Research* 25:963–977.

Levi, D. M. & Klein, S. A. (1990a). The role of separation and eccentricity in encoding position. *Vision Research* 30:557–585.

Levi, D. M. & Klein, S. A. (1990b). Equivalent intrinsic blur in spatial vision. *Vision Research* 30:1971–1993.

McFarlan, D., ed. (1991). *Guiness Book of World Records,* 27. New York: Bantam Books.

Mulligan, J. B. & Stone, L. S. (1989). Halftoning method for the generation of motion stimuli. *Journal of the Optical Society of America A* 6:1217–1227.

Nachmias, J. & Sansbury, R. V. (1974). Grating contrast: Discrimination may be better than detection. *Vision Research* 14:1039–1042.

Natrevali, A. N. & Haskell, B. J. (1988). *Digital Pictures: Representation and Compression.* New York: Plenum Press.

Peterson, H. A., Rajala, S. A. & Delp, E. J. (1989). Image segmentation using human visual system properties with applications in image compression. *Human Vision, Visual Processing, and Digital Display,* ed. Bernice E. Rogowitz. *Proceedings of the SPIE* 1077:155–163.

Pillai, S. U. & Elliott, B. (1990). Image reconstruction from one bit of phase information. *Journal of Visual Communication and Image Representation* 1:153–157.

Pratt, W. K. (1978). *Digital Image Processing.* New York: John Wiley & Sons.

Rabbani, M. & Jones, P. W. (1991). *Digital Image Compression Techniques,* Bellingham, Wash.: Engineering Press. vol. TT7 SPIE Optical.

Ross, J., Morrone, C., and Burr, D. C. (1989). The conditions under which Mach bands are visible. *Vision Research* 29:699–715.

Roufs, J. A. J. & Boschman, M. C. (1990). Methods for evaluating the perceptual quality of VDUs. *Human Vision and Electronic Imaging: Models, Methods, and Applications,* ed. Bernice E. Rogowitz, Jan P. Allebach. *Proceedings of the SPIE* 1249:2–11.

Silverstein, L. D., Krantz, J. H., Gomer, F. E., Yeh, Y. & Monty, R. W. (1990). Effects of spatial sampling and luminance quantization on the image quality of color matrix displays. *Journal of the Optical Society of America A* 7:1955–1968.

Simoncelli, E. P., Freeman, W. T., Adelson, E. H. & Heeger, D. J. (1992). Shiftable multi-scale transforms. *IEEE Transactions on Information Theory, Special Issue on Wavelets.* Forthcoming.

Stork, D. G. & Wilson, H. R. (1990). Do Gabor functions provide appropriate descriptions of visual cortical receptive fields? *Journal of the Optical Society of America A* 7:1362–1373.

Stromeyer, III, C. F. & Klein, S. A. (1974). Spatial frequency channels in human vision as asymmetric (edge) mechanisms. *Vision Research* 14:1409–1420.

Stromeyer, III, C. F. & Klein, S. A. (1975). Evidence against narrow-band spatial frequency channels in human vision: The detectability of frequency modulated gratings. *Vision Research* 15:899–910.

Stromeyer, III, C. F. & Chaparro, A. (1992). Display intensity-resolution required for measuring visual discriminations. *Society for Information Display 92 Digest* 23:247–250.

Watson, A. B. (1987). The cortex transform: Rapid computation of simulated neural images. *Computer Vision, Graphics and Image Processing* 39:311–327.

Witkin, A. (1985). Scale-space filtering. *Proceedings of International Joint Conference on Artificial Intelligence,* 1019–1021, Karlsruhe.

Yuille, A. L. & Poggio, T. (1983). Fingerprints theorems for zero-crossings. MIT A. I. Memo 730.

Zettler, W. R., Huffman, J. and Linden, D. C. P., (1990). Application of compactly supported wavelets to image compression. *Image Processing Algorithms and Techniques.* ed. Keith S. Pennington, and Robert J. Moorhead, II. *Proc. of the SPIE* 1244:150–160.

8

The Significance of Eye Movements and Image Acceleration for Coding Television Image Sequences

Michael P. Eckert
and Gershon Buchsbaum

The spatial acuity of the human visual system depends on the velocity of the image traveling across the retina, so as retinal image velocity increases, the spatial acuity of the visual system decreases. This is due primarily to the temporal integration time (limited temporal bandwidth) of visual processing, which limits the spatial resolution of quickly moving objects. Since the velocity of image motion in the real world can vary widely, the visual system is presented with the problem of viewing images that are often blurred because of fast motion. The visual system addresses this problem in part by tracking moving objects with smooth-pursuit eye movements. Smooth-pursuit eye movements accomplish two tasks: (1) They maintain the object of interest in the area of highest spatial acuity of the visual field and (2) they minimize the velocity slip of the image across the retina by matching eye velocity to image velocity. Thus, even with large absolute image velocities, the retinal velocity of the image can be small.

The ability of the visual system to compensate for object motion with smooth-pursuit eye movements is a significant factor in coding television image sequences. Girod (1988) points out a common misconception about visual perception, which is that substantial reduction in image spatial resolution is allowed in regions of motion, since the human visual system is insensitive to high spatial frequencies during fast motion. When eye movements are allowed, however, Girod found that human observers are actually highly sensitive to spatial blur with image velocities up to 9.4 deg/sec (the highest velocity measured). This means that fast image motion does *not* necessarily permit reduction of image spatial resolution when eyes are allowed to move freely. This result was corroborated by Westerink and Teunissen (1990), who investigated the perceived sharpness of complex images when the screen image was moved and degraded by camera blur, and when the image was moved but remained unblurred. They found that the camera blur was easily detectable and that the perceived sharpness of the image remained high for all velocities. Murphy (1978) and Flipse et al. (1988) measured spatial contrast sensitivity curves for moving sine-wave gratings when smooth pursuit was allowed and found no decrease in spatial acuity for moderate image velocities (less than 20 deg/s). They found that spatial acuity of the observer depends solely on retinal velocity rather than absolute image velocity. The effect of eye movements on observer spatial acuity is also discussed by B. Girod and P. Hearty in chapters 15 and 12, respectively. Since retinal image velocity is the difference between eye velocity and image velocity, then the spatial acuity of the observer is a function of the accuracy with which eye movements compensate for image motion.

In the first part of this chapter we show how eye movements modify the spatiotemporal spectrum of image sequences and consider the effectiveness of tracking under different image motion characteristics. We then address the circumstances under which the spatial resolution of moving television images can be reduced with no perceptual loss for the observer. This involves an analysis of known psychophysical results to identify the image motion conditions under which spatial resolution can be decreased. Finally, we examine four television sequences to identify the degree to which screen spatial resolution of moving images can be reduced because of image motion.

The Effect of Eye Movements on the Image

Spatiotemporal Spectrum of Image Sequences

Motion is a highly ordered space-time variation in a visual scene. A first-order approximation of motion in television images, as seen by the visual system, is a velocity field. The velocity field assigns a velocity vector to each point in space and arises from the projection of motion in the scene onto the image plane of the retina. The estimation of the velocity field serves as a basis for many computational models of human motion processing (Adelson and Bergen, 1985; van Santen and Sperling, 1985; Watson and Ahumada, 1983a, 1985; Heeger, 1987). Spatiotemporal variations of image intensity based on the velocity field can be described as

$$I(\boldsymbol{u}, t) = I_0\left(\boldsymbol{u} - \int_{t_0}^{t} \boldsymbol{v}(\boldsymbol{u}, t') \, dt', t_0\right), \quad (8.1)$$

where $I(\boldsymbol{u}, t)$ is the image intensity at spatial point $\boldsymbol{u} = (u_x, u_y)$ and time t, $I_0(\boldsymbol{u}, t_0)$ is the image intensity at time t_0

and $\boldsymbol{v}(\boldsymbol{u}, t)$ is the velocity field assigning a velocity vector, $\boldsymbol{v} = (v_x, v_y)$ to each point in space and time. Equation 8.1 is an approximation to the complex spatiotemporal variations found in actual images. It assumes conservation of image intensity and is valid only for small time periods (small $t - t_0$). This means that it fails to account for space-time variations at occlusion edges and for effects such as flicker or photometric motion. However, equation 8.1 does explicitly allow space and time variations of image velocity and so is more general than the commonly used formulation that assumes constant image velocity ($\boldsymbol{v}(\boldsymbol{u}, t) = \boldsymbol{v}$).

An image translating at constant velocity has energy located on a plane in the three dimensions of spatiotemporal frequency space, with the orientation of the plane determined by the velocity direction and magnitude (Watson and Ahumada, 1983a, 1985; Heeger, 1987; Girod, 1992). However, since images do not, in general, have constant velocity across the entire image, the orientation of the plane containing the image energy will also vary across space. Assuming that the velocity field is piecewise constant (image velocity changes drastically only at occlusion boundaries), then a space-time variant spectrum (Cohen, 1989) of time-varying image sequences derived from the model of equation 8.1 is

$$S(\boldsymbol{u}, t, \boldsymbol{k}, f) = S(\boldsymbol{k})\delta(f - \boldsymbol{v}(\boldsymbol{u}, t) \cdot \boldsymbol{k}), \quad (8.2)$$

where $\delta(\ )$ is the Dirac delta function, $\boldsymbol{v}(\boldsymbol{u}, t)$ is the velocity field, and $S(\boldsymbol{k})$ is the spatial power spectrum. To understand this equation we note that the spectrum is highly ordered in spatiotemporal frequency space (Watson and Ahumada, 1983a), with power lying on the plane $f - \boldsymbol{v}(\boldsymbol{u}_0, t_0) \cdot \boldsymbol{k} = 0$ in the region of spatial point $\boldsymbol{u}_0$ and time t_0. The spectrum described by equation 8.2 is a local spatiotemporal spectrum, since it can vary as a function of space and time because of changes in the velocity field.

Eye movements can be modeled as a linear, time-variant filter introduced between the image scene $I(\boldsymbol{u}, t)$ and the retina (figure 8.1). Inclusion of eye movements introduces a single, time-varying velocity vector to the image velocity field. The image that reaches the retina, ($I_r(\boldsymbol{u}, t)$ in figure 8.1), possesses a spatiotemporal spectrum of the form

$$S_r(\boldsymbol{u}, t, \boldsymbol{k}, f) = S(\boldsymbol{k})\delta(f - [\boldsymbol{v}(\boldsymbol{u}, t) - \boldsymbol{v}_e(t)] \cdot \boldsymbol{k}), \quad (8.3)$$

where $S_r(\boldsymbol{u}, t, \boldsymbol{k}, f)$ is the retinal spatiotemporal image spec-

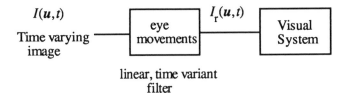

Figure 8.1
The image, $I(u, t)$, is filtered by eye movements before reaching the retina.

trum, and $v_e(t)$ is the velocity of eye movements. Eye movements shift all velocities in the image by the eye velocity. The difference between the image velocity field and eye velocity is the retinal velocity field and constitutes the velocity of the image on the retina:

$$v_r(u, t) = v(u, t) - v_e(t), \tag{8.4}$$

where $v(u, t)$ is the image velocity field, and $v_e(t)$ is eye velocity.

Spatial Acuity is a Function of Retinal Velocity

The decrease in spatial acuity (spatial frequency limit) due to motion is a result of the limited temporal frequency bandwidth of a channel or system. For the visual system, spatial acuity is a function of retinal velocity: A large translational velocity of the image across the retina decreases spatial acuity. This effect is illustrated in figure 8.2 using a rectangular "window of visibility" in spatiotemporal frequency space (Watson and Ahumada, 1983b). For velocities below the corner velocity v_c spatial resolution is limited by intrinsic spatial limitations. Above the corner velocity the temporal frequency limit causes the spatial resolution to drop off with the inverse of image velocity ($1/v$). A closer approximation for the relationship between spatial acuity and retinal velocity is found with the formula

$$k_0(|v_r(u, t)|) = k_{max} \frac{v_c}{|v_r(u, t)| + v_c}, \tag{8.5}$$

where k_0 is the reduced spatial acuity (spatial frequency limit) of the observer, $|v_r(u, t)|$ is the magnitude of the retinal velocity (from equation 8.4), v_c is the corner velocity, and k_{max} is the maximum spatial frequency limit of the system as determined by the contrast sensitivity function of the visual system (Kelly, 1979). If k_{max} is selected to be the maximum spatial frequency resolved by the visual system for a fixed low contrast level, then equation 8.5 fits Kelly's data for $v_c = 2$ deg/sec.

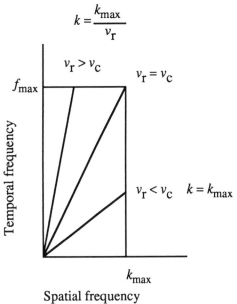

Figure 8.2
The reduction of spatial acuity because of motion is illustrated with a rectangular "window of visibility" (Watson, 1983b). The spatiotemporal spectrum of an image translating at velocity v has energy located on a line with slope v in two-dimensional spatiotemporal frequency space. For velocities less than the corner velocity v_c high spatial acuity is maintained. For velocities greater than v_c, spatial acuity drops off with the inverse of velocity ($1/v$). The corner velocity determined by human contrast sensitivity experiments (Kelly, 1979) is $v_c = 2$ deg/sec.

The reduction of observer spatial acuity (equation 8.5) from motion actually depends on the direction of the retinal velocity rather than simply the magnitude. Equation 8.5 can be accommodated to give the directionally specific spatial acuity. The spatial acuity of the observer is

$$k_0(\theta, v_r(u, t)) = k_{max} \frac{v_c}{|\cos \theta||v_r(u, t)| + v_c}, \tag{8.6}$$

where $0 \leq \theta \leq 180°$ is the angle from the direction of the retinal velocity. The image is maximally blurred in the direction of the retinal velocity ($\theta = 0°$ or $180°$) and unblurred in the direction orthogonal to the retinal velocity ($\theta = \pm 90°$). Figure 8.3 illustrates the relationship between the spatial acuity of the observer k_0, the angle from the retinal velocity θ, and the magnitude of the retinal velocity $|v_r(u, t)|$. The spatial acuity of the human visual system in directions other than that of the retinal velocity has not been extensively investigated, but psychophysical evidence indicates that the visual system exper-

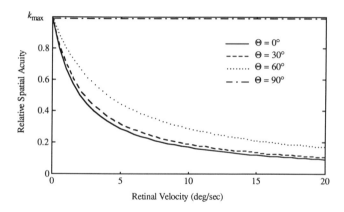

Figure 8.3
The relationship between spatial acuity of the observer and retinal velocity for different values of θ, the angle from the direction of motion (equation 8.6). The greatest loss of spatial acuity occurs in the direction of motion ($\theta = 0$). There is no loss of acuity in the direction orthogonal to motion ($\theta = 90$). For this graph, $v_c = 2$ deg/sec.

iences little or no loss of spatial acuity in the direction orthogonal to motion (Westheimer and McKee, 1975; Fahle and Poggio, 1981; Morgan and Benton, 1989; Prather and Ramachandran, 1991). Thus psychophysical evidence supports the directionally specific reduction of spatial acuity described by equation 8.6.

The visual system has maximum spatial acuity when there is little or no retinal velocity. It is not surprising, therefore, that smooth-pursuit eye movements attempt to set eye velocity equal to image velocity at the fovea (area of the retina with highest cone sampling density and thus highest spatial acuity). In other words, smooth-pursuit eye movements maximize spatial acuity at the fovea by minimizing foveal retinal velocity. Realistically, however, it is not possible to set eye velocity exactly equal to image velocity, so there is usually an error associated with smooth-pursuit eye movements, resulting in image movement across the fovea.

Since the spatial acuity of the visual system depends on retinal velocity rather than image velocity, the spatial resolution required for a coding system will depend on the effectiveness of smooth pursuit rather than directly on screen image velocity. Thus, any coding system that attempts to take advantage of the decrease in visual spatial acuity due to motion blur must rely on a priori knowledge about the ability of the smooth-pursuit system to track effectively.

Retinal Velocity Depends on Image Acceleration

We now consider the image motion characteristics that determine the accuracy of smooth pursuit and thus the retinal velocity. The performance of the smooth-pursuit system has received considerable attention (Westheimer, 1954; Stark et al., 1962; Hallett, 1986; Lisberger et al., 1987; Steinman et al., 1990). Smooth-pursuit eye movements depend on predictability of object motion, object size, background illuminance, prior expectations of motion, image velocity, and image acceleration (Lisberger et al., 1987; Gresty and Leech, 1977; Pola and Wyatt, 1980; Lisberger et al., 1981; Wyatt and Pola, 1983; Kowler et al., 1984; van den Berg and Collewijn, 1986; Barnes and Lawson, 1989). However, the most important and consistent factors determining the accuracy of smooth pursuit are image velocity, image acceleration, and predictability of image motion (Stark et al., 1962; Lisberger et al., 1981; Barnes and Lawson, 1989, see also Regan et al., 1986; Lisberger et al., 1987; Krauzlis et al. 1991). In particular, large accelerations and unpredictable image motion decrease the ability to pursue effectively, thereby increasing the retinal velocity.

Tracking occurs at the center of gaze, which is also the area of highest spatial acuity for human observers. Thus we consider only the center of gaze and assume that image velocity is constant within this region. This means that image velocity and acceleration are considered to be a single, time-varying vector. Furthermore, the experiments relating retinal velocity to image acceleration (Lisberger et al., 1981) were performed for one-dimensional motion. Because no data are available for motion in two dimensions, we consider only the magnitude of acceleration and velocity.

The relationship between retinal velocity and object acceleration for predictable motion is (Lisberger et al., 1981)

$$v_r(a) = \frac{a}{18},\tag{8.7}$$

where a is image acceleration in units of deg/s². For unpredictable motion, the relationship is

$$v_r(a) = \begin{cases} \dfrac{a}{8} & \text{for } a < 80 \\[2ex] \dfrac{a-80}{2.5} + 10 & \text{for } a > 80 \end{cases}\tag{8.8}$$

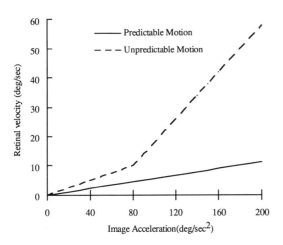

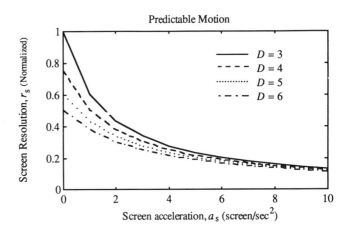

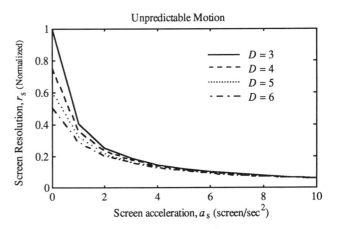

Figure 8.4
The relationship between image acceleration and retinal velocity for predictable and unpredictable motion (Lisberger et al., 1981).

The relationships described in equations 8.7 and 8.8 are depicted in figure 8.4.

Required Screen Resolution for Moving Images

The minimum screen spatial resolution (equivalent to spatial frequency bandwidth) required to display images in a perceptually lossless manner depends on both viewing distance and image acceleration. Spatial and temporal units for the observer are given in degrees of visual angle and seconds. Image (screen) units are given in screen heights and seconds. Thus retinal velocity has units of deg/sec, whereas screen velocity has units of (screen heights)/sec.

The screen spatial resolution (spatial frequency limit) required for perceptually lossless viewing depends on the spatial acuity of the viewer k_0 and the viewing distance. The relationship, from simple trigonometry, is

$$r_s(D) = k_0 \tan^{-1}\left(\frac{1}{D}\right), \tag{8.9}$$

where r_s is the minimum screen spatial resolution allowed for perceptually lossless viewing in units of cycles/screen, k_0 is the spatial acuity of the observer in units of cycles/deg, D is viewing distance in units of screen heights, and the term $\tan^{-1}(1/D)$ represents the relationship between distance and the angle of view that the screen subtends in units of deg/screen.

Therefore, the minimal allowable screen resolution as a function of image acceleration and viewing distance is

Figure 8.5
The relationship between screen spatial resolution r_s, screen image acceleration a_s, and observer viewing distance D. The curves are normalized to the screen resolution required for a static image at the closest viewing distance ($D_{\min} = 3$ screen heights).

found by combining equations 8.5, 8.7 or 8.8, and 8.9 to get

$$r_s(a_s, D) = \frac{k_{\max}}{v_r(a_s)/v_c + 1/\tan^{-1}(1/D)}, \tag{8.10}$$

where D is viewing distance measured in screen heights, a_s is image (screen) acceleration in units of (screen heights)/s², and v_c is the corner velocity ($v_c = 2$ deg/s). At a set viewing distance (D fixed) the required resolution drops off hyperbolically with image acceleration.

Figure 8.5 illustrates the relationship between the minimal allowable screen spatial resolution r_s, image acceleration a_s in screens/sec² and viewing distance D in screen

Table 8.1
Description of Television Sequences Analyzed for their Motion Content

Sequence Number	Sequence Description
IJ10833	Jungle scene with some 3-D object motion and a small amount of camera motion
IJ12426	Man walking. Some camera motion to keep man centered in visual field. The result is much background motion.
IJ01300	Man talking while moving head occasionally. No camera motion. Some slight motion in the background
IJ04454	Storm scene. No camera motion, but large amounts of nonrigid 3-D motion from waves. Intensity changes from lightning.

heights, for both predictable and unpredictable motion. In the figure the screen spatial resolution r_s is normalized to the maximum resolution required for a static image at the closest viewing distance D_{min} of 3 screen heights. The required screen spatial resolution decreases with both observer viewing distance and screen acceleration. The curves in figure 8.5 shift downward and flatten with increased viewing distance. The reason for this is that observer resolution scales differently for viewing distance than for the effect of screen acceleration. At large screen accelerations the required screen resolution is independent of viewing distance. However, r_s is always maximum at the nearest viewing distance for all accelerations, so this curve gives the minimum allowable screen spatial resolution for perceptually lossless coding.

Motion in Television Images

We calculated the acceleration of objects in four real-world image sequences. The sequences (256×256 pixels $\times$ 64 frames at 8 bits/pixel, 30 frames/s with no scene cuts) were taken from a video disk that contained scenes from movies (table 8.1). For each sequence, two objects (or areas in the scene) were selected and tracked through all 64 frames of the sequence. One of the selected areas was always a salient feature in the image, seemed to be the focus of action in the scene, and usually possessed the largest image velocity in the scene. The other tracked region was selected from the background and often had low screen velocities. Tracking of the objects was performed by minimizing the squared difference between 24×24 pixel blocks in each pair of sequential frames in

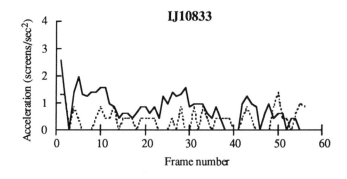

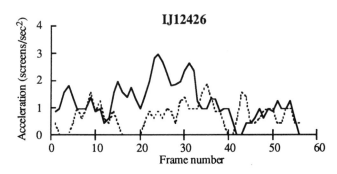

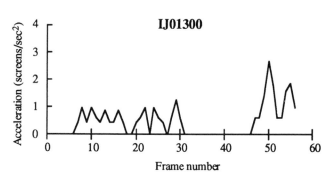

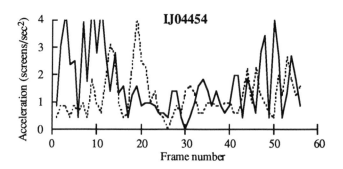

Figure 8.6
The acceleration of two selected tracked objects (indicated by solid and dashed lines) for the four sequences examined. The solid line represents the acceleration of the most salient feature in the image, the dashed line represents an arbitrary object in the background. There is only one line in sequence IJ01300 because one of the tracked objects did not move.

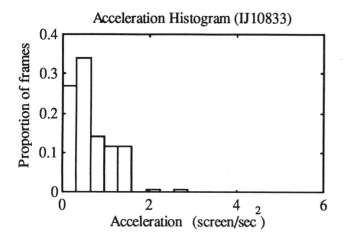

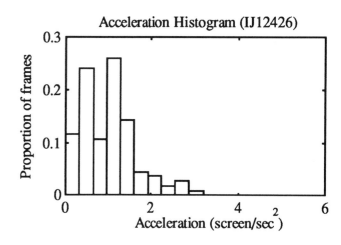

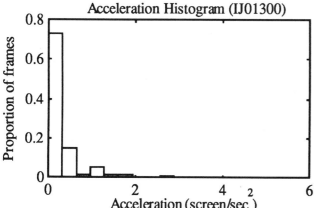

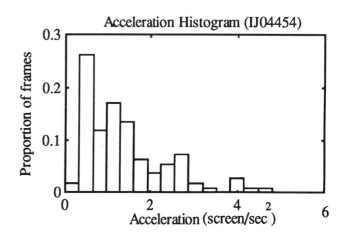

Figure 8.7
Acceleration histogram of the two spatial areas in the sequences. Most of the time, the screen acceleration is less than 2 screen/sec² for all the sequences.

the sequence (Jain and Jain, 1981). This algorithm accurately tracked image features, as long as the object did not become occluded. For three of the four sequences (IJ10833, IJ12426, and IJ01300) this algorithm worked well, because the scenes generally consisted of rigid, moving objects. It was difficult to judge the tracking effectiveness on the fourth scene, IJ04454, because the scene consisted mostly of ocean waves during a thunderstorm. Because none of the waves lasted for more than a few frames, there was nothing to consistently track in the sequence. The tracking algorithm gave a set of displacement vectors that were then smoothed with a linear filter of [0.25 0.5 0.25]. The

acceleration was computed using a second-order finite difference. This calculation gave the screen acceleration in pixels/frame², which was then translated into units of (screen heights)/sec².

The screen acceleration of the two 24×24 pixel areas in the sequences is presented in figures 8.6 and 8.7. The acceleration of three of the four sequences was almost always under 2 screen heights/s². The storm sequence had image accelerations that often exceeded this level, but this was probably due to spurious results of the algorithm, which did not work well with this sequence. The image acceleration found in the television sequences (figures 8.6 and 8.7) can be compared with the screen spatial resolution required for lossless viewing (figure 8.5). At the nearest viewing distance an acceleration of 2 screen heights/s² will allow only a 60 percent decrease in screen spatial resolution, assuming predictable motion. If the motion is considered to be unpredictable, then a 70 percent decrease in resolution is possible. Although a 60 percent to 70 percent reduction in spatial resolution is large, this level of image acceleration occurred only rarely in the sequences (figure 8.7). Most of the time, screen acceleration was low, so few coding gains could be obtained by taking advantage of the decrease of observer acuity with image motion.

Conclusion

The spatial acuity of the visual system depends on the velocity of the image across the retina. Essentially, spatial acuity is reduced for large retinal velocities. However, retinal image velocity is not equivalent to the screen image velocity, because eye movements filter the image before it reaches the retina. As a result, spatial acuity is a function of the ability of the visual system to track objects with smooth-pursuit eye movements and does not depend directly on the image velocity. The accuracy of smooth-pursuit eye movements depends on a variety of factors, many difficult to quantify. But the most consistent relationship between retinal velocity and image motion is through image acceleration and the degree of motion predictability (Lisberger et al., 1981; Barnes and Lawson, 1989). The dependence of spatial acuity on image acceleration rather than on image velocity explains the high spatial acuity of observers found by Girod (1988) and Westerink and Teunissen (1990) for large image velocities. In these experiments image acceleration was low, and the image motion was highly predictable. Smooth-pursuit tracking is accurate for these cases, so the motion of the image across the retina is small, and the visual system experiences little or no reduction of spatial acuity. These experiments also used scenes that consisted of a single translational velocity. The velocity field of most image scenes changes with space and time, which may reduce the ability of humans to pursue effectively.

One of the goals of television engineering technology is to display images in a perceptually lossless manner with a minimum screen spatial resolution (Watson, 1990). Since a decrease in screen spatial resolution is allowed for areas with large acceleration (figure 8.5), we computed the acceleration of areas in four television motion sequences

to determine whether image acceleration could provide any significant coding gains. For the sequences we considered, image acceleration only rarely exceeded the level that would allow significant decreases in screen spatial resolution.

The decrease of screen spatial resolution allowed because of motion is directionally specific, and no reduction in spatial resolution is allowed for the direction orthogonal to motion (figure 8.3). Directionally specific acuity has been confirmed by psychophysical experiments, which indicates that the visual system experiences no loss of spatial acuity in the direction orthogonal to motion (Westheimer and McKee, 1975; Fahle and Poggio, 1981; Morgan and Benton, 1989; Prather and Ramachandran, 1991). For example, spatial hyperacuity tasks remain possible for retinal velocities up to 6 deg/s, as long as the task requires spatial analysis along the direction unblurred by motion (Morgan and Benton, 1989). This last observation increases the complexity of a coder that attempts to take advantage of visual system motion blur. Not only must the image be segmented based on areas with large image acceleration, but a reduction in screen resolution due to image motion can be obtained only in the direction of motion. This type of coding can be accomplished using the motion-oriented tuned basis functions proposed by Watson (1990, 1992).

There are, of course, limitations to the analysis presented in this chapter. We used results of experiments that quantify smooth pursuit with relatively simple signals and velocity structures: moving spots, moving gratings, moving bars, full-field translation of images at constant velocity, and the like. We applied these results to complex stimuli such as television sequences by assuming that eye movements are matched to image velocity in a single, small spatial region of the image. However, eye movements in response to complex image motion may not be simple to quantify. They can be investigated in a straightforward manner with eye-tracking experiments using television sequences by correlating retinal velocity with image velocity and image acceleration at the point of gaze. These types of experiments are being done by Hearty (see chapter 12) and Stelmach et al. (1992).

Our observations suggest that care must be taken if coding gains are to be obtained by taking advantage of motion blur in the visual system. Tracking with smooth-pursuit eye movements minimizes the loss of visual system spatial resolution during image motion. Even when eye movements are not able to compensate for image motion effectively (large image acceleration), the visual system retains high spatial acuity in the direction orthogonal to motion, increasing the complexity of the coding system.

Acknowledgments

The research reported in this chapter was supported by AFOSR Grant #91-0082 and by NASA RTOP 506-71-51.

References

Adelson, E. J. & Bergen, J. R. (1985) Spatiotemporal energy models for the perception of motion. *Journal of the Optical Society of America A* 2(2): 284–299.

Barnes, G. B. & Lawson, J. F. (1989) Head-free pursuit in the human of a visual target moving in a pseudo-random manner. *Journal of Physiology* 410: 137–155.

van den Berg, A. V. & Collewijn, H. (1986) Human smooth pursuit: Effects of stimulus extent and of spatial and temporal constraints of the pursuit trajectory. *Vision Research* 26(8): 1209–1222.

Cohen, L. (1989) Time-Frequency Distributions: A Review. *Proceedings of the IEEE* 77(7): 941–981.

Fahle, M. & Poggio, T. (1981) Visual hyperacuity: Spatiotemporal interpolation in human vision. *Proceedings of the Royal Society of London B* 213: 451–477.

Flipse, J. P., Wildt, G. J., Rodenburg, M. & Knol, P. G. M. (1988) Contrast sensitivity for oscillating sine wave gratings during ocular fixation and pursuit. *Vision Research* 28: 819–826.

Girod, B. (1988) Eye movements and coding of video sequences. In *Visual Communications and Image Processing*. ed. T. R. Hsing. SPIE 398–405.

Gresty, A. & Leech, J. (1977) Coordination of the head and eyes in pursuit of predictable and random target motion. *Aviation, Space and Environmental Medicine* 48: 741–744.

Hallett, P. E. (1986) "Eye Movements." Chap. 10 *in Handbook of Perception and Human Performance*. New York: John Wiley and Sons.

Heeger, D. J. (1987) Model for the extraction of image flow. *Journal of the Optical Society of America A* 4(8): 1455–1471.

Jain, J. R. & Jain, A. K. (1981) Displacement measurement and its application in interframe image coding. *IEEE Transactions on Communications COM-29* 12: 1799–1808.

Kelly, D. H. (1979) Motion and vision II: Stabilized spatiotemporal threshold surface. *Journal of the Optical Society of America A* 69(10): 1340–1349.

Kowler, E., Martins, A. J. & Pavel, M. (1984) The effect of expectations on slow oculomotor control. IV, Anticipatory eye movements depend on prior target motions. *Vision Research* 24: 197–210.

Krauzlis, R. J. & Lisberger, S. G. (1991) Visual motion commands for pursuit eye movements in the cerebellum. Science 253: 568–571.

Lisberger, S. E., Evinger, C. & Johnson, G. W. (1981) Relationship between eye acceleration and retinal image velocity during foveal pursuit in man and monkey. *Journal of Neurophysiology* 46: 229–249.

Lisberger, S. G., Morris, E. J. & Tychsen, L. (1987) Visual motion processing and sensory-motor integration for smooth pursuit eye movements. *Annual Review of Neuroscience* 10: 97–129.

Morgan, M. J. & Benton, S. (1989) Motion-deblurring in human vision. *Letters to Nature* 340: 385–386.

Murphy, B. J. (1978) Pattern thresholds for moving and stationary gratings during smooth eye movement. *Vision Research* 18: 521–530.

Pola, J. & Wyatt, H. J. (1980) Target position and velocity: The stimuli for smooth pursuit eye movements. *Vision Research* 20: 523–534.

Prather, L. & Ramachandran, V. S. (1991) Direction specific deblurring of moving images. *Investigative Opthalmology and Visual Science Supplement*, 825.

Regan, D. M., Kaufman, L. & Lincoln, J. (1986) "Motion in Depth and Visual Acceleration." chap. 19 in *Handbook of Perception and Human Performance: Sensory Processes and Perception*. New York: John Wiley and Sons.

van Santen, J. P. H. & Sperling, G. (1985) Elaborated Reichardt detectors. *Journal of the Optical Society of America A* 2(2): 300–321.

Stark, L., Vossius, G. & Young, L. R. (1962) Predictive control of eye tracking movements. *IRE Transactions on Human Factors and Electronics*, 52–57.

Steinman, R. M., Kowler, E. & Collewijn, H. (1990) New directions for oculomotor research. *Vision Research* 30(11): 1845–1864.

Watson, A. B. & Ahumada, A. J., Jr. (1983a) A look at motion in the frequency domain. NASA Tech. Memo. 84352.

Watson, A. B. & Ahumada, A. J., Jr. (1983b) The window of visibility: A psychophysical theory of fidelity in time-sampled visual motion displays. NASA Tech. Paper 2211.

Watson, A. B. & Ahumada, A. J., Jr. (1985) Model of human visual motion sensing. *Journal of the Optical Society of America A* 2(2): 322–341.

Watson, A. B. (1990) Perceptual-components architecture for digital video. *Journal of the Optical Society of America A* 7(10): 1943–1954.

Watson, A. B. & Tiana, C. L. M. (1992) Color motion video coded by perceptual components. *Society for Information Display Digest of Technical Papers*, 23: 314–317.

Westheimer, G. & McKee, S. P. (1975) Visual acuity in the presence of retinal image motion. *Journal of the Optical Society of America A* 65: 847–850.

Westerink, J. H. D. M. & Teunissen, C. (1990) Perceived sharpness in moving images. In *Human Vision and Electronic Imaging: Models, Methods, and Applications,* ed. B. E. Rogowitz & J. P. Allebach. SPIE 78–87.

Westheimer, G. (1954) Eye movement responses to a horizontally moving visual stimulus. *A.M.A. Archives of Opthalmology* 52:932–941.

Wyatt, H. J. & Pola, J. (1983) Smooth pursuit eye movements under open-loop and closed-loop conditions. *Vision Research* 23(10):921–1206.

9

Visual System Considerations in the Coding of Natural Color Images

Gershon Buchsbaum

Historically all image media were first developed in black and white; only later, with advancements in technology, was color added. This was true of printing, photography, and electronic media such as television and image processors. A historical exception is artists who incorporated color in their art and within their artistic talent exploited the rules of color addition and mixture and spatial interactions of color. In contrast to technology, art experimented with color from the outset. Art thereby, immediately used the most general spectral composition relevant to the visual system, making black-and-white images only a special case.

The evolution of electronic media was quite different. Advances in technology enabled introduction of color into existing black-and-white monochrome media. Societal and economic constraints then limited the extent to which the switch from monochrome to color was possible. The most notable example is color television. This ubiquitous electronic color medium had an interesting evolution. Color television technology was faced with a difficult challenge at the time of its introduction into the consumer electronics market. Although technology was sufficiently developed, it was required (by the Federal Communications Commission) that the new color broadcasting system be compatible with the old black-and-white system. That meant that the two additional color channels had to be efficiently compressed into the electromagnetic spectrum allocated for television after the monochrome system (not anticipating color) had liberally consumed it. The additional chromatic information had to be "tacked on" to the black-white signal in a way that would not interfere with reception on a monochrome television receiver.

This addition of color signals to the existing spectrum was possible only by taking advantage of some properties of the visual system. For example, the visual system has lower spatial resolution in the color channels than in the luminance channel (Van der Horst et al., 1967; Van der Horst and Bouman, 1969; Granger and Heurtley, 1973; Mullen, 1985). This allows color television technology to allocate small fractions of the broadcast signal energy to the chrominance channels. The similarity of National Television Standards Commission (NTSC) color coding and opponent processing in the visual system is another example (Buchsbaum, 1987). However, because of the constraints imposed by the NTSC requirement for monochrome compatibility, the design was less than optimal.

Similar developments were made in image processing. With the availability of faster processors, diminishing price of memory, and advancements in color CRT monitors, color was introduced. Color was added in most cases by expanding the one-plane monochrome image into a three-plane color image. For all practical purposes this meant having three parallel image processors whose outputs were then combined on a color monitor. Color was added as an extension or a generalization of the already available technology for black-and-white images. For example, color specifications for image processors are often given in bits per color plane, and 2^{24} (8 bits per color plane), or 16 million colors is touted as solving the color presentation problem. This was an extension of the standard 8-bit monochrome plane. However, the complexities of perceptual color space and its information measures do not linearly translate to the number of bits allocated for color planes (Bedrosian and Xie, 1982; Xie and Bedrosian, 1984; Buchsbaum and Bedrosian 1984; Orchard and Bouman, 1991). A long list of phenomena such as simultaneous and successive color contrast and various effects of luminance affect color perception. Thus, even if colorimetric color coordinates are precisely coded by providing ample bits per plane, color appearance may differ from the original because factors other than color coordinates are not accurately duplicated. Walraven (1985) reviews these phenomena, where perception of color may differ on color displays from the intended and designed color specification.

The success of art, however, lies in its reliance on properties of the visual system and on properties of natural images as they pertain to perception. The design of high-definition television (HDTV) advanced imaging systems provides an opportunity to let "life imitate art." Following the example of the artists, we should take color imagery as the starting point. If the standards of HDTV and other future imaging systems can be reasonably divorced from constraints imposed on earlier designs, properties of the visual system and the inherent nature of real-world color images can be exploited. Identifying the image attributes that are significant for the visual system can serve as the basis for an efficient perceptually based coding system (Watson, 1990). Color cannot be taken as just a frill added to the spatial image—a luxury that is added when enough bits are available and when spatial and other design constraints limit the resources available to color. Rather, as in art, a holistic approach to the image should be taken—an approach that will not a priori separate color attributes from spatial features. Thus, color will be a natural part of the image incorporated into other features as they naturally occur and not just added on later. The biological visual system applies a holistic strategy for color that incorporates spatial and color coding, and we use it as an example here.

In this chapter we briefly highlight some points in the color coding strategy of the visual system. The underlying hypothesis is that the early visual system is an efficient coder that minimizes signal redundancy so that transmission resources are preserved but little information is lost (Barlow, 1961, 1981). We conclude with some observations about visual system color coding strategy and hope these can serve in concepts for better manufactured color systems.

Color Coding in the Visual System

Basic Color Strategy

Interestingly enough, as with the development of manufactured imaging systems, visual science was also late in combining spatial and color vision research. Such progenitors of modern color vision and color science as Newton, Young, Palmer, Helmholtz, and Schrödinger devised color spaces and relationships that essentially were mappings of three-dimensional color space into a three-dimensional geometric space and its corresponding line elements (see MacAdam, 1970). The theories were largely based on the observation that a three-dimensional geometric space is needed to account for the trichromatic nature of color vision. Constraints derived primarily from wavelength discrimination experiments determined metrics in a visual color space whose axes were defined by the cone action spectra combined with various psychophysical considerations (Vos and Walraven 1972a,b). These metrics could also be related to communication theory considerations (Buchsbaum and Goldstein, 1979; Buchsbaum, 1981). One of the most desirable properties of the geometric theories is that they can easily be related to colorimetry via the relation of the cone system response functions to Commission Internationale de L'eclairage (CIE) standards (Vos and Walraven, 1971; Walraven, 1974; Smith and Pokorny, 1975; Vos, 1978; Vos et al., 1990; Walraven and Werner, 1991).

However, the failure of the simple geometric theories to account for color sensation phenomena beyond those explained by simple color mixing led to the development of the concept of opponent processing. The basic premise of the opponent theory, in its various forms, is that additive and subtractive combinations of the initial three cone types are taken, respectively, to constitute a luminance and two chromatic channels in the visual system (Lennie and D'Zmura, 1988). The need of the visual system to apply this coding transformation is not immediately obvi-

ous. As in some image processors, the initial three color outputs could be transmitted throughout the system, from retina to cortex. But this transmission is known to be inefficient (Pratt, 1978). Efficient information transmission can be defined mathematically in terms of minimizing the channel capacity required to transmit the information at a given level of reliability. Pursuing the analogy of the visual system, we may consider the stages beyond the cone photoreceptors as an information channel comprising many nerve fibers that themselves are information channels. The optic nerve has a finite number of fibers, each with a finite dynamic range and thus limited information channel capacity; good design must optimize the use of this limited resource.

Figure 9.1 which models the first stage of color processing in the visual system (from Buchsbaum and Gott-

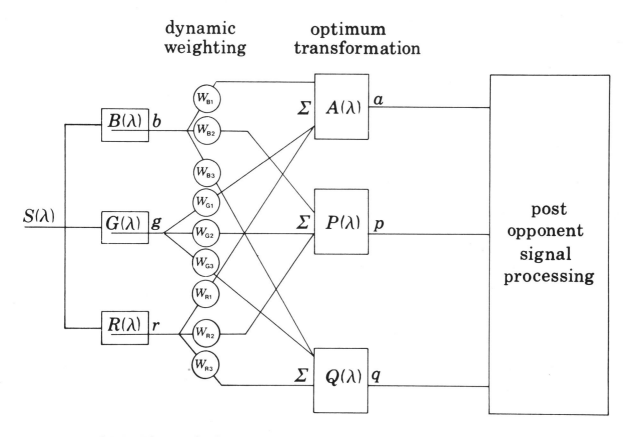

MODEL FOR FIRST STAGE OF COLOR PROCESSING IN THE VISUAL SYSTEM

Figure 9.1
Schematic diagram of color processing in the visual system. The three initial color mechanisms $B(\lambda)$, $G(\lambda)$, and $R(\lambda)$ are converted via opponent-type processing into the three channels $A(\lambda)$, $P(\lambda)$, and $Q(\lambda)$.

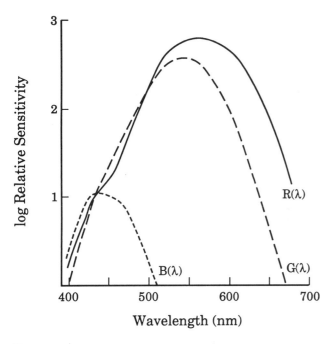

Figure 9.2
Cone system response functions (after Vos and Walraven, *Vision Res.*, 1971, 1974, 1978). These functions were used for computations of the eigenvector transformation. The relative heights of the Vos-Walraven response functions are adjusted so that their sum equals the luminous efficiency curve (figure 9.3).

the "red" and "green" mechanisms will have outputs that are correlated. Another source of correlation in the outputs of the cone systems is the statistics of wavelength distributions in the world. Many colors are slowly varying distributions of wavelength, so that, for instance, the distribution in one part of the spectrum is correlated with that in other parts of the spectrum and causes correlation in the output of the cones (Buchsbaum and Gottschalk, 1983). The transmission of the outputs of $R(\lambda)$, $G(\lambda)$, and $B(\lambda)$ to higher stages of perception without first transforming them would result in inefficient use of available channel capacity in the visual system.

Using the principal components, we can find a transformation that decorrelates the outputs of $R(\lambda)$, $G(\lambda)$, and $B(\lambda)$. The basic advantages of using principal components can be briefly summarized as follows: (1) The basis functions or vectors of the representation are orthogonal and have uncorrelated coefficients. (2) The expected square coefficients (eigenvalues) are minimum compared with other generalized Fourier representations. These properties make principal components attractive for efficient signal coding and representation, because decorrelation eliminates redundancy, and smaller coefficients require smaller dynamic ranges and hence fewer transmission resources. The principal-components transformation, which is also referred to as the Karhunen-Loève (or Hotelling or eigenvector) transformation, can also serve as a yardstick to evaluate other transformations (Jayant and Noll, 1984; Pratt, 1978).

For the purpose of decorrelating r, g, b and finding the optimum transformation, we form their covariance matrix as follows:

$$C = \begin{bmatrix} C_{rr} & C_{rg} & C_{rb} \\ C_{rg} & C_{gg} & C_{gb} \\ C_{rb} & C_{gb} & C_{bb} \end{bmatrix}, \tag{9.1}$$

where the diagonal terms are the variances of r, g, b, and the off-diagonal terms are the respective covariances. Because $B(\lambda)$, $G(\lambda)$, and $R(\lambda)$ are linearly independent, the covariance matrix C is nonsingular. It has three real eigenvalues, say, Γ_1, Γ_2, Γ_3, that are positive and three corresponding eigenvectors v_1, v_2, v_3. In the case of real symmetric matrices with distinct eigenvalues, the eigenvectors constitute an orthogonal set. The 3×3 matrix W, whose columns are the three normalized eigenvectors (W is an orthogonal matrix) fulfills

schalk, 1983), summarizes this issue. $B(\lambda)$, $G(\lambda)$, $R(\lambda)$ and r, g, b represent the spectral sensitivities of the initial retinal color mechanisms, and their outputs, respectively. We refer to the color mechanisms "red", "green", and "blue" for convenience. These are transformed into three channels $A(\lambda)$, $P(\lambda)$ and $Q(\lambda)$, with respective outputs a, p, q. The question is, What is the optimal transformation, given proper constraints, that the visual system should use? The transformation need not be a fixed one and can be dependent on adaptation conditions. The dynamic weighting (figure 9.1) indicates changes in the weights given to contributions from $B(\lambda)$, $G(\lambda)$, and $R(\lambda)$ under changing adaptation (Buchsbaum and Gottschalk, 1983). The optimum transformation is chosen to decorrelate r, g, b as delineated next.

To pursue this question we used the Vos-Walraven cone system response functions (figure 9.2). The need for a transformation is illustrated by the shape and position of the curves. The "red" and "green" action spectra overlap greatly, and spectrally broad-band color signals will excite both mechanisms. Largely because of this overlap

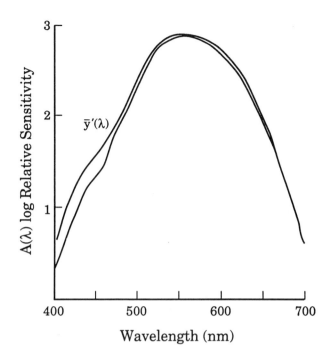

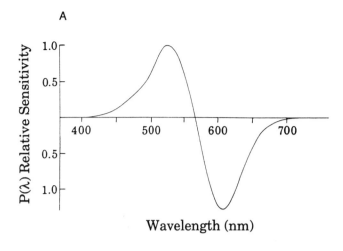

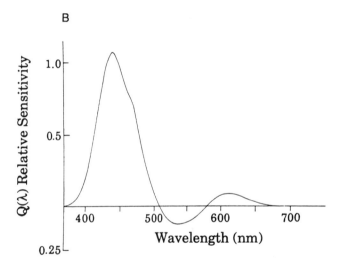

Figure 9.3
Achromatic channel derived by eigenvector transformation of the Vos-Walraven response functions. Also shown for comparison is the visual luminous efficiency curve, $\bar{y}'(\lambda)$. The curves are presented on an arbitrary scale for comparison.

$$W'CW = \begin{bmatrix} \Gamma_1 & 0 & 0 \\ 0 & \Gamma_2 & 0 \\ 0 & 0 & \Gamma_3 \end{bmatrix} \tag{9.2}$$

where W' is the transpose of W.

The eigenvector transformation of b, g, and r is

$$\begin{bmatrix} a \\ p \\ q \end{bmatrix} = W' \begin{bmatrix} r \\ g \\ b \end{bmatrix} \tag{9.3}$$

a, p, q, the response of the transformed channels $A(\lambda)$, $P(\lambda)$, and $Q(\lambda)$, are uncorrelated, and their covariance matrix is represented by equation 9.2. The eigenvector transformation can be parametrized in terms of λ when the expected response of the channels for monochromatic signals is considered.

$$\begin{bmatrix} A(\lambda) \\ P(\lambda) \\ Q(\lambda) \end{bmatrix} = W' \begin{bmatrix} R(\lambda) \\ G(\lambda) \\ B(\lambda) \end{bmatrix} \tag{9.4}$$

Using the Vos-Walraven cone system response functions in figure 9.2 as a numerical example, and computing

Figure 9.4(A,B)
Chromatic channels derived by eigenvector transformation of Vos-Walraven response functions (arbitrary linear scale).

the matrix C from the overlap of $R(\lambda)$, $G(\lambda)$ and $B(\lambda)$, we give the resulting transformed channels $A(\lambda)$, $P(\lambda)$, and $Q(\lambda)$ in figure 9.3 and 9.4. $A(\lambda)$, $P(\lambda)$, and $Q(\lambda)$ are orthogonal. The achromatic additive combination is similar to the visual luminous efficiency curve $\bar{y}'(\lambda)$, whereas the two chromatic subtractive combinations correspond to the color opponent channels in the visual system (Buchsbaum and Gottschalk, 1983). This suggests that a basic purpose of early vision is decorrelation of the color signal to reduce redundancy. This analysis predicts the need for the opponent transformation in vision and deduces it from basic signal coding principles.

To this point the principle underlying the opponent transformation in vision is similar both in concept and to some degree in detail to the NTSC color transformation (YIQ). A difference is in the adaptability of the visual transformation, as opposed to the fixed YIQ transformation. The eigenvector transformation of adapted cone system responses, simulated by changing the weights in figure 9.1, shows how $A(\lambda)$, $P(\lambda)$, $Q(\lambda)$ vary their wavelength responses (Buchsbaum and Gottschalk, 1983). The visual system adapts its color channels in response to changing stimulus conditions (e.g., Lennie and D'Zmura, 1988, provide a summary). The visual adaptation process itself is a multistage interactive complex process (see, e.g., the review by Walraven et al., 1990; Hayhoe and Wenderoth, 1991). Lee (1990) makes the point that opponent processing is also matched in an adaptive manner to daylight illumination. Such adaptability is not available in color television. Television color channels, for example, do not adjust their color coding, in terms of YIQ combinations, to compensate and match changes in the color-signal environment.

Spatiochromatic Coding: Strategy in the Visual System

A color-only based approach has the same limitation in the visual system as it has in image processing and television. Although the preceding analysis was successful in logically deriving the opponent transformation from the cone responses and efficiency consideration, it had several limitations.

1. Because no spatial constraints and only cone wavelength responses were considered in the visual problem definition, no spatial dependence could be found in the solution. As a result, the spatial characteristics of receptive field filters in the visual system and how they relate to the color responses were not considered. In other words, only the color combinations of the opponent transformation were revealed without their spatial realization. For example, in the retina color-opponent receptive fields comprise spatially weighted combinations of cone responses.

Unlike color television, the visual system must take combinations from different locations, since it does not have "red," " green," and "blue" pixel values at each spatial coordinate. The visual system has only one plane for sampling the image, and at each spatial coordinate there is only one type of photoreceptor. The spatial distribution

of the "red," "green," and "blue" photoreceptors, unlike that in color television cameras, is not identical .

2. Because only color stimuli were considered in earlier analyses, any signal distribution statistics could be considered only along the wavelength axis. Obviously, the statistics and autocorrelation of natural imagery must include the spatial dimension as well as the correlation between the color and spatial dimension. The cross correlation between color and space will constrain the combinations of color and spatial responses and how they emerge in the solution.

The need for a hybrid spatiochromatic coding method is illustrated in figure 9.5. Transform coding such as the principal-components transformation described earlier will reduce correlation and increase efficiency along the λ axis. Various spatial coding schemes could decrease correlation along the spatial dimension (Srinivasan, Laughlin, and Dubs, 1982). However, correlations between space and color along the curved axis are usually not considered. These correspond to the inherent nature of color images in the real world.

The representation in figure 9.5 takes us one step further in the direction of a holistic approach to the multispectral image. The image need not be separated by planes

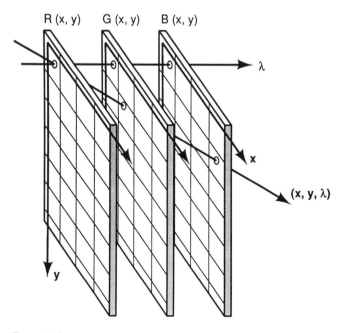

Figure 9.5
Illustration of a three-plane color image.

as has been done classically, but other partitions are possible (Buchsbaum 1987, 1991). For example, different processing can be applied to $B(\lambda)$ and to combinations of $R(\lambda)$ and $G(\lambda)$. Another obvious example is to consider processing by blocks of the color image. The visual system, for example, applies an array of receptive fields to cover the entire image. This enables the visual system to implement massive distributed parallel processing in retinal architecture. Block processing of images is not a new idea and has been tried before. Transform coding of a group of pixels has, of course, also been investigated, but only recently have attempts been made to take advantage of the multiplane structure of naturally occurring color images (Hunt and Kübler, 1984; Ohyama et al., 1988; Galatsanos et al., 1991a,b; Lee and Cok, 1991). These methods result in multiplane pixel operations, such as the cone combinations in the visual system.

To see how the principal-component transformation can be extended to multispectral structures in the context of visual color coding, we computed the principal components of a number of natural color images using small sections of the images (Hunt and Kübler, 1984, provide the theory for multiplane Karhunen-Loève transforms). We used small blocks of 4×4 pixels in each color plane. The reason for using small blocks was to be consistent with visual receptive-field arrays coding small segments of images. With 16 pixel values on each plane, the correlation matrix was 48×48 with 48 eigenvectors and corresponding eigenvalues. Projection and reconstruction using fewer than all 48 basis functions was performed. No further bit allocation or coding schemes were applied to the eigenvectors. The eigenvectors computed for the natural color images comprised basis functions with various spatial and color profiles. A rendition of the most significant eigenvectors is presented in figure 9.6. The results show that the most significant eigenvectors comprise achromatic basis functions with increasing frequency in the x- and y-directions and chromatic basis functions with low spatial frequency (Derrico and Buchsbaum, 1990; Buchsbaum and Derrico, 1992). Basis functions that have both a high spatial frequency and a chromatic response have very low eigenvalues. The achromatic eigenvectors are similar to those found for black-and-white images (Rosenfeld and Kak, 1982). We used four different color images, each having 1024 4×4 three-plane color blocks. The eigenvector configuration in figure 9.6 was common

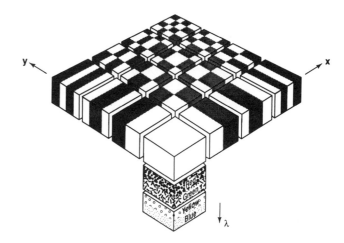

Figure 9.6
The eigenfunctions of color images. The x and y axes represent profiles with increasing spatial frequency. The λ axis shows color profiles. A color image can be recovered using these building blocks.

to all the images. Details and exact numerical values of the eigenfunctions differed, of course, depending on the image color and spatial content.

As in the visual system, the correlation between the responses of the "red," "green," and "blue" sensitivities originally making the three planes also affects the eigenvectors. Color plate 1 shows the projections of an image on the eigenfunctions. The projection in the center of color plate 1 shows the projection on the front corner eigenvector in figure 9.6, which includes mostly the average of the 4×4 blocks. The projections below the center are on the color eigenvectors. The projections around the center are on achromatic spatial eigenvectors of different spatial frequencies in the x- and y- directions. Color plate 2 shows an image reconstructed from the most significant eigenfunctions. The inset shows the number of eigenfunctions used. The absence of significant eigenvectors with both color response and spatial high frequency also suggests that color and space are nearly separable when small sections of natural images are considered. Another advantage of the small sections is their computational load. The computational load associated with an eigenvector transformation of whole images or large sections of images is immense (Hunt and Kübler, 1984).

Looking at the wealth of neurophysiological data in the early visual system one finds a correspondence between the eigenvectors of natural color images and certain visual system image operations in space and in color. In early cortical levels color-opponent units have mostly low spatial frequency response and high spatial frequency, and oriented units are mostly achromatic (Lennie and D'Zmura, 1988; T'so and Gilbert, 1988). High spatial frequency color-responsive ("doubly opponent") cells are rare, and there is debate about their existence. This correspondence suggests that the visual system has units that are tuned to the principal components of natural images. Psychophysically measured pathways also reveal a high spatial frequency achromatic and low spatial frequency color pathways (Van der Horst et al., 1967; Van der Horst and Bouman, 1969; Mullen, 1985). The response of these visual pathways adapts to changing signal conditions and can be modeled by relative changes in center and surround mechanisms such as those found in retinal receptive fields (Rohaly and Buchsbaum, 1988, 1989). The center-surround spatial architecture that underlies retinal receptive fields can be combined to form the achromatic and color systemic channels (Lennie and D'Zmura 1988, Derrico and Buchsbaum, 1991, Billock 1991). Oriented combinations can be made by adding retinal cells in the proper spatial configuration (Mullen and Kingdom, 1991). The center-surround retinal receptive field properties and how they combine to multiplex spatial and chromatic features have been investigated by Ingling and Martinez (1983, 1985) and Billock (1991). Retinal receptive fields serve as a basic multiplane architecture from which more complex spatiochromatic operations can be configured.

Conclusion

In the past I have made the statement that "...if there is anything good done in [color] coding, the visual system has already done it...." Naturally, I have drawn some challenges. Surely, my statement must have been be more than slightly influenced by my enthusiasm about the visual system. Notwithstanding, I do not apologize. In reviewing the strategy of color coding in the biological visual system the following points were made.

1. The visual system transforms the initial outputs of the color photoreceptor into a luminance and two color channels and decorrelates them. It does so in an adaptive manner. The ingenuity of NTSC engineering design in transforming RGB into Y (luminance) and I, Q (chrominance) channels with the constraints imposed at the time is well honored. But what's new?

2. The visual system allocates less spatial resolution to color channels. This allocation seems to be matched to images in the real world and their information content. This design has counterparts in image coding in manufactured systems. Many applications extract the spatial information from the luminance channel and then assign to color remaining low-acuity resources.

3. The visual system allocates resources in a differential manner among the different planes. For example, the sampling in the blue plane is markedly below the rate in other planes. This idea is also proposed in image processing. The visual system, though, does not always get the credit.

4. Small-block distributed parallel processing is implemented by receptive fields in the retina. Block processing is commonplace in image processing and coding. Does the visual system get any royalties?

5. The visual system applies multiplane operations in the sense that it combines cone responses from different spatial locations to create hybrid spatiochromatic filters. Such multispectral methods have only recently been explored as a more efficient alternative to single-plane operations.

Three additional points that are part of the visual system strategy are not fully exploited in manufactured vision systems.

6. The apparent tuning of some visual system units to certain spatiochromatic eigenfunctions of color images in the real world and the advantage it takes of the near-separability of color and space in small blocks needs to be explored. The choice of filter profile, and spatial block size and how it combines the different color planes is an open issue.

7. The visual system employs a planar sampling array with distribution of receptors of different types to sample the entire multiplanar structure of the multispectral signal. Within this structure, unlike in television cameras, the visual system does not allocate "red," "green," and "blue" receptors in each spatial coordinate (pixel location) and yet is able to extract both spatial and color detail from the image. Sampling properties of multiplane signals that correspond to natural images are not fully understood. The spatial similarity among the color planes enables special considerations in sampling that seem to exist in the visual system.

8. In all its operations the visual system adapts its color coding to changing stimulus conditions by varying gain,

spatial, and wavelength responses of its channels. Although certain adaptability, such as automatic gain control, is implemented in manufactured systems, there is no workable method for combined spatiochromatic adaptability.

All these points are a demonstration of the holistic approach used by the visual system. Manufactured systems and the mathematics underlying color processing usually begin by defining image planes as in figure 9.5. They carve the multidimensional structure by planes and separate, for coding purposes, color as an isolated attribute. The visual system carves the space in figure 9.5 into pieces that include all dimensions of the image. Color is not isolated from the structure, and the coding mechanisms multiplex all dimensions of the image.

Do my statements suggest that engineering solutions that differ from visual system implementation cannot be optimal, useful, or better than the visual system? Absolutely not. Engineering is the manipulation of solutions to a problem to meet constraints imposed by practicality, cost, and societal need. Although these may, of course, differ from biological constraints, one wonders about the similarity between some engineering solutions and the visual system. So, if natural images and their distribution are at issue and constitute the constraints for spatial and color coding, the visual system must have evolved to have some very useful solutions.

Acknowledgment

Writing of this chapter was supported by AFOSR Grant 91-0082. Processing of the color images was done by Joel Derrico.

References

Barlow, H. B. (1961). "Possible Principles Underlying the Transformation of Sensory Message." In *Sensory Communications*, 217–234. Cambridge, Mass. MIT Press.

Barlow H. B. (1981). The Ferrier Lecture, 1980: Critical Limiting Factors in the Design of the Eye and Visual Cortex, *Proceedings of the Royal Society of London B* 212:1–34.

Bedrosian, S. D. & Xie, W. (1982). Fuzzy measure justification of some grey tone experimental data. *Electronics Letters* 18:615–617.

Billock, V. A. (1991). The relationship between simple and double opponent cells. *Vision Res.* 31:33–42.

Buchsbaum, G. & Goldstein, J. L. (1979). Optimum probabilistic processing in colour perception. 1, Colour discrimination. *Proceedings of the Royal Society of London B* 205:227–248.

Buchsbaum, G. (1981). The retina as a two-dimensional photodector array in the context of color vision theories and signal detection theory. *Proceedings of the IEEE* 69:772–786.

Buchsbaum, G. & Gottschalk, A. (1983). Trichromacy, opponent colours coding and optimum colour information transmission in the retina. *Proceedings of the Royal Society of London B* 220:89–113.

Buchsbaum, G. & Bedrosian, S. D. (1984). Number of simultaneous colors versus grey levels. *Proceedings of the IEEE* 72:1419–1421.

Buchsbaum, G. (1987). Color signal coding: Color vision and color television. *Color Research Applications* 12:266–269.

Buchsbaum, G. (1987). Multidimensional signal coding in the visual system. CIE Wyszecki and Stiles Memorial Symposium, *Die Farbe* 34:145–149.

Buchsbaum, G. (1991). "Hybrid Spatio-Chromatic Coding in the Visual System." In *Channels in the Visual Nervous System. Neurophysiology. Psychophysics. Models*, ed. B. Blum. London: Freund. 139–150.

Buchsbaum, G. & Derrico, J. B. (1992). "The basic building blocks of color vision: A generalized view of the opponent colors transformation." In *Advances in Color Vision*. Optical Society of America 4:84–86.

Derrico, J. B. & Buchsbaum, G. (1990). Spatial and chromatic properties of cortical mechanisms in V1 correspond to the principal components of natural color images. *Investigative Ophthal. & Vis. Science (ARVO Sup.)* 31:1294.

Derrico, J. B. & Buchsbaum, G. (1991). A computational model of spatio-chromatic coding in early vision. *Journal of Visual Communication and Image Representation* 2:31–38.

Galatsanos, N. P., Katsaggelos, A. K., Chin, R. T. & Hillery, A. D. (1991). Least squares restoration of multichannel images. *IEEE Transactions on Signal Processing* 39:2222–2236.

Galatsanos, N. P. & Chin, R. T. (1991). Restoration of color images by multichannel kalman filtering. *IEEE Transactions on Signal Processing* 39:2237–2252.

Granger, E. M. & Heurtley, J. C. (1973). Visual chromaticity modulation transfer function. *Journal of the Optical Society of America* 63:1173–1174.

Hayhoe, M. & Wenderoth, P. (1991). "Adaptation Mechanisms in Color and Brightness." In *From Pigments to Perception*, ed. A. Valberg and B. Lee, 352–367. New York: Plenum Press.

Hunt, B. R. & Kübler, O. (1984). Karhunen-Loève multispectral image restoration. Pt. 1, Theory. *IEEE Transactions on Acoustics Speech & Signal Process.* ASSP-32:592–599.

Ingling, C. R. & Martinez, E. (1983). The relationship between spectral sensitivity and spatial sensitivity in the primate *r-g* X-channel. *Vision Research* 23:1495–1500.

Ingling, C. R. & Martinez-Uriegas, E. (1985). The spatiotemporal properties of the r-g X-cell channel. *Vision Research* 25:33−38.

Jayant, N. S. & Noll, P. (1984). *Digital Coding of Waveforms: Principles and Application to Speech and Video*. Englewood Cliffs, N.J.: Prentice Hall.

Lee, H. C. (1990). A computational model for opponent color encoding. *Proceedings SPSE Conference*. 178−181. Springfield, Mass: SPSE Press.

Lee, H. C. & Cok, D. R. (1991). Detecting boundaries in a vector field. *IEEE Transactions on Signal Processing* 39:1181−1194.

Lennie, P. & D'Zmura, M. (1988). Mechanisms of color vision. *CRC Critical Reviews Neurobiology* 3:333−400.

MacAdam, D. L. (1970). *Sources of Color Science*. Cambridge, Mass: MIT Press.

Mullen, K. T. (1985). The contrast sensitivity of human colour vision to red-green and blue-yellow chromatic gratings. *Journal of Physiology* 359:381−400.

Mullen, K. T. & Kingdom, F. A. A. (1991). "Color Contrast in Form and Perception." In *The Perception of Colour*, ed. P. Gouras, 198−217. London: Macmillan.

Ohyama, N., Yachida, M., Badique, E., Tsujiuchi, J. & Honda, T. (1988). Least squares filter for color-image restoration. *Journal of the Optical Society of America A* 5:19−24.

Orchard, M. T. & Bouman, C. A. (1991). Color quantization of images. *IEEE Transactions on Signal Processing* 39:2677−2690.

Pratt, W. K. (1978). *Digital Image Processing*. New York: John Wiley.

Rohaly, A. M. & Buchsbaum, G. (1988). Inference of global spatiochromatic mechanisms from contrast sensitivity functions. *Journal of the Optical Society of America A* 5:572−576.

Rohaly, A. M. & Buchsbaum, G. (1989). Global spatiochromatic mechanism accounting for luminance variations in contrast sensitivity. *Journal of the Optical Society of America A* 6:312−317.

Rosenfeld, A. & Kak, A. (1982). *Digital Picture Processing*, 2d edition. New York: Academic Press.

Smith, V. C. & Pokorny, J. (1975). Spectral sensitivity of the foveal cone photopigments between 400 and 500 nm. *Vision Research* 15:161−171.

Srinivasan, M. V. Laughlin, S. B. & Dubs, A. (1982). Predictive coding: A fresh view of inhibition in the retina. *Proc. R. Soc. London B* 216:427−459.

T'so, D. Y. & Gilbert, C. D. (1988). The organization of chromatic and spectral interaction in the primate striate cortex. *Journal of Neuroscience* 8:1712−1727.

Van der Horst, G. J. C., De Weert, C. M. M. & Bouman, M. A. (1967). Transfer of spatial chromaticity-contrast at threshold in the human eye. *Journal of the Optical Society of America* 57:1260−1266.

Vos, J. J. & Walraven, P. L. (1971). On the derivation of the foveal receptor primaries. *Vision Research* 11:799−818.

Vos, J. J. & Walraven, P. L. (1972a). An analytical description of the line element in the zone fluctuation of colour vision. I, Basic concepts. *Vision Research* 12:1327−1344.

Vos, J. J. & Walraven, P. L. (1972b). An analytical description of the line element in the zone fluctuation of colour vision. II. The derivation of the line element. *Vision Research* 12:1345−1365.

Vos, J. J. (1978). Colorimetric and photometric properties of a 2^0 fundamental observer. *Color Research Applications* 3:125−128.

Vos, J. J. (1979). Line elements and physiological models of color vision. *Color Research Applications* 4:208−216.

Vos, J. J., Estevez, O. & Walraven, P. L. (1990). Improved color fundamentals offer a new view on photometric additivity. *Vision Research* 30:937−943.

Walraven, J. (1985). The colours are not on the display, A survey of non veridical perceptions that may turn up on a colour display. *Displays* January 1985:35−42.

Walraven, J., Enroth-Cugell, Ch., Hood, D. D., MacLeod, D. I. A. & Schnapf, J. L. (1990). "The Control of Visual Sensitivity: Receptoral and Postreceptoral Processes." In L. Spillman and J. D. Werner, *Visual Perception: The Neurophysiological Foundations*, 53−101. San Diego: Academic Press.

Walraven, J. & Werner, J. S. (1991). The invariance of unique white: A possible implication for normalizing cone action spectra. *Vision Research* 31: 2185−2193.

Walraven, P. L. (1974). A closer look at the tritanopic Convergence Point. *Vision Research* 14:1339−1343.

Watson, A. B. (1990). Perceptual-components architecture for digital video. *Journal of the Optical Society of America A* 7:1943−1954.

Xie, W. & Bedrosian, S. D. (1984). An information measure for fuzzy sets. *IEEE Transactions on Systems Men and Cybernetics* SMC-14:151−156.

10

The Importance of Intrinsically Two-dimensional Image Features in Biological Vision and Picture Coding

Christof Zetzsche,
Erhardt Barth, and
Bernhard Wegmann

Image signals represent an extraordinarily large amount of information. In technical applications a typical value is 2 Mbit for a single gray-level picture of broadcast quality. In biology more than 1 million fibers carry the image information from the retina to the visual cortex (Potts et al., 1972). Reduction of the immense data load is, therefore, an essential requirement for any kind of image-processing system, be it biological or technical in nature. Data compression can rely on two essential sources for such a reduction: statistical redundancy and subjective irrelevance. Traditionally, research on statistical dependencies and their exploitation by redundancy reduction is related to communication engineering, whereas a basic method of visual psychophysics and physiology is the measurement of the limits of visual performance, that is, the determination of the irrelevance aspects. We argue that this view deserves some revision. In particular, we shall demonstrate that for the case of still images (1) no substantial further improvements in irrelevance reduction of images can be gained by a more detailed knowledge of static spatial visual sensitivities, and (2) the standard mathematical approaches to the redundancy reduction problem are severely limited in their ability to recognize essential structural aspects in natural images. In particular, we shall show that the efficient exploitation of "orientations" in images is beyond the scope of methods of optimum linear transform coding that are based on second-order statistics.

The main conclusion to be drawn from these considerations will be the following: Image coding scientists should not primarily see the visual system as determining irrelevance, that is, the limits of visibility of certain signals. Rather, they should take into account that it has adapted its information-processing strategies during millions of years to the statistics and structures of our environment. Hence, it seems suited as a heuristic guide to improved encoding procedures that may overcome the limits of the existing theoretical concepts. Vision scientists, on the other hand, can expect to gain an additional theoretical concept for the interpretation and explanation of structures found in psychophysical and physiological experiments. This is not to say, however, that irrelevance aspects, that is, the investigation of certain limits of biological structures, will play no role in the future development. Rather, redundancy and irrelevance should be seen as essential and equally important aspects of image information processing in both technical and biological systems.

Irrelevance

Definition

There is a long-standing debate on how a useful definition of the *perceptual lossless, transparent, subjectively perfect,* and the like, image can be arrived at. One unresolved issue behind this dispute is an unsharp definition of what the "true" signal is (the screen luminance? the world outside?). Another one is the insufficient consideration of human information processing as an inherently dynamic task for which bits/s play a more fundamental role than bits/deg^2. To avoid this discussion for the context of this paper, we rely on the following definition (which may also be extended to finite-duration image sequences):

A deviation of a reconstructed signal from the original is irrelevant in the strict sense if a critical observer given unlimited time cannot find any difference between the original and the reconstructed picture.

With respect to this "strict sense" definition, a main thesis of this chapter is that most of the potential savings that can be gained from knowledge of the absolute limits of spatial sensitivity are already incorporated into the current techniques. Thus, substantial progress in this direction cannot be expected.

Basic Limitations of Human Vision

Weber's Law

A basic finding with respect to the detection of differences in luminance signals is that the just-noticeable difference is not a fixed property but depends on the starting level. Here the relative increase and not the absolute difference (as in any linear system) is the relevant factor. It seems that the detailed modeling of this effect has to take into account something like local gain-control mechanisms (Shapley and Enroth-Cugell, 1984; Sperling, 1970). The

important point with respect to image coding, however, is that it can be approximated by a static saturating nonlinearity at the input of the system (Xie and Stockham, 1989). This type of irrelevance is (though in a suboptimal fashion) already taken into account by most of the conventional television equipment. Indeed, the relation between input and signal (camera) usually follows a compressive law, and the relation between the signal and the output (screen luminance) follows an expansive nonlinear law.

Spectral Sensitivity and Visual Acuity

The basic finding with respect to the sensitivity for the detection of spatial frequency (gratings) is a pronounced band-pass shape of the spatial contrast sensitivity function (CSF) of the human visual system with a peak at about 4 cycles/deg (e.g., Kelly, 1977). However, only the higher frequencies can be more coarsely quantized in frequency-specific encoding systems (e.g., pyramid coders), whereas in the lower-frequency range quantization has to be refined monotonically with decreasing frequency (Burt and Adelson, 1983). The reason for this may be the existence of a more low-pass-like CSF for suprathreshold signals (e.g., Georgeson and Sullivan, 1975) and the increase in the variance of filter outputs toward the lower frequency bands (cf. Wegmann and Zetzsche, 1991b).

An additional property of the CSF is its orientation anisotropy, that is, a preference for vertical and horizontal orientations, which is also known as the *oblique effect* (Appelle, 1972). It can easily be incorporated in frequency-specific coding schemes, for example, by an appropriate bit allocation in transform coding.

Spatial Masking

Contrast, and not the linear difference, determines the visibility of luminance variations. Yet even contrast is processed in a nonlinear fashion. *Masking* designates the reduction of detectability of a given stimulus by the (simultaneous) presence of an additional, in general suprathreshold stimulus. Masking occurs between periodic patterns (sinusoidal gratings) with similar orientation and radial frequency (Legge and Foley, 1980; Phillips and Wilson, 1984), and between aperiodic patterns, for example, at luminance borders (Fiorentini et al., 1955). The latter effect is often modeled by using some "masking signal" (e.g., the gradient) derived from the original image for a proportional reduction of an error signal (e.g., Lukas and Budrikis, 1982). Application of this concept to image coding may cause an overhead for the transmission of the masking signal needed to determine local quantization. However, we were able to show that both types of masking can be described within a single model by a frequency-specific channel splitting followed by saturating nonlinear transducer functions (Zetzsche and Hauske, 1989). This property is directly exploited by the companded quantizers in HVS-based image coders (e.g., Watson, 1987). A similar tendency is obtained by the Lloyd-Max quantization of subband outputs or transform coefficients.

Texture Perception

An even greater masking effect seems to occur in textured regions. In fact, certain variations in the microstructure of a texture are not readily visible if the macro properties are not changed. However, with attention directed to the right place (which is always possible, given unlimited time) a detailed analysis of the micro structure (vision with scrutiny, in the terms of Julesz, 1981) is possible. Visibility of a stimulus modification is then only slightly impaired by the simultaneous presence of similar elements. Loosely speaking, the problem is not that we *cannot see* the error but that the we have difficulties in *finding* it. Hence, no substantial savings beyond the "standard" masking effects can be expected from the point of view of "strict-sense irrelevance."

Semantics cause an additional complication, as becomes clear by noting that what you are currently looking at is probably fulfilling all signal statistical criteria for a texture. The only reason to care about the following Miss Print is in the semantics, but not in the statistics of the luminance signal.

Channels

It has been shown that under certain conditions the visual system has the ability to separate signals into different frequency ranges (Campbell and Robson, 1968). This channel concept is directly incorporated in HVS-based coding (Watson, 1987; Daugman, 1989; Martens, 1990; Wegmann and Zetzsche, 1990a,b), wavelet coding (Mallat, 1989), and, less directly, in subband coding schemes (Woods and O'Neill, 1987). It has been used in transform coding for frequency group bit assignment (Netravali and Haskell, 1988). However, the ability of independent detection does not exclude interactions between channels in human vision and does, therefore, not automatically favor an independent quantization of frequency-specific coefficients. In coding applications the joint (vector) quantization of subbands (Westerink et al., 1988), transform coefficients (e.g., Ramamurthi and Gersho, 1986), or orientation filter outputs (Wegmann and Zetzsche, 1990a,b) seems to be more efficient than their independent processing.

The Limits Are Limited

In conclusion, not much more can be gained from strict-sense irrelevance, that is, from the absolute limits biology imposes on the visibility of spatial stimuli. The basic effects are, more or less efficiently, included in the current techniques. A limited potential of irrelevance effects was also found in a recent rate-distortion analysis of basic nonlinear and filtering properties of human vision (Girod, 1989; also chapter 15). Totally new phenomena are not in sight. In fact, it would be surprising if there existed essential limits for the detectability of signal manipulations not yet recognized in the past century of scientific study.

If perfect invisibility of coding errors is not required, however, the strict irrelevance condition can be relaxed by consideration of *dynamic* properties of human visual information processing. For example, one may allow for errors that, though visible in principle, cannot be found rapidly in a structured display. Such dynamic aspects are often implicit in investigations of static image compression. However, the only systematic scientific exploration of dynamic aspects of visual processing has been conducted in experimental psychology in the form of visual search, scanning strategies, control of attention, and the like (e.g., Treisman and Gelade, 1980). Unfortunately, these experiments have been performed with abstract items like symbols and letters. Therefore, an adequate theory on the signal-processing level is still completely lacking. The topic deserves further exploration, but conceptually we should clearly distinguish between the disregard of a (detectable) signal deviation due to lack of attention and the impossibility of detection due to limitations of spatial sensitivity.

Although spatial irrelevance is no promising candidate for further savings, there is another potential source of data reduction: statistical redundancy.

Communication Engineering Approaches to Image Data Compression

Redundancy Reduction

Redundancy reduction (in its ideal form) means a unique, that is, invertible mapping from a sequence of input symbols to a (statistically) shorter sequence of encoded symbols. It is based on the statistical dependencies or correlations between the input symbols. Let is assume, for example, that symbol *A* is always followed by symbol *B*. We can then say that symbol *B* is *redundant or predictable*, since it suffices to transmit only *A* and reconstruct *B* at the receiver.

In real applications a unique mapping is often impossible or not desirable. One reason for this is the common need for encoding continuous-amplitude signals into discrete (e.g., binary) symbols. Obviously, the performance of an information-processing system has to be characterized by a function relating the amount of data used in the computation to the quality of the result. In an object-recognition system, for example, we may ask for the minimum number of features needed to achieve a certain classification performance. For data compression, a function relating the data rate to the quality of the reconstructed image is needed. Perfect separation of irrelevance and redundancy is often difficult, but redundancy reduction can be seen as the exploitation of statistical dependencies to enable the reproduction of the signal at a given level of quality with the minimum data rate possible. In the case of a human observer we may try to find the processing scheme that provides the minimum amount of data sufficient to obtain a physically measurable but just-invisible distortion.

The theory of information and communication (Shannon, 1948, 1959) deals with these issues. Because no alternative theories with comparable potential are in sight, we mainly follow the Shannon theory in this chapter. Information theory relies on a statistical concept. Accordingly, most of the work in image coding has also been based on statistical signal descriptions.

Some Basic Statistical Considerations

The basic assumption in the statistical description of images is that the formation of these signals is governed by certain not yet understood rules. These, in turn, cause

Figure 10.1
Basic statistical dependencies in images from the natural environment. The *homogeneity* of the interior object regions causes *isotropic* statistical dependencies. The *compactness* of objects and the related local straightness of object borders cause *anisotropic* dependencies.

statistical dependencies exploitable by appropriate coding schemes. Hence, an understanding of how physical and biological laws determine the formation and aggregation of matter would be highly desirable. Unfortunately, our knowledge in this area is more than limited. A major point of this chapter, however, is that even this restricted knowledge is not fully exploited in current theories.

Figure 10.1 demonstrates in a schematic fashion which elementary types of statistical dependencies are caused by the strikingly homogeneous and compact aggregation of matter in our environment. Basically, two kinds of dependencies can be observed. The most prominent one, a strong and roughly isotropic statistical dependency, is related to the *homogeneity* of the interior regions resulting from the projection of a three-dimensional object onto a two-dimensional image plane. This property can be loosely described as "neighboring points tend to be of similar luminance irrespective of the direction of their spatial relation," and we shall often speak simply of *isotropic statistical dependencies* (including both isotropic and separable image models; Jain, 1981b).

Most image regions are of the smoothly varying type, but some are textured, that is, they show a high degree of signal variation. They may also be described as homogeneous, although in a more complicated, higher-order sense. A detailed discussion of the texture issue is beyond the scope of this chapter, but some remarks can be found in a later section.

The second type of statistical dependency results from the *compactness* of objects and is restricted to the (statistically less frequent) points of the projected object boundaries, the *edges*. This second property is a highly anisotropic property that can be described as "edges tend to be straight" or "only a minority of edge points are highly curved." Such straight structures have often been referred to as *linear features* (a slightly misleading term, as we shall see later). The distribution of these anisotropic dependencies across orientations is weakly biased at horizontal and vertical orientations, probably due to the influence of gravity and solar radiation, which favor conditions like the horizontal flattening of the ground and the vertical "struggle for light" of plants.

The basic structural properties of images can also be described in a more deterministic view by defining idealized classes of signals according to their *intrinsic dimensionality* (Zetzsche and Barth, 1990a,b). Signals with strong isotropic statistical dependencies, being approximately constant, will be designated as *0D-signals*. Signals with strong anisotropic dependencies will be designated as *1D-signals*, since it is possible to find a coordinate transform $(x, y) \rightarrow (x', y')$ for which the two-dimensional image intensity $i(x, y)$ can be well approximated by $i'(x')$. Only the signals for which it is impossible to find such a mapping will be regarded as intrinsically two-dimensional, that is, as *2D-signals*. As stated above, the latter are a statistical minority. Nevertheless, they will play an important role in our theory of biological vision. We use both the statistical and the intrinsic dimensionality classifications as approximately equivalent, unless we state otherwise.

The following discussion utilizes the theory of stochastic processes (e.g., Papoulis, 1984). In the case of multidimensional signals, like images, such processes are also called *random fields*. We give a short introduction for readers with a nontechnical background.

Images as Random Fields

Once image signals are considered within the framework of random-field theory, a given signal can be seen as only one possible example of the "ensemble" (an infinity of possible "realizations" of the stochastic process). The probabilistic parameters of the random field are defined by expected values, that is, probability weighted averages across the ensemble. There are no a priori reasons that enforce the application of the framework of stochastic processes to the representation of image signals. However, having chosen this perspective, one should keep a consistent definition of how the signals are related to the entities of the theory. This is particularly relevant for the definition of what is seen as the coordinate axes of the random field and what is seen as the ensemble (even if the latter exists only as an assumption, i.e., within a model).

In the case of image signals the common assumption is that the ensemble consists of an infinite set of images (e.g., Rosenfeld and Kak, 1982). The luminance at each position (m, n) is an actual value of a random variable $\mathbf{u}(m, n)$ the ordered set of which constitutes the random field. A random field is said to be *stationary (in the "strict sense")* if the joint probability density functions of all tuples of random variables $(\ldots, \mathbf{u}(m, n), \ldots, \mathbf{u}(m + i, n + j), \ldots)$ depend only on the relative distances (i, j) and not on the absolute position (m, n). This means that the statistical properties of the actual or hypothetical ensemble are identical in all image regions. The issue of nonstationarity of image signals is a crucial point of this chapter. A random field is said to be weakly or *wide-sense* stationary if the above criterion is true only for combinations up to the second order, that is, for mean and covariance (Papoulis, 1984).

An essential point for many practical applications is the property of *ergodicity*. Only for an ergodic and stationary random field can the probabilistic parameters be reliably estimated by using only a single realization (a given image) instead of the ensemble. A simple example of this is that one can calculate the mean of the process by taking the limit of the average of the values of a single realization.

In the remainder of the chapter we concentrate on the question of how the statistical properties of natural images are taken into account by technical coding schemes in contrast with the biological visual system.

Optimum Linear Coding Based on Second-Order Statistics

The classical methods for the design of data compression schemes follow one common strategy: The optimum parameters of a linear device (coefficients of a linear predictor, basis (eigen) images of a linear transform) are determined from the second-order statistics (covariance) of the input signal (e.g., Jayant and Noll, 1984). An essential question, therefore, is whether this linear/second-order approach is suited to capture the basic statistical dependencies in natural images. This issue is discussed in the context of transform coding approaches, since the performance of predictive schemes is in general inferior, except for the high-quality coding of Markov-type signals (Jain, 1981a). However, similar arguments apply to predictive techniques.

A powerful theoretical tool for data compression is the Karhunen-Loeve transform (KLT), which is also known as the Hotelling transform or principal-component analysis. The KLT is often regarded as the theoretically optimal method for the exploitation of redundancies in signals. In particular, it can be shown mathematically that (1) it can transform a set of correlated input data into a set of uncorrelated output coefficients and (2) it provides among the unitary transforms the optimal "compaction of energy" if only a subset of the coefficients is retained for the reconstruction of the signal (e.g., Jain, 1989).

Due to this formal optimality it is often believed that the linear, second-order-based techniques would represent the suitable theoretical framework for data compression, were there not *practical* difficulties. The theoretical potential is seen to be hampered by several factors: Subjective quality cannot be adequately described by a mean-squared-error criterion, edges are isolated discontinuities that cannot be embedded in a purely statistical framework, and—the most general and serious obstacle—image signals are highly nonstationary. Due to this nonstationarity they cannot be efficiently coded by any fixed scheme optimized to global statistical properties, but deserve a locally adaptive processing. However, we shall show that this common view tends to hide an important general deficiency of the underlying theory and may, therefore, be potentially misleading in the search for further improvements.

We are aware that natural image signals represent an enormous variety and are hence difficult to handle in a discussion of specific properties of a theoretical approach. The available mathematical models, however, are known to be too restricted for an adequate description of image signals. We therefore use an idealized example with restricted and consistent properties for the illustration of our arguments.

Let us assume that the task is to design a picture database for a huge set of images that all belong to one restricted class, say, from an X-ray analysis of Jupiter cyclones. This is a typical task for an approach based on ensemble statistics. An example image is shown in figure 10.2. These images are of an *orientation-only* type, that is, they do not contain any of the isotropic statistical dependencies (0D-signals); however, they contain very strong and far-reaching anisotropic dependencies. Hence, they

Figure 10.2
Typical example image of a hypothetical image data base for which an optimum compression algorithm should be developed. The images are all of the orientation-only type, that is, they do not contain smooth regions (isotropic statistical dependencies).

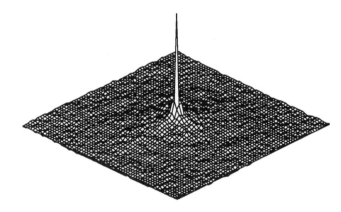

Figure 10.3
Autocorrelation function of the image in Figure 10.2. A 64 × 64 section is shown. Note the sharp decrease in the immediate vicinity of the origin. This implies that second-order statistics "see" this image as almost completely decorrelated.

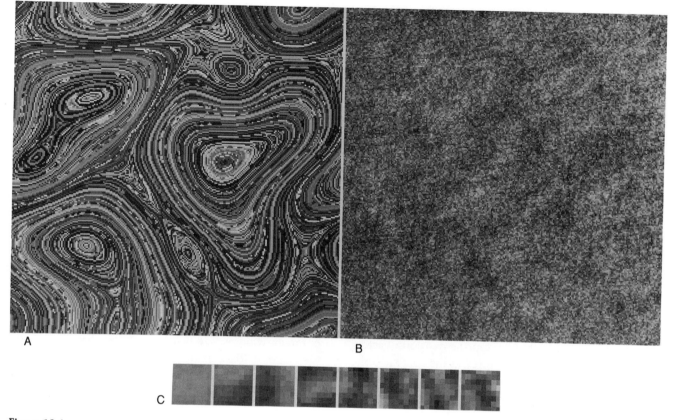

A

B

C

Figure 10.4

Two images with identical second-order properties. (A) an "orientation only" image from the hypothetical data base (see Figure 10.2); (B) an appropriately filtered white-noise process. The filter function has been chosen in a way that image (B) has the same autocorrelation as image (A). Note the completely different structures of (A) and (B) in spite of their common second-order statistics. (C) The first eight eigenimages (block size 8×8, zoomed for illustration) as derived from the second-order statistic (covariance matrix). Obviously, there can be no systematic relationship between the oriented nature of the eigenimages and the oriented structures in image (A), since (B) has the same eigenimages but does not contain any oriented structures.

seem ideally suited for an evaluation of whether the theoretical concept of the optimum linear transform is appropriate for the exploitation of statistical dependencies due to local oriented structures (linear features) in images.

The optimum transform (KLT) is completely determined by the second-order properties of the signal, more specifically by its covariance matrix. In the stationary case the covariance matrix is block Toeplitz and equivalent to the position-independent mean-free autocorrelation function. This function is shown in figure 10.3. Although statistical dependencies extend over more than 50 pixels,

the measured correlation drops down abruptly within the immediate neighborhood (it is easy to see that even the tiny rest of correlation results from the finite sampling). Hence, second-order statistics tell us that the image is nearly perfectly decorrelated: *second-order statistics are "blind" for the presence of "orientations" in images*. This is also corroborated by the structure of the image shown in figure 10.4(B), which is identical to figure 10.4(A) with respect to its second-order properties (it is an appropriately filtered white-noise process) but does not exhibit any oriented structures.

It is sometimes assumed that the occurrence of oriented eigenimages of the KLT is somehow related to the frequent presence of oriented structures in natural images. Therefore, it is instructive to take a look at the eigenimages of figures 4(A) and (B) shown in figure 4(C). From figure 4(B) it should be obvious that the oriented eigenimages have nothing to do with orientations in images. Rather, they result more or less automatically, due to the orthogonality requirement, as soon as some correlation is present and the matrix is approximately block Toeplitz. This does not imply that oriented eigen or basis images are useless in image coding, but it implies that there exists no theoretical explanation for how the exploitation of "oriented" statistical dependencies (1D-signals) can be related to second-order statistics and the derived optimal linear transform.

However, all the preceding reasoning rests on one basic assumption, namely, stationarity, the invalidity of which may put things into an entirely different perspective. Figures 4(A) and (B) make clear that there is indeed a fundamental difference between the two. Although image (B) is quite homogeneous, the local structural properties of (A) do vary considerably across the image. It may be a problem to obtain reliable estimates of probabilistic parameters of a random field by averaging within a single realization if the averaging is performed across positions with nonidentical statistical properties, as may be the case for image (A).

Nonstationarity is regarded as one of the key problems of the statistical approach to image coding. For example, only if the signal is stationary can the transform vectors be computed in advance and stored at the coder and the decoder. Otherwise, such a fixed set of transform vectors cannot be expected to yield the optimum result. Similarly, no fixed optimum quantization scheme for the transform coefficients can be derived, since their variances will not stay constant across the image. The solution of these problems is known as *adaptive coding* (e.g., Habibi, 1977; Netravali and Haskell, 1988). The general strategy is to obtain *local* estimates of the statistical properties that are then used for an updating of the parameters of the coding scheme (e.g., adaptation of transform vectors (expensive), adaptation of predictor coefficients, adaptive quantization, adaptive bit allocation, and adaptive classification). Most common is a blockwise estimation at the coder with the results being transmitted as additional "side information" to the decoder. In our example, provision of side information about the local orientation can be expected to yield a substantial improvement (cf. Wilson et al., 1983). In transform approaches (Wintz, 1972) *threshold coding* is better suited than *zonal coding* for an adaptation to local orientation, though at the price of considerable side information.

A central problem in adaptive signal processing is the determination of the appropriate window size for the estimation of local probabilistic parameters. Here it is important to remember that in random-field theory the probabilistic parameters are defined as (probability

weighted) ensemble averages. Perfectly reliable estimates needed for optimum coding efficiency can be obtained only if the signal is stationary and ergodic (Papoulis, 1984) and the estimation is based on as many samples as possible (i.e., the whole image or, even better, a set of images). Any reduction of estimation window size yields a suboptimal solution due to estimation errors.

For nonstationary signals, however, we are faced with a trade-off between two opposing tendencies. On the one hand, estimation window size should be small to prevent samples of regions with differing statistical properties from influencing the estimate (this may have happened in figure 10.3). On the other hand, the window should be large, since only with a large enough number of samples can a restricted average come close to the true probabilistic value. As a consequence, a convex dependency with an intermediate optimum will appear in the nonstationary case, not the monotonic decrease in performance with decreasing window size, as with stationary signals. The optimum window size is a compromise that depends on the rate of spatial variation of the parameters. This implies that, in contrast with the stationary case, performance can never reach the theoretical optimum in the nonstationary case, since this would require perfect knowledge of the nonstationary parameters, which cannot be obtained with finite windows. However, even a suboptimal adaptation will be superior to an erroneous stationarity assumption in the processing of a nonstationary signal. Hence, adaptive coding seems to be an adequate solution for the exploitation of oriented structures in images, and the only remaining problem is to find the best compromise for the window size.

In our example the solution can be greatly simplified, since the image has nothing to do with Jupiter cyclones (as may have been expected) but stems from an artificial computer source. In addition, it has not been chosen without hindsight. In fact, the nonstationarity is obvious only to the eye of the beholder. The source is perfectly stationary and ergodic. It is generated by a low-pass filtering of a white-noise source followed by a nonlinear but spatially homogeneous mapping of the filter output values by a lookup table containing uncorrelated output values. To avoid a widening of the curved lines, that is, the emergence of additional isotropic statistical dependencies (0D-signals), the resolution of the lookup table is controlled by the local gradient of the filtered signal. That is, the

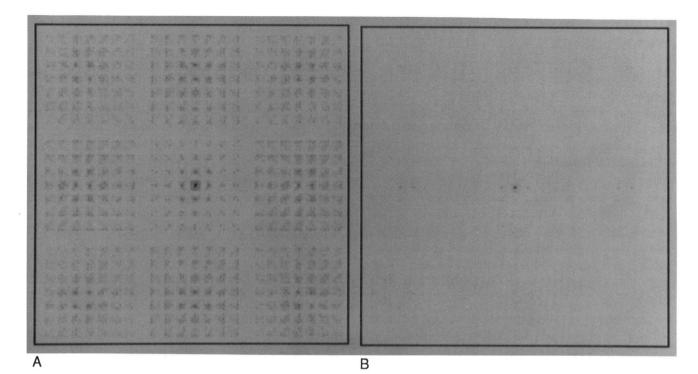

A   B

Figure 10.5
Fourth-order statistics (cumulants) of (A) the orientation-only image of figure 10.4(A) and (B) the equivalent-filtered-noise image of figure 10.4(B). The evaluated images are completely equivalent with respect to their second-order statistics, but it is evident from this figure that 4(A) contains relevant fourth-order statistical dependencies, whereas 4(B) is completely characterized by its second-order dependencies. Stationary fourth-order statistics of images depend on six variables $(\Delta x_1, \Delta y_1; \Delta x_2, \Delta y_2; \Delta x_3, \Delta y_3)$. The mapping of the six-dimensional fourth-order statistic (cumulant) into a two-dimensional picture results in an arrangement of small pictures, where each small picture represents one two-dimensional section $(\Delta x_1, \Delta y_1)$ through the six-dimensional cumulant function, and its position is indexed by the other four variables $(\Delta x_2, \Delta y_2; \Delta x_3, \Delta y_3)$.

new source results from spatially homogeneous operations applied to a stationary and ergodic source and is therefore itself stationary and ergodic.

If this source can be successfully encoded by an adaptive scheme, we are faced with a conceptual inconsistency. Because the source is stationary and ergodic, the optimum linear transform exists and is uniquely determined by the second-order properties of the process (note that the proof of the optimality properties does not require any additional assumptions, such as Gaussian properties or the like). These can be perfectly estimated by averaging within the optimum window size, which is infinite in the stationary case. Application of the resulting optimal trans-

form should yield the optimum coding efficiency obtainable by linear transforms. The theory predicts that this will be poor, however, since nearly nothing can be gained from the optimum transform of a highly decorrelated signal. If we now systematically decrease the estimation window size, due to our (definitely wrong) belief that the signal is nonstationary, we shall arrive at a point were the performance of the (now-adaptive) coding scheme is considerably better than the optimum performance. However, at this point the estimates are grossly incorrect and will show a random variation across spatial position. This should be no surprise, since it is well known that the reliability of parameter estimates is low if there exist substantial statistical dependencies within the window range used for the estimation. In particular, second-order estimates are known to depend on fourth-order moments (Papoulis, 1984). The oriented structures in our example do cause substantial fourth-order dependencies, as is demonstrated in figure 10.5. It should be recalled that the basic motivation for image coding is the assumption of strong statistical dependencies that could be exploited. Local window based parameter estimates, therefore, have to be expected to show substantial variation across the image, even in stationary environments.

The usual demonstrations of nonstationarity are hence not conclusive. It can be doubted whether statistical tests performed over *adequately sized* spatial regions or, even better, across a typical sample set of realizations from the ensemble for which the coding system is to be designed will yield substantial nonstationarities. What is even more intriguing, however, is that adaptive schemes can yield better performance than their nonadaptive counterparts in such stationary conditions. Since the theoretical justification of adaptive procedures is usually based on proving that the system converges toward the static optimum solution in a stationary environment (e.g., Haykin, 1986), it seems difficult to find a theory of optimum adaptive coding that yields an optimum better than this static optimum in the case of stationary signals.

We shall discuss these important problems in general form at the end of this section, after a short look at two important alternative image coding schemes.

Subband Coding

On a first look, subband (or wavelet) coding seems to be basically different from transform coding. In transform coding an input signal is taken and is converted into an entirely different representation in the transform (or spectral) domain. In subband coding the incoming spatial signal is split by a number of spatial filters into a set of again purely spatial signals (Vetterli, 1984; Woods and O'Neill, 1986). However, it is easy to see that there is no essential difference between the output coefficients of an $n \times n$ block transform as a function of block position and the *set* of channel outputs of a separable fixed bandwidth $n \times n$ filter bank at each subsampled position (e.g., Singhal et al., 1990). Consequently, quite similar arguments with respect to the exploitation of oriented structures in images will apply.

The theoretical justification of subband coding is that such coders can approach the rate-distortion limit for the redundancies imposed by the nonflatness of the power-spectral density (psd) (Jayant and Noll, 1984; see also Rao and Pearlman, 1991). The psd's of many images are roughly circular symmetric. Hence a band splitting by *isotropic* band-pass filters, as in the Laplacian pyramid, can be expected to give near-optimum performance for such signals. This is evident from the fact that the radial deviation from spectral flatness can be exploited with arbitrary precision by increasing the number of filters and decreas-

ing their bandwidth. Without a substantial orientation-specific deviation from spectral flatness there is no theoretical reason (besides sampling considerations) for any advantage of a further splitting into oriented subbands. The true reason for the emergence of orientation-specific subband schemes is rather an implementation issue: The straightforward extension of QMF filters to two dimensions is easier if separability is assumed, and this in turn automatically creates a certain degree of orientation specificity. Hence, orientation specificity results more as an accidental byproduct than from a theory-based optimization. We shall show later, however, that there are reasons beyond the scope of second-order theory that favor orientation-specific signal decompositions.

Vector Quantization

It is interesting to note that the nonstationarity used to motivate adaptive coding would be a disadvantage in vector quantization (VQ), which would yield optimum performance in the stationary case. This view seems to be supported by the reported difficulties of vector quantizers in the reproduction of the locally oriented edge patterns (e.g., Ramamurthi and Gersho, 1986). However, the minimum requirement for convergence toward an optimum is only asymptotically mean stationarity (Sabin and Gray, 1984), and the edge reproduction problems have been observed with schemes like LBG (Linde et al., 1980) that are not entropy optimized. If entropy is taken into account, it should be possible to increase the quantization resolution in regions with low probability without significantly affecting the rate.

Although the optimum transform approach is based solely on the second-order statistics and is therefore limited to the removal of pairwise correlations, vector quantization can take into account, at least theoretically, the complete multivariate statistics of an n-dimensional vector or image subblock. However, although there is *in principle* no limit to vector quantization performance within the scope of rate-distortion theory, that is, one can approach the distortion-rate function arbitrarily close by increasing the vector size, in practice a limit will be imposed by complexity. Even for moderate sizes (e.g., $n = 4 \times 4 = 16$) and amplitude resolutions (e.g., 4-bit) the combinatorial expansion (here to the order of 10^{19}) puts severe restrictions on the development of straightforward redundancy reduction methods as, for example, in form of entropy-coded lattice quantizers. All VQ schemes are in some way dependent on a correct adaptation to the multidimensional probability density function, and the mere provision of sufficient empirical data for the reliable estimation of proper learning will be a limiting factor. The exploitation of dependencies extending across a distance of more than 5 pixels seems hence to be impossible by unstructured brute-force spatial VQ approaches. An additional complication stems from the necessity to envisage complicated interactions of redundancy and irrelevance effects. This may be one reason for the emergence of a great variety of VQ schemes that all deviate substantially from the unstructured spatial approach (Nasrabadi and King, 1986). In general, it can be assumed that any additional knowledge about specific structural properties of the multivariate statistical dependencies can provide a basis for achieving a better performance, at given complexity, than the one achievable by an unstructured VQ.

Conclusion: Limits of the Formal Approach

A basic structural property of natural image signals—the frequent occurrence of locally oriented structures—seems to be difficult to incorporate into the framework of optimum linear coding schemes derived from second-order statistics. This has been demonstrated by an orientation-only image that, despite its far-reaching statistical dependencies, is "seen" as perfectly decorrelated by second-order measures.

The common explanation for the deficits of the statistical approach, the "obvious" nonstationarity of image signals, has led to the development of a variety of adaptive coding schemes. Although we do not dispute the heuristically and empirically evident fact that such adaptive schemes are superior to static ones, its theoretical justification seems to be difficult. We cannot see a theoretically convincing argument in favor of nonstationarity of image signals, since the arguments usually raised can also be raised in the case of perfectly stationary and ergodic sources, as shown by our example. There, the covariance matrix exists and can be reliably determined. Hence, the optimum linear transform can be uniquely derived, since its optimality in no way depends on additional a priori model assumptions (such as joint Gaussian or Markov). What is needed then is a theoretical justification for the superiority of the nonstationary over the optimum stationary solution in such stationary environments.

There seem to be two alternative approaches to resolving the apparent inconsistencies. These may be characterized as the *conservative* and the *nonlinear* interpretations. The basis for these interpretations is a recent important result by Fontana, Gray, and Kieffer (1981) on the stationarity properties of switched composite sources (Berger, 1972). In these processes each realization consists of segments from a number of distinct stationary sources. On the one hand, a consequence of their result is that it is in principle impossible to obtain reliable evidence for nonstationarity from the empirical data in this case, even if a large number of realizations are available. On the other hand, the result shows that the assumption of an intra-realization nonstationarity (a nonprobabilistic property being different for each realization) is not necessarily inconsistent with the factual probabilistic stationarity of the ensemble. In cases where the amount of side information needed is small, or where it is even possible to estimate this information at the decoder, the conservative view can provide some plausibility for the apparently inconsistent superiority of adaptive schemes in certain stationary environments. However, we know of no formally derived statistical criteria a stationary process must fulfill to enable such superiority.

The alternative, nonlinear view is more formal. In cases where no reliable evidence for nonstationarity can be obtained (since the criteria invoked would inevitably enforce the interpretation of statistical dependencies in perfectly stationary environments as nonstationarity, as in our example), the random field should, logically, be seen as stationary. This view, however, then necessitates an alternative explanation for the superiority of adaptive coding in certain stationary cases. The simple solution is that an adaptive coder should be interpreted as a *static nonlinear* instead of a *space-varying linear* device by regarding the combination of coder and adaptive control circuit as the nonlinear device.

The standard adaptive coding approach, then, is interpreted in the following way: Images are stationary (though not Gaussian) and do possess strong higher-order statistical dependencies for which the traditional linear/second-order approach is blind. Nonlinear coding schemes optimized with respect to the higher-order properties are needed; however, no suitable nonlinear/higher-order theory is yet known. Adaptive coding is a trick for the construction of nonlinear operations within the framework of a linear theory. The problem is "linearized" by reinterpreting higher-order statistical dependencies as a special type of intrarealization nonstationarity. This does then allow a partial exploitation of higher-order dependencies within the available framework of second-order statistical signal processing. It should be noted, however, that the linearization approach has its own restrictions, the most important one being the optimal determination of the borders between the segments of the composite source signal and the optimization of side information, which are not trivial problems in the case of image signals.

In a certain sense a theoretical framework for the stationary nonlinear approach does already exist: vector quantization. This is obvious, since any possible block coder can be seen as a special VQ. An adaptive, that is, space-varying linear transform coder can therefore be given a stationary nonlinear interpretation as a static VQ. This is easily seen in the case of adaptive quantization of transform coefficients, where the adaptation causes a specific, signal-dependent shape of the quantization regions, and the combination of adaptivity information and quantizer outputs constitutes a variable-length vector index.

The foregoing demonstrates that VQ should not be regarded as one specific coding method but rather as an important aspect of complex coder structures. It is evident that straightforward, unstructured VQ of the signal itself can always be outperformed, at given complexity, by the additional incorporation of structural knowledge. The simplest example of this is mean/shape VQ (Sabin and Gray, 1984). The structural knowledge, however, is difficult to obtain from analysis of the multidimensional probability density function, with respect to both the mere availability of sufficient data and the deduction of suitable rules and structuring principles. Only evolution, during millions of years and with billions of sensors, had a chance for making statistical observations and for learning appropriate structural principles that we can never get, even with a direct feeding of broadcast programs into supercomputers. Therefore, knowledge about the way in which the biological vision system deals with the multivariate statistics of natural images can be expected to provide important insights into an optimized design of complex coding schemes. In the following section we hence try to analyze the biological system from the viewpoint of redundancy reduction. As is evident from the preceding discussion, nonlinear operations will be of special interest in this analysis.

Redundancy Reduction in Biological Vision

The Primary Stage: Isotropic Processing

The isotropic statistical dependencies resulting from smoothly varying image areas can be described by a first-order Markov process with a correlation coefficient near unity. These properties can be efficiently exploited by a cosine transform, which comes close to the optimum KLT under these conditions (Jain, 1979).

Biology has chosen a different scheme, namely, isotropic lateral inhibition, for the primary processing stage (Kuffler, 1953). In technical terms this can be seen as the operation of an isotropic band-pass filter, and the corresponding multiresolution version has become famous as the Laplacian pyramid (Burt and Adelson, 1983). We saw earlier that a frequency-specific isotropic filter decomposition suffices for an efficient exploitation of the statistical redundancies imposed by the nonflatness of isotropic psd's (Jayant and Noll, 1984). More importantly, however, such an isotropic organization of the primary stages enables the provision of essential additional features.

We hope we have made clear that we do not suggest that the goal of primary visual processing is a mere compression of data. Rather, we maintain that the biological system should be seen as a multipurpose system pursuing diverse objectives, but with the manageability of data load as an ultimate constraint (without such a limitation many problems would become trivial). One such objective of early visual processing is the separation of information about object properties (reflectance) from the variation caused by the incident light (illumination). Unfortunately, both components enter the eye as a highly nonlinear, multiplicative combination. Interestingly, this basically semantic separation problem can be partially solved on the "primitive" signal-processing level. Both components can be seen as independent statistical processes that cause a combined process whose variance (apparently) fluctuates in a nonstationary manner. (This is a typical situation where a clear-cut distinction between higher-order properties and nonstationarity is difficult to make). In the biological system the two components are approximately separated by a *nonlinear type* of lateral inhibition that acts like an adaptive gain-control mechanism. Without prior semantic knowledge no preferable scale can be determined, hence the algorithm should work on several levels of resolution simultaneously (this simultaneity may arise on the cortical level; cf. Peichl and Wässle, 1979). The resulting structure can be described as ROG (ratio of gaussian) pyramid and can be shown to provide, in addition to the various desirable nonlinear properties, a complete and invertible representation of the input signal (Zetzsche and Hauske, 1989; see also Xie and Stockham, 1989; Peli, 1990). The initial stage of the visual system can hence be regarded as performing a clever mixture of predictive, transform, and adaptive coding strategies. Similar conclusions have also been reached for the insect eye (Laughlin, 1983).

Cortical Orientation Specificity

The discovery of orientation-specific units in the visual cortex (Hubel and Wiesel, 1962) is often regarded as one of the most important experimental results in sensory neurobiology. Although it may appear intuitively convincing that a decomposition of the image signal into local, oriented components is a good starting point for a visual analysis of the environment, it must be admitted that the usefulness of this property has not yet received undisputable theoretical support. There have been claims that special sets of functions can optimize a joint space/frequency localization criterion, but it is not clear what exactly should be optimized or why this kind of optimization should be essential for a vision system (Daugmann, 1985; Stork and Wilson, 1990; Yang, 1992; Klein and Beutter, 1992).

Could arguments from information theory (Field, 1987; Zetzsche and Schönecker, 1987) provide a basis for understanding cortical orientation specificity? We have already seen that the statistical redundancies imposed by the nonflatness of isotropic psd's can be efficiently exploited by an isotropic frequency-specific filter decomposition (Jayant and Noll, 1984). For a fixed number of filters the minimum rate-distortion function is indeed obtained with the biological, logarithmic frequency spacing, the only case for which the nonflatness resulting from the $1/f$ decrease of the spectra of natural images is identical in each frequency band. Hence, second-order theory predicts that no substantial advantage can be gained by a further orientation-specific decomposition. Even if we take into account the slight prominence of vertical and horizontal orientations, the remaining deviation from spectral flatness within an isotropic pass-band is still greater in radial than in angular direction. The only formal argument for orientation specificity then is that in the ideal limit a slightly greater number of samples (33 percent) is needed for an isotropic decomposition. However, this advantage can be obtained only with a biologically implausible orthogonal wavelet basis. Furthermore, a considerable oversampling in terms of retinal ganglion cells and nerve fibers already occurs in biological vision (Wässle et al., 1990).

Obviously, the second-order/linear systems approach cannot provide an answer. Furthermore, these considerations also show that the learning of oriented receptive fields in neural network approaches (e.g., Linsker, 1986; Sanger, 1990) corresponds closely to the decorrelating and orthogonality properties of KLT-like techniques but has no relation to the presence of oriented structures in the environment. This is also evident from the fact that isotropic (correlated) random-noise signals have been used for the network training.

So what are oriented filters good for? For redundancy reduction. Although second-order theory cannot provide arguments for this hypothesis, it is possible to find heuristic and empirical evidence for a superiority of orientation-specific over isotropic representations with respect to redundancy reduction (Field, 1987; Zetzsche and Schönecker, 1987). In addition, it will become clear in a subsequent section that orientation specificity is a *necessary prerequisite* for the nonlinear, higher-level processing of 2D-signals.

To get a heuristic understanding of the connection between the anisotropic statistical dependencies and orientation specificity we should consider the example shown in figure 10.6. We take an idealized image that consists simply of a bright square on a dark background. (We can think of this as one sample from a random process with realizations consisting of squares at different positions and with different luminance levels. Hence, all luminance levels are equally probable and first-order entropy will be close to the maximum value). An isotropic representation, for example, in one layer of a Laplacian pyramid, is illustrated in the lower left of figure 10.6 (top), with figure 10.6 (bottom) showing the appropriately subsampled version. The (trivial) second-order dependencies in the constant-image regions have been efficiently converted to a reduced first-order entropy (we always assume quantization on a fixed distortion level), since the probability distribution is peaked and variance is reduced (most samples have zero and only a few nonzero amplitudes). The influence of a further, anisotropic (orientation-specific) splitting of this

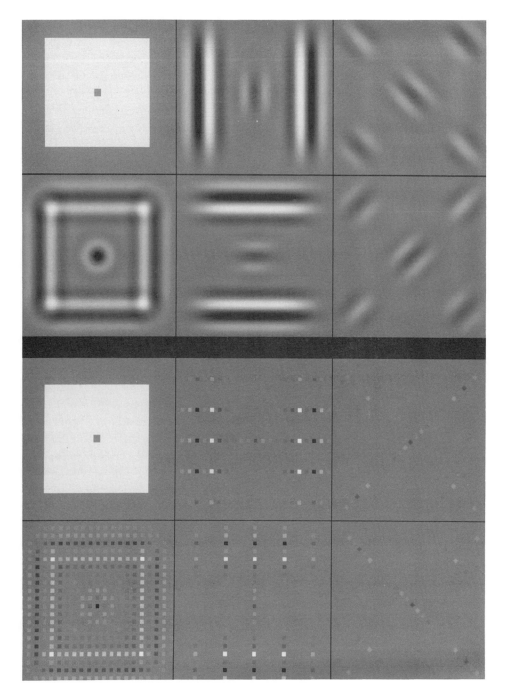

Figure 10.6

(Top) Comparison of different representations of the dark square on a gray background shown on the upper left side. The isotropic representation (lower left image) in comparison to its anisotropic representation (the four images on the right side). (Bottom) same as above but with the appropriately subsampled representations. It becomes evident by merely counting the active samples that the variance and the entropy are considerably reduced in the anisotropic representation.

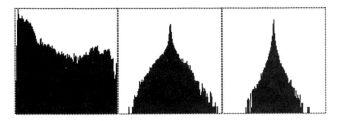

Figure 10.7
Probability density functions (logarithmic ordinates) obtained by simulations of an isotropic versus an anisotropic representation of natural images. (Left) Input; (middle) isotropic lateral inhibition (retina); (right) orientation specific (anisotropic representation (cortex). Variance and entropy are clearly reduced in the anisotropic representation.

frequency band is shown on the right of figure 10.6 (top) and (bottom). Simple counting of the "active" samples in figure 10.6 (bottom) reveals that for certain input signals an orientation-specific splitting can indeed further reduce first-order entropy. Loosely speaking, the application of an orientation-specific decomposition by n filters to image signals containing frequent locally straight structures results in a reduction of the number of active samples by a factor of about n. Thereby, the whole number of samples of all filters remains approximately equal to the isotropic case. This is because each straight segment will appear in only one filter output, and for each of the n orientation filters the sampling in the preferred direction can be reduced by a factor of n (in comparison with the single isotropic band-pass). Hence, an orientation-specific decomposition can reduce the variance and the first-order entropy of the representation provided the input image contains substantial anisotropic dependencies.

But are these properties present in natural images? Extended simulations of the biological processing of a wide variety of natural images have shown a substantial reduction of first-order entropy and variance (Field, 1987; Zetzsche and Schönecker, 1987; Wegmann and Zetzsche, 1990b). Figure 10.7 shows the probability of occurrence of different levels of activity in an isotropic representation compared with an anisotropic representation. Further confirmation comes from image-coding approaches using an orientation decomposition, be they motivated by human vision (e.g., Watson, 1987; Daugman, 1989; Martens, 1990; Wegmann and Zetzsche, 1990a) or by more formal considerations (Vetterli, 1984; Woods and O'Neill, 1986; Mallat, 1989).

Suboptimality of the "Matching" Approach

The orientation-specific coding schemes can be seen as examples of a more general coding strategy, namely, *coding by matching*, in which a local image part is represented by as few as possible (ideally one) template functions that provide a good fit (according to some criterion) to the form of the local signal. Transform coders as well as vector quantizers can also be seen as members of this class. What is necessary for an optimal exploitation of 1D-signals by the matching strategy? To completely specify a 1D-signal we need information about (a) its profile, that is, specification of a one-dimensional function; (b) its orientation; and (c) its position and length. This information can, in principle, be provided by the template-matching procedure. However, the matching strategy may easily run into combinatorial problems. First, a vast variety of templates has to be provided, then a decision has to be made about which combination of templates will give the best match, that is, one has to find the best subset among a huge set of templates with massive overlap in both space and frequency. This produces an optimization problem.

The problem may be simplified either by restricting it to the determination of the single "best" matching template within a small area (VQ) or by using a more-or-less orthogonal set of templates, as in the decomposition by orientation-and-size selective filters or in subband and transform coding. In the latter schemes the optimization problem can partially be avoided, since each matching coefficient can be determined independently of the other ones.

However, with a "small" set of orthogonal templates the matching efficiency will be suboptimal. This can be illustrated by regarding the problem of determining the optimal orientation bandwidth (and by that the optimal length of the kernel and the related spatial sampling) for the example of figure 10.6. It is evident that a maximal concentration of activity can be achieved if the orientation bandwidth and, correspondingly, the length of the filter kernel is matched to the length of the edges. If the kernel is too short, more nonzero samples are needed to represent the edges. If it is too long, several filters will jointly respond to all shorter-edge patterns. These conflicting demands will enforce a single "optimum" length matched to the statistics of natural image signals, which can only be a compromise, however. Simulations yield a compromise length corresponding to an orientation bandwidth around 30 deg, the value commonly encountered with cortical neurons (Field, 1987; Zetzsche, 1988).

The problem of optimal sampling along the preferred orientation cannot be solved by the provision of multiple scales, since the signal has to be split into orientation-specific channels on each level of resolution. In addition, these considerations indicate that the non-orientation-specific sampling scheme and the nonseparate processing of oblique orientations in subband coders may hinder a more efficient exploitation of 1D-signals.

To summarize, the "local straightness" of natural image signals causes important higher-order statistical properties that cannot be described by the available second-order theory. However, it can be shown by heuristic arguments that these higher-order dependencies can be exploited partially—and from the theoretical point of view "accidentally"—by any linear scheme using an orientation-specific decomposition of the image signal, be it by cortical simple cells and the corresponding HVS-based coders, or even by subband and transform coding schemes. However, even with an optimal compromise for the orientation bandwidth, the higher-order statistical dependencies cannot fully be exploited by matching schemes, because they would require a huge number of templates and of complicated optimization procedures. The basic alternative to the matching strategy is a special kind of nonlinear predictive coding, which we discuss in the next section. But first we analyze the statistical dependencies that remain (in spite of decorrelation) between the outputs of simple cells located at the same visual position but differing in symmetry, preferred size, or preferred orientation.

Statistical Dependencies between Uncorrelated Orientation Filter Outputs

Decorrelation and Statistical Independence

What would be most desirable for the exploitation of statistical dependencies is the mapping of the dependent input signal onto *statistically independent* output variables. What is obtained by the linear filtering properties of cortical simple cells (and similarly by predictive, transform, and subband schemes) are *decorrelated* output variables. Although statistical independence necessarily implies decorrelation, the reverse is true only for Gaussian signals (e.g., Papoulis, 1984). Unfortunately, the outputs of simple cells and image coders are definitely non-Gaussian. This

implies that there may remain substantial statistical dependencies between the outputs of simple cells that, however, cannot be exploited by any further linear processing. The redundancy reduction hypotheses will, therefore, predict that the subsequent cortical stages have to be nonlinear. For the extension of our theoretical concepts into this territory two points need to be considered: (1) the systematic evaluation of the multivariate statistics of filter outputs and (2) the derivation of appropriate nonlinear signal-processing models.

Complex Cells and the Analytic Signal

The biological system (in contrast with some technical subband schemes) uses both even- and odd-symmetric filters for signal decomposition. Although a filter pair in quadrature relationship is orthogonal and therefore produces perfectly uncorrelated output signals, our simulations with natural images have revealed a substantial remaining statistical dependency between the joint local outputs of cells with even- and odd-symmetric receptive fields (Wegmann and Zetzsche, 1990a). This is evident from the form of the measured two-dimensional pdf, which is circular symmetric but non-Gaussian. However, statistically independent variables can easily be generated by a *nonlinear* coordinate transform. Using the concept of the analytic signal (Bracewell, 1965), one can convert the local signals from a Cartesian (even/odd) to a polar (amplitude/phase) representation (Zetzsche and Schönecker, 1987; Morrone and Owens, 1987; Wegmann and Zetzsche, 1990a). Computation of the amplitude part of the analytic signal may be performed by "complex" cortical cells (Adelson and Bergen, 1985; Morrone and Burr, 1988).

The nonlinear transform of the analytic signal converts certain higher-order statistical dependencies into second-order dependencies that can then be exploited by linear operations (Field, 1989; Zetzsche, 1988). This becomes evident by considering, for example, the regularities in textures. The demodulating properties of the local-filter amplitude (energy) convert the strongly varying input texture signal into an internal representation in which each texture region is characterized by a homogeneous, nonvarying level of activity. This homogeneity is a second-order property that can be exploited by decorrelating operations on subsequent stages (edge detectors in biology, predictive, subband, or transform schemes in image coding).

Figure 10.8
Joint probability density function of four orientation filter outputs.
Shown is a pseudo three-dimensional visualization obtained by
projection of the four-dimensional space. 0D-signals are located at
the origin. 1D-signals are located on axes or on the horizontal plane,
that is, between axes with neighboring orientations. 2D-signals are
located in the residual space (the cube on the lower right), and it can
be seen that the occupation density of this residual space is very
low—That is, it is a rare event that several orientation filters respond
simultaneously at the same location.

In addition to the statistical dependencies between cells
with equal orientation and size preference there exist also
dependencies between cells with different tuning parameters. (These dependencies should be differentiated from
the small remaining correlation due to the imperfect
orthogonality of, e.g., Gabor-like visual filter functions).
The statistical dependencies across scales (radial frequencies) caused by the presence of edges have already
been recognized as coincidences of zero-crossings by Marr

and Hildreth (1980). The nonlinear transformation into an
amplitude/phase representation converts these interscale
dependencies into correlations between the amplitudes/
energies of filters from different scales. These may then be
exploited by subsequent linear operations, for example,
by simple summation across scales. Even more interesting,
however, are the interorientation dependencies between
neurons with different orientation preferences.

Interorientation Statistical Dependencies

The amplitudes of several filters with different orientations at joint spatial positions can be treated as a vector
source. The corresponding multivariate statistical distribution obtained by simulations with natural input images
revealed the existence of important interorientation statistical dependencies (Wegmann and Zetzsche, 1990b). The
main results were that: (a) In most cases a near-zero-length

vector is obtained (i.e., no filter responds at all, as expected due to the isotropic dependencies). (b) In many cases the signals are straight (anisotropic statistical dependencies), that is, a single filter responds and the vector falls directly on one axis, or two neighboring filters respond, and the vector falls in the plane spanned by the corresponding axes. (c) The remaining space (i.e., joint responses of several filters) is far less densely populated than would be expected from the assumption of statistical independence. A three-dimensional-projection of the multidimensional pdf is shown in figure 10.8.

This specific form of the pdf implies that in technical procedures such as LBG vector quantization most "resources" (vectors) will get allocated to the origin region, some to the axes, but only very few (if any) to the multi-filter-response region. However, such an allocation strategy has been shown to be suboptimal with respect to perceived quality (Wegmann and Zetzsche, 1991a). The suboptimality in the region around the origin is due to an unnecessarily precise representation of low-contrast stimuli and can be straightforwardly explained by the threshold properties of the biological system. However, finding a reason why the removal and/or manipulation of a few, statistically rare patterns should cause strong visual impairments is a more intricate problem.

Intrinsically Two-Dimensional Signals

Psychophysical and Neurophysiological Evidence

What are those seldomly occurring structures that are nevertheless so important for perception? It is simply the class of local signals that are not straight, that is, *intrinsically two-dimensional* or *2D-signals* in our notation. Indeed, such signals play a special role in biological vision. Massive evidence for the relevance of 2D-signals in visual information processing has been accumulated during the last three decades.

A well-known example from psychology is the famous *Attneave cat* (figure 10.9). Attneave performed a series of experiments in which subjects had to rate the importance of the various points in a line drawing. The main result was that extrema of *curvature* were rated to be most "informative" (Attneave, 1954). The Attneave cat is a striking example of this effect, since it resulted from simply joining the corresponding sparse set of informative

points by straight-line segments. Hence, it was as early as 1954 that the relation between intrinsic dimensionality and information theoretical redundancy, and the importance of these phenomena for human vision were recognized. Attneave's concept was later successfully extended to topics like eye-movement control (Mackworth and Morandi, 1967) and human object recognition (Biedermann, 1985).

In the "opposite" branch of vision research, in visual neurophysiology, evidence for the importance of intrinsically two-dimensional signals is equally old. The famous "bug detector" is an early example of a neuron that is completely insensitive to any kind of 0D- or 1D-signal, be it a straight line, a straight border, a sinusoidal grating, or whatever kind of constant or straight pattern (Lettvin et al., 1959). The same is true for hypercomplex or end-stopped cells in the primary areas of the visual cortex (Hubel and Wiesel, 1965) and for the recently discovered dot-responsive cells (Saito et al., 1988). It has been suggested that end-stopped cells also provide the input for higher-order neurons capable of "seeing" illusory contours (von der Heydt et al., 1984). There is also an interesting and hitherto unnoticed relationship between the end-stopping property and the unique determination of optic flow (Zetzsche et al., 1991).

Various kinds of psychophysical phenomena associated with 2D-signals and posing serious problems for the standard filter approach have been reported. These comprise

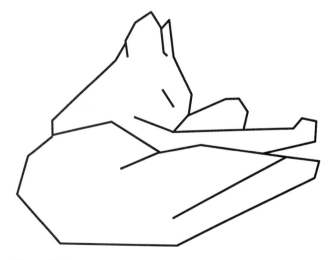

Figure 10.9
The famous Attneave cat (redrawn after Attneave, 1954). This was an early demonstration of the importance of 2D-signals. The drawing resulted from simply joining curvature extrema.

effects due to superimposed gratings found with evoked potentials (Regan and Regan, 1987), discrimination and detection (Olzak and Thomas, 1991), and masking (Derrington and Henning, 1989).

Why is it that biological vision systems treat 2D-signals as something special? As late successors of Attneave (1954), Barlow (1960), and other authors, we suggest that it is their potential for the reduction of redundancy that makes 2D-signals so important. In the following we therefore try to show in which sense 2D-signals capture non-redundant information in images and why the extraction of this information necessitates a quite specific kind of nonlinear operation.

Basic Requirements for 2D-Detectors: Nonlinear Operations and Differential Geometry

It is interesting to note that the detection of 2D-signals has to be an essentially nonlinear operation (Zetzsche and Barth, 1990a). The reason for this is that linear systems can be seen to perform an *or*-type of operation (a weighted superposition) on their strictly one-dimensional eigenfunctions. For such systems it is always possible to find a suitable 1D-signal that will cause a nonzero output. Finding the adequate nonlinear operation is no trivial problem.

Nonlinear systems are not simply some special subset but comprise the major part of all possible systems, excluding the small class of linear systems. Obviously, a structuring principle is needed for the development of a theory for 2D-signal detectors. Differential geometry can provide an adequate starting point.

The connection between surface differential geometry and images has been employed in technical image processing for quite a long time (e.g., Beaudet, 1978; Haralick et al., 1983; Besl and Jain, 1988). In theories of biological vision it has only recently appeared (Koenderink and van Doorn, 1987; Zetzsche and Barth, 1990a,b). Differential geometry is relevant for 2D-signal detection because it contains a concept closely related to intrinsic dimensionality, namely, Gaussian curvature.

The only conceptual step needed for the application of differential geometry to images is to regard the two-dimensional luminance function as a surface in three-dimensional space. The image can then be characterized in terms of surface properties. This is schematically illustrated in figure 10.10 for a band-limited image consisting of a bright square on a dark background. This picture can also serve as a demonstration for the connection between the information content of certain signal types (in terms

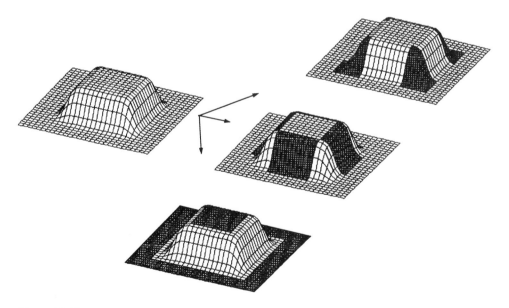

Figure 10.10
Surface representation of a bright square on a dark background. The basic surface types can be classified as (top) planar (0D-signals); (middle) parabolic (1D-signals); and (bottom) elliptic/hyperbolic (2D-signals).

of statistical dependencies) and the corresponding surface types. Planelike surfaces (e.g., the interior of the square or the surround) show no signal variation at all. They can hence be seen as 0D-signals and exhibit an extreme type of isotropic statistical dependency. These surfaces are called *planar*. Surfaces that show a variation along one orientation but are perfectly constant along the other one (like the straight edges of the square) are called *parabolic*. They correspond to 1D-signals and constitute strong higher-order, anisotropic statistical dependencies. It is interesting to note that planar and parabolic are *extrinsic* surface properties, that is, they are determined by the *embedding* of the surface and are equivalent with respect to their *intrinsic* structure. The extrinsic properties can be differentiated by linear operations; hence, linear filters and transforms can perfectly exploit the isotropic statistical dependencies imposed by 0D-signals. However, the most important distinction is not between 0D- and 1D-signals but between 1D- and 2D-signals. This distinction refers to intrinsic surface properties. In differential geometry the central intrinsic concept is Gaussian curvature. Surfaces for which it is impossible to find an orientation along which they are constant (e.g., the corners of the square) have nonzero Gaussian curvature. They are called *elliptic* or *hyperbolic*, depending on the type of variation.

We can think of the planar and parabolic surfaces as consisting of sheets of paper or metal. Such surfaces can be bent (i.e., the embedding can be changed) without changing their intrinsic properties. Curved surfaces, however, can be generated only by distorting deformations (paper will be creased or even torn; metal will be embossed). We claim that these regions represent the essential information in images. We discuss this point in more detail later in this section.

There is no perfect one-to-one relationship between the concept of intrinsic dimensionality and the surface classification in differential geometry (Zetzsche and Barth, 1990b). Loosely speaking, the dimensionality concept is less rigid than the geometrical one. We discuss the benefits of this in the following section.

General Detectors for 2D-Signals

The modeling of the variety of 2D-specific cells and the development of efficient 2D-signal-processing algorithms requires the availability of an adequate nonlinear theory. Differential geometry, though a good starting point, is too restricted for a general signal-processing framework, mainly due to its limitation to infinitesimal calculus. For example, in cases where the 2D-detector output should be the only information to be retained, the low sensitivity and the extreme invariance properties of Gaussian curvature may cause too unspecific a representation (Zetzsche and Barth, 1990b). Due to their low sensitivity, curvature operators based on second-order derivatives can detect only high-contrast, sharply curved features like isolated spots and corners. Furthermore, the inherent instability of the differentiation may enforce an unspecific, extensive smoothing of the data to obtain stable results. Another important point is that the pure, geometrically intrinsic information seems not to be sufficient for intensity image-processing applications. Gaussian curvature is invariant not only with respect to a rotation in the $(x\text{-}y)$ plane but also with respect to the orientation of the surface normal in $(x\text{-}y\text{-}z)$ space, making, for example, both "peaks" and "pits" equivalent.

It appears that these problems are also relevant in biological vision. Hypercomplex cells, for example, are not rotation invariant but show a definite anisotropic behavior. Our analysis revealed that increased curvature sensitivity can be obtained only if more narrowly tuned, orientation-specific receptive fields are used instead of first- or second-order-derivative operators with their extremely broad orientation tuning. Furthermore, end-stopped cells seem to come up with various phase relationships, thereby enabling a more specific representation of the form of 2D-signals. Also, even visual cells of lower animals can easily differentiate between peaks and pits, as is apparent from the famous bug detector in the frog retina.

Obviously, a more general theoretical framework has to be developed to cope with these problems. However, the concept of Gaussian curvature is ideally suited as a starting point and for illustration of the basic requirements for more general 2D-detectors. The classification properties of Gaussian curvature are completely determined by the determinant of the Hessian $\text{DET} = l_{xx}l_{yy} - l_{xy}^2$, where $l = l(x, y)$ denotes the two-dimensional luminance function, and subscripts denote partial differentiation (e.g., $l_{xy} = \partial l/\partial x\,\partial y$) in the respective direction. (Note that some extrinsic information is already incorporated by the DET-operator, which, unlike Gaussian curvature, is not invariant to all rigid motions of the surface). From the above formula the essential requirements for general 2D-detectors may be identified. The first requirement is the provision of at least two elementary measurements of signal variation (l_{xx} and l_{yy}). In the general case these may be linear filter operations that may or may not overlap in their orientation tuning (the measurements must not be completely independent) but have to comprise some nonoverlapping orientations. It should be noted that this implies that both cannot be isotropic. An important consequence of this is that anisotropic, orientation-selective operations are a *necessary prerequisite* for the extraction of 2D-information. This is a new aspect of the functional role of cortical orientation specificity (Barth and Zetzsche, 1991).

The results of the elementary measurements then have to be combined in an *and*-like fashion, for example, by multiplication (remember the restriction to *or*-operations in linear systems). Obviously, a necessary condition for the detection of 2D-signals is the joint indication of a signal variation by at least two measurements. However, this is not sufficient in general. If the elementary measurements overlap, as in case of the second-order derivatives in DET, a 1D-signal may cause a simultaneous output from both measurements that, by the *and*-rule, will lead to an erroneous response. This can be avoided by a suitable control term (a kind of bias estimate) with which the result of the *and*-combination has to be compared. In case of Gaussian curvature the subtraction of the second term $l_{xy}{}^2$ can be seen as an appropriate "coordinate rotation."

Starting from these considerations we have developed a generalized theoretical framework for 2D-specific signal processing based on our concept of *intrinsic dimensionality* (Zetzsche and Barth, 1990a,b). This concept is more flexible than the rigid geometric definition and seems to be gaining acceptance for the characterization of neurons with end-stopping and related properties (e.g., Heitger et al., 1992). The generalized framework provides three essential advantages over the differential geometry approach:

1. It enables use of arbitrary filter operations instead of derivatives.

2. It provides an alternative interpretation of the influence of $l_{xy}{}^2$. Since the description as coordinate rotation is valid only for certain isotropic 2D-detectors, we have introduced the more general concept of the *compensation principle* for the description of such an "inhibitory" interaction

(Zetzsche and Barth, 1990a,b). With this formal concept it is possible to avoid the main problem of a heuristic development of 2D-detector models (e.g., Dobbins, Cynader, and Zucker, 1989), that is, the risk of "false responses" (Zetzsche and Barth, 1990a; see also Heitger et al., 1992).

3. The present approach enables a simple differentiation between peaks and pits in a biologically realistic setting. This can be obtained using a special kind of 2D-detector, the *clipped eigenvalues* (Zetzsche and Barth, 1990b). These are derived from the eigenvalues of the Hessian matrix that represent the second-order derivatives in the direction of the principal axes. Loosely speaking, the eigenvalues can be seen to encode certain extrema of 2D-signal variation. Generalized biological analogues can be obtained by nonlinear combinations of orientation filter outputs. The eigenvalues themselves are obviously not 2D-detectors, since one of them will always give a nonzero response to 1D-signals. However, a suitably chosen one-way rectification (the naturally occurring data format in physiology!) will yield a peak and a pit detector. These detectors can be seen as "measuring" the signal variation along the orientation with the smallest amount of variation (in the case of 1D-signals this amount will be zero). This automatic adjustment to an optimal axis is of special conceptual importance because it reveals that the nonlinear 2D-detectors can equivalently be seen as locally adaptive linear orientation filters. This should be no surprise, since we have already seen that the exploitation of the statistical dependencies imposed by orientations (1D-signals) in images can be achieved only by nonlinear or adaptive linear schemes. This observation indicates that principles derived from biological structures may constitute a starting point for the development of nonlinear image-coding algorithms.

Based on these properties, the approach allows the design of a variety of 2D-detectors with adjustable tuning properties, phase relationships, and classification characteristics. These comprise models for bug detectors, dot-responsive cells, and various sorts of hypercomplex cells, including a curvature energy detector (Zetzsche and Barth, 1990a,b). Examples are shown in figure 10.11. Furthermore, the approach can be seen as a first step toward a general theoretical framework for 2D-specific signal processing. The curvature detectors suggested by Koenderink and Richards (1988), for example, can be interpreted as a special case by realizing that they cannot be seen as linear

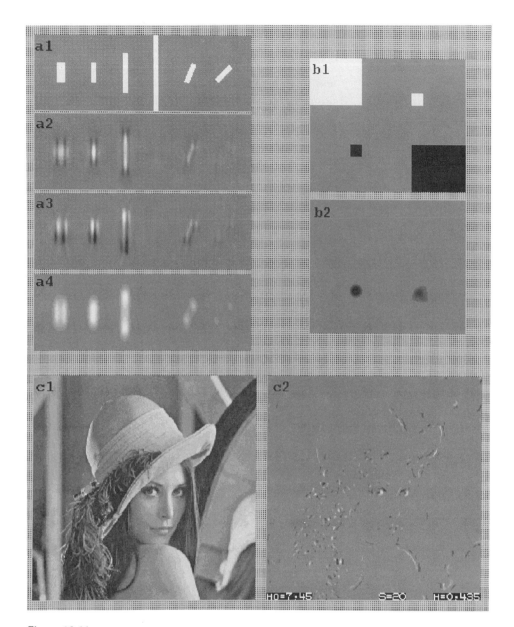

Figure 10.11
Various examples of 2D-detectors. (a) Hypercomplex cell, (al) input
image, (a2),(a3) responses of cells with different symmetry
combinations (even-even and odd-even); note the anisotropic
properties (lowered response to tilted bar) and the end-stopping (no
response to extended straight line), (a4) phase-independent curvature
amplitude can also be computed from these cells. (b) Bug detector,
(b1) input, (b2) response. The detector responds to neither straight
patterns nor to bright spots or edges. (c) Clipped eigenvalues of a
natural image, (c1) input, (c2) response. Even with strong
thresholding the significant information is preserved.

filters (or receptive fields of the simple cell type) but require a highly nonlinear, *and*-like interaction of orientation filters as a prerequisite (Zetzsche and Barth, 1990b). Similarly, the operators suggested by Heitger et al. (1992) fit our compensation principle, since false responses are avoided by inhibitory interactions of orientation filters.

A central question with respect to the redundancy reduction hypothesis is how much information can be retained by the representations obtained from 2D-detectors and how this depends on the specific properties of the 2D-detectors employed.

Predictability of 1D-Signals from 2D-Information

We have already seen that linear operations can only partially exploit the anisotropic statistical dependencies introduced by the common occurrence of locally straight patterns (1D-signals) in natural images, since the matching strategy will be either suboptimal or will run into combinatorial problems.

The alternative is an indirect specification of 1D-signals by *boundary information:* If we connect 1D-signals that are not collinear, we need 2D-signals for the "junctions." If the position and shape of these 2D-signals is completely specified, the possible 1D-signals in between are also specified. This can be conceived most easily by considering again the example in figure 10.10. How can the curved parts of figure 10.10 be connected by using only planar or parabolic surfaces (i.e., with sheets of paper that are allowed only to be smoothly bent)? It is obvious that there cannot exist many possibilities to do this; there might even exist only a unique solution. This implies that non-curved surface parts are highly redundant, since they are predictable from the knowledge of the 2D-signals. Once the 2D-information is specified, only a few additional bits (if any) are needed to resolve the remaining uncertainty.

The two complementary approaches, matching versus providing two-dimensional boundary information, are basically equivalent in their potential to uniquely specify image signals. However, the 2D-approach can cope with the optimum-length problem without running into combinatorial problems, and it can be expected to work with a fixed, comparably small set of form parameters for the description of the shape of the junction points. The only remaining problem is the detection and representation of this 2D-information by local operations, and this seems to be exactly what end-stopped cells in the visual cortex are

doing. A redundancy reduction, however, can be obtained by 2D-features only if their probability of occurrence is low compared with the 0D- and 1D-signals, that is, if they are "sparse." White noise, for example, consists entirely of 2D-signals. Fortunately, as we have already seen, the physical and biological tendency toward a compact and homogeneous aggregation of matter is in favor of a sparse distribution of 2D-signals in natural images. This has also been verified empirically by analysis of the corresponding multivariate statistics (Wegmann and Zetzsche, 1990b).

Uniqueness and Invertibility

The ability to extract essential or even unique information from images does not imply that an invertible transform is easily available. For general information-processing systems this is not necessary, since there the determining factor is the potential for deriving inferences, generalizing, generating hypotheses to guide further actions, and the like. The visual system has an interest in, for example, the selection of informative points to guide its eye movements or in the inference of three-dimensional shape from luminance data but has no need to reconstruct the retinal image. In such a context, invertibility is only of theoretical interest in the sense that the inverted signal may be regarded as an indicator of the significance or non-redundancy of the features extracted. Of course, invertibility is of direct interest for image-coding applications.

In the case of linear operations, as in predictive, transform, and filter-based coding schemes the inversion problem reduces to some form of weighted integration, but not so for essentially nonlinear transformations. Basically, a moderate and an extreme way of incorporating the concept of intrinsic dimensionality into image-coding applications can be distinguished. In the moderate version bit allocation is matched to intrinsic dimensionality, that is, more bits per area are allocated to 2D- than to 1D- or even 0D-signals. In the extreme version, reconstruction has to be based on a 2D-only representation.

A tendency toward dimensionality-specific bit allocation is already present in HVS-based filter decompositions followed by entropy coding. By using short code words for zero outputs and longer ones for nonzero outputs most bits are allocated to 2D-signals, since it is only for these signals that several orientation filters jointly respond at the same location. Fewer bits are allocated to 1D-signals, to which only one (or two neighboring) orientation filters respond. 0D-signals get allocated the least number of bits per area, since only filters from a lower level of resolution may respond.

For an extreme version, namely, 2D-only coding by the DET operator, reconstruction corresponds to the solution of the Monge-Ampère differential equation for which solutions only for restricted cases are known (e.g., Gilberg and Trudinger, 1983). Also, in general, only convex surfaces are determined by their Gaussian curvature values (Chern, 1957; Efimov, 1957). This is closely related to the more general problem of how the embedding of a manifold into a higher-dimensional space is restricted by its intrinsic properties. Theoretically, it is known that there exist certain ambiguous cases where different surfaces have equal Gaussian curvature, but it is not known how strongly this ambiguity is reduced for extended sets of connected "patches" with varying properties and, eventually, additional boundary conditions. Intuitively, however, ambiguity seems to be drastically reduced for the latter case.

Between the extreme ends—reconstruction from purely intrinsic information on one side, and implicit bit allocation in HVS-based orientation filter decompositions on the other side—a variety of mixed approaches can be considered. For example, certain extrinsic properties, but only from 2D-regions, may be included. For luminance itself, reconstruction would correspond to the interpolation of irregularly spaced samples. Alternatively, or in addition, higher-order information from 2D-regions may be used, for example, in the form of coefficients obtained by linear and/or nonlinear operations. In the perfect limit, reconstruction corresponds to the problem considered in figure 10.10: How to connect completely specified 2D-regions using solely 0D- and 1D-signals (paperlike surfaces).

In realistic applications, however, neither the classification and description nor the connecting process will be perfect. Of course, then, the amount of specification has to be traded-off against the number of samples selected. From the conceptual point of view, however, the extreme 2D-only representations are the most interesting ones.

Reconstruction from a 2D-Scale-Space Representation

We investigated reconstruction from a 2D-only representation. For this representation we used two modifications with respect to the geometric intrinsic information provided by Gaussian curvature. First, we used additional extrinsic information about whether a 2D-signal is positive or negative elliptic, that is, of the peak or the pit type. This information can be obtained from the clipped eigenvalues, discussed previously. In addition, we provided this 2D-information on several scales of resolution. The resulting representation can be seen as a *2D-scale space* or, appropriately subsampled, as a *two-dimensional pyramid*. We expect that for some of the arguments in favor of zero-crossings from scale-space a counterpart for the 2D-scale-space can be found. From this point of view the essential structure of an image can be seen to be determined by the treelike ramification of "2D-veins" in 2D-scale-space.

For the reconstruction we employed a relaxation paradigm that minimizes a cost-function defined as the difference between the 2D-scale-space representations of the reconstructed and of the original image. Additional energy terms ensure the spatial and scale continuity. The algorithm works from low to high resolution, so that at each new scale it starts with the expanded results from the previous, lower scale. A detailed description of the reconstruction procedure can be found in Barth et al. (1992).

An example for the reconstruction from a 2D-scale-space representation is shown in figure 10.12. On the left side the original input image is shown. The series of images in the upper right part is the 2D-scale-space representation based on the clipped eigenvalues. It can be seen that this representation is considerably more sparse than, for example, a Laplacian pyramid. (In the two-dimensional representation a threshold of 4 percent leads to 93 percent zero-valued samples at the highest resolution level. To obtain the same degree of sparseness in the Laplacian pyramid a threshold of 15 percent is needed.) In the lower half the corresponding reconstruction is shown. The reconstruction demonstrates that, in spite of its sparseness, the two-dimensional representation captures the essential image information.

However, the conditions for an optimal reconstruction are not yet fully understood. For example, we have not yet succeeded in enforcing an appropriately increasing "stiffness" of the non-two-dimensional regions during the relaxation process. It can therefore be expected that even better reconstructions can be obtained with a deeper insight into the optimal tailoring of energy terms.

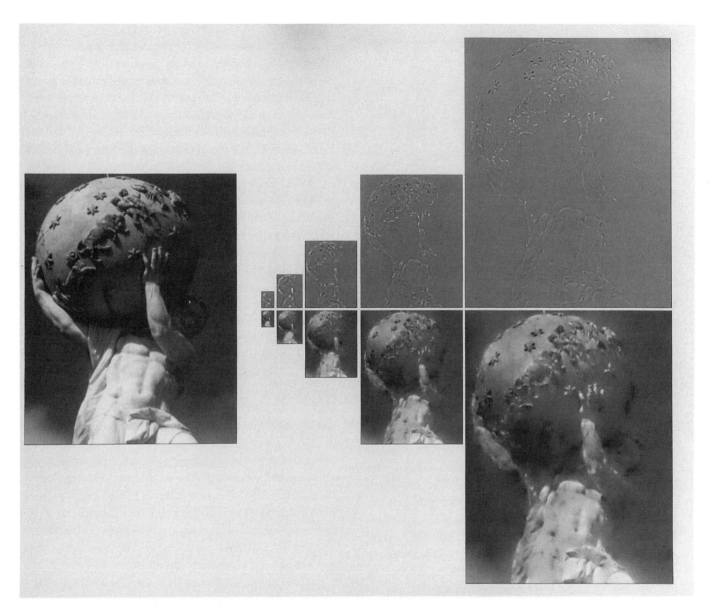

Figure 10.12
Reconstruction from a 2D-scale-space representation. The original image is shown on the left side. The corresponding 2D-scale-space representation is shown as an appropriately subsampled pyramid on the upper right side. The reconstruction, as proceeding from lower to higher resolution, is shown below.

Conclusion

It is commonly believed by vision scientists and communication engineers that the relevant properties of biological spatial vision are given by its limits, for example, by absolute and increment thresholds of spatial visibility. In this chapter we have argued for an alternative view, namely that an essential feature of biological vision is the reduction of redundancy. Although there have been early claims in that direction (e.g., Barlow, 1960), only recently have the processing structures found in early vision received a more thorough analysis in terms of information and communication theory (Field, 1987; Zetzsche and Schönecker, 1987; Wegmann and Zetzsche, 1990a,b). An important quantitative confirmation for the appropriateness of such an approach was obtained by extensive simulations of the biological processing of natural images. These showed that the transformation of natural image signals into the corresponding internal representations yields a significant reduction of redundancy. An indirect confirmation of this observation can also be seen in the success of HVS-based coding schemes in recent years (e.g., Watson, 1987).

A somewhat surprising result, from the viewpoint of psychophysics and biology, was that neither a description of the most elementary structural properties of natural image signals nor the appropriate methods for their exploitation can be easily derived from modern communication theory. This has been illustrated by the "blindness" of second-order statistics with respect to orientation in images. A related result was that it seems impossible to find any theoretical relationship between orientation specificity (of kernels or basis images in modern image-coding schemes or of receptive fields in artificial neural networks) and the frequent occurrence of oriented structures in images, if such a relation is sought within the available framework of linear systems and second-order statistics.

The statistical properties caused by orientations in images can be analyzed in two complementary fashions that cannot be differentiated on the basis of observable data. One view is that images are generated by a composite source with a nonprobabilistic intrarealization nonstationarity. Although the resulting ensemble is indeed stationary, a suitable linearization may enable the con-struction of adaptive coding schemes that are superior to the optimal stationary solution as obtainable by second-order theory. An alternative and more general view is that the statistical properties caused by local oriented structures are regarded as higher-order statistical dependencies that require nonlinear operations for their exploitation. Together with the observation of the special status of 2D-signals in biological vision this indicates that the derivation of two-dimensional-specific nonlinear operations is relevant to both image data compression and the modeling of biological vision. Differential geometry was identified as providing a suitable starting point for the development of the necessary nonlinear concepts. However, having in mind the fruitless efforts spent in the Fourier/feature debate, it seems unwise to expect from a single mathematical theory a complete explanation of visual perception. Rather, we should ask for the essential properties of the theory with respect to the modeling of visual functions. With respect to the derivation of suitable nonlinear operations the essential principle may be identified as *intrinsic dimensionality*, a sufficiently structuring but not too restrictive concept for the exploration of the relevant subregion of the vast diversity of nonlinear operations. This is so due to its close relationship to the important theoretical concepts of statistical redundancy and adaptive processing. The connection between redundancy reduction and nonlinear 2D-detectors has been demonstrated empirically by the reconstruction of an image from its 2D-scale-space representation. The development of a comprehensive nonlinear, higher-order theory remains a challenge for the future.

Unlike communication technology, however, biology cannot be interested in a mere compression of the incoming data. The type of entropy reduction performed in biological vision does not per se reduce the numbers of fibers and neurons needed to transport and to represent the retinal image (this would require a biologically implausible variable-word-length coding). That simple data compression cannot be the essential goal is also evident from the enormous extent and complexity of cortical machinery, which provides about 1000 cortical neurons per retinal cone for the primary processing of visual information (Kronauer and Zeevi, 1985). Rather, relevant criteria for a biological, multipurpose image-processing and pattern recognition system are the limitation of wiring complexity, the minimization of energy consumption, and the optimization of memory functions. These requirements are supported by the linear and nonlinear transformations of early vision. They provide a sparse distribution of activity, that is, a representation well suited to reducing the immense combinatorial problems in further processing. Typical advantages of such a representation are, for example, the simplification of feature extraction and of classificationlike operations, which can operate on reduced signal-subspaces (i.e., with fewer "wires") without a significant loss in discriminatory power (e.g., Tou and Gonzalez, 1974; see also Zetzsche and Caelli, 1989); the efficient use of storage capacities by associative memories (Zetzsche, 1990); and the simplified extraction of invariances (Zetzsche and Caelli, 1989; Zetzsche and Barth, 1990b).

Taken together, these considerations lead us to propose a *convergence hypothesis:* We expect that models and theoretical concepts in biological vision research and image coding will continuously converge toward a substantial common basis. The main reason for this is the common "interest" of technical and biological systems to "explain" as much as possible of a given input signal by providing as compact a code as possible. We are aware that planes are not birds, however. What we expect is not a simple structural identity of image coders and models of biological vision, although this may happen to a surprising degree at the low-level stages. Rather, we look forward to the development of a general theoretical framework for two-dimensional-feature extraction that may be useful in a variety of image-processing problems. The analysis of biological vision in terms of redundancy reduction should not be seen as an alternative but as an extension of current research strategies. Communication engineers will have a valuable source of heuristics that, we hope, may help them further to extend the scope of their theories. Vision scientists, meanwhile, will obtain a valuable set of theoretical and practical concepts that will allow them a deeper insight into an essential aspect of visual information processing.

Acknowledgment

We thank G. Krieger for programming assistance and I. Rentschler and the reviewers for helpful comments.

This work has been supported by DFG grant Re337/7-1 to I. Rentschler and C.Z.

References

Adelson, E. H. & J. R. Bergen (1985). Spatiotemporal energy models for the perception of motion. *Journal of the Optical Society of America* A2:284–299.

Ahmed, N. & K. R. Rao (1975). *Orthogonal Transforms for Digital Signal Processing*. New York, Heidelberg: Springer.

Appelle, S. (1972). Perception and discrimination as a function of stimulus orientation: The oblique effect in man and animals. *Psychological Bulletin* 78:266–278.

Attneave, F. (1954) Some informational aspects of visual perception. *Psychological Review* 61:183–193.

Barlow, H. B. (1960). "The Coding of Sensory Messages." In W. H. Thorpe and O. L. Zangwill (Eds.), *Current Problems in Animal Behavior* Cambridge: Cambridge University Press, 331–360.

Barth, E. & C. Zetzsche (1991). The functional role of orientation selectivity revisited. *Perception* 20:70.

Barth, E., T. M. Caelli & C. Zetzsche (1992). Image encoding, labelling and reconstruction from differential geometry. *Computer Vision, Graphics, and Image Processing*. Forthcoming.

Beaudet, P. R. (1978). Rotationally invariant image operators. *4th International Joint Conference on Pattern Recognition* ICPR-78:578–583. Kyoto, Japan.

Berger, T. (1972). *Rate Distortion Theory*. Englewood Cliffs, N. J.: Prentice Hall.

Besl, P. J. & R. C. Jain (1988). Segmentation through variable-order surface fitting. *IEEE Transactions on Pattern Analysis and Machine Intelligence* PAMI-10:167–192.

Biedermann, I. (1985). Human image understanding: Recent research and a theory. *Computer Vision Graphics and Image Processing* 32:29–73.

Bracewell, R. N. (1965). *The Fourier Transform and its Applications*. New York: McGraw-Hill.

Burt, P. J. & E. H. Adelson (1983). The Laplacian pyramid as a compact image code. *IEEE Transactions on Communications* COM-31:532–540.

Campbell, F. W. & J. G. Robson (1968). Application of Fourier analysis to the visibility of gratings. *Journal of Physiology* 197:551–566.

Chern (1957). A proof of the uniqueness of Minkowski's problem for convex surfaces. *American Journal of Mathematics* 79:949–950.

Dobbins, A., S. W. Zucker & M. S. Cynader (1989) Endstopping and curvature. *Vision Research* 29:1371–1387.

Daugman, J. D. (1985). Uncertainty relation for resolution in space, spatial frequency, and orientation optimized by two-dimensional visual cortical filters. *Journal of the Optical Society of America* A2:1160–1169.

Daugman, J. D. (1989). Entropy reduction and decorrelation in visual coding by oriented neural receptive fields. *IEEE Transactions on Biomedical Engineering* 36:107–114.

Derrington, A. M. & G. B. Henning (1989). Some observations on the masking effects of two-dimensional stimuli. *Vision Research* 29:241–246.

Dobbins, Efimov, N. W. (1957). *Flächenverbiegung im Großen*. Berlin: Academie.

Field, D. J. (1987) Relations between the statistics of natural images and the response properties of cortical cells. *Journal of the Optical Society of America A*4:2379–2394.

Field, D. J. (1989). What the statistics of natural images tell us about visual coding. In B. E. Rogowitz (Ed.), *Human Vision, Visual Processing, and Digital Display, Proc. SPIE* 1077: 269–279.

Fiorentini, A., M. Jeanne & G. Toraldo di Francia (1955). Measurement of differential threshold in the presence of spatial illumination gradient. *Atti. Fond. Georgio Ronchi* 12: 371–379.

Fontana, R. J., R. M. Gray & J. C. Kieffer (1981). Asymptotically mean stationary channels. *IEEE Transactions on Information Theory* IT-27(3): 308–316.

Gardner, W. A. (1986). *Introduction to Random Processes with Applications to Signals and Systems*. New York: Macmillan.

Georgeson, M. A. & G. D. Sullivan (1975). Contrast constancy: Deblurring in human vision by spatial frequency. *Journal of Physiology, London* 252:627–656.

Gilberg, D. & N. Trudinger (1983). *Elliptic Partial Differential Equations of Second Order*. Berlin, New York: Springer.

Girod, B. (1989). The information theoretical significance of spatial and temporal masking in video signals. In B. E. Rogowitz (Ed.), *Human Vision, Visual Processing, and Digital Display, Proc. SPIE* 1077: 178–187.

Habibi, A. (1977) Survey of adaptive image coding techniques. *IEEE Transactions on Communication* COM-25:1275–1284.

Haralick, R. M., L. T. Watson & T. J. Laffey (1983). The topographic primal sketch. *International Journal of Robotics Research* 2:50–72.

Haykin, S. (1986). *Adaptive Filter Theory*. Englewood Cliffs, N. J.: Prentice Hall.

Heitger, F., L. Rosenthaler, R. von der Heydt, E. Peterhans & O. Kübler (1992) Simulation of neural contour mechanism: From simple to end-stopped cells. *Vision Research* 32:963–981.

von der Heydt, R., E. Peterhans & G. Baumgartner (1984). Illusory contours and cortical responses. *Science* 224:1260–1262.

Hubel, D. H. & T. N. Wiesel (1962). Receptive fields, binocular interaction and functional architecture in the cat's visual cortex. *Journal of Physiology* 160:106–154.

Hubel, D. H. & T. N. Wiesel (1965). Receptive fields and functional architecture in two nonstriate visual areas (18 and 19) of the cat. *Journal of Neurophysiology* 28:229–289.

Jain, A. K. (1979). A sinusoidal family of unitary transforms. *IEEE Transactions on Pattern Analysis and Machine Intelligence* PAMI-1:356–365.

Jain, A. K. (1981a). Image data compression: A review. *Proceedings of the IEEE* 69:349–389.

Jain, A. K. (1981b) Advances in mathematical models for image processing. *Proceedings of the IEEE* 69:502–528.

Jain, A. K. (1989). *Fundamentals of Digital Image Processing*. Englewood Cliffs, N. J.: Prentice Hall.

Jayant, N. S. & P. Noll (1984) *Digital Coding of Waveforms*. Englewood Cliffs, N. J.: Prentice Hall.

Julesz, B. (1981). Textons, the elements of texture perception, and their interactions. *Nature* 290:91–97.

Kelly, D. H (1977). Visual contrast sensitivity. *Optica Acta* 24:107–129.

Klein, S. A. & B. Beutter (1992). Minimizing and maximizing the joint space–spatial frequency uncertainty of Gabor-like functions: Comment. *Journal of the Optical Society of America A*9: 337–340.

Koenderink, J. J & A. J. van Doorn (1987). Representation of local geometry in the visual system. *Biological Cybernetics* 55:367–375.

Koenderink, J. J. & W. Richards (1988). Two-dimensional curvature operators. *Journal of the Optical Society of America A* 5:1136–1141.

Kronauer, R. E. and Y. Y. Zeevi (1985). Reorganization and diversification of signals in vision. *IEEE Transactions on Systems, Man, and Cybernetics* SMC-15:91–101.

Kuffler, S. W. (1953). Discharge patterns and functional organization of the mammalian retina. *Journal of Neurophysiology* 16:37–68.

Laughlin, S. (1983) Matching coding to scenes to enhance efficiency. In O. J. Braddick and A. C. Sleigh (Eds.) *Physical and Biological Processing of Images*, Berlin: Springer, 42-52

Legge, G. E. & J. M. Foley (1980). Contrast masking in human vision. *Journal of the Optical Society of America* 70:1458–1470.

Lettvin, J. Y., H. R. Maturana, W. S. McCulloch & W. H. Pitts (1959). What the frog's eye tells the frog's brain. *Proceedings IRE* 47:1940–1951.

Linde, Y., A. Buzo & R. M. Gray (1980). An algorithm for vector quantizer design. *IEEE Transactions on Communication* COM-28:84–95.

Linsker, R. (1986). From basic network principles to neural architecture: Emergence of orientation selective cells. *Proceedings of the National Academy of Science USA* 83:8390–8394.

Lukas, F. X. J. & Z. L. Budrikis (1982). Picture quality prediction based on a visual model. *IEEE Transactions on Communications* COM-30(7): 1679–1692.

Martens, J.-B. (1990). The Hermite-transform: Applications. *IEEE Transactions on Acoustics, Speech, and Signal Processing* ASSP-38:1607–1618.

Mackworth, N. H. & A. J. Morandi (1967). The gaze selects informative details within pictures. *Perception and Psychophysics* 2:547–552.

Marr, D. & E. Hildreth (1980). Theory of edge detection. *Proceedings of the Royal Society of London* B207:182–217.

Mallat, S. G. (1989). A theory for multiresolution signal decomposition. *IEEE Transactions on Pattern Analysis and Machine Intelligence PAMI*-11:674–693.

Mallat, S. G. (1989). Multifrequency channel decompositions of images and wavelet models. *IEEE Transactions on Acoustics, Speech, and Signal Processing ASSP-37*:2091–2110.

Morrone, M. C. & R. A. Owens (1987). Feature detection from local energy. *Pattern Recognition Letters* 6:303–313.

Morrone, M. C. & D. C. Burr (1988). Feature detection in human vision: A phase dependent energy model. *Proceedings of the Royal Society of London B235*:221–245.

Nasrabadi, M. N. & R. A. King (1988). Image coding using vector quantization: A review. *IEEE Transactions on Communications COM-36*:957–971.

Netravali, A. N. & B. G. Haskell (1988). *Digital Pictures: Representation and Compression*. New York: Plenum Press.

Olzak, L. A. & J. P. Thomas (1991). When orthogonal orientations are not processed independently. *Vision Research* 31:51–57.

Papoulis, A. (1984). *Probability, Random Variables, and Stochastic Processes*. New York: McGraw-Hill.

Peli, E. (1990). Contrast in complex images. *Journal of the Optical Society of America A7*: 2032–2040.

Peichl, L. & H. Wässle (1979) Size, scatter and coverage of ganglion cell receptive field centres in the cat retina. *Journal of Physiology* 291:117–141.

Phillips, G. C. & H. R. Wilson (1984). Orientation bandwidths of spatial mechanisms measured by masking. *Journal of the Optical Society of America A1*(2):226–232.

Potts, A. M., D. Hodges, C. B. Shelman, K. J. Fritz, N. S. Levy & Y. Mangnall (1972). Morphology of the primate optic nerve: I, Method and total fibre count. *Investigative Ophtalmology* 11:980–988.

Ramamurthi, B. & A. Gersho (1986). Classified vector quantization of images. *IEEE Transactions on Communications COM-34*:1105–1115.

Rao, R. P. & W. A. Pearlman (1991). On entropy of pyramid structures. *IEEE Transactions on Information Theory IT-37*:407–413.

Regan, D. & M. P. Regan (1987). Nonlinearity in human visual responses to two-dimensional patterns and a limitation of Fourier methods. *Vision Research* 27:2181–2183.

Rosenfeld, A. & A. C. Kak (1982). *Digital Picture Processing*, 2d ed. New York: Academic Press.

Sabin, M. J. & R. M. Gray (1984). Product code vector quantizers for waveform and voice coding. *IEEE Transactions on Acoustics, Speech, and Signal Processing ASSP-32*(3):474–488.

Saito, H., K. Tanaka, Y. Fukada & H. Oyamada (1988) Analysis of discontinuity in visual contours in area 19 of the cat. *Journal of Neuroscience* 8:1131–1143.

Sanger, T. D. (1990). Analysis of the two-dimensional receptive fields learned by the generalized Hebbian algorithm in response to random input. *Biological Cybernetics* 63:221–228.

Shannon, C. E. (1948) A mathematical theory of communication. *Bell Systems Technical Journal* 27:379–423, 623–656. (Reprinted in Shannon, C. E. & E. Weaver (1949). *A Mathematical Theory of Communication*. University of Illinois Press)

Shannon, C. E. (1959) Coding theorems for a discrete source with a fidelity criterion. *IRE National Convention Record, p. 4*, 142–163. (Reprinted in Shannon, C. E. (1960). "Coding Theorems for a Discrete Source with a Fidelity Criterion." In R. E. Machol (Ed.), *Information and Decision Processes* New York: MacGraw-Hill.)

Shapley, R. & C. Enroth-Cugell (1984). Visual adaptation and retinal gain controls. *Progress in Retinal Research* 3:263–346.

Singhal, S., D. LeGall & C. T. Chen (1990). Source coding of speech and video signals. *Proceedings of the IEEE* 78:1233–1249.

Sperling, G. (1970) Model of visual adaptation and contrast detection. *Perception and Psychophysics* 8(3):143–157.

Spivak, M. (1975) *A Comprehensive Introduction to Differential Geometry*, Boston, Mass: Publish or Perish.

Stockham, T. G., Jr. (1972) Image processing in the context of a visual model. *Proceedings of the IEEE*, 828–842.

Stork, D. G & H. R. Wilson (1990). Do Gabor functions provide appropriate descriptions of visual cortex receptive fields? *Journal of the Optical Society of America A7*:1362–1373.

Tou, J. T. & R. C. Gonzalez (1974). *Pattern Recognition Principles*. Reading, Mass: Addison-Wesley.

Treisman, A. & G. Gelade (1980) A feature-integration theory of attention. *Cognitive Psychology* 12:97–136.

Vetterli, M. (1984). Multi-dimensional sub-band coding: Some theory and algorithms. *Signal Processing* 6:97–112.

Wässle, H., U. Grünert, J. Röhrenbeck, & B. B. Boycott (1990). Retinal ganglion cell density and cortical magnification factor in the primate. *Vision Research* 30:1897–1911.

Watson, A. B. (1987). Efficiency of a model human image code. *Journal of the Optical Society of America A4*:2401–2417.

Wegmann, B. & C. Zetzsche (1990a). Visual system based polar quantization of local amplitude and local phase of orientation filter outputs. In B. E. Rogowitz and J. P. Allebach (Eds.), *Human Vision and Electronic Imaging Models, Methods, and Applications, Proc. SPIE* 1249. Bellingham, Wash. SPIE, 306–317.

Wegmann, B. & C. Zetzsche (1990b) Statistical dependence between orientation filter outputs used in a human vision based image code. In M. Kunt (Ed.), *Visual Communications and Image Processing, Proc. SPIE* 1360. Bellingham, Wash. SPIE, 909–1923.

Wegmann, B. & C. Zetzsche (1991a) Comparison of LBG based and perceptually motivated vector quantization of orientation filter outputs. In J. Morreale (Ed.) *Proceedings of the International Symposium of the Society for Information Display*. Playa del Rey, C A: Society for Information Display, 611–614.

Wegmann, B. & C. Zetzsche (1991b) Local amplitude irrelevance thresholds in a human vision image code. In *Proc. Picture Coding Symposium PCS 91*. Tokyo, Japan, 333–336.

Westerink, P. H.; J. Biemond; D. E. Boekes & J. W. Woods (1988). Subband coding of images using vector quantization. *IEEE Transactions on Communications COM*-36:713–719.

Wilson, R., H. Knutsson & G. Granlund (1983) Anisotropic non-stationary image estimation and its applications. *IEEE Transactions on Communication COM*-31:388–406.

Wintz, P. A. (1972). Transform picture coding. *Proceedings of the IEEE* 60:809–820.

Woods, J. W. & S. D. O'Neill (1986). Subband coding of images. *IEEE Transactions on Acoustics, Speech, and Signal Processing ASSP*-43:1278–1288.

Xie, Z. & T. G. Stockham, Jr. (1989). Toward the unification of three visual laws and two visual models in brightness perception. *IEEE Transactions on Systems, Man, and Cybernetics* 19(2):379–387.

Yang, J. (1992). Do Gabor functions provide appropriate descriptions of visual cortical fields?: Comment. *Journal of the Optical Society of America A*9:334–336.

Zetzsche, C. & W. Schönecker (1987). Orientation selective filters lead to entropy reduction in the processing of natural images. *Perception* 16:229.

Zetzsche, C. (1988) Statistical properties of the representation of natural images at different levels in the visual system. *Perception* 17:359.

Zetzsche, C. & T. Caelli (1989). Invariant pattern recognition using multiple filter image representations. *Computer Vision, Graphics, and Image Processing* 45:251–262.

Zetzsche, C. & G. Hauske (1989) Multiple channel model for the prediction of subjective image quality. In B. E. Rogowitz (Ed.), *Human Vision, Visual Processing, and Digital Display, Proc. SPIE* 1077:209–216.

Zetzsche, C. (1990). "Sparse Coding: The Link between Low Level Vision and Associative memory." In R. Eckmiller, G. Hartmann & G. Hauske (Eds.), *Parallel Processing in Neural Systems and Computers*. Amsterdam: Elsevier, 273–276.

Zetzsche, C. & E. Barth (1990a). Fundamental limits of linear filters in the visual processing of two-dimensional signals. *Vision Research* 30:1111–1117.

Zetzsche, C. & E. Barth (1990b). Image surface predicates and the neural encoding of two-dimensional signal variations, In B. E. Rogowitz and J. P. Allebach (Eds.), *Human Vision and Electronic Imaging: Models, Methods, and Applications, Proc. SPIE* 1249. Bellingham, Wash. SPIE, 209–216.

Zetzsche, C. & E. Barth (1991). Direct detection of flow discontinuities by 3D curvature operators. *Pattern Recognition Letters* 12:771–779.

Zetzsche, C., E. Barth & J. Berkmann (1991). Spatio-temporal curvature measures for flow-field analysis. In B. C. Vemuri (Ed.), *Geometric Methods in Computer Vision, Proc. SPIE* 1570. Bellingham, Wash. SPIE, 337–350.

Part III

Measurement and Prediction of Visual Quality

In previous chapters we have seen how various aspects of human vision have been acknowledged or incorporated into image coding and compression algorithms. The ultimate goal of such schemes is, of course, to render imagery with optimal visual quality, given constraints on computation, memory, bit rate, and display. This goal is complicated, however, by the difficulty of defining exactly what is meant by "visual quality." As pointed out in the chapters by Ahumada and Null, and by Hearty, visual quality may have more than a single dimension. As noted in chapter by Lubin, these dimensions may be weighted differently, depending on the use to which the imagery is put. Nonetheless, these authors suggest meaningful ways of measuring this elusive but precious commodity.

Few researchers or developers of imaging systems have the facilities or expertise to measure image quality in reliable ways (Stein, Watson, and Hitchner, 1989; Watson, 1987). Furthermore, while large variations in image quality may to some degree be self-evident to the nonexpert viewer, production of prototype imaging hardware is extremely expensive and time-consuming. For both these reasons there is a need for so-called objective measures, that is, mathematical formulas or algorithms that will predict the visual quality of an imaging system before any physical prototype is built (Zetzsche and Hauske, 1989). Such predictions necessarily incorporate models of human vision.

Almost invariably, objective measures of image quality are measures of image *fidelity:* the accuracy with which some standard image can be reproduced. The most common objective measure of image fidelity is the root-mean-squared (RMS) error between a source (original) image and a compressed or otherwise rendered image. This may be thought of either as a complete lack of a visual model or as a model that assumes that all errors of equal magnitude are equally visible and that errors combine perceptually in a quadratic fashion. The simplest refinement to this measure is the addition of a contrast sensitivity function, which weights errors in different frequency bands in proportion to visual sensitivity. Pratt (1978) provides an excellent discussion of a number of such measures.

However, as discussed in chapter 15, the RMS approach requires many other modifications before it can serve as an accurate measure of image quality or fidelity. In general, these modifications consist of various sorts of channeling and non-linear processing of the image. Two examples of recent approaches to the problem of predicting visual quality are provided in chapters 13 and 14. Both these approaches incorporate multiple channels selective for spatial frequency and orientation, as well as various nonlinearities such as light adaptation, contrast adaptation, and probability summation.

References

Pratt, W. K. (1978). *Digital Image Processing*. New York: John Wiley & Sons.

Stein, C. S.; Watson, A. B. and Hitchner, L. E. (1989). Psychophysical rating of image compression techniques. *SPIE Proceedings* 1077:198–208.

Watson, A. B. (1987). Efficiency of an image code based on human vision. *Journal of the Optical Society of America A* 4(12):2401–2417.

Zetzsche, C. & Hauske, G. (1989). Multiple channel model for the prediction of subjective image quality. *Society of Photo Instrumentation Engineering Proceedings* 1077:209–216.

11

Image Quality: A Multidimensional Problem

Albert J. Ahumada, Jr., and Cynthia H. Null

The design of displays and image compression methods could proceed more efficiently if one could predict observer ratings of display quality from physical properties of displayed images. Zetzsche and Hauske (1989) report correlations between their image-quality model predictions and mean subjective ratings ranging from 0.95 down to 0.74, depending on the types of distortion in the images. Although they suggest that improvements in their models might allow adequate predictions, it is equally easy to suppose that models of image quality based on fixed visual system properties are fundamentally limited in their ability to predict subjective image-quality ratings. Even if the ratings reflect only the detectability of artifacts, there is significant variation in observers' contrast sensitivity functions and other critical visual parameters (Ginsburg, Evans, Sekuler, and Harp, 1982; Owsley, Sekuler, and Siemsen, 1983).

When the display artifacts are suprathreshold, the observers' different experiences with artifacts are bound to lead to differential weighting of the artifacts. Also, images are used for a range of purposes, so the objectionability of artifacts should also depend on the observers' presumptions as to the use of the display. The presumed use would also be expected to vary with the observers' past experiences. Because different groups of observers are bound to differ systematically, there is little likelihood that a measure calibrated for one group could perfectly predict results for all other groups.

The dimensions to which different observers give different weight should be more stable than the weightings over different groups of observers. It may be easier to generate predictions for these dimensions based on physical properties of the displays. The methods described here do not average out observer variability; they use interobserver variability to extract dimensions of image quality. We describe one such method in detail, give an example of how it can find multiple dimensions of image quality, and describe some of the problems associated with the method. The method, a multidimensional scaling one, is a variant of the MDPREF method (Carroll, 1972). In many multidimensional scaling methods, observers provide estimates of the similarities or distances between stimuli in perceptual space (Kruskal and Wish, 1978; Shepard, Romney, and Nerlove, 1972). All that is needed for the methods described here are quality ratings.

Preference Factoring

An Imaginary Example

To see how dimensions of image quality can be recovered when observers weight them differently, imagine four displays that vary on two dimensions, as illustrated in figure 11.1. An observer who pays attention only to the first dimension might rate the quality of the displays as in the first row of ratings in the figure. The second row of ratings shows the ratings of an observer who attends only to the second dimension, and the third row shows ratings of an observer who pays equal attention to both dimensions. Figure 11.2 shows a lightly edited transcript of a Mathematica dialogue, with the input in bold type (Wolfram, 1991). The input is the data matrix from the previous figure. First, the mean rating for each observer is subtracted from the ratings by that observer. Next, the singular value decomposition (SVD) routine is called. The output is three matrices: a 2×3 matrix giving weights for our three observers on two new dimensions, a 1×2 list giving the weights of the two dimensions, and a 2×4 matrix giving the weights of the four displays on the two dimensions. Figure 11.3 is a plot of these results. The symbols representing the four displays are in the same configuration as in figure 11.1, but this configuration has been rotated, reflected, and translated. Dimension 1 now represents the overall average quality, the single dimension that can best (in a least squares sense) represent the input data matrix. The new dimension 2 does not have such a nice name; it represents the difference between the two original dimensions. The observer weights are also shown, scaled by the two dimension weights so that all the SVD information is contained in the graph. The first subject is represented by the solid point in the lower right hand corner. The normalized ratings are the dot product of a subject's vector with each of the display vectors. These dot products are the projections onto the observers dotted line multiplied by the distance from the origin.

The SVD analysis has factored the data matrix into a display matrix and an observer matrix representing the directions of the observers' preferences in display dimensions. The output dimensions are not the original dimensions, but they are related to them by a linear transformation.

Some Theory

Imagine now an experiment in which n_o observers are asked to give quality ratings to n_d displays, resulting in a

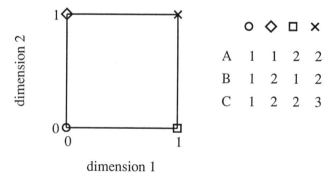

Figure 11.1
The positions of the symbols indicate the values of four imaginary displays on two hypothetical quality dimensions. The three rows of the table represent ratings of these displays by three observers (A, B, and C) who differentially weight the two quality dimensions as described in the text.

```
Mathematica 2.0 for SPARC
Copyright 1988-91 Wolfram Research, Inc.
In[1]:= Needs["Statistics `DescriptiveStatistics`"]

In[2]:= rawdata = {{1.,1.,2.,2.},
                    {1.,2.,1.,2.},
                    {1.,2.,2.,3.}};
In[3]:= data = rawdata - (Mean /@ rawdata)
Out[3]= {{ -0.5, -0.5,  0.5, 0.5 },
         { -0.5,  0.5, -0.5, 0.5 },
         { -1.0,  0.0,  0.0, 1.0 }}

In[4]:= SingularValues[data]

Out[4]= {{{-0.408, -0.408, -0.816},
          { 0.707, -0.707,  0.   }},

         {1.732, 1.},

         {{0.707, 0.    , 0.    , -0.707},
          {0.    , -0.707, 0.707, 0.    }}}
```

Figure 11.2
A computer dialogue in Mathematica. Keyboard inputs are in bold.

matrix R of ratings

$$(R)_{i,j} = r_{i,j}, \quad i = 1, \ldots, n_o, \quad j = 1, \ldots, n_d. \quad (10.1)$$

One Dimension

If everyone agrees on the ratings perfectly, so that

$$r_{i,j} = q_j, \quad i = 1, \ldots, n_o, \quad j = 1, \ldots, n_d, \quad (10.2)$$

all the rows of R are the same, and the rank of R (the smaller of the number of linearly independent rows or columns) is 1. In this case it will be possible for some single-valued function of the displays to predict the ratings, since they depend only on the display.

Suppose all the subjects have the same underlying quality ratings but use different numerical scales, so that

$$r_{i,j} = a_i q_j + b_i, \quad i = 1, \ldots, n_o, \quad j = 1, \ldots, n_d. \quad (10.3)$$

R now has rank 2, since the rows are linear combinations of a column (q_j) and a column of 1's. An SVD analysis would find two dimensions even though there is really only one of interest. Subtracting the observer's mean rating from each rating leaves a data matrix of differences with elements

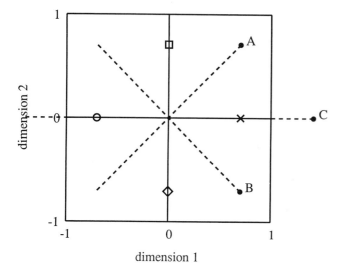

Figure 11.3
Results of the SVD example of Figure 11.2 plotted as in Figure 11.1. The positions of the same four symbols indicate the values of four imaginary displays on the two quality dimensions found by the SVD. The solid points are the subject weights of the three observers (A, B, and C) multiplied by the singular values. The dashed lines indicate the directions of the observers' preferences in the two-dimensional space.

$$r'_{i,j} = r_{i,j} - \bar{r}_i$$

$$= a_i(q_j - \bar{q}), \quad i = 1, \ldots, n_o, \quad j = 1, \ldots, n_d. \quad (11.4)$$

R' again has rank 1, and the SVD analysis returns observer weights and display weights that can be obtained simply by averaging.

Multiple Dimensions

The preference factoring model assumes that there are a number n_q of different quality dimensions that observers, in general, weight differently, so that

$$r_{i,j} = \sum_{k=1}^{n_q} a_{i,k} q_{j,k}, \quad i = 1, \ldots, n_o, \quad j = 1, \ldots, n_d, \quad (11.5)$$

where $q_{j,k}$ is the quality of display j on dimension k, and $a_{i,k}$ is the weight that observer i gives to that dimension. The rank of this rating matrix is now, in general, the smaller of n_o, n_q, and $n_d - 1$, assuming each observer's mean rating has been subtracted out. If the observers use the weightings and qualities of equation 11.5, and we find two matrices that multiply together as in equation 11.5 to give the matrix $R = (r_{i,j})$, we have probably not found the same dimensions used by the observers. There are many equivalent factorizations of a matrix R, since any invertible $n_q \times n_q$ matrix T can postmultiply $A = (a_{i,k})$ and then its transposed inverse postmultiply $Q = (q_{j,k})$, and the resulting matrices satisfy equation 11.5. In general, we can find only the dimensions up to an arbitrary invertible linear transformation T.

The Rating Matrix

If observers use numbers to report quality, it is not reasonable to assume that the numerical scales are the same for different observers. Subtracting the mean rating for an observer from the ratings for that observer can help in two ways. As we saw earlier, it makes the results blind to differences among observers in the absolute positioning of their scales, removing an additive factor dimension from the analysis. Second, the additive model has only to fit the smaller range of variations in the region of the mean, analogous to the improved functional fit of a Taylor expansion about the center of the desired region, rather than about zero.

The results can also be made independent of the scale factor used by the observer by dividing the observers' ratings by their standard deviations. This normalization (the default for most factor-analysis programs) can cause problems if the scales were originally reasonably comparable, since then differences that one observer found inconsequential can be made as large as the important differences of another observer. If repeated judgments are available, their variability can be used to normalize the scale factors. Dividing an observer's ratings by the pooled repeated-judgment standard deviation allows each observer's responses to be weighted by an estimate of their precision. More complicated unidimensional scaling procedures such as Thurstone scaling allow the observers to use nonuniform rating functions, but these methods usually require more responses (Torgerson, 1958).

A rating matrix can also be generated from ranking or paired-comparison experiments. If ranks are used, the only source of differential spacing is the different ordering, not accounted for by the multiple dimensions, so the results benefit from many closely spaced displays. Paired-comparison data can be converted to ratings by scaling procedures, of which the simplest is computing the percentage of time each stimulus was chosen over the others (Torgerson, 1958).

Singular Value Decomposition

As was shown in the preceding example, the SVD can solve the problem of finding the rank n_r of a rating matrix and then finding observer weights and display values that can be multiplied together to recreate the ratings as in equation 11.5. The SVD represents the rating matrix as the sum of the products of three numbers,

$$r_{i,j} = \sum_{k=1}^{n_r} u_{i,k} v_{j,k} w_k, \quad i = 1, \ldots, n_o, \quad j = 1, \ldots, n_d, \tag{11.6}$$

where $U = (u_{i,k})$ is a matrix of normalized weights for each observer on each quality dimension, $V = (v_{j,k})$ is a matrix of normalized values for each display on each quality dimension, and $W = (w_k)$ is an array of strengths for each dimension (the singular values). Equation 11.6 can be put in the same form as equation 11.5 by arbitrarily associating the dimension strengths with the observer weights, that is, setting $a_{i,k} = u_{i,k} w_k$ and $q_{j,k} = v_{j,k}$. A defining property for the SVD is that for any $n_q < n_r$, the first n_q rows of U and V and the first $n_q w_k$'s are dimensions for a least squares representation of R by a matrix of rank n_q (Eckart and Young, 1936). In other words, if we con-

strain ourselves to a preference model with only n_q quality dimensions, then the best (least squares) version is given by the first n_q rows of U and V and the corresponding values of W. The sum of squares of the singular values w_k for k greater than n_q is the squared error of the representation. Another resulting property is that the rows of U are orthogonal to each other, as are the rows of V. The w_k values allow the vector lengths of all these rows to be set to 1. The resulting representation is unique except for the signs of the rows of U and V, if the w_k are assumed positive.

Although the SVD is readily available in matrix operation subroutine collections (Dongarra et al., 1979; The Mathworks, Inc., 1991; Becker and Chambers, 1984; Wolfram, 1991), its results can also be obtained from a principal-components factor analysis or eigenvector and eigenvalue analysis available in many statistical packages (Wilkinson, 1987; Dixon et al., 1977; Nie et al., 1975). Some programs will accept the data matrix as input and can subtract the observers' means (covariance about the mean option) and divide by the observers' standard deviations (correlation about the mean). Some will output the display weights multiplied by the singular values (test factor loadings). Some also output the observer weights (factor scores), and some also provide transformations (rotations) to possibly more interpretable dimensions. In the worst case one you must subtract the means and form the symmetric covariance matrix,

$$o_{i,i'} = \sum_{j=1}^{n_d} r_{i,j} r_{i',j}, \quad i, i' = 1, \ldots, n_o, \tag{11.7}$$

to get the program to output the subject weights; and then provide

$$d_{j,j'} = \sum_{i=1}^{n_o} r_{i,j} r_{i,j'}, \quad j, j' = 1, \ldots, n_d, \tag{11.8}$$

to get the display image configuration. The singular values are the square roots of the eigenvalues of either covariance matrix.

Some authors view each observer as selecting a preference direction in the stimulus space, represented by his or her unit length row vector in the U matrix. They leave the rows of U alone and multiply the rows of V by the w_k. Others prefer to leave the stimulus representation normalized and consider the w_k to represent the relative weights that the observers place on the dimensions. When the w_k span a large range, it is convenient to leave the model in

Measurement and Prediction of Visual Quality

the three separate parts so that plots of both subject weights and stimulus values can be scaled uniformly.

Error

Suppose that the ratings are all based on a single underlying quality value q_j, but that other unsystematic factors affect the ratings.

$$r_{i,j} = q_j + e_{i,j}, \quad i = 1, \ldots, n_o, \quad j = 1, \ldots, n_d, \qquad (11.9)$$

where $e_{i,j}$ is independent Gaussian noise,

$$e_{i,j} \equiv N(0, \sigma). \qquad (11.10)$$

Now, with probability 1 the matrix $r_{i,j}$ has full rank, but if we use SVD to factor it, the dimension corresponding to the largest singular value will correspond most closely to the noise-free ratings, and the other dimensions will represent the noise. Although the true noise dimensions are equal in their singular values, the SVD will place the estimates of their singular values in descending order, so that the actual number of dimensions is not obvious even in this simple case.

Let us return to the case of n_q dimensions of display quality (equation 11.5), but with added noise as above.

$$r_{i,j} = \sum_{k=1}^{n_q} a_{i,k} q_{j,k} + e_{i,j}, \quad i = 1, \ldots, n_o, \quad j = 1, \ldots, n_d. \qquad (11.11)$$

If σ is small enough, the SVD may result in a large drop in the singular values w_k after w_{n_q}, but dimensions that we recover will not be exactly a linear transformation of the original dimensions. We are then left with the problem of recovering "true" dimensions that has plagued practitioners of factor analysis and multidimensional scaling. Solutions to these problems have been proposed and shown to do well in certain cases (Harmon, 1967; Torgerson,

1958). Statistical packages that include factor analysis usually also provide options to attempt to rotate the dimensions to make them more meaningful or interpretable.

A Real Example

Farrell, Trontelj, Rosenberg, and Wiseman (1991) reported rankings of 12 displays by 18 observers. The displays were compressed versions of the classic 512×512 monochrome Lena image (the woman with the hat) from the USC data base. Six of the images were compressed using a discrete cosine transform (DCT) method (Wallace, 1991), and six images were compressed using the non-uniform sampling and interpolation (NSI) method of Rosenberg (1990). The bit rate of the compressed images ranged between 1.7 and 0.3 bits/pixel. At low bit rates, the DCT method created visible blocklike patterns, whereas the NSI method produced vertical and horizontal smearing. Figure 11.4 illustrates the nature of the artifacts in the highest compression (lowest bit rate) conditions. Observers viewed all 66 pairwise comparisons of the 12 images three times. Ratings were formed by computing the average proportion of times each display image was chosen to be more like the original, which was displayed with the two compressed images.

Table 11.1 shows the 11 singular values from the SVD of the ratings. (Only 11 remain after the mean response (0.5) is first subtracted from all ratings.) Although it is not clear from the pattern of sizes in table 11.1, it is clear from the plot of the stimulus weights in figure 11.5 that the SVD recovers at least two meaningful dimensions differentially weighted by the observers. The first dimension correlates with the amount of compression in bits/pixel, and the second distinguishes between the two types of compression. The observer weights have been multiplied by the corresponding singular values and then plotted on

dct

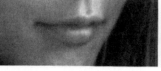
original

nsi

Figure 11.4
Sections of the original image, a DCT compressed image, and an NSI compressed image from the study by Farrell et al. (1991), enlarged to illustrate the nature of the compression artifacts.

Table 11.1
Singular Values w_k from the Data of Farrell et al. (1991)

k	1	2	3	4	5	6	7	8	9	10	11
w_k	4.28	0.61	0.37	0.34	0.31	0.22	0.22	0.13	0.13	0.08	0.05

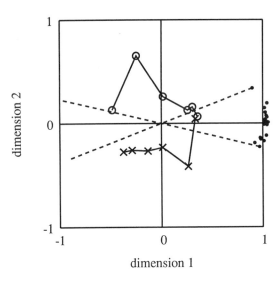

Figure 11.5
The first two dimensions from the SVD of the data of Farrell et al. (1991). Circles indicate the $v_{j,k}$ of the six DCT compressed images; $\times$'s indicate the $v_{j,k}$ of the six NSI compressed images. Solid lines link neighboring compression levels, which decrease from left to right. Solid points are 18 subject weights $u_{i,k}$ multiplied by the singular values w_k. The orders of the rankings for two very different observers can be obtained by dropping perpendiculars to the dashed lines through their points.

the same figure. The order of the predictions for an observer can be seen by dropping perpendiculars from the compressed image points to the line through the origin and the observer point. These points of intersection can be converted to numerical predictions of proportion of times chosen by multiplying their distance from the origin by the distance of the observer's point (here nearly unity) and then adding 0.5.

Unfortunately, the data do not tell us the direction of the dimensions that the observers used. For example, the observers could have had two dimensions, "blockiness" and "blurriness," or the observers could have had one dimension of "quality" and another dimension of "near-sightedness," presuming (for the sake of argument) the NSI artifacts to be less visible to nearsighted observers. Whether the multidimensionality is important depends on the lability of the observer weights. If the observer

weights are stable, representing something like the distribution of acuity in the population, the second dimension has little importance, since most of the observers weights are close to zero on dimension 2. If the weights are easily modified by experience or task, the relative quality of the two compression methods can change greatly if the predicted ratings can change as much as the difference between the two most extreme observers.

INDSCAL

Carroll and Chang's INDSCAL procedure (Carroll, 1972; Arabie, Carroll, and DeSarbo, 1987) is a variant of preference factoring that puts greater demands on the form of the data and makes stronger assumptions about the rating process, but provides, in return, dimensions with uniquely determined directions. The data must have three fully crossed factors: observers, displays, and conditions. That is, every observer must rate each display in each condition. The additional assumption is that the effect of the conditions on either the observer weights or the display weights is purely multiplicative in each dimension, so that equation 11.5 becomes

$$r_{i,j,m} = \sum_{k=1}^{n_q} a_{i,k} q_{j,k} c_{m,k}, \quad i = 1, \dots, n_o,$$
$$j = 1, \dots, n_d, \quad m = 1, \dots, n_c, \quad (11.12)$$

where $c_{m,k}$ are weights for the n_c conditions on the n_q quality dimensions. Because the $c_{m,k}$ vary with both m and k, this equation does not in general reduce to equation 11.5. Also, in general, except for normalizations and reflections, the directions of the dimensions satisfying equation 11.12 are unique.

An Example

The same data used to illustrate two-way preference factoring can be used to illustrate three-way factoring by arbitrarily letting the two types of compression represent two condition levels for six display types, which then are the compression levels. The resulting INDSCAL analysis is illustrated in figure 11.6. In this example only two dimensions can result, since INDSCAL cannot extract more dimensions than the smallest of n_o, n_d, and n_c. The configuration of the six compressions for the two dimensions is shown for both the DCT and the NSI compressed

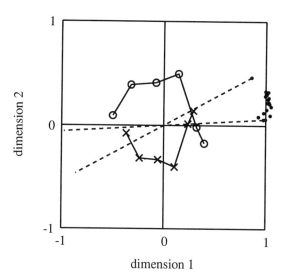

Figure 11.6

The data of Figure 11.5 analyzed by the INDSCAL procedure. Circles indicate the $q_{j,k}c_{m,k}$ for the six DCT compressed images; ×'s indicate these products for the six NSI compressed images. Solid lines link neighboring compression levels, which decrease from left to right. The solid points are 18 observer weights $a_{i,k}$. The dashed lines have the same interpretation as in Figure 11.5 and are drawn for the same two observers.

images in figure 11.6. They are the same configuration scaled by the $c_{m,k}$ for the two different conditions. The configurations of figures 11.5 and 11.6 are extremely similar; both show the same general pattern. When there is little compression, the methods are of course similar. Of more interest, the method differences get smaller again for the largest compressions. The shape similarity prevents figure 11.6 from showing the apparent difference for the two methods in the level of compression at which the observer differences are maximal.

The major possible advantage of the INDSCAL analysis is not well illustrated by this example. The directions of the dimensions in figure 11.6, although similar to those of figure 11.5 are determined by the functional interaction of equation 11.12 rather than being determined by which dimension can predict the most variance in the data. When there are only two dimensions, one can easily transform to another coordinate system by drawing in the new axes and projecting onto one axis using lines parallel to the other. For more dimensions, it is difficult to find "best" axes, and the fixed solution of the INDSCAL method can be very helpful.

Summary

Preference factoring can be easily performed using readily available computer programs. This multidimensional scaling procedure allows dimensions of image quality to emerge if there is a variance in the relative weights that observers give to the dimensions. An example analysis of preference data for images compressed by two different methods showed that the method can find multiple dimensions even when there is strong agreement about the ratings from most of the observers. Dimensions found by these methods are likely to be better predicted by image properties. In addition to demonstrating the multidimensional nature of the quality ratings, the analyses showed that the differential effect of the two compression methods on different observers is greatest at moderate levels of compression.

Acknowledgments

We are grateful to J. Farrell, H. Trontelj, and their colleagues at Hewlett Packard for the data and encouragement, and to H. Peterson for helpful comments. This work was supported by NASA RTOP 505-64-53 and 506-71-51.

References

Arabie, P., Carroll, J. D., and DeSarbo, W. S. (1987). *Three-Way Scaling and Clustering*. Sage University Paper series on Quantitative Applications in the Social Sciences, 07–065. Beverly Hills and London: Sage Publications.

Becker, R. A., and Chambers, J. M. (1984). *S: An Interactive Environment for Data Analysis and Graphics*. Belmont, Calif.: Wadsworth.

Carroll, J. D. (1972). "Individual Differences and Multidimensional Scaling." In *Multidimensional Scaling. Vol. I, Theory*, ed. R. N. Shepard, A. K. Romney, and S. B. Nerlove. New York: Seminar Press.

Dixon, W. J., Brown, M. B., Engelman, L., Frame, J. W., and Jennrich, R. I. (1977). *BMDP-77: Biomedical Computer Programs, P Series*. Berkeley: Univ. of California. Press.

Dongarra, J., Moler, C. B., Bunch J. R., and Stewart, G. W. (1979). *LINPACK User's Guide*. Philadelphia, Pa.: SIAM.

Eckart, C., and Young, G., (1936) The approximation of one matrix by another of lower rank. *Psychometrika* 1:148–158.

Farrell, J., Trontelj, H., Rosenberg, C., and Wiseman, J. (1991). Perceptual metrics for monochrome image compression. *Society for Information Display Digest* 22:631–634.

Ginsburg, A. P., Evans, D. W., Sekuler, R., and Harp, S. A. (1982). Contrast sensitivity predicts pilots' performance in aircraft simulators. *American Journal of Optometry and Physiological Optics* 59:105–109.

Harmon, H. (1967). *Modern Factor Analysis.* New York: McGraw-Hill.

Kruskal, J. B., and Wish, M. (1978). *Multidimensional Scaling.* Sage University Paper series on Quantitative Applications in the Social Sciences, 07-011. Beverly Hills and London: Sage Publications.

MathWorks, The Inc. (1991). *MATLAB User's Guide.* Natick, Mass.: The MathWorks, Inc..

Nie, N. H., Hull, C. H., Jenkins, J. G., Steinbrenner, K., and Bent, D. H. (1975). *SPSS: Statistical Package for the Social Sciences,* 2d ed. New York: McGraw-Hill.

Owsley, C., Sekuler, R., and Siemsen, D. (1983). Contrast sensitivity throughout adulthood. *Vision Research* 23:689–699.

Rosenberg, C. (1990). A lossy image compression algorithm based on nonuniform sampling and interpolation of the image intensity surface. *Society for Information Display Digest* 21:388–391.

Shepard, R. N., Romney, A. K., and Nerlove, S. B. (1972). *Multidimensional Scaling. Vol. I, Theory.* New York: Seminar Press.

Torgerson, W. S. (1958). *Theory and Methods of Scaling.* New York: Wiley.

Wallace, G. (1991). The JPEG still picture compression standard. *Communications of the ACM* 34:31–44.

Wilkinson, L. (1987). *SYSTAT: The System for Statistics.* Evanston, Ill.: SYSTAT, Inc..

Wolfram, S. (1991). *Mathematica: A System for Doing Mathematics by Computer.* Redwood City, Calif.: Addison-Wesley.

Zetzsche, C., and Hauske, G. (1989). Multiple channel model for the prediction of subjective image quality. In *Human Vision, Visual Processing, and Digital Display,* ed. B. Rogowitz, Proc. 1077, 209–216, Bellingham, Wash. SPIE.

12

Achieving and Confirming Optimum Image Quality

Paul J. Hearty

The television broadcast standard currently in use in North America, NTSC,[1] has existed without appreciable change since its adoption in the 1950s. Although it was a considerable technological achievement for the 1950s, this system provides a narrow picture with limited spatial resolution and a number of intrinsic artifacts, such as a difficulty in maintaining independence between the luminance and chrominance information in the video signal.

During the past 15 years the research and development community, stimulated by the shortcomings of NTSC in comparison to film and supported by developments in image processing, has undertaken new initiatives in television design. The goal of these developments is to provide, not only in the production studio or the cinema but also in the home, wider-and higher-resolution images that exhibit no perceptible artifacts. In concrete terms the objective is to provide wider images (i.e., ones with a width-to-height ratio of 16:9 rather than 4:3 as in NTSC), with twice the horizontal and vertical resolution of NTSC, and with no compensatory reduction in temporal resolution. Systems that subscribe to this objective are referred to as high-definition (HDTV) or advanced television (ATV) systems.

The challenge in broadcasting HDTV or ATV to the home is to transmit images that comply with this objective within the constraints of the existing 6-MHz broadcast channel. In simple numerical terms this requires that the number of points sampled from the scene be increased by a factor of 5 or more and that the ensuing information be transmitted with no increase in channel bandwidth. In practical terms this requires the development of realizable schemes that compress the video data by a factor of 5 or better yet provide images that, when viewed, are *perceptually equivalent* to the original, uncompressed images.

Central to developments in HDTV/ATV, the criterion of perceptual equivalence highlights the role of perceptual, and related, research in the development of HDTV/ATV systems. Two classes of such research provide the "tools" for systems design, namely,

- models and data that describe visual processes involved in the perception of images; and
- assessments that measure the quality of images by using judgments by potential viewers.

The former refers to fundamental theoretical and empirical knowledge of the performance of the human visual system and, in particular, of the ways in which the visual system processes the television image. The latter refers to the use of potential viewers, under highly controlled conditions and with rigorously applied methods, to measure the quality of images. As we shall make clear in the remainder of this chapter, both tools are required but serve complementary roles.

This chapter is not intended to provide a review of perceptual and assessment research related to the development of conventional or advanced television systems. Rather, it is intended primarily to describe some of the work of the Advanced Television Evaluation Laboratory.[2] Part of the work described provides guidance for the design of optimum systems, whereas part measures the extent to which systems approach optimum performance.

The work undertaken to provide guidance for the design of optimum systems is done to support developments in a variety of real-time video systems, including advanced television. The work undertaken to measure the extent to which systems approach the optimum is done, in large part, in a joint U.S./Canada effort to examine ATV systems and to set standards for terrestrial broadcasting (i.e., off-air and by cable) of advanced television.

Perceptual Models and Data

In attempting to develop a system that approaches the optimum, a designer uses perceptual data and models to identify how best to approach the objective of *perceptual equivalence* with the reference image stream (i.e., a series of uncompressed, wide-aspect images with twice the sampling density of NTSC).

The use of perceptual models and data is neither new nor unique to advanced television. The earliest work in television was guided by the consideration of perceptual data. For example, in NTSC, color information is represented more sparsely than luminance information because early perceptual data showed that small-area changes in

color are less apparent than corresponding changes in luminance. Similarly, NTSC images are presented at a rate of about 60/sec because early perceptual data showed that large-area flicker is less perceptible at rates on the order of 60 Hz.

Since the emergence of NTSC there have been significant advances in perceptual knowledge relevant to the development of television and other real-time imaging systems. For example, early research in human spatial and temporal processing addressed the spatial and temporal domains separately (e.g., Carlson and Cohen, 1980; DeLange, 1958), but more recent work has established resolving capacities jointly in the spatial and temporal domains (e.g., Watson, Ahumada, and Farrell, 1986).

Such advances support the development of optimum systems by providing a sound and readily interpreted basis for developing artifact-free source-coding (i.e., compression) algorithms that more fully exploit the perceptual sensitivities of the viewer as a function of image content. Moreover, they also provide guidance for systems that are not optimum (e.g., ones that must compress to the point that information is visibly lost) in that they suggest ways of minimizing the perceptibility of coding deficiencies.

Such research represents a significant step forward in support of systems development. Based on such work, advanced television systems dynamically allocate processing resources according to procedures that explicitly relate image content and viewer sensitivities. It should be noted, however, that many such procedures (and the theories from which they are derived) assume that the viewer maintains a fixed gaze with respect to the images displayed. The remainder of this section of the chapter describes studies that (1) illustrate the importance of accounting for shifts in gaze during viewing and (2) examine the feasibility of using predicted gaze patterns to optimize source-coding procedures.

Resolution, Motion, and Eye Movements

Two experiments are described in this section. Both experiments demonstrate the importance of considering possible viewer eye movements when estimating the resolution required for the optimum rendition of image sequences. However, the first experiment explores the consequences of eye movements for *spatial resolution*, whereas the second does so for *temporal resolution*.

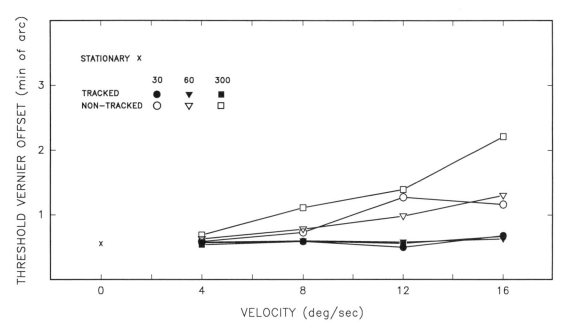

Figure 12.1
Threshold estimates for spatial acuity as a function of velocity for nontracked and tracked movement. Spatial acuity decreases with increased velocity for nontracked movement but remains high for all velocities for tracked movement.

The first experiment (Stelmach and Hearty, 1991) investigated the effects of viewers' eye movements on the spatial resolution required to represent optimally stationary and moving objects in displays sampled at 30, 60, or 300 Hz. In the experiment, viewers were shown two vertically oriented lines that were stationary or that moved at velocities up to 16 deg/sec. One of these lines was spatially continuous, whereas the other was discontinuous (i.e., a horizontal offset had been introduced midway along its length). From trial to trial, the location of the discontinuous line was varied randomly, while the extent of the offset was varied according to a maximum-likelihood threshold-tracking procedure (Taylor and Creelman, 1967). The viewers' task was to determine which of the two lines was discontinuous. The measure taken was the threshold, in minutes of arc, needed to reliably (at 75 percent accuracy) identify the spatially discontinuous line.[3]

The manipulation of primary interest, however, concerned directions given the viewers about eye movements. In half the trials with moving lines, viewers were instructed to hold their eyes stationary and to maintain a gaze locked on a centrally located fixation point (i.e., nontracked movement); in the remaining trials with moving lines, viewers were instructed to move their eyes and to maintain a gaze locked on the moving lines (i.e., tracked movement).

As is shown in figure 12.1, the minimum offset required to discriminate the spatially discontinuous line varied as a function of velocity of movement, tracked versus non-tracked movement, and temporal sampling rate. The offset required for stationary displays at the 30-, 60-, and 300-Hz temporal sampling rates was about 0.6 min. For nontracked movement this value increased to an average of about 1.6 min as the velocity of movement was increased to 16 deg/sec, which indicated a progressive loss in spatial acuity with increasing velocity (for similar findings, see Burr, Ross, and Morrone, 1986; Kelly, 1979). In contrast, for tracked movement the value remained about the same as that for stationary displays regardless of velocity, which indicated a retention of high spatial acuity (for similar results, see Girod, 1988; Glenn, Glenn, and Bastian, 1985; Westerink and Teunissen, 1990).

Some compression approaches (e.g., spatiotemporal subsampling) assume that viewers are less able to detect fine detail in moving images and, consequently, represent the moving portions of images with reduced resolution. The reduced spatial acuity reported here for higher velocities of untracked movement is consistent with such approaches. However, the maintenance of high acuity despite increases in velocity when movement is tracked indicates that such approaches may result in a visible

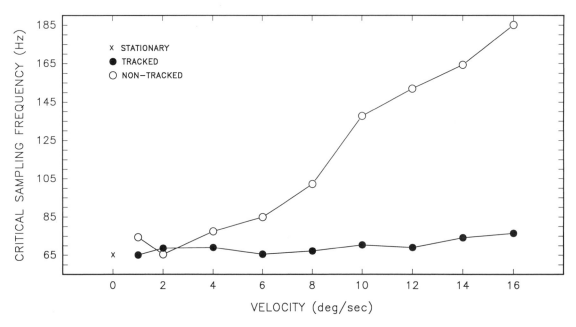

Figure 12.2
Critical temporal sampling rates as a function of velocity for nontracked and tracked movement. The rate increases with increased velocity for nontracked movement but remains low for all velocities for tracked movement.

loss in resolution that will be unacceptable to viewers, a hypothesis borne out in assessments (see Image Quality).

The results also showed the effect of temporal sampling rate. Specifically, for tracked movement, sampling rate did not affect measured acuity. However, for nontracked movement the loss in measured acuity was greater at 300 Hz than at the two lower rates. For example, at a velocity of 16 deg/sec, the threshold offset at 300 Hz was 2.2 min, whereas the corresponding offsets at 30 Hz and 60 Hz were 1.2 min and 1.3 min, respectively (for similar results, see Fahle and Poggio, 1984). At first glance this outcome may appear counterintuitive. However, for a given velocity of movement, the distance between successively displayed lines decreased with increased sampling rate. Accordingly, it is possible that at 300 Hz successive lines were displayed sufficiently close to one another that the lines appeared blurred, thereby undermining the viewers' ability to detect vernier offsets. Alternatively, it is possible that because displays were intentionally not filtered, aliasing at the lower sampling rates enhanced the viewers' ability to detect offsets.

The second experiment (Hearty and Stelmach, in preparation) was in a similar vein but investigated the effects of viewers' eye movements on the *temporal resolution* required to optimally represent stationary and moving objects. In this experiment, viewers also were shown two vertically oriented lines that were stationary or that moved at velocities up to 16 deg/sec. In this case, however, one of the lines was sampled temporally at 300 Hz, whereas the other was sampled at a lower rate. From trial to trial the location of the line sampled at the lower rate was varied randomly, while the rate at which it was sampled was varied according to a maximum-likelihood threshold-tracking procedure (Taylor and Creelman, 1967). The viewers' task was to determine which of the two lines exhibited temporal artifacts of any kind (e.g., flicker or judder). The measure taken was the sampling rate, in hertz, at which the two lines could not be distinguished (i.e., the critical sampling rate). Again, however, the manipulation of primary interest concerned directions given viewers about eye movements, which were as in the first experiment.

As is shown in figure 12.2, the critical sampling rate varied as a function of velocity of movement and tracked versus nontracked movement. On average the critical sampling rate was about 65 Hz for stationary displays (for similar findings, see Kelly, 1979). For nontracked movement this value increased to an average of about 185 Hz as the velocity of movement was increased to 16 deg/sec, which indicated that the sampling rate needed to avoid visible spatiotemporal artifacts increases with velocity (for

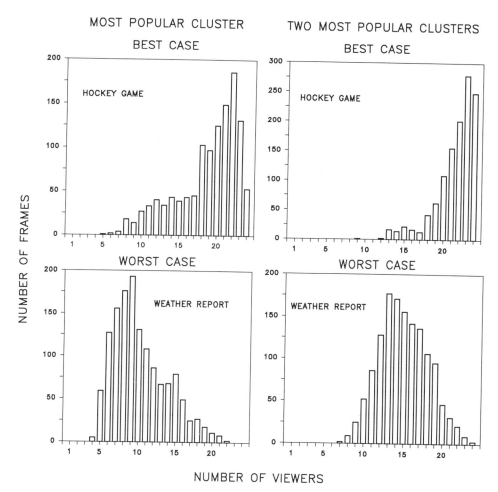

MOST POPULAR CLUSTER · BEST CASE

TWO MOST POPULAR CLUSTERS · BEST CASE

NUMBER OF FRAMES

NUMBER OF VIEWERS

Figure 12.3

Number of video frames in which a given number of viewers directed their gazes to the single most popular cluster, and the two most popular clusters for the best and worst cases of consistency in direction of gaze. Of 24 viewers, the number whose gazes were directed to the single most popular cluster ranged from 18.7 to 10.2; corresponding numbers for the two most popular clusters ranged from 21.5 to 15.0.

similar results, see Burr, Ross, and Morrone, 1986, and Watson, Ahumada, and Farrell, 1986). In contrast, for tracked movement the value remained approximately the same as that for stationary displays regardless of velocity. The latter result suggests that visible spatiotemporal artifacts result from the successive stimulation of discrete retinal locations (or their projections), an occurrence that is minimized when movement is tracked visually.

Both of the foregoing experiments demonstrate the importance of considering not only the contents of the image stream and the fixed-gaze acuities of viewers but

also the ways in which viewers move their eyes while viewing (for other views on these issues, see Girod, 1988 and chapters 8 and 15 in this text). It remains to be seen, however, whether eye-movement patterns are sufficiently predictable to support the development of source-coding algorithms.

Eye Movements in Television Viewing

It is generally assumed that eye movements during television viewing are idiosyncratic to the individual viewer and therefore unpredictable in a global sense. The following study addresses the validity of this assumption.

The study (Stelmach, Tam, and Hearty, 1991) identified the locations in television images to which viewers directed their gazes at various points in time. The television material used consisted of fifteen 45-s segments selected to represent the types of programs (e.g., news, sports, and weather) found in a large random sample of televised material. The material was displayed on a professional video monitor so that the images shown subtended viewing angles of 18 deg vertically and 24 deg horizontally.

Twenty-four viewers between 20 and 40 years of age watched the material. The viewers were asked to watch the material as they would at home. However, as the viewers watched, the locations in the images to which their gazes were directed were determined to an accuracy of 0.5 deg every $\frac{1}{30}$ sec by an eye-monitoring system.

The results of the study were analyzed to identify "clusters" in the locations to which viewers' gazes were directed in each television frame. To ensure a conservative measure, a cluster was constrained to cover no more than 6 percent of the total area of the image (i.e., about 25 deg^2). The measure taken was the number of viewers (maximum = 24) whose gazes fell in a given cluster.

As is shown in figure 12.3, the results of the study showed good agreement among viewers in direction of gaze. The number of viewers whose gazes were directed to the single most popular cluster varied from 18.7 (of 24) in the best case to 10.2 (of 24) in the worst case; the number of viewers whose gazes were directed to the two most popular clusters were 21.5 (of 24) in the best case and 15.0 (of 24) in the worst case.

If optimum systems are to be developed, the first two studies suggest that it is necessary to consider not only the contents of images and the fixed-gaze sensitivities of viewers but also the likely eye movements of viewers. The third study indicates that direction of gaze during viewing is not idiosyncratic to individual viewers and suggests that it may be possible to develop practical source-coding schemes that consider all three factors.

Assessments

Once a video system has been developed to the point at which its performance (in whole or in part) can be measured, the extent to which its performance approaches the optimum can be established either by the application of a perceptual/assessment model or by the application of procedures involving judgments by possible viewers (i.e., subjective assessments).

Assessments by Perceptual Model

As a first stage of analysis, assessment models typically compare source (i.e., uncompressed) and encoded (e.g.,

compressed) images and determine the extent to which the two differ in terms of previously established features. The extent and nature of the differences observed in this feature space are then used to estimate image quality as it would be judged by human observers.

Although significant advances have been made in developing assessment models, the following are some limitations to their use:

1. The most successful assessment/perceptual models have been developed to deal with specialized processing or transmission environments. Although these models can be used with reasonable success in the environments for which they were developed, they often do not yield fully convincing outcomes in other environments.

2. To the extent that a model is successful in predicting judgments in a particular environment, it tends to become a dominant factor in development in that environment. That is, as processing is progressively optimized in terms of model outcomes, it begins de facto to incorporate the basic premises of the model. Consequently, the model's value in identifying problems will decline with use, as the problems it identifies are alleviated, but those it does not identify will remain in the systems developed.

Assessments by Viewer Judgment

The only approach to determining the extent to which a processing scheme is optimum that, in principle, can be fully convincing involves judgment by the viewer. This is not to say that judgment methods are without problems. However, they do involve assessment by a "model" (the viewer) that is external to the processing domain and thus can convey new information.

Assessments by viewer judgment involve decisions in three areas:

1. *Assessment method.* This is the means used to solicit viewer judgments. The issues here concern the validity, reproducibility, and sensitivity of judgments and the extent to which the method adequately responds to the problem at hand. In principle, any of a variety of possible methods can be used in assessments. In practice, however, the need for convincing results favors the use (or adaptation) of methods that are already widely accepted (e.g., CCIR, 1990 a,b, present the details of methods currently recommended for assessments in television together with

guidance concerning their application to particular assessment problems).[4]

2. *Assessment participants.* These are the individuals selected to judge the performance of the system as illustrated by the assessment materials. The issues here concern the type of participants (e.g., experts or nonexperts), the validity and sensitivity of their judgments, and the extent to which their judgments can be thought to represent those of possible viewers.

3. *Assessment materials.* These are the video materials used to illustrate, for judgment by viewers, the performance of the system. The issues here concern the sensitivity of the materials (i.e., the likelihood that they will reveal deficiencies), the extent to which the materials are representative of the population of material to which the system is likely to be applied, and the extent to which the materials suit the assessment problem at hand.

Traditionally, subjective assessments have tended to be used to derive overall indexes of the picture quality achieved by systems. Such indexes have been used to examine the adequacy of individual systems, to compare and select among systems in terms of overall performance, and to provide assurance that systems will not yield unacceptable outcomes in practice.

Recent developments in subjective assessment, in which the Advanced Television Evaluation Laboratory is deeply involved, reflect the desire to address more directly and more thoroughly the two concerns that may be thought to be addressed in traditional assessments, namely, (1) to "diagnose" deficiencies and strengths in system performance and (2) to confirm that systems will perform acceptably "in the long run."

The next two sections deal with these two approaches. The first is presented in the context of work on advanced television that is currently well underway at the laboratory. The second is exemplified by work that currently is at an exploratory stage.

Performance Diagnosis

The research described in this section is carried out as part of a joint U.S./Canadian effort to set terrestrial broadcast standards for advanced television. In a process of examination initiated by the FCC's Advisory Committee on Advanced Television Service, six advanced television systems have shown sufficient promise to be considered

for adoption.[5] These systems exemplify widely differing approaches and consequently afford a rich "menu" for selection. For example, one is an enhanced-NTSC system that offers a wide aspect ratio and improved resolution but allows for reception (with reduced quality) by conventional NTSC receivers.[6] The remaining five systems offer a wide aspect ratio and increased resolution but are not compatible with NTSC. Of these, one uses digital techniques for image representation and processing and analog techniques for transmission; the remaining four systems use digital techniques for image representation and processing and digital techniques for transmission. Collectively, the six systems incorporate four different scanning standards and, potentially, provide four different levels of perceived resolution.

The research described in this section of the chapter being is done in collaboration with the Advanced Television Test Center (U.S.) and the Cable Television Laboratories (U.S.).

Image Quality

Diagnostic assessments of image quality are intended to identify specific areas in which systems should be improved as well as areas in which systems can "ease off" without appreciable loss in perceived quality. The assessments conducted at the Advanced Television Evaluation Laboratory represent the first significant application of the diagnostic approach.

The assessment method used is the one recommended by the CCIR, the double-stimulus, continuous quality-scale method (CCIR, 1990a,b). In this method each assessment trial involves two pairs of 10-sec presentations. The first pair presents a segment of the assessment material in an HDTV studio format and in the transmission format being assessed, allowing viewers to identify differences between the high-quality studio format (reference) and the transmission format (test). The second pair is a repetition of the initial pair, intended to allow viewers to confirm their initial impressions and to form and express their judgments. The order of presentation (i.e., reference-test or test-reference) is varied from trial to trial to eliminate potential sources of bias in judgments.

Viewers are instructed to examine the first pair of presentations and to identify deficiencies in the rendition of the assessment material; judgments are made during or after display of the second pair. Judgments are made individually for the reference and test formats by marking the appropriate points on two continuous-line scales divided into five equal segments labeled "excellent," "good," "fair," "poor," and "bad." The measure of interest is the difference between judgments given the reference format and those given the format under consideration.

The participants used in the assessments are selected to exhibit "normal" (i.e., perfect) visual acuity, contrast sensitivity, and color vision. As such, they can be considered to represent the visually most discerning members of the viewing public. Expert viewers are not used, as they may not be typical of the overall viewing population.

The video assessment materials have been developed expressly to respond to the goals of the diagnostic approach.[7] Each segment has been designed to stress a particular aspect of system performance and thus to evoke viewer reactions that can be related to particular strengths and deficiencies in design. These reactions may reflect performance on a design factor directly (e.g., relate to a visible loss of resolution in the moving portions of the image) or indirectly (e.g., relate to a secondary artifact, such as enhanced quantization noise, that results from an inability to handle high levels of detail in the moving portions of images). The performance factors assessed are as given in table 12.1; the table also provides descriptions of the dominant content in the corresponding segments of assessment material.

The intent of the assessments is to derive a performance profile for each system examined that identifies design factors that meet or exceed the quality of the high-quality reference format as well as those that fail to achieve this level of quality and thus that can be improved. A sample performance profile, based on assessments of one of the systems currently under consideration, is presented in figure 12.4 (for a fuller description of the results, see Advanced Television Test Center, Cable Television Laboratories & Advanced Television Evaluation Laboratory, 1992).

As the figure shows, the system tested was judged less favorably than the reference format on all 11 performance factors. However, the difference in performance observed between system and reference was appreciably larger for motion sequences than for stills. The latter outcome is particularly interesting in that the system tested used spatiotemporal subsampling, a compression approach that assumes that viewers are less able to detect fine detail in moving images and, consequently, represents the moving

Table 12.1
Diagnostic Material in Advanced Television Subjective Assessments

Performance Factor	Dominant Content of Material
Static luminance resolution	Fine detail defined by luminance differences
Static chrominance resolution	Fine detail defined by color differences
Luminance rendition	Fine changes in luminance over wide range
Luminance dynamic range	Fine changes in luminance in areas of different average luminance
Color rendition	Fine variations in color throughout full color gamut
Color dynamic range	Fine variations in color in areas of different average luminance
Depth portrayal	Variations in detail, size, luminance, and color reflecting extreme depth in composition
Peripheral performance	Sharp edges and fine luminance and color detail at lateral extremities of image
Dynamic luminance resolution	Sharp contours and fine detail defined by luminance differences in moving parts of images
Dynamic chrominance resolution	Sharp contours and fine detail defined by color differences in moving parts of images
Rendition of image motion	Single-object, multiple-object, complex, and full-frame movement in different scenes

portions of images with reduced resolution. However, the study on eye movements and spatial resolution reported previously in this chapter suggests that this approach may result in a visible loss in resolution that will be unacceptable to viewers, a hypothesis borne out by the results of the quality assessment (see Resolution, Motion, and Eye Movements).

Quality assessments are to be conducted system-by-system for the six advanced television systems under consideration. Systems will be compared, factor-by-factor, in terms of performance in relation to the fixed, high-quality reference format.

Transmission Robustness

Thus far, this chapter has treated television in terms of *achievable* picture quality. It is essential, however, to remember that television is a *transmission* service. Thus, the assessments also establish the performance of systems when subjected to a variety of impairments typical of off-air and cable transmission channels.

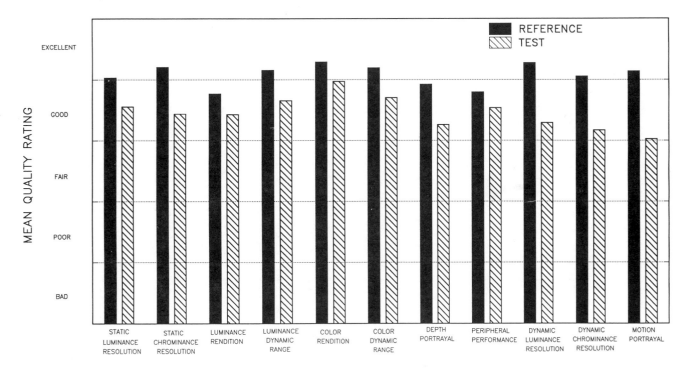

Figure 12.4
Performance profile showing mean quality ratings given the reference (studio) format and a sample test (transmission) format for 11 performance factors. The test format was inferior to the reference format for all factors, with deficiencies most pronounced for those factors related to movement.

For assessments of response to impairments, the method used is that recommended by the CCIR, the double-stimulus, impairment-scale method (CCIR, 1990a,b). In this method each judgment trial involves two 10-sec presentations. The first shows a segment of material as it would be received via the system under consideration if the transmitted signal was not subjected to the source of impairment under test; the second shows the same segment of material as it would be received via the system if the transmitted signal was subjected to a measured amount of impairment from the source under test.

The viewer is instructed to compare the pair of presentations and to judge the severity of any additional deficiencies in the second presentation; judgments are made during or after display of the second presentation. Judgments are expressed by selecting one of the following responses: "imperceptible," "perceptible, but not annoying," "slightly annoying," "annoying," and "very annoying."

The measure of interest is the rate at which the judgments become increasingly negative as the level of the impairing source is increased.

The participants used in the assessments are selected to exhibit normal (i.e., perfect) visual acuity, contrast sensitivity, and color vision. As such, they are considered to represent the visually most discerning members of the viewing public. Expert viewers are avoided as not typical of the overall viewing population.

The video materials used in impairment assessments have been developed with great care. Each is designed to be particularly sensitive to the effects of transmission impairments.

The intent of the assessments is to determine the rate at which the test system's performance degrades as the level of impairment is increased. A sample "failure characteristic," based on assessments of one system currently under consideration, is given in figure 12.5 (for a fuller description of the results, see Advanced Television Test Center, Cable Television Laboratories & Advanced Television Evaluation Laboratory, 1992).

As the figure shows, the test format did fail in response to random noise in the transmission channel. However, the system exhibited a graceful (i.e., gradual) failure over

Hearty: Achieving and Confirming Optimum Image Quality

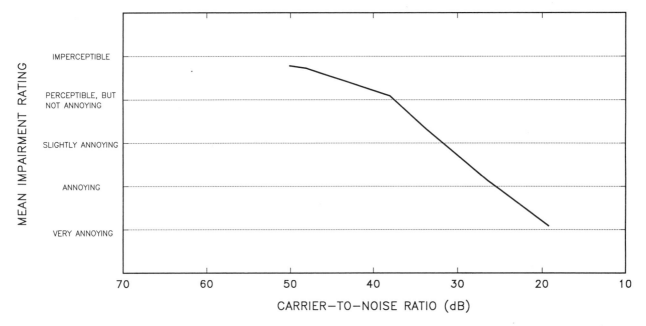

Figure 12.5
Failure characteristic showing mean impairment ratings as a function of transmission-channel signal-to-noise ratio for a sample test (transmission) format. The test format exhibited a graceful (i.e., gradual) failure over a broad range of signal-to-noise ratios.

a broad range of impairment due to reduced signal-to-noise ratios.

The assessments are conducted system-by-system for the six advanced television systems under consideration. Systems will be compared in terms of the rates at which their performance degrades as the level of impairment is increased.

Long-Run Performance

Complete analysis of a system's potential requires knowledge of the performance it is likely to exhibit over the course of its use (i.e., in the long run). Knowledge of quality exhibited under ideal conditions and of rate of failure given particular deficiencies in the transmission channel are essential to decision making but do not *fully* satisfy the requirements of a complete analysis. In contrast, *probabilistic* determinations, which establish the likelihood with which particular levels of performance will occur, will support more thorough analysis either in confirming that a system will perform to acceptable standards or in selecting among systems according to likely performance in use.

Assessments of long-run performance represent a new approach in subjective assessment, one in which the Advanced Television Evaluation Laboratory is actively involved. The discussion in this section explores procedures for implementing such an approach.

In general, there are two possible sources of reduced performance in a television, or other video transmission, system.[8]

1. Limitations in source-coding performance. This refers to the likelihood and severity of visible artifacts introduced by the source-coding algorithm when it is exposed to the range of possible program content.

2. Limitations in channel-coding performance. This refers to the likelihood and severity of artifacts that penetrate, or are introduced by, the channel-coding algorithm when it is exposed to the range of possible transmission conditions.

The thrust of the long-run approach is to determine the *probabilities* with which particular levels of performance (i.e., perceived quality or, equivalently, judged impairment) will occur in practice. In theory, a function defining such probabilities could be determined empirically by a brute-force approach. This would require that each system considered be subjected to a random sample of program content *and* transmission conditions that was sufficiently extensive to represent the population of possible outcomes. In practice, however, this approach would tend to require assessment experiments that would be too large for practical implementation.

The fundamental problem, then, is to identify procedures by which the basic objectives of the long-run approach can be achieved more efficiently. In addressing this problem it is useful to consider separately the two sources of potential problems for systems—program content and transmission conditions.

Program Content

As we indicated previously, the effects of program content could be determined using a sample of randomly selected segments of program material. The ensuing assessment experiment would allow performance probabilities to be estimated directly from the frequencies with which different impairment judgments were observed but would result in large, if not intractable, experiments, particularly if the effects of transmission conditions also must be considered.

The advantage in using random-selection procedures is that performance probabilities can be determined in the absence of knowledge about the population of program material. However, if such knowledge can be brought to bear, material can be chosen more selectively and more tractable experiments are possible.

To do this, it is first necessary to develop a statistic to measure characteristics on which program material differs. However, because this statistic will be used to anticipate performance in source coding, it must capture the level of stress imposed by program content on the encoding process (e.g., differential entropy for discrete cosine transform schemes). In essence, a statistic is required whose values relate monotonically to the perceived quality of the encoded material.

Once an appropriate statistic has been developed, it is necessary to determine the probabilities with which values of the statistic occur in the population of program material. To achieve this, the statistic must be applied to a random sample of program material that is sufficient in size to represent the overall population.

If this approach was successful, assessments would use the smaller number of segments of material needed to sample values of the content statistic rather than the larger number of segments required to represent the population of program content. Moreover, the number of segments

could be reduced further if values of the statistic were sampled in a nonuniform manner, with sampling skewed toward values of the statistic associated with greater stress for encoding.

The content-statistic procedure appears to offer a basis for more practical implementations of the long-run approach. However, the following fundamental issues concerning the feasibility of the procedure remain to be resolved:

1. Feasibility of the statistic. Here, there are two related issues. First, is it possible to develop a statistic that captures all aspects of program content that would relate to stress in source coding? Second, is it necessary to develop different statistics for different source coding algorithms (or classes of source-coding algorithms)? Clearly, the statistic(s) must take account not only of the distributions of luminance and chrominance values in images but also of the rates at which local luminance and chrominance values change both spatially within an image and temporally across successive images. For practical reasons, it would be advantageous to use a generic scheme to characterize the program material and, as needed, coding-specific "transfer functions" to relate different values in the characterization to perceptible consequences for particular coding schemes (or classes of coding schemes).

2. Availability of program material. Access to the population of program material is required to determine the probabilities with which different values of the statistic occur. This is a straightforward, if demanding, task if systems are to be applied to an existing base of programs (e.g., NTSC). However, if systems are to be applied to a new or emerging base of programs (e.g., HDTV), it will be necessary to adapt procedures. For example, it may be acceptable to extrapolate from an existing base of material, if adequate provision can be made for a priori differences between the existing and new/emerging populations (e.g., to extrapolate from NTSC to HDTV, allowing for differences in sampling density, or from film to HDTV, allowing for differences in sampling density, dynamic range, and sampling rate). Alternatively, it may be acceptable simply to accept the emerging base of program material as representative of the eventual population and to derive probabilities from that limited base. (*Note:* This fails to account for improvements in image-capture technologies and for increases in production experience, both of which extend the range of the program material).

3. Availability of value-specific material. In the assessments it will be necessary to find segments of test material that represent particular values of the statistic. However, because assessments require segments of material that are 10 s or more in duration, this will be difficult unless the statistic itself is based on 10 s samples of material. If such is not the case, it may be acceptable to select segments of material that exhibit a distribution of values of the statistic that is centered on the targeted value and that meets some minimum-variance constraint.

Transmission Conditions

The second, statistically independent source of problems for systems involves the condition of the transmission channel through which the signal is received. As with program content, the effects of transmission conditions could be determined using a large random sample. Again, however, such an approach would result in large, intractable experiments.

However, the procedures described previously for program content can be applied equally to consideration of the effects of transmission conditions. Thus, it would be necessary to develop a statistic that captured the level of stress imposed by transmission conditions on the channel-coding process and to determine the probabilities with which values of that statistic occurred in transmission. Then, assessments would use a selection of transmission conditions sufficient to sample values of the statistic, preferably in a nonuniform manner.

Like the program-content procedure, this procedure appears to offer a basis for more practical implementations of the long-run approach. However, this procedure also faces a number of unresolved issues. Because these are directly analogous to those for the program-content procedure, we will not repeat them here.

Assessment Procedures

In the assessments, segments of program material selected to sample values of the program-content statistic would be subjected to transmission conditions selected to sample values of the transmission-condition statistic. Because program content and transmission conditions are independent in practice, assessment materials and transmission conditions would be combined independently to elicit judgments of total impairment.

The assessment method used would be the double-stimulus, impairment-scale method (see Transmission Robustness). The reference condition would show a 10-s segment of material in the appropriate source (i.e., non-encoded) format, whereas the test condition would show the same segment of material as it would be received via the system under consideration if the transmitted signal was subjected to transmission impairment. Criteria for the selection of assessment participants would be as described previously for performance diagnosis methods.

Participants would judge the visibility and severity of impairments introduced in each segment of material, whether by source coding, transmission condition, or both. The ensuing judgments would then be used to derive a probabilistic, program-content/transmission-condition failure characteristic. This characteristic would be based on observed occurrences of different impairment judgments, weighted by the underlying probabilities for program content and transmission conditions.

It remains for further research to establish the viability of the long-run approach and of the methods by which it can be implemented. Clearly, it would be advantageous in decision making if information of the sort offered by the long-run approach was available. However, it is necessary to determine whether valid statistics for program content and transmission conditions can be established.

Summary

This chapter provides a brief summary of research done, or underway, at the Advanced Television Evaluation Laboratory. The research described includes the following:

- Psychophysical research that relates the spatial and temporal resolution required in advanced television and other video systems to viewers' gaze patterns while viewing;

- Examinations of viewers' gaze patterns during television viewing to determine the extent to which eye-movement behavior is consistent across viewers and thus can be predicted sufficiently to develop optimum source-coding methods;

- Subjective assessment research, as part of a joint U.S./Canadian advanced television standardization effort, that diagnoses the performance of advanced television systems in terms of image-quality attributes and robustness on transmission; and

• Research on methods of establishing the performance of systems in the long run that consider the performance of both source-coding and transmission schemes.

Acknowledgments

The research described in this paper is supported by the Broadcast Technologies Research Branch of the Communications Research Centre, Department of Communications (Canada), and by a consortium of broadcasting interests in Canada. The author acknowledges the contributions of his collaborators, Lew B. Stelmach and W. James Tam, to work described in the earlier sections of this chapter. The author expresses his appreciation to Phillip Corriveau and the other members of the team at the Advanced Television Evaluation Laboratory, and to Michael Sablatash and other colleagues in Broadcast Technologies Research. And, finally, the author expresses his special appreciation to A. B. Watson and to A. J. Ahumada, Jr., for their helpful and insightful reviews of this chapter. Correspondence should be addressed to Paul J. Hearty, Communications Research Centre, 3701 Carling Avenue, Ottawa, Canada K2H 8S2.

Notes

1. NTSC is an acronym for the National Television Systems Committee, an industry body that, in the 1950s, was responsible for establishing a color television standard for broadcast in the United States. The acronym is used conventionally to refer to the system recommended, which currently is in use in North America. Images presented by this system have a nominal 525 scanning lines and have a width-to-height (aspect) ratio of 4:3; of the nominal 525 lines, half are displayed each 1/59.94 sec.

2. The Advanced Television Evaluation Laboratory is a facility of the Canadian Department of Communications that is managed by the Communications Research Centre.

3. The use of a vernier acuity task in this context may seem controversial inasmuch as it has been shown that if the orientation of the vernier target is held constant (as in the present experiment), reasonable vernier acuity can be maintained despite low-pass filtering of the image (e.g., Watt, Morgan, and Ward, 1983). However, because the intent of the experiment was principally to demonstrate the importance of eye movements, and because losses in vernier acuity do occur in the experiment, the task does appear sufficient to requirements.

4. CCIR is an acronym for the International Radio Consultative Committee, an organ of the International Telecommunications Union of the United Nations. The CCIR is responsible for the promulgation of international broadcasting standards.

5. The FCC's Advisory Committee on Advanced Television Service was established in 1987 by the Federal Communications Commission to examine possible advanced television systems and to recommend a terrestrial broadcast standard for consideration by the commission.

6. After commencement of the testing program, this system was removed from consideration.

7. The description given here considers only one aspect of the video quality assessments, that relating to performance diagnosis. However, the assessments also serve a confirmatory role. To that end, additional segments of assessment material were included to confirm the performance of systems with electronically generated material (i.e., graphics) and with filmed material (i.e., 24, 30, and 60 frame/sec film).

8. The dichotomy introduced here between source coding and channel coding is a simplification intended to promote a clearer presentation of the long-run approach. In fact, some systems adaptively "trade off" quality in source coding with robustness in channel coding. However, complications of this sort promote, rather than invalidate, the long-run approach.

References

Advanced Television Test Center, Cable Television Laboratories & Advanced Television Evaluation Laboratory (1992). *Narrow-MUSE: Record of test results.* Alexandria, Va: Advanced Television Test Center.

Burr, D. C., Ross, J. & Morrone, M. C. (1986). Smooth and sampled motion. *Vision Research* 26:643–652.

CCIR (1990a). Recommendation 500: Method for the subjective assessment of the quality of television pictures. *Recommendations of the CCIR, vol. 11, pt. 1.* Geneva: International Radio Consultative Committee.

CCIR (1990b). Recommendation 710: Subjective assessment methods for image quality in high-definition television. *Recommendations of the CCIR, vol. 11 pt. 1.* Geneva: International Radio Consultative Committee.

Carlson, C. R. & Cohen, R. W. (1980). A simple psychophysical model for predicting the visibility of displayed information. *Proceedings of the Society for Information Display* 21:229–246.

DeLange, H. (1958). Research into the dynamic nature of the human fovea-cortex systems with intermittent and modulated light: I, Attenuation characteristics with white and colored light. *Journal of the Optical Society of America* 48:777–784.

Fahle, M. & Poggio, T. (1984). Visual hyperacuity: Spatiotemporal interpolation in human vision. In S. Ullman and W. Richards (Eds.), *Image Understanding.* Norwood, N.J.: Ablex.

Girod, B. (1988). Eye movements and coding of video sequences. *SPIE Proceedings, 1001.*

Glenn, W. E., Glenn, K. G. & Bastian, C. J. (1985). Imaging system design based on psychophysical data. *Proceedings of the Society for Information Display* 26:71–78.

Hearty, P. J. & Stelmach, L. B. Requirements for static and dynamic temporal resolution in advanced television systems: A psychophysical evaluation. Unpublished manuscript.

Kelly, D. H. (1979). Motion and vision. II, Stabilized spatio-temporal threshold surface. *Journal of the Optical Society of America* 69:1340–1349.

Stelmach, L. B. & Hearty, P. J. (1991). Requirements for static and dynamic spatial resolution in advanced television systems: A psychophysical evaluation. *Journal of the Society of Motion Picture and Television Engineers* 100:5–9.

Stelmach, L. B., Tam, W. J. & Hearty, P. J. (1991). Static and dynamic spatial resolution in image coding: An investigation of eye movements. *SPIE Proceedings* 1453:147–152.

Taylor, M. M. & Creelman, C. D. (1967). PEST: Efficient estimates on probability functions. *Journal of the Optical Society of America* 41:782–787.

Watson, A. B., Ahumada, A. J. Jr. & Farrell, J. E. (1986). Window of visibility: A psychophysical theory of fidelity in time-sampled visual motion displays. *Journal of the Optical Society of America, A* 3:300–307.

Watt, R. J., Morgan, M. J. & Ward, R. M. (1983). The use of different cues in vernier acuity. *Vision Research* 10:991–995.

Westerink, J. H. D. M. & Teunissen, C. (1990). Perceived sharpness in moving images. *SPIE Proceedings* 1249:78–87.

13

The Use of Psychophysical Data and Models in the Analysis of Display System Performance

Jeffrey Lubin

A Hierarchy of Vision Models

It is often important to know how well a display system is performing. For display designers developing a new system, this knowledge allows them to optimize the system performance under a set of hardware constraints. For display users trying to choose a system for a particular application, this knowledge allows them to determine if a particular display would suit their needs.

In both cases the performance of the display system must ultimately be measured in terms of the ability of a person using that system to perform desired tasks. Although display performance is traditionally measured in terms of physical parameters such as brightness, contrast, or bandwidth, these parameters are useful only to the extent that measured values can be correlated with predictions of human visual task performance.

In this chapter we address the problem of translating between the physical performance of a display system and the task performance of the display user. We shall argue that the appropriate translation technique depends on the specific performance analysis needed. In some cases, direct psychophysical measurement as a function of physical display system parameters is warranted. However, it is often the case that a mathematical model of human visual response can effectively guide performance analysis when direct psychophysical measurement is impractical or impossible. In fact, even when direct measurement is possible, a reliable model can provide a means of interpreting the data, so that the performance effects of different display manipulations can be better understood.

Thus, one question is the extent to which vision models can be used in conjunction with or instead of data collection to analyze display system performance. However, because vision models vary in their scope and level of complexity, another important consideration is how to choose a particular vision model for the display performance analysis issue at hand.

To help answer these questions, this chapter presents a hierarchy of vision models; that is, a description of a range of different approaches to the modeling and collection of psychophysical data. Four distinct levels of this hierarchy are described:

1. Model-free data collection;
2. Task modeling;
3. Performance modeling;
4. Mechanistic modeling.

Each of these terms is defined in the appropriate section. For each level of the hierarchy, one or more examples are shown that illustrate the application of each modeling approach to the analysis of particular display performance questions.

Data Collection

At one end of the model hierarchy is no model at all. As we mentioned in the introduction, one way to translate from physical display system parameters to user performance is simply to measure the ability of human observers using the system to perform desired tasks. Suppose, for example, that a radiology department is considering the purchase of a softcopy (e.g., CRT-based) display system to replace the traditional film-based hardcopy system. One could evaluate the system by asking a number of radiologists to perform diagnoses using softcopy outputs and then comparing the results with performance using hardcopy. Relevant performance measures might include the probability of correct diagnosis or the time needed to perform the task.

The main virtue of this technique is that it can be applied even when a reliable model of performance on a specific task does not exist. This is often the case when subjective judgments of viewer preference for home entertainment applications are needed.

The main problem with this technique is its cost. Reliable data collection is a time-consuming process, especially when substantial training is necessary to adapt the experimental observer to inherent differences among the different display media. Such training would certainly be necessary in the radiology example cited, since even subtle changes in the processing of hardcopy can adversely affect diagnostic performance until the radiologist has become accustomed to the new images.

Moreover, when performance analysis is required during display system development, the costs of psychophysical data collection must often include the construction of one or more prototype systems on which task performance is evaluated. Device simulation can in some cases reduce the cost of prototype construction, but to the extent that a simulated display output is an imperfect rendering, some additional guidance is needed to determine under what conditions performance evaluations using simulated imagery are accurate. Such guidance will generally come from a vision model.

Costs of psychophysical data collection for display development also increase with the number of physical display parameters to be optimized. For a single parameter, optimization is relatively easy, because a performance maximum can be determined from data collected at a range of values of this one parameter. However, the amount of data needed can grow exponentially with the number of physical parameters, since the parameter values can interact in unexpected ways in determining task performance. Here again, a vision model can provide guidance, in this case by indicating regions of the parameter space within which independence among the parameters determining task performance can be expected. For example, if the vision model indicates that human sensitivity to changes in contrast is independent of mean display luminance over some range of luminances, then it is not necessary to collect data at every combination of luminance and contrast within that range.

One conclusion from these considerations is that data collection for display system optimization is difficult in the absence of a vision model unless the number of optimization parameters is small, and the display output imagery can be conveniently and accurately rendered. These conditions are met in the following example, in which subjective quality ratings were collected for images differing along the dimensions of resolution and brightness. Here, data collection is especially appropriate, because a model that accurately predicts subjective image quality ratings in this context does not yet exist.

Resolution Versus Brightness Study

Current CRT technology imposes a cost trade-off between resolution and brightness of the display, as shown in the schematic plot of figure 13.1. In this figure, peak brightness of the display is plotted along the abscissa, and

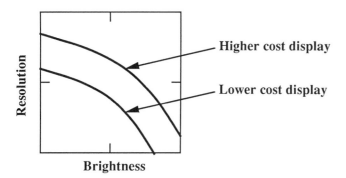

Figure 13.1
Iso-cost contours. In this schematic plot the abscissa is peak brightness of the display, and the ordinate is a resolution measure such as the area under the modulation transfer function of an average spot. Each curve indicates the achievable values on these two parameters for a given fixed cost.

resolution along the ordinate, with "iso-cost" contours showing the achievable values of these parameters at each of two different fixed costs. The trade-off is indicated by the negative slopes of these contours: At constant cost, resolution goes down as brightness goes up.

Given this trade-off, a display manufacturer needs to choose a point on the curve when building a display. For consumer television sets, a good point is that which maximizes the perceived quality of the displayed imagery.

This is a reasonable application for model-free data collection, for all three of the reasons mentioned above. First, the number of stimulus parameters is small (2), so that the stimulus space can be adequately sampled without excessive effort. Second, the experimental imagery can be conveniently rendered, using standard digital filtering techniques to produce different resolution settings, and CRT beam current manipulations to produce different brightness settings.[1] Third, the dependent measure of image quality is sufficiently ill defined so that accurate modeling in the absence of data collection is not a viable alternative.

To generate the appropriate data, Lubin, Pica, and Barbin (1992) conducted a set of experiments in which subjects were presented still images on a high-definition CRT display. In all experiments subjects were asked to rate each image on a scale from 1 to 10, low to high, based on the degree to which they would like images of a similar quality on their home televisions.

In one experiment for which sample results are shown here, four different images, chosen to span a range of

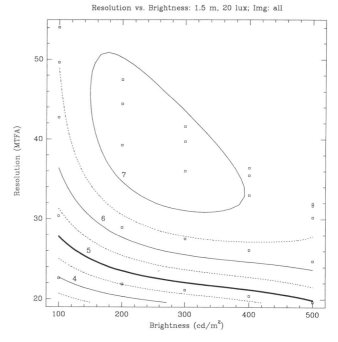

Figure 13.2
Subjective rating contour data for resolution versus brightness experiment. Viewing distance was 1.5 m, ambient illumination was 20 lux. Open squares show points at which data were collected on four different images; contours are from a polynomial approximation to these data. Numbers on plot indicate the rating associated with each solid contour line: the dashed lines are at half-rating increments.

common television scenes, were used. These included a city street scene, a male portrait, a scene with text, and an outdoor harbor scene. Each of the four different images was presented at each of a set of five different resolutions and five different brightnesses. Each subject participated in two experimental sessions, one at each of two ambient light settings: 300 lux (showroom conditions) and 20 lux (dim home lighting). Both sessions for each subject were at a single viewing distance. For half the subjects, this distance was 1.5 m, for the other half, 3.0 m. This corresponded to approximately 3.5 and 7 picture heights from the 86-cm diagonal, 16 × 9 aspect ratio tube used in the experiments.

Figure 13.2 shows a representative contour plot of subjective ratings as a function of resolution and brightness, averaged across the four images. As in the iso-cost plot of figure 13.1, the abscissa shows peak brightness, and the ordinate shows resolution, defined here as the area under the modulation transfer function of an average spot for the displayed brightness level. This plot is from the

1.5-m, 20-lux viewing condition, approximating the conditions for home television viewing; the other three combinations of viewing distance and ambient lighting show similar results.

Notice that because this contour plot has the same axes as the iso-cost plot of figure 13.1, a simple design optimization procedure presents itself: By overlaying the iso-cost curve for a given cost onto a contour plot of rating data, the designer can simply choose the point on the iso-cost curve that corresponds to the maximum subjective rating.

One potential problem with this enterprise is that substantial differences exist among the rating data for different images. For example, if one examines for each image the histogram of number of pixels at each gray level, the intuitively plausible pattern emerges that preferred brightness is higher for images with a higher percentage of pixels at the lower gray levels (e.g., a dimly lit interior scene) than for images with more pixels at the higher gray levels (e.g., an outdoor scene with a bright sky). In one sense, such results are not a problem and simply indicate that no single combination of physical display parameters will be subjectively optimal for all possible displayed images. In this sense, the best that can be done is to collect rating data over a sufficiently large and representative range of imagery and then choose the display parameter settings that maximize the combined ratings across this range. However, the problem is that the larger the variance in ratings from image to image, the larger is the set of images required to produce reliable data, so that the cost of data collection may grow to prohibitive levels.

An interesting solution to this problem is to stabilize the variance across images by plotting the rating data in terms not of the physical parameters of the display but of transformed parameters that include the effects of the relevant differences among images. For example, in the case of the differences in preferred brightness mentioned above, it was found that by using as the abscissa of the contour plots the brightness at the 95th percentile of the image histogram, rather than the peak brightness of the display, the plots for the different images became much more similar.

This solution generates its own problem, though, since the transformed brightness axis is no longer in a form that relates directly to a physical parameter of the display. However, by measuring this histogram-based brightness value for a large range of imagery, an average brightness can be determined that is expressible in terms of the peak brightness of the display, and the link to the physical parameter is reestablished. Notice that here, as is the case with the more direct data collection strategy outlined above, measurements are required across a representative range of imagery. The difference is that rather than a subjective quality rating, an image statistic is measured from which the quality rating can be predicted. Because it is easier to measure a large number of image histograms than a large amount of rating data, the efficiency of the process is improved.

Notice also that this strategy of establishing a functional relationship between psychophysical data and a computation on the input image is itself a simple form of psychophysical modeling in which hypotheses are made and tested concerning which features of the stimulus contribute to the subjective quality judgement. This stimulus analysis strategy can be seen as a simple form of the task analysis strategy to be discussed in detail in the following section. There, in addition to the extraction of relevant stimulus features, the methodology consists of hypothesizing simple psychophysical detection tasks on which complex judgements such as image quality ratings are based.

Task Modeling

It is often the case in display performance analysis that the visual task is not well defined. This is most commonly true when the desired performance measure is a subjective estimate of image quality for home entertainment or other applications. As the previous example demonstrates, direct psychophysical measurement can sometimes solve this problem by removing the need for a vision model and hence for the objective task definitions that these models generally require.

As noted above, one potential problem with the data collection approach is that subjective quality ratings can vary widely with image content. If, however, one could determine the particular image features on which viewers based their subjective ratings, the accuracy of predicted ratings on arbitrary imagery would increase. This strategy, discussed briefly at the end of the previous section, can be taken further: Given these image features, it is also sometimes possible to relate ill-defined tasks such as subjective image quality rating to psychophysically well-defined measures such as detection thresholds for these features. The term *task modeling* in this section thus refers to this decomposition of an ill-defined task into simple component tasks for which data collection and/or simple visual modeling can then provide accurate performance estimates as a function of the physical parameters varied.

A critical and sometimes difficult question in this context is how to choose the task decomposition. One approach is to use standard techniques of multidimensional scaling, such as those described by Ahumada and Null in chapter 11. However, in many cases, a suitable decomposition can be obtained by knowledge of the application, by direct inspection of sample imagery, or by other a priori considerations. One such consideration is the assumption that perceived image quality will suffer to the extent that processing by the display system produces visible artifacts in the output imagery. Given this assumption, image quality can be measured and optimized by first characterizing the artifacts that can result from particular physical processes of the display system and then measuring and/or modeling psychophysical thresholds for the visibility of these artifacts as a function of the display parameters in question. This approach will be clarified in the two examples that follow.

Designing an Optimal Quantizer

Increasing the brightness range of a display system introduces another image quality problem beyond the resolution trade-off discussed above, namely that luminance quantization artifacts can begin to appear on displayed digital imagery. For example, in an image region that should change gradually in intensity, the luminance steps from one gray level to the next can become detectable, resulting in visible contours. The design problem is this: Assuming design control over the function mapping gray level to luminance (i.e., the quantizer), and a cost associated with increasing the number of gray levels in this quantizer, determine the lowest cost quantizer (i.e., the quantizer with the fewest number of gray levels) that maximizes image quality for a given brightness range of the display.

This problem, addressed in detail in Lubin and Pica (1991), is an appropriate application for the task modeling methodology described in this section. In this case the detectability of contouring edges in the image is assumed to be the simple psychophysical task with which image-

quality judgments are associated. Based on this assumption, a quantizer that minimizes the detectability of these edges will maximize the perceived image quality. Moreover, because the luminance step required for edge detectability increases with the average luminance around the step (as will be shown in data to be presented shortly), it follows that the optimal quantizer is similarly nonuniform, with larger luminance steps at higher gray levels: Although a uniform quantizer could be designed with enough gray levels to prevent contouring artifacts from appearing, a nonuniform quantizer matched to human visual performance on edge detection will provide the same image quality with fewer gray levels, and hence, lower cost.

Figure 13.3 shows the relevant psychophysical data (see Lubin and Pica (1991) for details of the psychophysical procedure). For these data, the size of a luminance change required for detectability of a vertical step edge halfway across a 17-deg wide by 5.25-deg high rectangle was

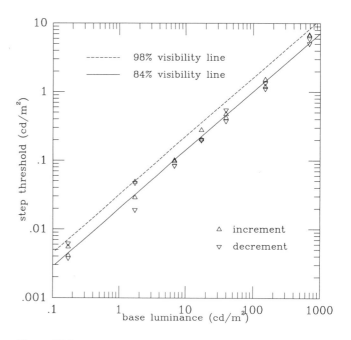

Figure 13.3

Thresholds for step-edge visibility. The points represent threshold data for an 84 percent detection criterion. Pairs of points at each base luminance represent two replications each for increments and decrements. The solid line through the plot is the best fitting regression line: $dL = aL^b$, where L is the base luminance, dL is the increment or decrement threshold, and the fitted values of a and b are 0.01667 and 0.8502, respectively. The dashed line represents a 98 percent detection criterion.

measured at several different luminances, with the eye fully adapted to each. The plotted points and the solid line fitted through them represent the set of step edges detectable on 84 percent of the trials. Under normal conditions such edges are very difficult to see. The dashed line parallel to and above the solid line represents the set of edges detectable on 98 percent of the trials. An edge from a point along this line is almost always detectable; its presence as an artifact in an image would therefore tend to degrade image quality.

These data can be used to construct an optimal quantizer, such that each quantization step is guaranteed to be as large as possible without leading to visible contouring artifacts. The procedure, a simplification of a technique by Sharma and Netravali (1977), is as follows:

1. The first quantization level Q_0 is put at I_0 (the lowest luminance level required.)

2. The second quantization level Q_1 is put at $I_1 = I_0 + \Delta(I_0)$, where $\Delta(I)$ is defined as the threshold luminance increment from luminance level I.

3. The third quantization level Q_2 is put at $I_2 = I_1 + \Delta(I_1)$.

This procedure continues until the desired luminance I_n is reached.

Using a simple plotting technique, one can use the data to assess the visibility of contouring artifacts that occur in existing displays, as is illustrated in figure 13.4. Here, with the same axes as for the data plot in figure 13.3, luminance steps for each of several hypothetical display designs are plotted as a function of the luminance from which each step occurs. Because these functions show the size of the step edge produced by the display for a one gray level increment at each of the possible displayed luminances, they can be compared directly with the 98 percent step-edge visibility line, reproduced on this plot from figure 13.3. For those points on the display functions at higher ordinate values than the 98 percent line, an increment of one gray level is predicted to produce a highly visible contouring artifact. For the three specific designs shown in figure 13.4, the results show that for a screen gamma of 2.2 (where gamma is the exponent in the power function relating input voltage and output luminance) and a luminance range of 0.05 to 100 cd/m², at least 10 bits are required in a linear DAC for contouring artifacts to remain invisible.

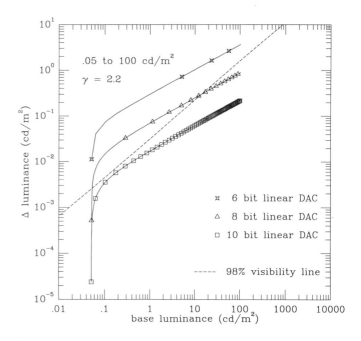

Figure 13.4
Δ luminance versus luminance is shown for displays with 6-, 8-, and 10- bit linear DACs, a display gamma of 2.2, and a 0.05 to 100 cd/m² luminance range. The dashed line is the 98 percent human threshold visibility estimate, obtained from the experimental data shown above. Plotted points represent every sixteenth quantization level on the display.

Psychophysical Requirements for Tiled LC Displays

Tiled liquid crystal displays are currently being developed for applications for which large, bright, high-resolution, low-profile displays are required. In this technology a number of smaller liquid crystal (LC) displays are tiled together to create a single larger display screen. Here, the display performance evaluation problem is to determine the physical requirements of the tiling process such that image quality is not compromised due to the segmentation of the display.

The strategy used by Alphonse and Lubin (1992) to perform these evaluations is another example of task modeling. Based on empirical knowledge of the manufacturing process and visual inspection of some sample displays, they constructed the following list of artifacts potentially visible as result of the tiling process:

1. Visible seams between adjoining tiles;

2. Visible variations in average luminosity and/or chromaticity among tiles;

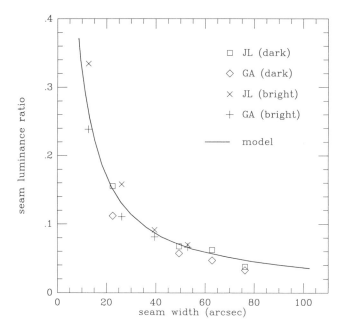

Figure 13.5
Experimental data for seam visibility thresholds. See text for details.

3. Vernier misalignments between tiles, resulting in apparent segmentation of extended-line objects.

With this list it is possible to determine a set of physical requirements, based on the measurement of simple psychophysical thresholds, that will guarantee that the described artifacts will not be seen. For example, figure 13.5 shows seam visibility data from Alphonse and Lubin (1992). In this experiment the contrast required to detect a thin vertical line on a CRT was measured as a function of line width. Viewing distance was 564 cm. The abscissa of the plot shows line width in arcsec, while the ordinate shows contrast, defined as $|\Delta I|/I_0$, where I_0 is the background luminance (always 17 cd/m^2 in this experiment), and $|\Delta I|$ is the absolute value of the change in luminance between the background and the line. Positive values of ΔI thus refer to lines brighter than the background. Plotted points are for two observers (the authors) for both bright and dark lines.

The curve through these points shows the contrast thresholds predicted by the Carlson and Cohen (1980) JND Model, a model similar to the performance model by Barten (1990) to be described in the next section. As shown in Alphonse and Lubin (1992), this curve has the form

$$\theta \approx \frac{3.5}{|\Delta I|/I_0}$$

where θ is the threshold seam width (in arcsec). Notice that this curve relates threshold seam width to threshold contrast and can thus be used as in figure 13.5 to predict threshold contrast for a given seam width or, alternatively, to predict threshold seam width for a given contrast. For example, for a completely dark seam (i.e., with a contrast of 1.0), this model predicts a maximum allowable seam width of 3.5 arcsec, which corresponds to a 9-μm seam at a 50-cm viewing distance.

The use of the Carlson and Cohen model predictions in this example illustrates an additional benefit of task modeling: When a complex visual task is decomposed into simpler psychophysical tasks, there is a higher probability that a simple vision model such as that of Carlson and Cohen will be able to generate reliable predictions, obviating the need for additional data collection. For example, after verifying the goodness of the model fit using the data collected for figure 13.5, one can reasonably extrapolate the model predictions for the threshold seam width calculation of the preceding paragraph without collecting additional data. In the next section the use of simple vision models like that of Carlson and Cohen are discussed in detail.

Performance Modeling

A vision model, as traditionally defined, computes predictions of human visual task performance from input imagery. The discussions and examples in the previous two sections have shown cases in which useful display performance information can be obtained at reasonable cost from psychophysical data alone, without the use of such a model. However, for any application in which a vision model produces reliable performance predictions, its use is almost always preferable to data collection. As already mentioned, one reason for this preference is that running a model generally costs much less than running a psychophysical experiment to generate the same display performance information, especially when the display system in question is still in the design phase.

In this and the following section, examples of these vision models are discussed. The distinction to be made between the models presented in the two sections is based on the level at which components of the visual system are primarily modeled: Although the distinction is more a continuum than a strict dichotomy, the performance models in this section tend to treat the entire visual system as a "black box" for which input/output functions need to be specified. For the mechanistic models in the next section, physiological and psychophysical data are used to open the black box. As a result, input/output functions are needed not only for the system as a whole but for a number of component mechanisms within.

An additional advantage of mechanistic modeling is the greater ease of generalization to new stimuli and tasks. This is discussed in detail in the Mechanistic Modeling section.

SQRI Model

In the Carlson and Cohen (1980) JND Model, an input image is decomposed by partitioning its one-dimensional power spectrum into a number of discrete adjacent frequency bands. The output from each band is then subject to a static nonlinearity that is accelerating for small input values and compressive for large values. Changes in the output of this process from one member of a pair of images to the other provides a simple perceptual measure of the visibility of differences between the two images. This model can successfully predict the visibility of changes in edge sharpness and of various display artifacts, for example, the seam visibility data described above. However, the model is somewhat complicated to compute, among other reasons because a noise parameter must be adjusted for each change in display parameters such as luminance or display size.

A similar but computationally simpler model is the SQRI (square root integral) model of Barten (1987, 1990), which has been successfully applied to a number of different display evaluation problems. A typical example of a performance model (for reasons to be discussed shortly), the SQRI model can be thought of a simplified version of the Carlson and Cohen (1980) model in which the separate frequency-selective bands are replaced by a single integral over spatial frequencies. This integral is

$$J = \frac{1}{\ln 2} \int_0^{v \max} \sqrt{\frac{M(v)}{M_t(v)}} \frac{dv}{v},$$

where $v_{\max}$ is the maximum spatial frequency displayed, $M(v)$ is the modulation transfer function of the display,

and $M_t(v)$ is the threshold modulation transfer function of the human visual system, that is, the threshold contrast for grating detection as a function of the spatial frequency of the grating. The value of $M_t(v)$ is also approximated by a simple computational expression, to be discussed shortly. The integral evaluates to J, the number of JNDs (just-noticeable differences) in the display. So, for example, if a particular display manipulation resulted in a unit change in the value of J, the model would predict that this manipulation would be just detectable to the human observer.

This model, like the Carlson and Cohen model, is spatially one-dimensional, and Barten himself does not generally give details on how the second dimension is handled for specific model applications. Still, the model gives impressive results in predicting subjective image quality, showing a linear relationship between model output and subjective ratings. Some sample predictions from Barten (1990) are shown in figure 13.6, where subjective image quality measured by Westerink and Roufs (1989) is plotted as a function of the model output J for a number of different slide images differing in resolution and size.

The SQRI Model is a good example of a performance model, because unlike the mechanistic models to be discussed next, it does not attempt to model the visual system at the level of neural input-output functions. Instead. it computes a quantity that is shown empirically to provide a good fit to the input-output function of the system as a whole. This feature of the SQRI model is most strikingly illustrated by considering the approximation it

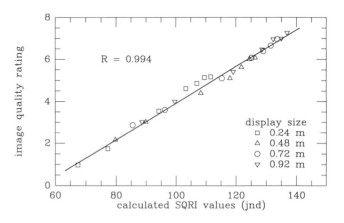

Figure 13.6
Linear regression between measured subjective image quality and output of the Barten SQRI model for slide images differing in resolution and size. From Barten (1990).

computes for the threshold function $M_t(v)$:

$$\frac{1}{M_t(v)} = av\exp(-bv)\sqrt{1 + c\exp(bv)},$$

where

$$a = \frac{540(1 + 0.7/L)^{-0.2}}{1 + 12/[w(1 + v/3)^2]},$$

$$b = 0.3(1 + 100/L)^{0.15},$$

$$c = 0.6,$$

and L and w are display luminance in cd/m² and display width in degrees.

This expression provides a good fit to data on contrast sensitivity as a function of frequency for different display sizes (Carlson, 1982) and different display luminances (van Meeteren and Vos, 1972). However, it is simply a curve fit, for which no claims are made concerning isomorphism to underlying mechanisms. For example, although a great deal of psychophysical and physiological data suggest that grating detection is governed by different mechanisms at different frequencies (e.g., Graham and Nachmias, 1971), there is nothing in the Barten $M_t(v)$ expression to indicate the operation of these established mechanisms.

This lack of mechanistic structure is not a problem when using the model for the simple detection applications for which it was designed. However, it becomes a distinct disadvantage when trying further to develop the model for application to other, more complex stimulus or task domains. For example, there is increasing evidence (e.g., Tolhurst and Barfield, 1977; Sagi and Hochstein. 1983; Olzak, 1985; Lubin and Nachmias, 1990) that individual neural mechanisms differing in frequency selectivity are not independent at superthreshold stimulus contrasts but instead interact in highly nonlinear ways. Lubin and Nachmias (1990) found evidence that the interaction consists of a divisionlike operation of mechanism outputs on each other; similar results among mechanisms tuned to different orientations are discussed later. For the SQRI model, incorporation of these effects would require a significant restructuring of the calculation, with the new model probably bearing little similarity to the old. However, for a model in which the calculation is already in terms of mechanism outputs, interactions among these outputs are much easier to incorporate. In the next section

an example of this model-refinement process is examined in the context of a prototypical mechanistic model.

Mechanistic Modeling

A vision model is mechanistic to the extent that components of the model have the same functional response as physiological mechanisms in the visual pathways of the brain. Because there is currently substantial agreement on the general form of some of these mechanisms, many proposed vision models of simple detection and discrimination task performance share a similar basic architecture. In these models the outputs of linear filters tuned to different frequencies, spatial positions, and orientations are passed through a sigmoid-shaped point nonlinearity and then to a summation mechanism that converts the outputs of these many channels into a single scalar value. Models sharing these features have been introduced into the basic psychophysics literature by Wilson and his colleagues (see Wilson, 1991, for a review), and by Legge and Foley (Legge and Foley, 1980; Foley and Legge, 1981), among others.

Physiological justification for this model architecture is not attempted in this section, except in passing. Instead, the discussion focuses on how to develop a mechanistically motivated model into a usable tool for display system performance analysis. To this end, the computational architecture for a typical, basic model of this kind is described in more detail. Then, the advantage of a mechanistic model is illustrated by describing the process by which this basic model can be refined to improve its predictions on new data sets, without requiring major changes in the basic architecture.

Basic Model Architecture

The following model (Lubin and Bergen, 1991) was developed to quantify the visibility of cockpit display information so that display designers might accurately assess the effect that specific design choices would have on crew performance over a broad range of flight scenarios.

Figure 13.7 shows a block diagram of the basic model architecture. The model takes as input one or two digitized images, expressed as sampled luminance distributions on a planar surface. In addition, several observer parameters

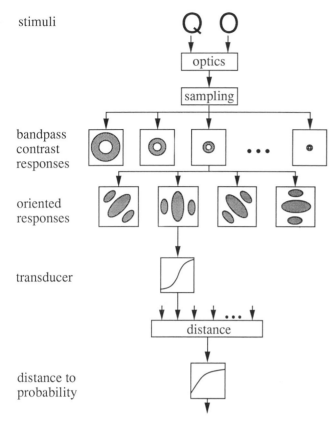

stimuli

optics

sampling

bandpass
contrast
responses

oriented
responses

transducer

distance

distance to
probability

Figure 13.7
Flow diagram for mechanistic model described in the text.

are entered, including distance of the observer from the images, fixation depth, and eccentricity of the images in the observer's visual field (expressed in degrees of visual angle.) The model ultimately returns a prediction of the probability that an observer will be able to discriminate between the two images or, in the case of a single image input, that the observer will be able to discriminate between that image and a uniform field of the same mean luminance. Another optional output is a spatial map of discrimination probabilities that provides a point-by-point measure of the discriminability of two images. This output is especially useful for determining the effect of specific display or image-coding artifacts on particular image features.

At the first stage, labeled "optics" in the block diagram, standard geometrical optics calculations are used to blur the input image if the fixation distance differs from the image distance. That is, the appropriate size blur circle is computed, and then each input image is prefiltered with this circular convolution kernel. The blur circle calculation

requires knowledge of the distance from the exit pupil to the imaging surface (i.e., the retina), which was taken as 20.3 mm from Westheimer (1986). It also requires an estimate of pupil size. For this, a simple interpolation routine was written to estimate pupil diameter as a function of light level, from a table in Hood and Finkelstein (1986).

Next, the image is resampled, to model the sampling by the cones. For images with an eccentricity of 0 deg, the image is resampled on a square grid of 120 pixels/deg, to generate a modeled retinal image of 512×512 pixels, covering approximately 4.25 deg of visual space in each linear dimension. This pixel density approximates that of foveal cones (e.g., Young, 1971). For eccentricities greater than 0 deg, the retinal pixel density is not 120 pixels/deg, but $120/(1 + ke)$, where e is the eccentricity, and k is a parameter set at 0.4, the value estimated from psychophysical data by Watson (1983).

This resampling operation allows the model to predict effects such as the fact that grating size must be scaled up linearly as a function of eccentricity to maintain threshold detection performance at a fixed contrast (see for example Watson, 1987). However, we shall show shortly that refinements of this basic model architecture will be necessary to predict eccentricity dependencies on character discrimination and other tasks.

In the next model stage, labeled "bandpass contrast responses" in the diagram, the raw luminance signal is converted to units of local contrast as follows, using a technique similar to that of Peli (1990). First, the image is decomposed into a Laplacian pyramid (Burt and Adelson, 1983), resulting in seven bandpass levels with peak frequencies from 32 through 0.5 cycles/deg, each level separated from its neighbors by one octave. Then, at each point in each level, the Laplacian value is divided by the corresponding point up-sampled from the Gaussian pyramid level two levels down in resolution. The result is a local difference divided by a local mean; that is, a local measure of contrast, localized in both space and frequency. For a sine grating within the frequency range of one pyramid level, the resulting contrast measure is approximately equivalent to the Weber contrast; that is, $(L_{max} - L_{min})/L_{mean}$.

In the following stage, marked "oriented responses" in the diagram, each pyramid level is convolved with eight spatially oriented filters; that is, a Hilbert transform pair for each of four different orientations. Then, the two

Hilbert pair outputs at each point are squared and summed to compute a local energy measure e_i, where i indexes over position, pyramid level, and orientation. For convenience and speed of operation, the linear filtering is performed with steerable filters of Freeman and Adelson (1991). The specific filters used are a second derivative of a Gaussian and its Hilbert transform, which have a log bandwidth at half-height of approximately 0.7 octave, a value within the range of bandwidths inferred psychophysically (e.g., Watson and Robson, 1981). The orientation bandwidth of these filters (i.e., the range of angles over which filter output is greater than one-half the maximum) is approximately 65 deg. This figure is slightly larger than the 40-deg tuning of monkey simple cells reported by Devalois et al. (1982b), and the 30- to 60-deg range reported psychophysically by Phillips and Wilson (1984).

At the "transducer" stage, each energy measure e_i is first normalized by the grating contrast detection threshold for that position and pyramid level. This threshold is calculated from the Barten expression $M_t(v, L, w)$, described in the Performance Modeling section. Here v is the peak frequency for the pyramid level, L is the local luminance value used in the contrast calculation described above, and w is the image width in degrees. This normalization allows the model to correctly predict the shape of the contrast sensitivity function.

Next, in the "transducer" stage, each normalized energy measure $\hat{e}_i$ is put through a sigmoid nonlinearity of the form

$$T(\hat{e}_i) = \frac{(k + 2)|\hat{e}_i|^n}{k|\hat{e}_i|^{n-w} + |\hat{e}_i|^m + 1},$$

where as currently fit, $n = 1.5$, $m = 1.1$, $w = 0.068$, and $k = 0.1$. This nonlinearity T is required to reproduce the dipper shape of contrast discrimination functions (Nachmias and Sansbury, 1974). The normalization by contrast detection threshold is justified by the contrast discrimination data of Bradley and Ohzawa (1986), which show that the dipper curves for different grating frequencies all superimpose when normalized by the detection threshold for each frequency.

After the transducer stage, each image's model output for each spatial position can be thought of as an m-dimensional vector, where $m = 28$ is the number of frequency levels (7) times the number of orientations (4). In the box marked "distance" in the diagram, the distance between these vectors for the two input images is calculated as follows. First, the smaller pyramid levels are upsampled to the full 512×512 size, the result being a set of twenty-eight 512×512 spatial arrays of transducer outputs for each of the two input images. Next, for each of the 512×512 spatial positions, a distance measure D is calculated as follows:

$$D_j = \left\{ \sum_{k=1}^{m} |T_{j,k}(s_1) - T_{j,k}(s_2)|^Q \right\}^{1/Q},$$

where j indexes over spatial position, k indexes over the 28 frequencies and orientations, s_1 and s_2 are the two input images, T is the transducer output, and Q is a parameter currently set to 2.4. The result of this stage is thus a spatial map of distance values.

At the final stage, labeled "distance to probability," each computed distance measure is converted to a probability value. Each of these values represents the probability that an observer will be able to discriminate between the two input images, based on the information in that spatial location. As we noted previously, this entire spatial map is an optional model output. Alternatively, the maximum of these probability values can also be returned. This maximum represents the overall probability that an observer will be able to detect any difference between the two images.

The transformation from distance to probability is performed as follows. During initial model calibration of transducer parameters on Legge and Foley (1980) 2 c/d grating contrast discrimination data, a distance of 1 is arbitrarily set to correspond to threshold performance; that is, a 75 percent probability of correct response. The form of the transducer thus fixed, the model's distance value is computed for a single 2 c/d grating as a function of grating contrast. Next, a Foley and Legge (1981) 2 c/d contrast detection psychometric function is used to obtain probability correct as a function of contrast. Thus there are two functions: one relating transducer distance to grating contrast, and the other relating probability correct to grating contrast. So, we have simply to invert one and substitute into the other to obtain probability correct as a function of transducer distance. This was done computationally, and the result was stored in the model software in a lookup table.

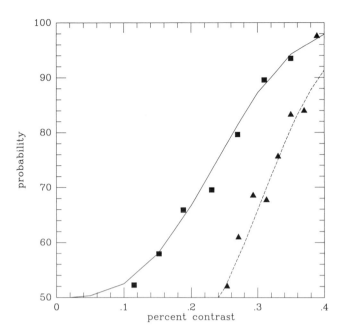

Figure 13.8
Model fit to Foley and Legge (1981) contrast detection and discrimination psychometric functions. Squares are contrast detection data for a 2 c/d sine grating, with the solid curve through these points showing the model fit. Triangles are contrast discrimination data, with the dashed line showing model predictions.

To test this mapping, the model was applied to predict a psychometric function for near-threshold contrast discrimination, also published in Foley and Legge (1981). In this function, probability for detecting a change in contrast of a sine grating at threshold is plotted against that change in contrast. As shown in figure 13.8, the predictions are quite accurate.

With no further parameter adjustment, the model also produces accurate predictions on other data sets, for example, the edge sharpness discrimination data from Carlson and Cohen (1980) (figure 13.9).

Some differences exist between this and other mechanistic models. For example, in this model a raw luminance signal is converted to units of local contrast, whereas in many models the input signal is assumed already to be in contrast terms. Also, in the pyramid-based frequency decomposition used here, frequency and orientation bandwidths of the oriented mechanisms are constant across the different frequency bands, even though evidence suggests (e.g., Devalois et al.. 1982a) that bandwidths decrease as frequency increases. In other models (e.g., Wilson, 1991), the oriented linear filters for different frequency bands

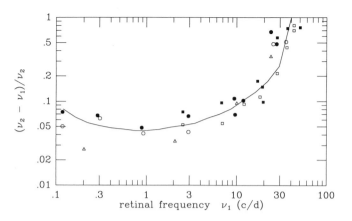

Figure 13.9
Data and model predictions for edge sharpness discrimination experiment. Data points from Carlson and Cohen (1980) show the minimum detectable change in the high frequency cut-off of a blurred step edge, as a function of the starting cut-off frequency ν_1. Different symbol types are for different subjects. Solid curve shows the fit of the mechanistic model described in the text.

vary in shape to take such data into account; the simplification was chosen here for efficiency of computation.

Differences like these will lead to different predictions in some data sets. An important question for application to display performance analysis is the extent to which the chosen model can be easily tuned to provide good performance predictions for specific problems of interest. In the discussion that follows, this tuning process is illustrated for the model just described.

Model Refinements

In a cockpit environment an important display performance measure is the legibility of displayed text at different positions in the visual field. As a first step toward providing such a measure, the model just described was applied to the task of discriminating between highly confusable alphanumeric characters: for example, *O* vs. *Q*. Psychophysical data were obtained on the confusability of small (12 arc-min width), briefly presented (167 ms), high-contrast characters at different eccentricities. The subject was asked to choose *O* or *Q* on each trial, and the probability of correct identification was recorded. These data are shown as the filled symbols in figure 13.10. Interestingly, the model predicted perfect identification out past 16 deg, even though the data show a fall-off to near-chance performance by 6 deg. This model prediction is not shown in the figure.

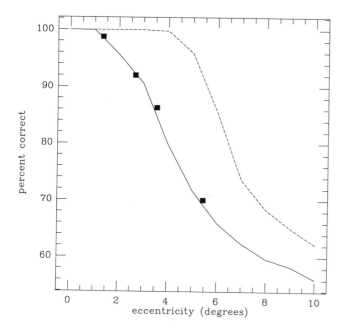

Figure 13.10
Data and model fits for discrimination of O and Q as a function of eccentricity. Solid symbols show the data. Dashed curve shows the predictions of a model with eccentricity-dependent pooling. Solid curve shows the predictions of a model with pooling and gain control among different orientations. See text for description of these model variants.

This dramatic discrepancy is a clear failure of the model and therefore requires some refinement of the basic architecture. The scaling of filter size with eccentricity, which allows accurate prediction of grating contrast sensitivity in the periphery, is obviously not sufficient to predict eccentricity dependencies in the character discrimination task. Some suggestion about the critical difference between these two tasks comes from observing eccentricity dependencies for other simple tasks, as shown in figure 13.11, taken from Levi et al. (1985).

The circular and square symbols in figure 13.11 show the increase in stimulus size required as a function of eccentricity to maintain constant task performance for grating acuity (open symbols) and vernier acuity (filled symbols). The solid line on this same plot shows the increase with eccentricity of the *inverse cortical magnification factor* (i.e., degrees of visual angle per millimeter of cortical surface), as estimated by Dow et al. (1981) from anatomical data in the macaque. The dashed line shows the increase in cone spacing with eccentricity, based on data from Rolls and Cowey (1970).

An interesting observation from this figure is that the vernier acuity data fit along the cortical magnification line, whereas the grating resolution data fit along the cone density line. Eccentricity dependencies in stimulus size scaling for other simple tasks also tend to group along one or the other of these two lines. For example, grating contrast sensitivity follows the lower line (e.g., Watson, 1987), whereas phase discrimination (Klein and Tyler 1981), optimal three-dot bisection (Yap et al., 1987), and character discrimination (Farrell and Desmarais, 1990) follow the upper line. A plausible generalization of these results is that for tasks requiring the accurate localization of stimulus features, the size scaling required for constant performance as a function of eccentricity follows the inverse cortical magnification factor. Thus, the loss of spatial localization ability with eccentricity may reflect an increase in the area over which retinal information is pooled in the cortex.

Although there is currently some controversy about the apparent difference in slope between the cone density function and the inverse cortical magnification factor (e.g., Wässle et al., 1989), additional results from Dow et al. (1981) show that cortical receptive field *overlap* decreases as eccentricity increases. So, if accurate localization requires a comparison of the response from several receptive fields, an additional deterioration in localization performance would be expected over that resulting from cortical magnification alone.

In any case, this link to a physiological substrate suggests a mechanistically motivated refinement to the basic model architecture. Specifically, an eccentricity-dependent spatial pooling stage was inserted after the transducer stage to increasingly blur out the spatial localization of detected features in the filter output maps as eccentricity increased. Note that this refinement does not degrade the grating contrast detection and discrimination performance of the model: Because the filter output maps for these stimuli are already relatively uniform, a blurring operation on them has no significant effect.

With the eccentricity scaling of the pooling function set to produce accurate predictions on the vernier acuity data in figure 13.11, the predictions of the model for the O versus Q data are now substantially improved, as shown by the dashed curve in figure 13.10. Further improvement was obtained by adding a gain-setting operation across the four oriented energy responses at each spatial point.

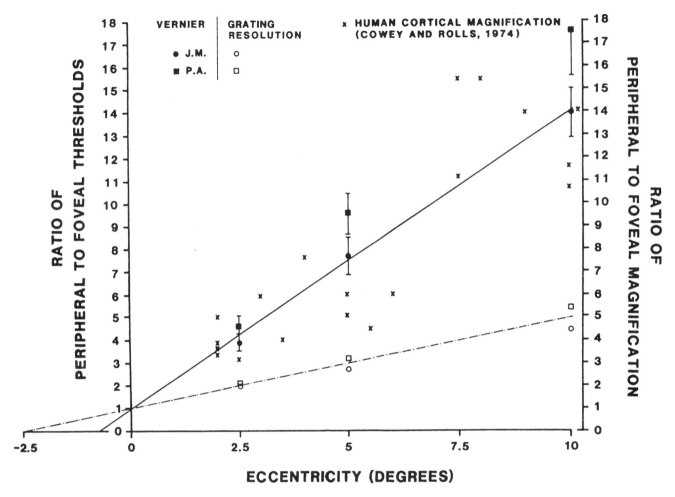

Figure 13.11
Scaling of task performance and physiological measures as a function of eccentricity. Dashed line shows increase in cone spacing as a function of eccentricity, from Rolls and Cowey (1970). Solid line shows inverse cortical magnification factor, from measurements on macaque by Dow et al. (1981). Cross symbols show estimates of human inverse cortical magnification factor, from Cowey and Rolls (1974). Open symbols show variation in grating acuity with eccentricity, for two observers; solid squares and circles show change in vernier acuity, for the same observers. From Levi et al. (1985).

That is,

$$e'_j = \frac{e_j}{\alpha \sum_{k \neq j} e_k + 1},$$

where the subscripts j and k on the energy responses e index over the four different orientations for each spatial position and frequency. This formulation is supported by physiological data from Bonds (1989); a similar expression was found by Lubin (1988, 1989) to fit psychophysical data using different spatiotemporally oriented patterns. The model fit is now quite good, as shown by the solid curve in figure 13.10.

Notice also that if only one orientation is present in the signal, so that $e_k = 0$ for $k \neq j$, then $e'_j = e_j$, and the model reduces to its earlier simpler form. Here again, as in the pooling refinement discussed above, the predictions for the contrast detection and discrimination data are preserved as the model is further developed.

Summary and Conclusions

In this chapter various techniques for psychophysically assessing display system performance have been described. These techniques included model-free data collection, task modeling, performance modeling, and mechanistic modeling.

Model-free data collection is appropriate when the number of display parameters over which performance measurements are needed is small and when the necessary imagery can be easily rendered. It especially appropriate when no accurate model exists for the task performance under investigation. This is often the case when subjective judgments of image quality are required.

Task modeling is useful as a means of decomposing an ill-defined task, such as image-quality rating, into one or more simple detection or discrimination tasks for which data collection and/or simple performance or mechanistic modeling can then provide performance estimates. Task modeling is easiest when the display system manipulations under consideration result in simple, easily quantifiable visual artifacts. Thresholds for artifact visibility can then be used to assess the image-quality impairments resulting from specific display system processes.

Although sometimes motivated by mechanistic considerations, performance modeling is defined here as a form of curve-fitting to the input-output function of the visual system as a whole. The advantage of performance models is that they are usually easy to compute. The disadvantage is that they are not easily generalizable.

Mechanistic modeling, in which the model components are proposed to be isomorphic to physiological mechanisms in the brain, is useful when performance predictions on simple stimuli and tasks must be generalized to other more complex conditions. Although often complicated and therefore slower to compute than performance models, mechanistic models provide rational paths for accurate generalization, as illustrated in the previous section. They therefore often represent the only viable alternative to the prohibitive costs of data collection for some display performance analysis questions.

Note

1. One complication here is that beam current manipulations also have an effect on resolution. However, this effect can be measured and taken into account when plotting the data, as has been done in the data plot Figure 13.2

References

Alphonse, G. A., and Lubin, J. (1992). Psychophysical requirements for seamless tiled large-screen displays. *Society for Information Display International Symposium Digest of Technical Papers* 23:941–944.

Barten, P. G. J. (1987). The SQRI method: A new method for the evaluation of visible resolution on a display. *Proceedings of the Society for Information Display* 30:253–262.

Barten, P. G. J. (1990). Subjective image quality of high-definition television pictures. *Proceedings of the Society for Information Display* 31:239–243.

Bonds, A. B. (1989). Role of inhibition in the specification of orientation selectivity of cells in the cat striate cortex. *Visual Neuroscience* 2:41–55.

Bradley, A., and Ohzawa, I. (1986). A comparison of contrast detection and discrimination. *Vision Research* 26:991–997.

Burt, P. J., and Adelson. E. H. (1983). The Laplacian pyramid as a compact image code. *IEEE Transactions on Communications* COM-31: 532–540.

Carlson. C. R. (1982). Sine-wave threshold contrast sensitivity function: dependence on display size. *RCA Review* 43:675–683.

Carlson, C. R., and Cohen, R. (1980). A simple psychophysical model for predicting the visibility of displayed information. *Proceedings of the Society for Information Display* 21:229–245.

De Valois, R. L., Albrecht, D. G.; and Thorell, L. G. (1982) Spatial frequency selectivity of cells in macaque visual cortex. *Vision Research* 22:545–559.

De Valois, R. L., Yund, E. W., and Hepler, N. (1982). The orientation and direction selectivity of cells in macaque visual cortex. *Vision Research* 22:531–544.

Dow, B. M., Snyder, A. Z., Vautin, R. G., and Bauer, R. (1981). Magnification factor and receptive field size in foveal striate cortex of the monkey. *Experimental Brain Research*, 44:213–228.

Farrell, J. E., and Desmarais, M. (1990). Equating character-identification performance across the visual field. *Journal of the Optical Society of America A* 7:152–159.

Foley, J. M., and Legge, G. E. (1981). Contrast detection and near-threshold discrimination in human vision. *Vision Research* 21:1041–1053.

Freeman, W. T., and Adelson, E. H. (1991). The design and use of steerable filters. *IEEE Transactions on Pattern Analysis and Machine Intelligence* 13:891–906.

Graham, N., and Nachmias, J. (1971). Detection of grating patterns containing two spatial frequencies: A comparison of single channel and multiple channel models. *Vision Research* 11:251–259.

Hood, D. C., and Finkelstein, M. A. (1986) "Sensitivity to light." In *Handbook of Perception and Human Performance*, ed. K. Boff, L. Kaufman, and J. Thomas. New York: Wiley.

Klein, S. A., and Tyler, C. W. (1981) Phase discrimination using single and compound gratings. *Investigative Ophthalmology and Visual Science Supplement* 20:124.

Legge, G. E., and Foley, J. M. (1980) Contrast masking in human vision. *Journal of the Optical Society of America* 70:1458–1470.

Levi, D. M., Klein, S. A., and Aitsebaomo, A. P. (1985). Vernier acuity, crowding and cortical magnification. *Vision Research* 25:963–977.

Lubin, J. (1988). Sub-additivity of masking among opponent motion signals. *Investigative Ophthalmology and Visual Science Supplement* 29:251.

Lubin, J. (1989) Discrimination contours in an opponent motion stimulus space. *Investigative Ophthalmology and Visual Science Supplement* 30:426.

Lubin, J., and Bergen, J. R. (1991) Pattern discrimination in the fovea and periphery. *Investigative Ophthalmology and Visual Science Supplement* 32:1024.

Lubin, J., and Nachmias, J. (1990) Discrimination contours in an f/3f stimulus space. *Investigative Ophthalmology and Visual Science Supplement* 31:409.

Lubin, J., and Pica, A. P. (1991). A non-uniform quantizer matched to human visual performance. *Society for Information Display International Symposium Digest of Technical Papers* 22:619–622.

Lubin, J., Pica, A. P., and Barbin, R. L. (1992) Resolution vs. brightness trade-offs in CRT image quality. In preparation.

Meeteren, A. van, and Vos, J. J. (1972) Contrast sensitivity at low luminances. *Vision Research* 12:825–833.

Nachmias, J., and Sansbury, R. V. (1974) Grating contrast: Discrimination may be better than detection. *Vision Research* 14:1039–1042.

Olzak, L. A. (1985). Interactions between spatially tuned mechanisms: Converging evidence. *Journal of the Optical Society of America A* 2:1551–1559.

Peli, E. (1990). Contrast in complex images. *Journal of the Optical Society of America A* 7:2032–2040.

Phillips, G. C., and Wilson, H. R. (1984). Orientation bandwidths of spatial mechanisms measured by masking. *Journal of the Optical Society of America A* 1:226–232.

Rolls, E. T., and Cowey, A. (1970). Topography of the retina and striate cortex and its relationship to visual acuity in rhesus and squirrel monkeys. *Experimental Brain Research* 10:298–310.

Sagi, D., and Hochstein, S. (1983). Discriminability of suprathreshold compound spatial frequency gratings. *Vision Research* 23:1595–1606.

Sharma, D. K., and Netravali, A. N. (1977). Design of quantizer for DPCM coding of picture signals. *IEEE Transactions on Communications* COM-25 11:1267–1274.

Tolhurst, D. J., and Barfield, L. P. (1977). Interactions between spatial frequency channels. *Vision Research* 18:951–958.

Wässle, H., Grünert, U., Röhrenbeck, J., and Boycott, B. B. (1989). Cortical magnification factor and the ganglion cell density of the primate retina. Nature 341:643–646.

Watson, A. B. (1983). "Detection and Recognition of Simple Spatial Forms." In *Physical and Biological Processing of Images*, ed. O. Braddick and A. Sleigh. Berlin: Springer-Verlag.

Watson, A. B. (1987). Estimation of local spatial scale. *Journal of the Optical Society of America A* 4:1579–1582.

Watson, A., and Robson, J. G. (1981) Discrimination at threshold: Labelled detectors in human vision. *Vision Research* 21:1115–1122.

Westerink, J. H. D. M., and Roufs, J. A. J. (1989). Subjective image quality as a function of viewing distance, resolution, and picture size. *SMPTE Journal* 98:113–119.

Westheimer, G. (1986). "The Eye As an Optical Instrument." In *Handbook of Perception and Human Performance*, ed. K. Boff, L. Kaufman, and J. Thomas. New York: Wiley.

Wilson, H. R. (1991). "Psychophysical Models of Spatial Vision and Hyperacuity." In *Vision and Visual Dysfunction*, ed. D. Regan. Vol. 10. *Spatial Vision*. Boston: CRC Press, Inc.

Yap, Y. L., Levi, D. M., and Klein, S. A. (1987). Peripheral hyperacuity: Three-dot bisection scales to a single factor from 0 to 10 degrees. *Journal of the Optical Society of America A* 4:1557–1561.

Young, R. W. (1971). The renewal of rod and cone outer segments in the rhesus monkey. *Journal of Cell Biology* 49:303–318.

14

The Visible Differences Predictor: An Algorithm for the Assessment of Image Fidelity

Scott Daly

The visible differences predictor (VDP) is an algorithm for describing the human visual response. It is motivated by the need quantitatively to describe the visual consequences of decisions regarding the design and quality control of imaging products. Intended to be used in the development of image-processing algorithms, imaging system hardware, and imaging media, it is a design tool that can find wide areas of application. The differences due to the imaging systems may begin as *mathematical differences* (i.e., incorrect code values) but ultimately end up as *physical differences* (i.e., incorrect luminances and chrominances) once the image is displayed. The goal of the VDP is to determine the degree to which these physical differences become visible differences. Commonly used techniques [3, 5, 11, 21, 24] analyze parameters such as the system's MTF and noise power spectra and calculate a single number describing image quality. Although these techniques perform reasonably well for many aspects of analog media, they have not been particularly successful for describing digital image quality, the effects of adaptive algorithms, or the nonlinear aspects of analog media. The problems with these techniques lie in their lack of phase information in the analysis, their inability to deal effectively with the nonlinearities of the media, and their simplicity relative to the complexity of the visual system.

To solve these problems the VDP uses a digital image-processing approach. Using actual images, rather than just parameters of the imaging system, enables the preservation of phase information. This information is necessary to predict visual distortion because of the masking properties of the visual system, in which the location of the image error is as important as the magnitude. Further, nonlinearities in the media or algorithms pose problems for the current approaches that use power spectra and MTF, because of their implications of linearity. An image-processing approach can easily incorporate such systems parameters as MTF and noise power spectra through simulation, yet it also allows for more exact simulation of

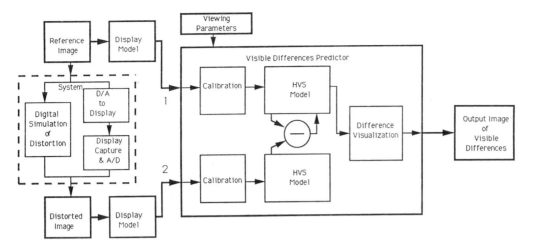

Figure 14.1
This block diagram describes the creation of the distorted image from the reference, and the input of the two images to the VDP algorithm to create the output image of visible differences.

the nonlinearities of both the media and the visual system. These features of the VDP approach are necessary to predict the visibility of imaging effects that are adaptive or nonlinear.

The VDP is a relative metric because it does not describe an absolute metric of image quality but instead addresses the problem of describing the visibility of differences between two images. Figure 14.1 shows the use of the VDP, which consists of components for calibration of the input images, a human visual system (HVS) model, and a method for displaying the HVS predictions of the visible differences. The input to the algorithm includes two images and parameters for viewing conditions and calibration, whereas the output is a third image describing the visible differences between them. Typically, one of the input images is a reference image, representing the image quality goal, and the other is a distorted image, representing the system's actual quality. The VDP is used to assess the image fidelity of the distorted image compared with the reference. The block components outside the VDP generically describe the simulation of the distortion under study. The output image is a map of the probability of detecting the differences between the two images as a function of their location in the images. This metric, *probability of detection*, provides a description of the threshold behavior of vision but does not discriminate among different suprathreshold visual errors. This metric does not limit the input images, however, which are expected to be suprathreshold. The VDP can therefore be summarized as

a threshold model for suprathreshold imagery, capable of quantifying the important interactions among threshold differences and suprathreshold image content and structure.

Unlike most image-quality metrics, including other recent image-processing-based approaches [28, 29, 60], the VDP does not collapse its output into a single number, which has advantages as well as disadvantages. An advantage is that an imaging system designer can see the nature of the difference and use this information to further improve the design. A disadvantage is that it cannot be used for suprathreshold ranking. Nevertheless, we feel this model is an initial step toward the aim of a complete suprathreshold model. As a result of the approach taken, the VDP can be used for all types of image distortions including blur, noise, algorithm artifacts, banding, blocking, pixellation, and tone-scale changes.

Overview of the Algorithm

Calibration

The input images represented by unitless digital numbers must be calibrated for the subsequent HVS model to have any meaning. One calibrating input parameter is the viewing distance for which the VDP algorithm will make its visual prediction. Other parameters include the physical pixel spacings, which along with the viewing distance map the visual frequencies expressed in cycles/degree (c/deg) to frequencies expressed digitally as a fraction of the Nyquist frequency. Although not formally a calibration parameter, the digital code values must be converted to physical luminances in the display device. The display

Figure 14.2
A reference image.

model is an entire field in itself, and the user will generally supply his or her own model for the application.

Human Visual System Model

The HVS model concentrates on the lower-order processing of the visual system, such as the optics, retina, lateral geniculate nucleus, and striate cortex. The overall approach we have taken to model the visual system has been to treat it as a number of processes that limit visual sensitivity. Without these limitations only a physical model of the displayed image would be needed. The necessity for an HVS model can be provided by demonstrating the severe failure of a common physical error metric: mean-squared error (mse). In figure 14.2 we show a reference image, whereas two distorted versions having identical mse appear in figures 14.3(a) and (b), with their associated error images in figures 14.3(c) and (d). Although these images have the same physical distortion as measured by the mse, the degree of visibility of the distortion is vastly different.

The HVS model addresses three main sensitivity variations, namely, as a function of light level, spatial frequency, and signal content. Sensitivity S is defined as the inverse of the contrast required to produce a threshold response,

$$S = \frac{1}{C_T},\qquad(14.1)$$

where C_T is generally referred to as simply the threshold. The Michelson definition of contrast,

$$C = \frac{(L_{\max} - L_{\mean})}{L_{\mean}},\qquad(14.2)$$

is used, where $L_{\max}$ and $L_{\mean}$ refer to the maximum and mean luminances of the waveform. Sensitivity can be thought of as a gain, although various nonlinearities of the visual system require caution in the use of this analogy. The variations in sensitivity as a function of light level are primarily due to the light-adaptive properties of the retina and are referred to as the *amplitude nonlinearity* of the HVS. The variations as a function of spatial frequency are due to the optics of the eye combined with the neural circuitry, and these combined effects are referred to as the *contrast sensitivity function (CSF)*. Finally, the variations in sensitivity as a function of signal content are due to the postreceptoral neural circuitry, and these effects are referred to as *masking*.

The HVS model consists of three main components that essentially model each of these sensitivity variations, and these three components are sequentially cascaded as shown in figure 14.4. The first component is the amplitude nonlinearity, implemented as a point process; the second is the CSF, implemented as a filtering process; and the final component in the cascade is the detection process, which models the masking effects. It is implemented as a combination of filters and nonlinearities.

Difference Visualization

We use two ways for visualizing the VDP output, which is a map of detection probabilities. One of the visualization techniques is called the *free-field difference map*. In this technique the visible difference predictions appear on a uniform field with a gray value near the system mean, in a way similar to the technique of creating mathematical error images commonly used in image compression. Unfortunately, with this method it is sometimes difficult to see where the predicted errors correspond in the input images. The second method, the *in-context difference map* is meant to overcome this limitation by mapping the output probabilities in color on the reference image.

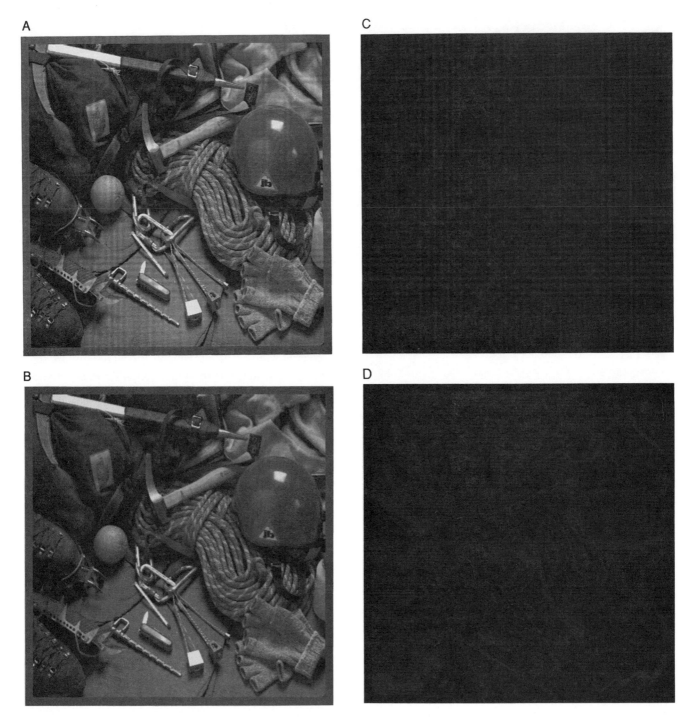

Figure 14.3
Two distorted versions of the reference image with identical mse.
The distortion in (A) is caused by a two-dimensional banding artifact,
whereas (B) suffers from a tone-scale distortion. The mse is 10.0
(38-dB PSNR). (C) The banding error shown in isolation; (D) The
isolated error due to the tone-scale distortion. These error images are
scaled by 1.0.

Plate 1. Projection of a color image on the first eight eigenfunctions using 4×4 color image blocks. The color eigenfunctions correspond to their location in figure 9.6.

Plate 2. Image reconstruction using the eigenvectors. The number of eigenvectors used is shown in the inset.

A

Plate 3. Results of the VDP algorithm shown in the *in-context difference map* format for the banding distorted image (A) and the tone-scale distorted image (B) that appear in figure 14.3. Red indicates where the distorted image looks lighter than the reference with a detection probability of 1.0, and cyan indicates where the distorted image looks darker than the reference with a detection probability of 1.0.

B

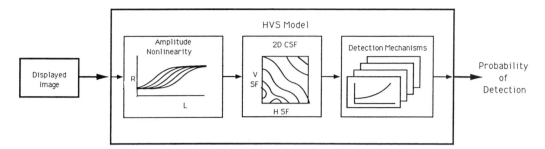

Figure 14.4
Block diagram of the three main components of the HVS model within the VDP.

HVS Model: Amplitude Nonlinearity

It is well known that visual sensitivity and perception of lightness are nonlinear functions of luminance. The amplitude nonlinearity of the VDP describes the sensitivity variations as a function of the gray scale, as well as the changes that occur due to different illumination levels, and is based on a model of the early retinal network [38]. The retinal response is modeled with the following equation,

$$\frac{R}{R_{max}} = \frac{L^n}{(L^n + \alpha^n)}, \quad 0.7 \le n \le 1.0, \tag{14.3}$$

where R/R_{max} is the normalized response, L is the luminance falling on the retina, and α is the semisaturation constant. The semisaturation constant is a function of the steady-state light level L_a to which the retina is adapted,

$$\alpha = c_1 L_a^b + c_2. \tag{14.4}$$

In the original model, L_a is determined by convolving the optical psf with small involuntary eye movements. This results in a shift-variant nonlinearity having the problem of noninvertibility.

We have developed a simplified version that is shift-*invariant*, invertible, and implemented as simple point nonlinearities [45]. It assumes a state of adaptation resulting from an observer fixating a small image area by reducing eye movements. Referred to as the local amplitude nonlinearity, it is implemented in the VDP as a function of pixel location (i, j),

$$\frac{R(i,j)}{R_{max}} = \frac{L(i,j)}{(L(i,j) + (c_1 L(i,j))^b)}, \tag{14.5}$$

where b is 0.63 and c_1 is 12.6 for the units of cd/m².

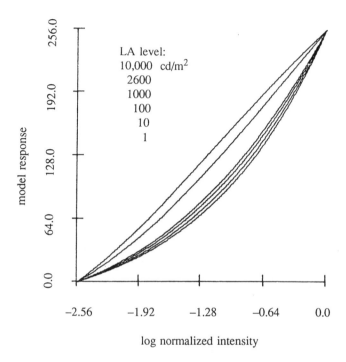

Figure 14.5
The local amplitude nonlinearity model responses are shown as a function of log luminance for a 2.55 log unit dynamic range. The series of curves show the effects of long-term adaptation on the instantaneous response curves. Each response curve is normalized by its maximum response to the 2.55 log range.

For this model the adaptation level for an image pixel is solely determined from that pixel. Although physiological data indicate that the visual system cannot adapt to indefinitely small areas of an image, we assume that the observer may view the image at any arbitrarily close distance. This removes any frequency attributes from the amplitude nonlinearity component and allows us to model all spatial frequency aspects separately in the CSF component. Although shift-invariant, the local amplitude nonlinearity *is* an adaptive function. Its behavior is shown in figure 14.5 for a series of illumination levels.

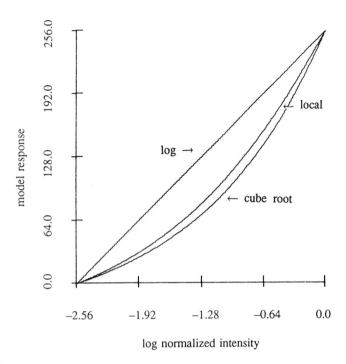

Figure 14.6
Common models are compared to the local amplitude nonlinearity model (at 100 cd/m²). The curve for a linear model (not shown) would lie to the right of the cube-root model.

Most of the other models used in the literature to describe this aspect of the visual system's nonlinearity with respect to gray level are also shift-invariant. These include the density domain or log model [22, 48], various power laws [4, 30] such as cube root [32, 36], and linear range assumptions. Figure 14.6 shows a comparison of these models against the local amplitude nonlinearity model. Even though it is similar to the cube root function for light levels near the practical range of 100 cd/m², the cube root function does not change shape with illumination level. The slopes of the curves in figure 14.6 describe the change in sensitivity as a function of the gray level and these sensitivities are compared across models in figure 14.7. Although this component of the VDP gives the shape of the nonlinearity, the actual sensitivity is determined by the CSF.

HVS Model: Contrast Sensitivity Funtion

The CSF describes the variations in visual sensitivity as a function of spatial frequency. These variations are primarily due to the optics of the eye, the sampling aperture of

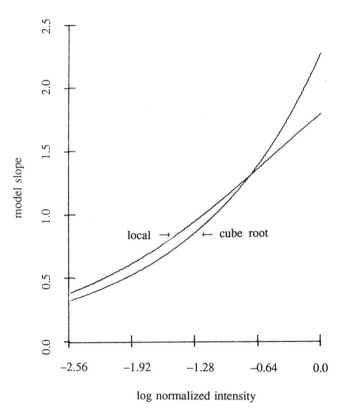

Figure 14.7
The slopes from fig.14.6 are shown in this figure. Because the slopes are calculated in the log domain, the slope of the log model would be a constant with a value of 1.0 (not shown).

the cone photoreceptor, and both passive and active neural connections. All these contributing biological components are highly adaptive, with the result that the CSF changes as a function of light adaptation, noise, color, accommodation, eccentricity, and image size. All global spatial frequency effects are modeled in this component, whether they actually occur due to the optics, cones, cortical neurons, or elsewhere in the visual system.

The following equations model the sensitivity S as a function of radial spatial frequency ρ in c/deg, orientation θ in degrees, light adaptation level l in cd/m², image size i^2 in visual degrees, lens accommodation due to distance d in meters, and eccentricity e in degrees:

$$S(\rho, \theta, l, i^2, d, e)$$

$$= P \cdot \min\left[S_1\left(\frac{\rho}{r_a \cdot r_e \cdot r_\theta}, l, i^2\right), S_1(\rho, l, i^2) \right], \quad (14.6)$$

where P is the absolute peak sensitivity of the CSF.[1] The parameters r_a, r_e, and r_θ, model the changes in resolution

Measurement and Prediction of Visual Quality

due to the accommodation level, eccentricity and orientation, respectively, via the following equations.[2]

$$r_a = 0.856 \cdot d^{0.14},$$ where d is the distance in meters

$$r_e = \frac{1}{1 + ke},$$ where e is the eccentricity in visual degrees, $k = 0.24$

$$r_e = \left(\frac{(1 - ob)}{2}\right)\cos(4\theta) + \frac{(1 + ob)}{2}, \quad \text{where } ob = 0.78$$

(14.7)

Remaining to be modeled are the effects of the image size and the light adaptation level,[3]

$$S_1(\rho, l, i^2) = ((3.23(\rho^2 i^2)^{-0.3})^5 + 1)^{-1/5}$$
$$\cdot A_l \varepsilon \rho e^{-(B_l \varepsilon \rho)} \sqrt{1 + 0.06 e^{B_l \varepsilon \rho}}$$
$$A_l = 0.801 \left(\frac{1 + 0.7}{l}\right)^{-0.2}$$
$$B_l = 0.3 \left(\frac{1 + 100}{l}\right)^{0.15}$$

(14.8)

where l is the light adaptation level in cd/m^2, i^2 is the image area in deg^2, and ε is a frequency scaling constant that equals 0.9 for the luminance CSF. The sensitivity as a function of image size and the changes in sensitivity and

bandwidth as a function of light adaptation level are modeled by the first and second halves of the equation, respectively. Figure 14.8 shows a typical CSF for the two-dimensional frequency plane.

In the VDP algorithm, the CSF is modeled in the units of c/deg and then mapped to the two-dimensional digital frequency domain by using the calibration parameters of viewing distance, horizontal pixel spacing, and vertical pixel spacing. The other calibration parameters (maximum light level, image size, and the like) also affect the CSF, according to the adaptive model. Noise is not input as a parameter, since it is modeled explicitly in the external image simulation steps, and its effects on the VDP model appear in the detection mechanisms. Although it is unrealistic to use a single distance in most applications, it is not unrealistic to assume the observer will remain within a range of viewing distances. For the VDP we have developed an extension of the CSF model, which is appropriate for a range of viewing distances, such that the input parameter to the VDP will include a minimum and a maximum viewing distance. This extended CSF model is shown in figure 14.9. The CSF model for a range of distances is shown as the dashed line and is formed as the envelope of all CSFs mapped to the digital frequency

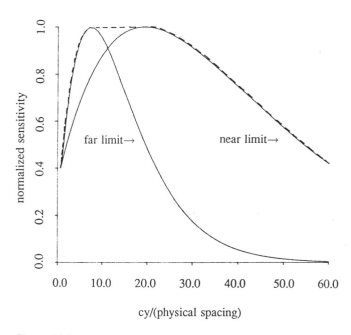

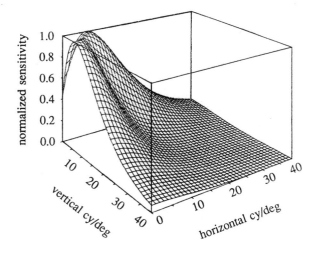

Figure 14.8
The normalized two-dimensional CSF model for one quadrant of the frequency plane is shown.

Figure 14.9
The normalized CSF for a range of viewing distances specified by a minimum and maximum distance (smooth curves) is shown as the envelope of all CSFs within that range (dashed curve).

domain for the range of distances specified by the minimum and maximum distances.[4] An observer would need to view the image for the entire range of distances to see as well as the VDP model's prediction, but this approach can ensure that no visible distortions are perceived within the applications range. For most applications, the critical parameter tends to be the nearest distance specification, since most distortions have a higher frequency than the peak frequency of the CSF.

Although the CSF is often described as the MTF of the visual system, this thinking can be misleading in many cases. Only the optical component of the CSF is amenable to linear systems analysis and can be regarded as an MTF. A better understanding of the CSF is reached by treating it as a description of the equivalent noise of the visual system [2], and one way of modeling it is to add an actual random realization of noise with a spectral shape provided by the inverse of the CSF. Another approach is for the CSF to act as a frequency normalization process for the subsequent detection mechanisms. The normalization approach was used in the VDP, where the images fed to the detection mechanisms are modified so that the threshold is the same for all frequencies. The CSF normalization is implemented as a two-dimensional filtering operation, but the net effect is *not* a linear MTF operation because of the subsequent nonlinearities in the detection mechanisms. The overall HVS model will display the same nonlinear behavior as that measured psychophysically, such as a flattening in the shape of the CSF as a function of suprathreshold contrast or noise level.

HVS Model: Detection Mechanisms

The final HVS component comprises the multiple detection mechanisms, which are modeled with four subcomponents as shown in figure 14.10. The subcomponents include the *spatial frequency hierarchy*, which models the frequency selectivity of the visual system and creates the framework for the multiple detection mechanisms; the *masking function*, which models the magnitude of the masking effect; the *psychometric function*, which describes the threshold in a detailed manner; and the *probability summation*, which combines the responses of all the detection mechanisms into a unified perceptual response.

Spatial-Frequency Hierarchy

The spatial-frequency selectivity of the visual system refers to the existence of specialized mechanisms that are selective for, or tuned to, narrow ranges of spatial frequency. This property has been known for a long time from both neurophysiological recordings [17, 26] and psychophysical studies in adaptation and masking [7, 50]. Although the masking studies originated as a tool to elucidate properties of the visual cortex, they are directly relevant to image-fidelity assessment. These studies have found a radial frequency selectivity that is essentially symmetrical on a log frequency axis with bandwidths nearly constant at one octave. In addition, these studies have revealed an orientation selectivity with symmetry about a center peak angle and tuning bandwidths[5] varying as a function of

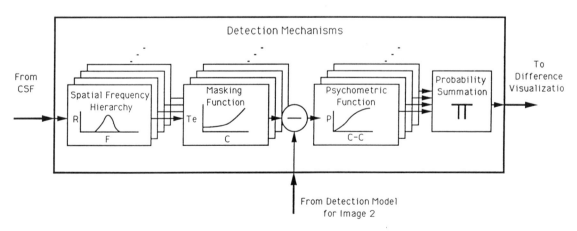

Figure 14.10
Block diagram of the four components comprising the detection mechanisms.

radial frequency, ranging from 30 deg for high frequencies to 60 deg for low frequencies [41]. The current understanding of these important mechanisms is that they are limited in both frequency and space, thus giving rise to the popularity of Gabor and Wavelet modeling approaches [14, 15, 31, 33, 54, 55].

The frequency selectivity of the visual system is modeled here by using a hierarchy of filters. This assumption of discrete spatial-frequency channels is merely an approximation to the visual system. By operating on the filtered spatial images from such a model, we can model the space-frequency localization aspects of the visual system. Of the many filter sets proposed to model the visual system [14, 15, 28, 54, 55, 60], this work uses a modification of the Cortex transform [55], so named because neurons demonstrating these effects are found in the striate cortex.

In the Cortex transform, the radial frequency selectivity and the orientational selectivity are modeled with separate classes of filters. As shown in figure 14.11(a), the effects of these filters are cascaded to describe the combined radial and orientational selectivity of cortical neurons. This combined filter has been termed the *cortex* filter, and the dissection of the frequency plane by these filters is shown in figure 14.11(b), where the lines indicate the half-amplitude frequencies of the radial frequency and orientation filters. To ensure that the filter set sums to 1.0, the radial frequency filters are formed as differences of a series of two-dimensional low-pass *mesa* filters, characterized by a flat pass-band, a transition region, and a flat stop-band region. In the VDP the transition region is modeled with a Hanning window, so that the mesa filter can be completely described by its half-amplitude frequency $\rho_{1/2}$ and the transition width tw as follows:

$$\text{mesa}(\rho) = 1.0 \qquad \text{for } \rho < \rho_{1/2} - \frac{tw}{2}$$

$$= \frac{1}{2}\left(1 + \cos\left(\frac{\pi(\rho - \rho_{1/2} + tw/2)}{tw}\right)\right)$$

$$\text{for } \rho_{1/2} - \frac{tw}{2} < \rho < \rho_{1/2} + \frac{tw}{2}$$

$$= 0.0 \qquad \text{for } \rho > \rho_{1/2} + \frac{tw}{2}. \qquad (14.9)$$

The radial frequency selectivity is modeled by dom filters (differences of mesas) formed from two mesa filters evalu-

ated with different half-amplitude frequencies. The kth dom filter is given by

$$\text{dom}_k(\rho) = \text{mesa}(\rho)|_{\rho_{1/2}=2^{-(k-1)}} - \text{mesa}(\rho)|_{\rho_{1/2}=2^{-k}}, \qquad (14.10)$$

where the | symbol means the mesa filter is to be calculated with the indicated half-amplitude frequency $\rho_{1/2}$.[6] Increasing values of k correspond to higher levels of the hierarchical pyramid, which are consecutively lower frequency bands as denoted in figure 14.11b.

The lowest-frequency filter is referred to as the *baseband*, and we deviate from the formulation to determine its shape. We have found that if a mesa filter is used, an unacceptable amount of ringing occurs in the baseband (5 percent of the signal amplitude at 10 pixels from edge and 2 percent at 20). Our solution is to use a truncated Gaussian function for the baseband, as given by

$$\text{base}(\rho) = e^{-(\rho^2/2\sigma^2)} \quad \text{for } \rho < \rho_{1/2} + \frac{tw}{2}$$

$$= 0 \qquad \text{for } \rho \geq \rho_{1/2} + \frac{tw}{2}, \qquad (14.11)$$

where the sum of the parameters $\rho_{1/2}$ and tw is used to describe the truncation point, which corresponds to the peak frequency of the lowest-frequency dom filter. In the current implementation,

$$\sigma = \frac{1}{3}\left(\rho_{1/2} + \frac{tw}{2}\right); \qquad \rho_{1/2} = 2^{-K}, \qquad (14.12)$$

so that the Gaussian is at its 3σ amplitude where the baseband filter is truncated. To retain the property that the radial filter set (doms plus baseband) sums to 1.0, the change in the baseband filter must also be reflected in the equation for its contiguous dom filter (the lowest-frequency dom). The equations for the whole set of dom filters are therefore

$$\text{dom}_k(\rho) = \text{mesa}(\rho)|_{\rho_{1/2}=2^{-(k-1)}} - \text{mesa}(\rho)|_{\rho_{1/2}=2^{-k}}$$

$$\text{for } k = 1, K - 2$$

$$= \text{mesa}(\rho)|_{\rho_{1/2}=2^{-(k-1)}} - \text{base}(\rho)|_{\rho_{1/2}=2^{-k}}$$

$$\text{for } k = K - 1, \qquad (14.13)$$

where K is the total number of radial filters.

In the current implementation, the transition width tw of each filter is a function of its defined half-amplitude

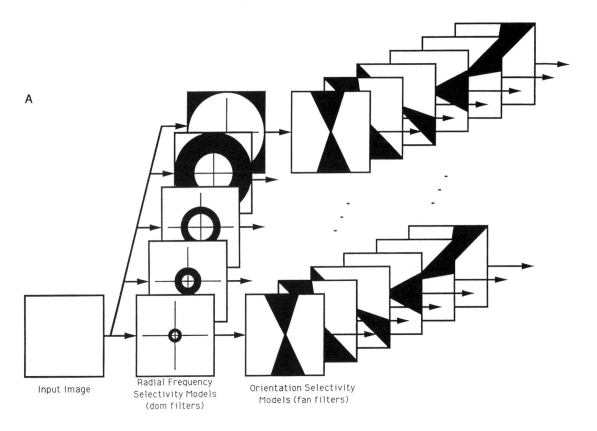

A

Input Image

Radial Frequency
Selectivity Models
(dom filters)

Orientation Selectivity
Models (fan filters)

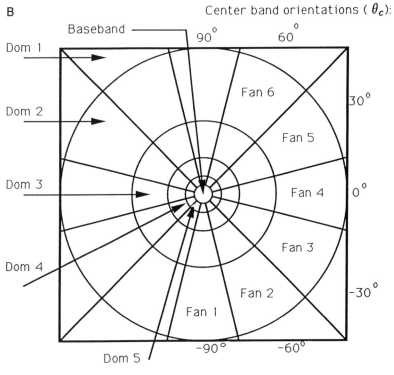

Center band orientations (θ_c):

B

Baseband

Dom 1

Dom 2

Dom 3

Dom 4

Dom 5

$90°$ $60°$

$30°$

Fan 6

Fan 5

Fan 4 $0°$

Fan 3

Fan 2 $-30°$

Fan 1

$-90°$ $-60°$

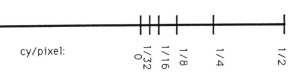

cy/pixel: 1/32   1/16   1/8   1/4   1/2
             0

Figure 14.11
Both these figures are views of the cortex transform's decomposition
of the frequency plane. In (A) the formation of the cortex filters are
shown, and in (B) the details of the radial frequencies and orientations
are shown along with the index notation used in this paper.

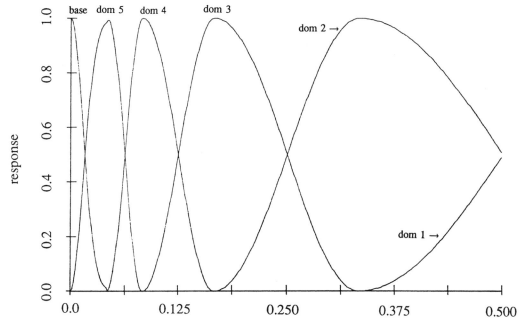

A

spatial frequency (cy/pixel)

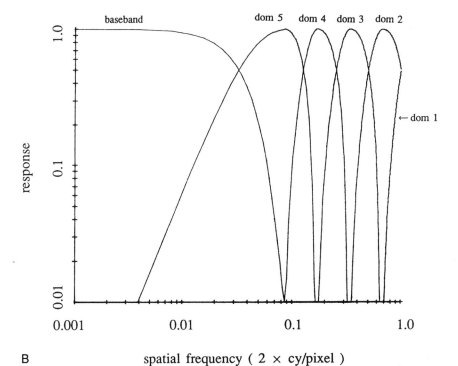

B

spatial frequency (2 × cy/pixel)

Figure 14.12
The dom filter series is shown for both linear (A) and log (B)
spatial-frequency axes.

frequency as follows:

$$tw = \frac{2}{3}\rho_{1/2},\qquad(14.14)$$

and the resulting radial frequency set is shown in figure 14.12 for both linear and logarithmic axes. This transition-width configuration gives constant behavior on a log frequency axis[7] with a bandwidth of 1.0 octave and symmetrical responses, as shown in the figure.

The orientation attributes of the spatial frequency selectivity are modeled with *fan* filters. As with the dom filter set, an integer number of fan filters are used to approximate the nearly continuous orientation selectivity of the visual system. A Hanning window is also used for these filters, which is determined in angular degrees θ in the Fourier plane. The equation for fan l as a function of orientation is

$$\mathrm{fan}_l(\theta) = \frac{1}{2}\left\{1 + \cos\left[\frac{\pi|\theta - \theta_c(l)|}{\theta_{tw}}\right]\right\}$$

$$\text{for } |\theta - \theta_c(l)| \le \theta_{tw}$$

$$= 0.0 \qquad \text{for } |\theta - \theta_c(l)| > \theta_{tw},\quad(14.15)$$

where θ_{tw} is the angular transition width and $\theta_c(l)$ is the orientation of the center, or peak, of fan filter l given by

$$\theta_c(l) = (l - 1)\cdot\theta_{tw} - 90.\qquad(14.16)$$

If we set the transition width equal to the angular spacing $\theta_{\Delta c}$ between adjacent fan filters,

$$\theta_{tw} = \theta_{\Delta c} = \frac{180}{L},\qquad(14.17)$$

where L is the total number of fan filters, then the filter set sums to 1.0, and the resulting orientation bandwidth also equals the angular spacing. The number of fan filters L in the current implementation is 6, which gives an orientation bandwidth of 30 deg. The fan filter set is shown in figure 14.13.

The cortex filters are formed as the polar separable product of the dom and fan filters as

$$\mathrm{cortex}_{k,l}(\rho,\theta) = \mathrm{dom}_k(\rho)\cdot\mathrm{fan}_l(\theta)$$

$$\text{for } k = 1, K - 1; l = 1, L$$

$$= \mathrm{base}(\rho)\ \text{ for } k = K,\qquad(14.18)$$

where the particular cortex filter can be denoted by the

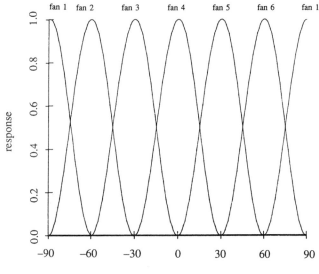

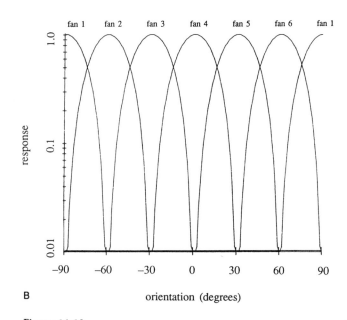

Figure 14.13
The set of six fan filters are shown for both linear (A) and logarithmic (B) responses axes.

dom and fan filter indices, k, l, respectively.[8] The total number of cortex filters in the set is $(\{K - 1\}^{*}L + 1)$, which in the current implementation is 31 ($K = 6, L = 6$). The set of cortex filters is invertible. That is,

$$\sum_{k=1,K}\sum_{l=1,L}\mathrm{cortex}_{k,l}(\rho,\theta) = 1\quad\text{for all }\rho, \theta,\qquad(14.19)$$

and a contour plot of a typical cortex filter pass-band ($k = 3, l = 5$) is shown in figure 14.14.

Measurement and Prediction of Visual Quality

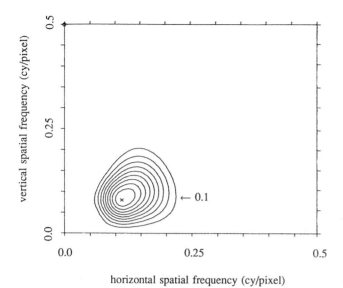

Figure 14.14
A contour plot of a cortex filter ($k = 3, 1 = 3$). The contours span from 0.1 to 0.9, with 1.0 indicated with an X.

Four modifications to the original Cortex transform [55] appear in the preceding model. The first modification is that the filter transitions use Hanning functions, whereas the original version used a Gaussian amplitude distribution function. We have found that the Hanning transition results in less ringing, especially if the Gaussian is truncated as in the original description. Another modification is that the orientation transitions are defined in polar degrees, whereas the original transitions were Euclidean. A third modification is our use of a Gaussian baseband to reduce ringing in the baseband. A final change was that we abandoned the use of a high-frequency residual, where all the radial frequencies greater than 0.5 c/pixel were either lumped in a single filter or merely discarded. In the model presented here, these high frequencies are split into a series of orientation bands as with all the other doms, despite the truncation of their shape by the Nyquist limits. This was necessary for blur prediction and other high-frequency distortions

Contrast Units in the Cortex Filtered Images

The two input images are filtered by the cortex filter set after they have been modified by the amplitude non-linearity and CSF models described previously. Thus each image is expanded to a set of filtered images, called cortex bands. To utilize data from psychophysical and physio-logical experiments the filtered images must be related to the units of contrast given in equation 14.2. For arbitrary waveforms, contrast should be defined as a function of location, since the waveform may change its entire character from one region to the next. With this definition it is also useful to allow the contrast to be both positive and negative, to delineate points on the waveform greater or less than the mean. The contrast for the cortex bands is modified from equation 14.2 into a function of pixel location $[i, j]$ given by

$$C_{k,l}[i,j] = \frac{(B_{k,l}[i,j] - \overline{B_{k,l}})}{\overline{B_{k,l}}}, \tag{14.20}$$

where $C_{k,l}[i,j]$ is the contrast in band k, l; $B_{k,l}[i,j]$ is the value of the filtered image; and $\overline{B_{k,l}}$ is the mean of band k, l. However, for all but the baseband image, the mean of the cortex bands $\overline{B_{k,l}}$ is zero, making the equation indeterminate. There are two solutions to this problem, both involving a redefinition of the mean term in the denominator of the contrast equation. The first of these, termed *global contrast*, uses a constant value for the denominator based on the input image mean, which can conveniently be found from the baseband mean $\overline{B_K}$ and leaves the numerator mean as zero:

$$C_{G_{k,l}}(i,j) = \frac{B_{k,l}(i,j)}{\overline{B_K}}. \tag{14.21}$$

The other approach, termed *local contrast*, uses the baseband image to define the mean as a function of pixel location. The equation is

$$C_{L_{k,l}}(i,j) = \frac{B_{k,l}(i,j)}{B_K(i,j)}, \tag{14.22}$$

where $B_K(i,j)$ is the baseband. Unfortunately, the available psychophysical image structure experiments do not allow us to determine which equation is more correct, because the type of imagery used in such experiments results in baseband images that are constant. However, some new experiments have recently begun to investigate this matter [39].

The local contrast metric, like the shift-variant retinal model [38], assumes that the eye can adapt to smaller local areas in the image. The small local area of adaptation is determined from the psf of the baseband, which can easily be chosen to give a psf similar to that in the shift-variant retinal model. However, there are significant differences between the two approaches due to the order of the nonlinearity with respect to the filtering processes. In the current implementation of the VDP, we have used the global contrast definition, since we are using the local amplitude nonlinearity model to describe differences in sensitivity as a function of gray level. The differences due to the order of the nonlinearities and the CSF between these two approaches are under investigation.

Masking Function

Masking refers to the decreased visibility of a signal due to the presence of a suprathreshold background. The masking function quantifies this effect as a function of the background contrast. The basic effect of the masking experiments holds for all types of signals and masks and can be summarized in a generic masking plot, shown in figure 14.15(a). In this log-log plot, the horizontal axis is the contrast of the mask, and the vertical axis is the threshold of the signal in the presence of the mask. We can see that the curve has two asymptotic regions: one with a slope of zero and the other with a slope near 1.0. The zero slope occurs for low mask contrasts, indicating that there is no masking effect, since the threshold is the same as for a uniform field. This uniform field threshold is a function of frequency and is equal to the inverse of the CSF. As the mask contrast increases, the threshold rises, and for high-contrast masks the data fall on the asymptotic region with a slope near 1.0.

Although the masking curve described in the plot occurs for nearly all signal and mask combinations, the actual locations of the asymptotes and other specifics of the curve critically depend on the frequencies in the test signal and mask. Both the CSF and the spatial frequency selectivity of the visual system play key roles in modeling the specifics of masking. In the following development we start with the simplest case, where both the signal and

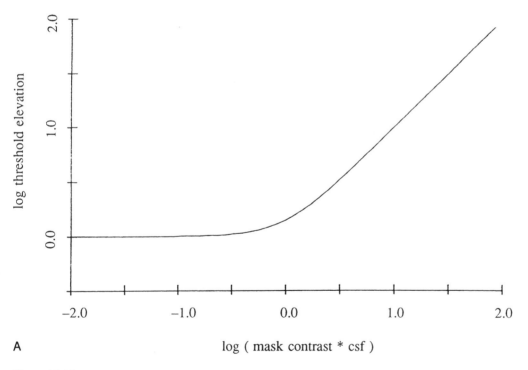

A

log (mask contrast * csf)

Figure 14.15
(A) The masking function normalized on both axes by the inverse of the CSF. The vertical axis, $T_E = T(m)/T(0) = T(m) \cdot csf$, is generally referred to as threshold elevation. (B) The generic behavior of the masking curves when the test and mask frequency are not equivalent. The normalization is the same as used in (A). (C) The effect of additional normalization by the cortex filter.

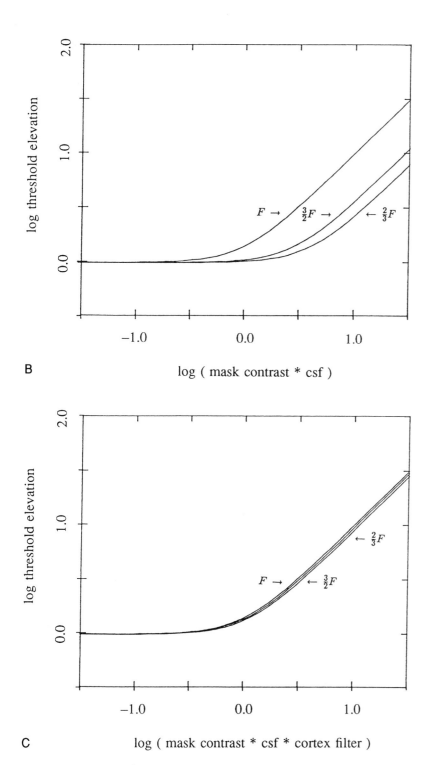

B   log (mask contrast * csf)

C   log (mask contrast * csf * cortex filter)

Figure 14.15 (continued)

mask consist of a single frequency. From this point we work toward a description of the masking effects for the signal and mask consisting of different arbitrary collections of frequencies.

If we normalize both the test threshold and mask contrast axes by the test frequency's threshold in a uniform field (i.e., $1/\text{csf}$), the curve in figure 14.15(a) can describe all frequencies, provided the test and mask are the same frequency. This normalization removes the CSF, and the vertical axis can be relabeled as threshold elevation T_e,

$$T_e(\rho, m) = \frac{T(\rho, m)}{T(\rho, 0)} = T(\rho, m) \cdot \text{csf}(\rho), \qquad (14.23)$$

which describes the degree of masking as a function of frequency ρ and mask contrast m. The same normalization of the horizontal axis causes the high mask contrast asymptote (and consequently the intersection of the two asymptotes) to be the same for all frequencies.

If we change the frequency of the mask while leaving the test frequency unchanged, the curve in figure 14.15a shifts to the right while retaining the same shape.[9] This shift is shown in figure 14.15(b), which compares the threshold elevation due to three masking frequencies $(\frac{2}{3}F, F, \frac{3}{2}F)$ on a test frequency of F. This shift is due to the spatial frequency selectivity of the visual mechanism responsible for detecting the frequency F. The detecting mechanism acts as if the mask is of frequency F but of lower contrast (thus the curve shifts to the right).

If we change the horizontal axis by normalizing for the filter shape of the visual mechanism responsible for detecting the test of frequency F, the curves will realign as indicated in figure 14.15(c). The mask contrast axis now represents contrast as seen by the detecting mechanism, and one curve completely describes the masking effects for all signal and mask combinations. The cortex filter set is used to model the detection mechanism's frequency response, and like the normalization performed by the CSF, the cortex filter normalizes all frequencies in the band to their effective contrast seen by the detection mechanism of the band. Therefore, once we have filtered the images into the separate bands, we need no longer concern ourselves with their specific frequencies, since all the activity in the band has been normalized (by the CSF and cortex filters) such that a single curve can describe all the masking in the band. Although this discussion has been limited to single frequencies, similar experiments have been performed for noise fields of different bandwidths,

and the essential results have held. The incorporation of the cortex filters along with the CSF is done by using the normalized mask contrast term,

$$m_n(\rho_t, \theta_t) = m(\rho_m, \theta_m) \cdot \text{csf}(\rho_m, \theta_m) \cdot \text{cortex}_{k,l}(\rho_m, \theta_m),$$
$$(14.24)$$

which describes the mask contrast at frequency (ρ_m, θ_m) seen by the mechanism that detects the test signal at frequency (ρ_t, θ_t). The indices k, l on the cortex filter correspond to the filter that is centered on the test signal frequency.[10]

Before we can generalize from noise fields to natural image textures, we need to discuss two major types of experiments to determine the shape of the masking function. These can be classified as experiments using sinusoidal masks and experiments using noise masks. Although these two experimental techniques both give masking functions with the frequency-shifting properties as described in figure 14.15, there are key differences in the results. These differences lead to two different kinds of models proposed for describing the masking function.

Phase-Coherent Masking

The experiments using *sine* waves as masks were the earliest studies of masking. The special case where the test and the mask are the same frequency and phase is known as *contrast discrimination*, because the detection task simplifies to discriminating the differences in contrast between the signal and the signal plus mask. In this case the threshold actually drops below the uniform field threshold near the intersection of the asymptotes, an effect known as *facilitation* or the *dipper effect*. Although many visual models rely on this specific experiment to model suprathreshold vision [28, 57, 59], we consider the broader class of sine masking studies, where the facilitation rapidly diminishes as the difference between the frequencies increases [27]. Other experiments involving brief temporal offsets between the test and mask found a complete disappearance of facilitation [19], suggesting the tenuous nature of this effect. However, nearly all the results from this class have two features in common. The first is that the intersection of the two asymptotes occurs where the mask contrast equals the threshold contrast, corresponding to a value of 1.0 on the normalized horizontal axis. The second is a high mask contrast asymptote with a slope near 0.7. The results have led to power-law models of suprathreshold perception, where the masking function is modeled [57] as a function of normalized mask contrast m_n,

$$T_e(m_n) = \frac{T(m_n)}{T(0)} = \left[\frac{m_n}{T(0)}\right]^s \quad \text{for } m_n > T(0)$$

$$T_e(0) = 1.0 \quad \text{for } m_n \leq T(0), \quad (14.25)$$

with the slope of the high contrast asymptote, typically 0.7, given by s. In these equations the CSF model will appear via the term $T(\rho, 0)$, but the frequencies are omitted from the equation because they are assumed to be equivalent.

Phase-Incoherent Masking

The *noise* experiments performed to date include a wide variety of combinations of noise masks and tests signals, including one-dimensional dynamic noise fields [50], one-dimensional static noise fields [51], two-dimensional static noise fields [35], and two-dimensional dynamic noise fields [42, 40]. A common feature of the experiments using noise is that for high mask contrasts, the data follow a slope of 1.0, indicating Weber-law behavior, rather than the slope of 0.7 found for the sine-wave masks. In addition, the facilitation effect does not occur for noise masks. The data for these experiments are commonly fit with the following equation [42]:

$$T = W\sqrt{n_i^2 + m^2}, \quad (14.26)$$

where T is the threshold, m is the rms contrast of the mask, W is the detection signal-to-noise ratio, and n_i^2 is proportional to the internal visual noise of the visual mechanisms responsible for detecting the signal. This expression is a straightforward representation of a signal-to-noise ratio detection process with two noise sources. The detector efficiency is inversely proportional to W, since a higher value of W corresponds to a higher signal-to-noise ratio required for detection. The parameters W and n_i can be determined from the asymptotes of the experimental data as

$$W = \frac{T(m_n)}{m_n} \quad \text{when } n_i \ll m_n \text{ (high-contrast asymptote)}$$

$$ (14.27)$$

$$n_i = \frac{T(0)}{W} \quad \text{when } m_n = 0 \text{ (zero-slope asymptote)}$$

Because we are working with a normalized relationship in the VDP algorithm (provided by the CSF and cortex filters), we rewrite equation 14.26 in terms of threshold elevation, normalized mask contrast, and equation 14.27,

$$T_e(m_n) = \sqrt{1 + (Wm_n)^2}. \quad (14.28)$$

It is worth noting that in most of the applications of the VDP, the notations of signal and noise are reversed from their normal usage. Normally, the image is regarded as the signal, and the distortions as noise, but our goal is to determine if a distortion is visible in the context of the image. The image content is the source of masking and is therefore regarded as noise, whereas the distortion is regarded as the signal whose detectability we wish to predict.

Learning-Effect Model

The differences in the results of these two types of experiments, with the two distinct slopes for the high-contrast asymptote, pose problems for those trying to use the data in applied visual models. The question arises as to which type of synthetic structure (sine waves or noise fields) is more appropriate to describe the masking effect in actual images. A study that seems to unify the disparate results between the noise and sine-wave experiments has been performed by Smith and Swift [47]. By clever design of experiments, they were able to obtain slopes of 1.0 for sine masks and slopes of 0.7 for noise fields, which are reversed from usual. This reversal shows that the difference in slopes was not inherent in the noise or sinusoidal waveforms. The source of the difference in slopes between the two masks seems to lie in the differing degrees of uncertainty caused by the masking pattern, an uncertainty that can be reduced through learning. Because the sine masking pattern is fairly easy to learn, one must merely look for differences in the expected appearance of the mask to detect the added signal. On the other hand, the pattern in the noise mask is difficult to learn, which results in a higher slope that is indicative of more masking and a lower detector efficiency. Because most experimenters using noise fields used different realizations of the noise throughout the experiment, the observer had no opportunity to learn the noise field, and the learning effect was obscured.

In Smith and Swift's study, the same noise field was used repeatedly, and the slope of the high-contrast

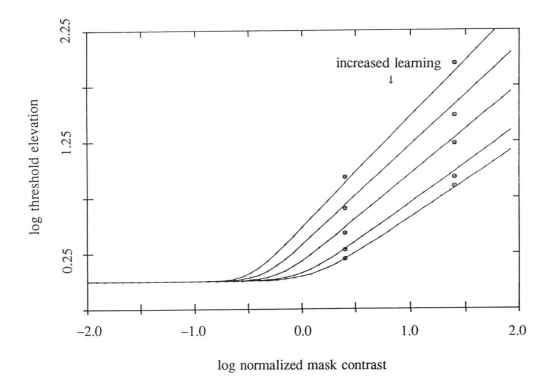

increased learning
↓

Figure 14.16
The masking model's change in shape with increased learning (smooth curves with slopes specified as 1.0, 0.9, 0.8, 0.7, and 0.65) are compared with data from [47].

asymptote was measured over a large number of trials. As the observer's familiarity with the noise mask increased, the slope dropped from 1.0 to about 0.65. Further proof that uncertainty was limiting the detection for the noise masks was ascertained by using a 3AFC technique. In this technique three identical noise fields were presented simultaneously, and the signal was added to one of them. The task was simply to pick the field that looked different, and for this experiment the slopes obtained were between 0.65 and 0.80, despite the changing noise field for each presentation. Because the uncertainty was removed for the observer, no learning was necessary. To obtain slopes of 1.0 for the sine-masking case, Smith and Swift used naive observers and collected data during the customary training sessions. Although they could measure only two points on the asymptote, the measured slopes were initially 1.0 before dropping to the usual 0.65. This was similar to the effect found for the noise masks, but faster, since the sine masks were easy to learn. The results of this learning experiment for sine masks are shown as data points in figure 14.16.

No equations for this uncertainty/learning effect were presented by Smith and Swift, but it was necessary to develop one for use in the VDP. The masking function in equation 14.28 has been extended to include the learning effect, and the masking function used in the VDP is

$$T_e(m_n) = (1 + (k_1(k_2 \cdot m_n)^s)^b)^{1/b}, \qquad (14.29)$$

where T_e is the threshold elevation, and s corresponds to the slope of the high masking contrast asymptote, which ranges between 0.6 and 1.0. The parameters k_1 and k_2 determine the pivot point of all the learning slopes shown in figure 14.16. They are also related to the parameter W by

$$k_1 = W^{(1-1/(1-Q))}$$
$$k_2 = W^{(1/(1-Q))}, \qquad (14.30)$$

where Q is the slope of the high-contrast asymptote when the intersection of the two asymptotes is 1.0 on the normalized mask contrast axis. This equation is shown fitting the data in figure 14.16 by using values of s ranging from 1.0 to 0.65, and it can be simplified to the noise model in equation 14.26 or the sine-mask model in equation 14.25. The value for W used in the current implementation of the VDP is 6, the value for Q is 0.70, and the value for b is 4. Although we have unified the different experiments, we are still left with the problem of choosing a slope or, consequently, the expected degree of learning. After many experiments with natural and synthetic images, we have chosen a value for the learning slope that depends on the cortex band. The values range from 0.7 for the baseband to 1.0 for the middle frequencies.

Masking in Cortex Bands

We now turn our attention to the role of the masking function in the context of the cortex filters. The previous discussion of the masking function was described in the context of the visual system's spatial-frequency selectivity rather than the cortex filter's discrete-channel approximation. The main difference in the discrete-filter approach is that there is not a detector centered on every test frequency. We need to broaden our concept of the test frequency to include all the frequencies present in the cortex band. Likewise, our concept of the masking frequency should now encompass all the possible frequencies in the band. This generality allows the model to describe local image regions, when combined with the activity in the other cortex bands. In the algorithm, many frequencies contribute to the normalized mask contrast m_n within a particular band k, l as a function of location $[i, j]$. It is calculated as,

$$m_n^{k,l}[i, j] = \mathscr{F}^{-1}\{\mathscr{L}[u, v] \cdot \text{csf}[u, v] \cdot \text{cortex}^{k,l}[u, v]\}, \quad (14.31)$$

where $\mathscr{L}$ is the Fourier transform of the input image processed by the amplitude nonlinearity, and u, v are the Cartesian frequency components. Although the normalized mask contrast may be positive or negative, It is its magnitude that affects the masking function, so that the threshold elevation in equation 14.29 implemented as a function of location becomes

$$T_e^{k,l}[i, j] = (1 + (k_1(k_2|m_n^{k,l}[i,j]|)^s)^b)^{1/b}. \quad (14.32)$$

The band-specific threshold elevation $T_e^{k,l}[i, j]$ is a function of pixel location and is referred to as the *threshold elevation image*.

Mutual Masking

Our initial approach was to derive the threshold elevation image solely from the reference image. This approach has failed in the prediction of bandwidth changes (in particular, blur). To explain this, we consider two complementary types of image distortions. The first of these is blur, where the basic effect is to change a step into a smooth ramp, and the other is contouring, which has the effect of changing a smooth ramp into a step.

For the case of blur, the step is the reference, and the smooth ramp is the distorted image. If the reference is used to form the masking image, there will be a high degree of masking along the edge, enough that the small differences due to blur will fall below the elevated threshold. With a model of this sort we have found that large amounts of easily visible blur are not predicted by algorithm. The problem with deriving the masking image from the reference image is that when the distorted (blurred) image is viewed, there is no edge signal present to cause any masking on the smooth ramp. To solve this problem, one might suggest deriving the masking image from the distorted image. In this case there is little masking along the edge (since it blurred), and the difference between the two images is correctly predicted.

However, this simple solution fails when the distortion is contouring. In this case the distorted images will have sharp steps in place of the smooth ramps, and these steps will mask out the differences between the two images near the steps, which is the main location of the error due to contouring. But when the contoured image with false steps is observed, those regions are expected to be smooth, and the false step edges do not mask the expectation of smoothness. It is clear from this discussion that the masking image cannot be derived solely from either the reference or the distorted image. One solution to this problem is to form the masking image from both the reference and distorted images, using the minimum of the two threshold elevations. We have termed this technique *mutual masking*, since the only masking that occurs is that which is mutual to both input images. With this approach there is no need to delineate the reference and distorted images; the algorithm's goal is to determine only the visible difference between them. The masking threshold elevation image is given by

$$T_{em}^{k,l}[i, j] = \min[T_{e1}^{k,l}[i, j], T_{e2}^{k,l}[i, j]], \quad (14.33)$$

where the subscripts 1 and 2 refer to the two images input to the algorithm. The development of the mutual masking technique was necessary for the VDP algorithm to predict blur as well as other special cases such as noise reduction and vernier acuity.

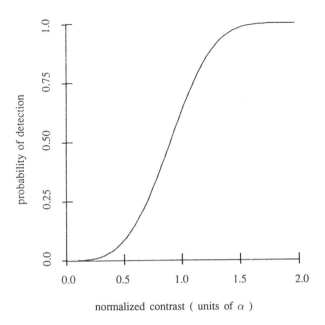

Figure 14.17
The psychometric function is shown in linear coordinates with an abscissa normalized by the threshold α.

Psychometric Function and Probability Summation

The psychometric function, shown in figure 14.17, describes the increase in the probability of detection as the signal contrast increases. It is given by the following equation [37], which can describe data for nearly all combinations of spatiotemporal frequencies:

$$P(c) = 1 - e^{-(c/\alpha)^\beta} \tag{14.34}$$

where $P(c)$ is the probability of detecting a signal of contrast c. The threshold is given by the parameter α, which shifts the function along the contrast axis. The slope of the pyschometric function is described by the parameter β and is largely invariant across many experiments [34]. This has enabled the single parameter α to retain the information describing the entire psychometric function region.

The probability of detection as a function of location is calculated as follows. First the contrast difference as a function of location is calculated using the global contrast equation,

$$\Delta C_{k,l}[i,j] = C1_{k,l}[i,j] - C2_{k,l}[i,j]$$

$$= \frac{B1_{k,l}[i,j]}{\overline{B}_K} - \frac{B2_{k,l}[i,j]}{\overline{B}_K}, \tag{14.35}$$

where $\Delta C_{k,l}(i,j)$ is the contrast difference for band k, l as a function of pixel location, and $B1_{k,l}$ and $B2_{k,l}$ are the two filtered input images for band k, l. This value is then input along with the threshold $T(0)$ and the threshold elevation from equations 14.31–33 for band k, l into equation 14.34,

$$P_n[i,j] = 1 - e^{-(\Delta C_{k,l}[i,j]/(T_{em}[i,j] \cdot T(0)))^\beta}, \tag{14.36}$$

to determine the probability of detection in band k, l as a function of location, $P_n[i,j]$. As we mentioned earlier, the role of the CSF in the VDP algorithm is to normalize all frequencies so that their thresholds are equal as seen by the subsequent spatial filter hierarchy. By the calibration techniques chosen, a code-value excursion of 1.0 corresponds to the uniform field threshold contrast in each band of the hierarchy, so that $T(0)$ in equation 14.36 equals 1.0. This approach assumes that the psychometric function does not change shape when the threshold is elevated by masking, which is a simplification from actual data. The sign of the error is also calculated, which indicates whether the error appears lighter or darker than the reference image. It is used to give shape to the predicted error in the visualization section of the algorithm. The signed probability of detection SP is simply calculated from

$$SP_{k,l}[i,j] = \text{sign}(\Delta C_{k,l}[i,j]) \cdot P_{k,l}[i,j]. \tag{14.37}$$

Once the detection probabilities are computed for each band of the spatial filter hierarchy, these probability images are combined into a single image that describes the overall probability of detecting an error for every pixel in the image. The technique of probability summation is used, with the equation given by the product series,

$$P_t[i,j] = 1 - \prod_{k=1,K; l=1,L} (1 - P_{k,l}[i,j]), \tag{14.38}$$

where P_t is the total probability of detection resulting from all bands as a function of location. Similar to the case for the individual bands, where the sign of the error was preserved, the sign of the total probability of detection of differences between the two input images is preserved. For most distortions the nonzero detection probabilities from different bands will agree in sign at every pixel. Occasionally, however, different cortex bands detect errors at the same pixel with different signs. This problem is resolved by summing the signs for each layer weighted by their probability of detection for that location and then taking the sign of the result. This works well in predicting the shape of most visible distortions.

Visualization and Interpretation of the Detection Maps

The output of the probability summation is a map of the probability of detecting visible differences and is a function of pixel location. Disregarding the sign of the detection map, which describes the polarity of the visible difference, the magnitude ranges from 0 to 1. All suprathreshold visual differences will map to the value of 1, since the algorithm cannot distinguish between visual differences that are easily detectable yet have different degrees of perceived contrast error. Thus the probability-of-detection map does not describe the contrast appearance of the visual differences, it only indicates their location. The range between 0 and 1 corresponds to the threshold detection region whose perceptual qualities of

visual differences in the threshold region can be described as very faint or unstable. Because the range of the probability map extends from -1 to 1, it must be remapped to be viewed on most current display devices. There are currently two methods of displaying the detection map.

Free-Field Difference Map

The first of these methods, the *free-field difference map*, displays the predictions on a uniform field of gray, free of image structure. This method merely uses a linear mapping of the code values of the detection map, with the equation given by

$$FF[i,j] = SP_t[i,j] * \left(\frac{max - min}{2}\right) + \left(\frac{max + min}{2}\right),$$

$$(14.39)$$

where FF is the free-field difference prediction, SP is the signed probability of detection from equation 14.31, and max and min are the display's maximum and minimum

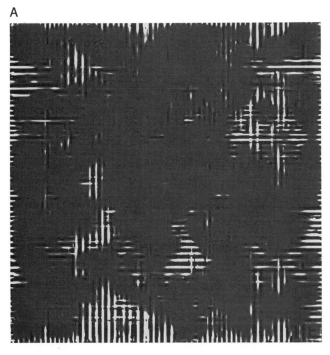

A

B

Figure 14.18
Results of the VDP algorithm shown in the *free-field difference map* format for the banding distorted image (A) and the tone-scale distorted image (B) that appear in figure 14.3. The viewing distance is for a range between 2.5 and 10 times the image height. White indicates where the distorted image looks lighter than the reference

with a detection probability of 1.0, and black indicates where the distorted image looks darker than the reference with detection probability of 1.0. A pedestal of gray value of 128 indicates zero detection probabiliy, and shades of gray between these extremes indicate threshold region detection.

values, respectively. This map is monochromatic, and an example of the VDP's output in this format is shown in Figures 14.18a and (b) for the distorted images of figures 14.3(a) and (b), respectively. Pixels that are lighter than the pedestal of (max + min)/2 indicate where the distorted image appears lighter than the reference, and vice versa for the darker pixels. Full-white or full-black pixels are detected completely, that is, with a probability of 1.0. These regions have a clipped appearance because all the suprathreshold differences are mapped to their values of −1.0 and 1.0. The pixels with shades of gray between these two extremes indicate where the visible differences are solely within the threshold region. The VDP results match the visibility of the distortions in figures 14.3(a) and (b) in that the banding distortions (a) are easily visible in many areas of the image, whereas the tone scale distortions (b) are extremely difficult to see, since they all lie within the threshold region.

In-Context Difference Map

With the method just described it is sometimes difficult to judge the correspondence between the predicted differences and the differences actually observed between the two input images. The second method, the *in-context difference map*, was designed to overcome this problem. It does so by displaying the predicted differences in the context of the reference image. So that the suprathreshold image content of the reference image does not mask the predicted results, we expanded the monochromatic output to color, so that the predicted differences appear in color on the original monochromatic reference image. The reference image is copied to all three RGB planes, and the detection image is scaled and added to one of the color planes as follows:

$$IC[i,j] = SP_t[i,j] \cdot \left(\frac{max - min}{2}\right) + ref[i,j], \qquad (14.40)$$

where *IC* is the in-context difference prediction, *ref* is the reference image, and the other terms are as described in equation 14.39. In this example the red layer was used, so that red indicates where the distorted image appears lighter than the reference, and the cyan indicates where it appears darker. The VDP's output is shown in this format in color plate 3 (a) and (b) for the two distorted images of figures 14.3(a) and (b), respectively. The map for the

banding distortion (a) makes it easy to judge the accuracy of the VDP, especially with respect to the location of the visible errors. On the other hand, the tone-scale distortions (b) are insignificant, which should agree well with most readers' perceptions.

The Use and Interpretation of the Maps

Although not an application, the initial use of the output detection maps is to evaluate the success of the algorithm. The maps indicate the shape and location of the predicted visual differences, which can be roughly verified by observation. One image with distortions equals many experiments, since there is essentially an experiment for each local artifact. Because the algorithm is a threshold model, the detection output maps can be analyzed and verified much more easily than for a suprathreshold model, in which it is difficult for individuals to quickly and consistently rank magnitudes. As a result, we relied on informal psychophysical testing to determine the parameters of the algorithm in the developmental phases. This allowed us to perform more time consuming formal psychophysical tests after completing of the model.

Of course, the primary function of the VDP is to aid in the design of imaging systems. The output detection maps can be used directly by imaging systems designers to see the nature of the distortion they are adding, which allows them to concentrate on the distortions that are visible. The shapes and locations of the predicted differences also may give the designer insight into ways to improve the performance/cost attributes of the system.

The potential of the VDP is diminished if the designer must always look at the detection map in the form of an image, since one can argue that the designer can gain similar information from looking at the simulated (distorted) image directly, except in the cases where the display system is not yet built. The number of applications for the VDP would be increased if the multidimensional detection map could be integrated into a single-number metric that could then be used as a cost function in automated optimization routines and other related design approaches. Once confidence is established in the accuracy of the VDP for threshold results, it can be used as a framework to study potential metrics that reduce the prediction to a single number. With the establishment of such metrics it would no longer be necessary to display the simulated image or visualize the detection maps, because the VDP output could be mathematically analyzed directly.

To date we have developed one straightforward method of reducing the detection map to a single number. This is done by finding the maximum magnitude of all the pixels in the detection map. If this number, the *peak probability of detection,* is less than 1.0, we know any visual differences are entirely in the threshold region. If the number is less than 0.5, the images are *visually equivalent* for our purposes. We then perform the VDP for a number of viewing distances to determine the minimum distance at which the two images are visually equivalent. We refer to this distance as the *critical distance* and use it to compare competing designs, with a lower number indicating a superior design. However, with the exception of this one approach, methods to combine the map of detectabilities into a single number are still under research. We hope this model will be instrumental in such research.

Comparisons with Other Visual Models

In this section we discuss other approaches used to develop an image-processing-based model of the visual system. Some of these are from published models for image-quality assessment, while others are from models developed for understanding the visual system. These other approaches are discussed with respect to their analogous components in the HVS model described here. Some of the differences in approaches are the result of data that are in disagreement, often due to second-order effects. In such cases of conflict, the approach used for the VDP was to model the simpler data.

Other Amplitude Nonlinearity Approaches

The first image-processing models of the HVS used a logarithmic front end [48, 22, 18]. This was a reasonable approximation, but it overestimated the detectability of differences in the dark areas for all but the brightest light adaptation levels. Conversely, linear front end models overestimated the detectability of differences in the light areas. Consequently, image-processing models began using the cube-root front end [36, 32], which performs very closely to the nonlinearity used in the current VDP. None of these models, however, had any mechanisms to account for spatial-frequency selectivity.

Two very recent image-processing models take unique approaches to modeling the front-end adaptation properties. One of these [60], combines the front end non-linearity with the generation of the multiple channel filters by using the ratio-of-Gaussians (ROG) rather than the more typical difference-of-Gaussians (DOG). Although this appears to be a better approach with regard to visual experiments studying harmonic distortion products, the overall model fails to predict the difference between quantization in the linear and log domains. The other model [28] uses a normalization process to center the signal on a "retinal transducer function" that precedes the generation of the multiple frequency channels. Curiously, the role of the retinal transducer function is to model the masking process, whereas adaptation is modeled by the normalization step. This is the only model that places the masking function before the multiple channel filtering, which is not well supported by psychophysics.

Other CSF Approaches

Several models ignore the effect of the CSF altogether [60, 55, 15]. In their defense, however, there are some applications where the primary effects of the CSF are minimized, making the deficiencies of these models less pronounced. In visual models based on spatial-frequency mechanisms, the most common approach is to weight the sensitivities of the discrete channels so that the sum is close to a target CSF [29, 57, 59, 12]. An advantage of the VDP technique of separating the CSF model from the multiple channel generation is that it allows for more flexibility in modeling the CSF adaptivities, distance changes, and range effects. A disadvantage is that the VDP's technique of preceding the cortex filtering with a CSF causes a slight distortion in the shape of the frequency channels from that described by the cortex filters.

A few models have separated the CSF into its neural and optical components, sandwiching a nonlinearity between these effects [22, 28]. The first of these is an older model, and it does not include spatial-frequency selectivity. Although the second reference uses this more advanced strategy of multiple CSFs in conjunction with a spatial-frequency hierarchy, the actual CSF used is very simple and does not include light adaptation, anisotropy, eccentricity, image size, accommodation, or a number of other important parameters.

Other Spatial-Frequency Hierarchy Approaches

The spatial-frequency hierarchy is the base algorithm necessary to model the signal dependency of masking. Currently, there is a vast array of choices for implementing the hierarchy. In this section we discuss the advantages and disadvantages of these approaches.

The *cortex transform* was selected as the basic structure to implement the spatial-frequency selectivity in the VDP. Its basic structure in the frequency domain, referred to as log-polar, was based on the combination of the spatial-frequency selectivity measured psychophysically and the measurements of two-dimensional cortical receptive fields. It was introduced by Watson [55], who later incorporated it into a more complete visual model (by adding masking) [57]. Some of the advantages of the cortex transform include its invertibility, its ease of implementation, and its flexibility. Because the filter set sums to 1 for all frequencies, it is one of the few filter sets that is invertible, which allows the two-dimensional CSF to be modeled independently. Flexibility ensues from its modular construction, which allows parameters such as bandwidths and specific shapes of the radial frequency and orientation responses easily to be varied. This enables more accurate modeling of the visual system by better matching to the available data. Since the purpose of the VDP is to analyze other imaging systems and algorithms (which may themselves be visually based to various degrees), the emphasis is on accuracy and not on efficiency. The cortex transform is not without its disadvantages, which include its nonorthogonality and computational complexity. Another problem is that bands cannot overlap with other than their direct neighbors, which imposes some constraints on the orientation and radial frequency bandwidths.

The *Gabor function* is optimal for space-frequency localization. As a result, a number of visual models based on the Gabor function have been proposed [28, 54, 15]. All these use the Gabor function in a log-polar structure similar to the cortex transform, but there are two major approaches. The simplest approach [28] is to filter the image by a bank of Gabor filters to produce an expanded set of images that overrepresent the image yet are not complete. The other approach is the Gabor transform [15], which creates a set of coefficients for the basis set of Gabor functions. These functions sample the image with multiple rates such that the total number of degrees of freedom is preserved. This representation is complete, for the image can be exactly reconstructed by summing all the Gabor functions weighted by their coefficients. There have been two main attempts at calculating the coefficients of the basis set, which is difficult since the transform is nonorthogonal. The first of these [6] uses a one-dimensional closed-form solution that has three main problems: Its extension to two-dimensions must be Cartesian separable; it cannot generate log-frequency basis sets; and the resulting analysis filter is physiologically unrealistic. The second [15] is a neural network solution that has the desired log-polar properties. Unfortunately, for computational reasons, the Gabor function is truncated at $1\ \sigma$, which causes the algorithm to lose its property of invertibility and can give rise to tiling artifacts in images.

All the Gabor approaches have a number of disadvantages. The filter sets of the simple filtering approaches do not sum to 1, which limits the visual model as a research tool and poses problems with regard to the CSF. Another problem with the Gabor techniques is that the filters are not symmetrical on a log-frequency axis. Also, the purported ideal property of joint space-frequency uncertainty minimization is only for a *definition* of uncertainty, in particular, one involving the second-order moments. There is debate whether this metric is appropriate for the visual system [49]. In addition, newer models have been proposed that are better fits to recent neurophysiological data for cortical receptive fields [23].

The *QMF subband transform* has been used as a structure for perceptually based image compression [1, 46], and we considered using it instead of the cortex transform. The main advantage of the QMF subband is that it is the most computationally efficient approach for generating the spatial-frequency bands. It is also orthogonal and reversible, although most narrowly tuned implementations typically lose the reversibility due to amplitude distortions in the reconstruction process. It can be set up to have the desired log spacing of frequency bands, by implementing it in a pyramid fashion. Its main problem is what is referred to as a mixed orientation band, in which the diagonal band contains frequencies near 45 deg and 135 deg. This leads to significant failures in its prediction of visual masking effects, because this mixed band assumes that contrast energies from these distant orientations mask each other as well as similar orientations. A version of pyramidal subband coding on a hexagonal grid [46] has been developed that removes the mixed orientation band, but then the orientation channels are either limited to three (60 deg apart) or bear no relationship to the shape of the frequency selectivity found psychophysically or physiologically. Although the QMF approach may be a reasonable framework for perceptually based compression, its limitations for visual models are significant.

The hexagonal orthogonal oriented pyramid *(HOP) transform* [58] begins with a hexagonal sampled image that was physiologically motivated by the hexagonal structure of the cones in the fovea. Difference-of-Gaussian (DOG) functions are applied to the samples in the hexagonal array. This model has proved useful in understanding how the cortical receptive fields are formed from the retinal inputs. Its disadvantage, similar to that of the hexagonal version of the QMF subband transform, is that there are only three orientation channels, and as a result, the tuning is too broad for use in a visual model. The visual system may indeed perform processing very similar to this model, but the hexagonal structure of the fovea undergoes apparently random shifts in local orientation about every 20 cones [43]. This allows more orientation channels to be formed in the cortex. Unfortunately, implementation of this property in the HOP model has not yet been worked out.

Another recent approach is the *wavelet* representation [31], which is a multiresolution decomposition with space and frequency localization properties like those of the other described approaches, but it is orthogonal and complete. Wavelets are based on a set of dilated and translated scaling functions that are consequently self-similar from one resolution to the next. There is overlap between the channels as in the other approaches, but the orthogonality allows better control of the overlap. Wavelets have been developed that have compact support and are continuously differentiable, and as in subband coding, the number of pixels remains the same in the representation. Most of the wavelet implementations are Cartesian separable and consequently have a mixed orientation band, as in the QMF subbands. There is also still debate regarding the definition of wavelets, so that most of the pyramid schemes proposed to model the spatial-frequency selectivity of the HVS can be loosely be regarded as wavelets, due to their self-similarity across resolutions.

A continuous-domain approach is the matched filter or *cross-correlation* approach, which is suggested by the masking data, since the mask becomes more effective as the signal and mask come closer together in the two-dimensional Fourier domain. Although some experiments [8] found support for this idea, they were very limited and used only spectrally flat noise as the mask. This work triggered another set of experiments [9] to further investigate this idea. These used "natural scenes" as the masking background and found that cross correlation failed to predict the observed results. In terms of applying any cross-correlation approach to the VDP application, the main problem occurs in the many applications where the observer does not know what he or she is looking for, and it is not known what should be used as the signal in the cross-correlation operation.

Other Masking Function Approaches

There are three main ways to model the masking effect, given that the image is decomposed into the appropriate spatial-frequency bands. One of these is to use a threshold elevation image, as was done in the VDP. Another is to use a contrast transducer function [29, 57, 59] to modify the pixel-dependent contrast of a band.[11] This technique has the advantage of being able to retain the degree of suprathreshold differences, and is easier to incorporate in image-compression algorithms. A third approach is to model the masking effects with uncertainty models, which take into account the uncertainty in position, frequency, and the like, of a signal in the context of a background pattern. This approach is typically modeled by using internal noise sources in the HVS model, which unfortunately requires noise realizations and Monte Carlo simulations. There is ongoing debate on whether masking is caused by a contrast transducer function, an uncertainty, or a combination of the two [13]. The threshold elevation approach, as implemented in the VDP, seems the most direct approach for threshold prediction, which is our primary application at the present.

Other Channel Summation Approaches

Although we have used probability summation in the VDP, the most common method used to combine the outputs from the different frequency mechanisms uses a vector summation of differences across bands and pixels [60, 28, 29], which gives a single-number output. This approach works in conjunction with the contrast transducer function described previously and has the capability of describing suprathreshold differences. However, its verification is much more difficult in the context of images where the distortion may be visible in several parts of the image and does not lend itself well to being described as a single signal. Like all single-number-output models, this approach treats the entire physical difference image as a single signal and then calculates objectionability of the global distortion. It does not tell you what parts of the distorted image are above and what parts are below threshold, nor whether the local distortions are lighter or darker than the reference. This makes it much more difficult to develop the algorithm as compared with the approach we have taken. Another problem with a single-number-output approach at this level of modeling is that we would eventually like a single-number metric to include the relative importances of certain image areas (such as faces), and methods that integrate their results into a single number would be more difficult to extend to include such higher-order attributes. For image-fidelity assessment our initial concern was to model the threshold accurately, and our current approach makes it more feasible to test the algorithm parameters for natural images. Having established the algorithm parameters with the threshold model, one can retain the parameters for the majority of the components and plug in the alternate components (contrast transducer function and vector summation in place of the masking function and probability summation) and concentrate on the adjustment of their parameters.

Summary

An algorithm for the prediction of visible differences between two digital images has been developed. This chapter provides a detailed description of the algorithm, its intended goals, and its utility as a design aid for imaging systems. The algorithm has been tested for a wide variety of image distortions including synthetic images designed after psychophysical experiments and natural images with practical distortions. These have included blur, noise, data compression artifacts, banding, blocking, contouring, low-frequency nonuniformities, hyperacuity, and tone-scale changes. The VDP's performance with these tests has been promising enough to warrant formal psychophysical tests that will help to quantify its degree of success.

Notes

1. The peak value of the CSF, P, depends on the individual. We can refer to two studies that measured the CSF for a large population of ob-

servers [52, 20]. Based on these, the value of 250 is used in the current implementation of CSF.

2. The resolution shift due to accommodation is based on data from [16, 44], the resolution shift due to eccentricity is based on [56], and the resolution shift due to orientation is based on data from [10, 53]. These resolution changes act to shift the entire CSF along the frequency axis. However, we would like these changes to affect only the high-frequency portion of the CSF, as suggested by the data. This is accomplished by taking the minimum of the shifted and nonshifted versions of the CSF as indicated in equation 14.6.

3. The image size effect is based on data from [25], and the function for the light adaptation effects is based on [3].

4. This method is a shortcut, since the range CSF is used with the rest of the algorithm only once, whereas the proper way would be to run the algorithm multiple times with viewing distances spanning the range and then combining the results. In testing of the VDP, however, we use single distances rather than ranges.

5. In this chapter we use the bandwidth as measured from the upper to the lower half-amplitude frequencies.

6. This frequency is expressed in the units of cy/pixel, which are the units used in the detection mechanisms model. It does not use cy/deg because of the separate modeling of the detection mechanisms and the CSF.

7. Except for the baseband, its neighboring dom filter, and where the high-frequency doms have been truncated by the Nyquist limit.

8. Because no orientation selectivity is attributed to the baseband ($k = K$), its index l is a dummy parameter.

9. Not all data support this exactly [27], but it is a simplification that aids modeling.

10. Since we have a discrete model, the test frequency does not always fall on a cortex filter peak. Other model components not yet described will cover such case.

11. Most of these approaches use a contrast transducer function calculated from the masking curve of the contrast discrimination experiment. As we stared earlier, we feel the contrast discrimination experiment is not appropriate for the majority of practical distortions in real-world images, whose image characteristics are more phase incoherent.

References

[1] E. H. Adelson, E. Simoncelli, and R. Hingorami (1987). Orthogonal pyramid transforms for image coding. *Society of Photo Instrumentation Engineering Proceedings*, vol. 845. *Visual Communications and Image Processing II*, 50–58.

[2] A. J. Ahumada and A. B. Watson (1985). Equivalent-noise model for contrast detection and discrimination. *Journal of the Optical Society of America* 2(7): 1133–1139.

[3] P. G. J. Barten (1987). The SQRI method: A new method for the evaluation of visible resolution on a display. *Proceedings of the Society for Information Display* 28:253–262.

[4] C. J. Bartleson (1975). Optimum tone reproduction. *Journal of the Society of Motion Picture and Television Engineering* 84:613–618.

[5] C. J. Bartleson (1985) Predicting graininess from granularity. *Journal of Photographic Science* 33:117–126.

[6] M. J. Bastiaans (1981). A sampling theorem for the complex spectrogram, and Gabor's expansion of a signal in Gaussian elementary signals. *Optical Engineering* 20:594–598.

[7] C. Blakemore and F. W. Campbell (1969). On the existence of neurones in the human visual system selectively sensitive to the orientation and size of retinal images. *Journal of Physiology* 203:237–260.

[8] A. Burgess and H. Ghandeharian (1984). Visual signal detection II. Signal-location identification. *Journal of the Optical Society of America A* 1:906–910.

[9] T. Caelli and G. Moraglia (1986). On the detection of signals embedded in natural scenes. *Perception and Psychophysics* 39:87–95.

[10] F. W. Campbell, J. J. Kulikowski, and J. Levinson (1966). The effect of orientation on the visual resolution of gratings. *Journal of Physiology* 187:427–436.

[11] C. R. Carlson and R. W. Cohen (1980). A simple psychophysical model for predicting the visibility of displayed information. *Proceedings of the Society for Information Display* 21(3):229–246.

[12] C. R. Carlson and R. W. Klopfenstein (1985). Spatial frequency model for hyperacuity. *Journal of the Optical Society of America A* 2:1747–1751.

[13] T. Cohn and D. Macleod (1991). Effect of stimulus area on psychometric function slope. *Investigative Ophthalmology and Visual Science, Supplement* 32(4):1023.

[14] J. Daugman (1985). Uncertainty relation for resolution in space, spatial frequency, and orientation optimized by two-dimensional visual cortical filters. *Journal of the Optical Society of America A* 2:1160–1169.

[15] J. Daugman (1988). Complete discrete 2-D Gabor transforms by neural networks for image analysis and compression. *IEEE Transactions on Acoustics, Speech, and Signal Processing* 36:1169–1179.

[16] J. J. DePalma and E. M. Lowry (1962) Sine-wave response of the visual system. II, Sine-wave and square-wave contrast sensitivity. *Journal of the Optical Society of America* 52:328–335.

[17] R. L. DeValois, D. G. Albrecht, and L. G. Thorell (1982) Spatial frequency selectivity of cells in the macaque visual cortex. *Vision Research* 22:545–559.

[18] O. D. Faugeras (1979). Digital color image processing within the framework of a human visual model. *IEEE Transactions on Acoustics, Speech, and Signal Processing* ASSP-27:380–393.

[19] M. A. Georgeson and J. M. Georgeson (1987). Facilitation and masking of briefly presented gratings: Time course and contrast dependence. *Vision Research* 27:369–379.

[20] A. P. Ginsberg and D. W. Evans (1984). Rapid measurement of contrast sensitivity using new contrast sensitivity vision test chart system: Initial population data. *Proceedings of the Human Factors Society, 28th Annual Meeting.* 123–127.

[21] E. M. Granger and K. N. Cupery (1972). An optical merit function (SQF), which correlates with subjective image judgements. *Photographic Science and Engineering* 16(3):221–230.

[22] C. F. Hall and E. L. Hall (1977). A nonlinear model for the spatial characteristics of the human visual system. *IEEE Transactions on Systems, Man, and Cybernetics* SMC-7(3):161–170.

[23] M. J. Hawken and A. J. Parker (1987). Spatial properties of neurons in the monkey striate cortex. *Proceedings of the Royal Society of London B* 231:251–288.

[24] G. Higgins (1977). Image quality criteria. *Journal Applied Photographic Engineering* 3(2):53–60.

[25] E. Howell and R. Hess (1978). The functional area for summation to threshold for sinusoidal gratings. *Vision Research* 16:957–968.

[26] D. H. Hubel and T. N. Wiesel (1962). Receptive fields, binocular interaction and functional architecture in the cat's visual cortex. *Journal of Physiology* 160:106–154.

[27] G. E. Legge and J. M. Foley (1980) Contrast masking in human vision. *Journal of the Optical Society of America* 70:1458–1471.

[28] C. Lloyd and R. Beaton (1990). Design of a spatio-chromatic human vision model for evaluating full-color display systems. *Society of Photo Instrumentation Engineering Proceedings* 1249:23–37.

[29] J. Lubin and J. Bergen (1991). Pattern discrimination in the fovea and periphery. *Investigative Ophthalmology and Visual Science, Supplement* 32(4):1024.

[30] J. Lubin and A. P. Pica (1991). A non-uniform quantizer matched to the human visual performance. *Society of Information Display International Symposium Technical Digest of Papers* 22:619–622.

[31] S. Mallat (1989). A theory for multiresolution signal decomposition: The wavelet representation. *IEEE Pattern Analysis and Machine Intelligence* 11:674–693.

[32] J. L. Mannos and D. J. Sakrison (1974). The effects of a visual fidelity criterion on the encoding of images. *IEEE Transactions on Information Theory.* IT-20:525–536.

[33] S. Marcelja (1980). Mathematical description of the responses of simple cortical cells. *Journal of the Optical Society of America* 70:1297–1300.

[34] M. J. Mayer and C. W. Tyler (1986). Invariance of the slope of the psychometric function with spatial summation. *Journal of the Optical Society of America A* 3:1166–1172.

[35] A. van Meeteren and J. M. Valeton (1988). Effects of pictorial noise interfering with visual detection. *Journal of the Optical Society of America A* 5:438–444.

[36] J. J. McCann, S. P. McKee, and T. H. Taylor (1976). Quantitative studies in retinex theory. *Vision Research* 16:445–458.

[37] J. Nachmias (1981). On the psychometric function for contrast detection. *Vision Research* 21:215–223.

[38] R. A. Normann, B. S. Baxter, H. Ravindra, and P. J. Anderton (1983). Photoreceptor contributions to contrast sensitivity: Applications in radiological diagnosis. *IEEE Transactions on Systems, Man, and Cybernetics* SMC-13(5):946–953.

[39] E. Peli (1990). Contrast in complex images. *Journal of the Optical Society of America A* 7:2032–2040.

[40] D. Pelli (1981). Effects of visual noise. Ph.D. diss., Cambridge University, England.

[41] G. Phillips and H. Wilson (1984). Orientation bandwidths of spatial mechanisms measured by masking, *Journal of the Optical Society of America A* 1:226–232.

[42] H. Pollehn and H. Roehrig (1970). Effect of noise on the modulation transfer function of the visual channel. *Journal of the Optical Society of America* 60:842–848.

[43] D. Pum, P. K. Ahnet, and M. Grasl (1990). Iso-orientation areas in the foveal cone mosaic. *Visual Neuroscience* 5:511–523.

[44] H. A. W. Schober and R. Hilz (1965). Contrast sensitivity of the eye for square wave gratings. *Journal of the Optical Society of America* 55:1086–1091.

[45] M. I. Sezan, K. L. Yip, and S. Daly (1987). Uniform perceptual quantization: Applications to digital radiography. *IEEE Transactions on Systems, Man, and Cybernetics* SMC-17 (4):622–634.

[46] E. Simoncelli and E. Adelson (1989). Nonseparable QMF pyramids. *Society of Photo Instrumentation Engineering Proceedings*, vol. 1199. *Visual Communications and Image Processing*, 1242–1246.

[47] R. A. Smith and D. J. Swift (1985). Spatial-frequency masking and Birdsall's theorem. *Journal of the Optical Society of America A* 2:1593–1599.

[48] T. G. Stockham (1972). Image processing in the context of a visual model. *Proceedings of the IEEE* 60(7):828–841.

[49] D. G. Stork and H. R. Wilson (1990). Do Gabor functions provide appropriate descriptions of visual cortical receptive fields? *Journal of the Optical Society of America A* 7:1362–1373.

[50] C. F. Stromeyer, III, and B. Julesz (1972). Spatial-frequency masking in vision: Critical bands and spread of masking. *Journal of the Optical Society of America* 62:1221–1232.

[51] J. P. Thomas (1985). Effect of static-noise and grating masks on detection and identification of grating targets. *Journal of the Optical Society of America A* 2:1586–1592.

[52] V. Virsu, P. Lehtio, and J. Rovamo (1981). Contrast sensitivity in normal and pathological vision. *Documents in Ophthalmology Proceedings Series*, ed. by L. Maffei. 30:263–272.

[53] A. Watanabe, T. Mori, S. Nagata, and K. Hiwatashi (1968) Spatial sine-wave responses of the visual system. *Vision Research* 8:1245–1263.

[54] A. B. Watson (1983). Detection and recognition of simple spatial forms. In *Physical and Biological Processing of Images*, ed. O. J. Braddick and A. C. Sleigh, 100-114. New York: Springer-Verlag.

[55] A. B. Watson (1987). The cortex transform: Rapid computation of simulated neural images. *Computer Vision Graphics and Image Processing* 39:311–327.

[56] A. B. Watson (1987). Estimation of local spatial scale. *Journal of the Optical Society of America A* 4:1579–1582.

[57] A. B. Watson (1987). Efficiency of a model human image code. *Journal of the Optical Society of America A* 4:2401–2417.

[58] A. B. Watson and A. J. Ahumada (1989). A hexagonal orthogonal-oriented pyramid as a model of image representation in visual cortex. *IEEE Transactions on Biomedical Engineering* 36:97–106.

[59] H. Wilson and J. Bergen (1979) A four mechanism model for threshold spatial vision. *Vision Research* 19:19–32.

[60] C. Zetzsche and G. Hauske (1989) Multiple channel model for the prediction of subjective image quality. *Society of Photo Instrumentation Engineering Proceedings* 1077:209–216.

15

What's Wrong with Mean-squared Error?

Bernd Girod

Compression algorithms for the transmission or storage of video signals have made impressive progress in the last few years [4]. Practically all this progress stems from a more elaborate modeling of the statistical properties of the video source. The properties of the human visual system are rarely taken into account with the same sophistication. The reason for this neglect seems to be a practical one: Although it is straightforward to evaluate a new source model by computer simulations with digitized video signals, models of the human observer have to be tested in tedious psychovisual experiments that are time-consuming and often influenced by factors beyond the experimenter's control. Today the distortion measure mean-squared error is still widely used for the design of practical image communication systems, but it is equally widely criticized.

In this chapter we review some of the known perceptual effects that are relevant for image coding. We restrict ourselves to luminance signals and to the perception of impairments at the threshold of visibility. Threshold effects are well studied, and they are especially relevant for the design of communication systems with high image quality. In the section on the spatiotemporal frequency response of the human visual system we emphasize the importance of eye movements. As application examples, we will look at temporal sampling and at noise shaping in a differential pulse code modulation (DPCM) system. In the section on subthreshold summation we show that error integration is a local rather than a global effect. Looking at DPCM as an example again, we discuss why the "masking function" does not neccessarily reflect the psychovisual masking effect. Also, we show why isotropic coders make sense perceptually. Finally, we discuss masking at luminance edges, where we discover that the γ-shift due to the picture tube has to be taken into account, and that more errors can be hidden on the dark side of a luminance edge.

This chapter is intended to be a critical discussion of some of the more important psychovisual aspects of image communication. For readability, we have avoided mathematics wherever possible. For a more formal treatment, the reader is referred to the literature. Due of the breadth of the field, the topics treated can be only a selection. The chapter is partly tutorial in nature, but we have largely restricted ourselves to areas where we were able to gather experimental evidence in the course of our own work.

Spatiotemporal Frequency Response

The brightness range in real-world scenes is much larger than can be transmitted over single fibers of the optic nerve. Various-gain control mechanisms act in the human retina to deal with this problem. One of these is a center-surround mechanism known as *lateral inhibition,* by which luminance integrated over a larger receptive field non-linearly inhibits the activity of the optic nerve fiber excited by a smaller central receptive field [3]. In the human fovea the central receptive field has a diameter of approximately 2 arc-min, which corresponds roughly to the optical point spread function of the eye [2]. The surrounding inhibiting field has three to five times the diameter [3]. Although the inhibition mechanism is nonlinear and space-varying, an isotropic band-pass filter can serve as a useful first-order approximation.

Contrast Sensitivity Function

Extensive psychovisual measurements have been carried out using spatial sine-wave patterns. The contrast sensitivity function (CSF) is defined as the reciprocal of the just-visible modulation depth of a sine wave. The spatial CSF curve is typically presented like the one shown in figure 15.1 [3, 21, 30].

It shows the band-pass characteristic of lateral inhibition discussed in the previous paragraph. The maximum sensitivity is at 2 to 4 cycles per degree (cpd). The curve shown in figure 15.1 is correct, but unfortunately misleading. The low-frequency drop-off appears to be as important as the high-frequency drop-off, but in practice, it is almost neglible. This is due to two reasons:

- The frequency axis in figure 15.1 is logarithmic.

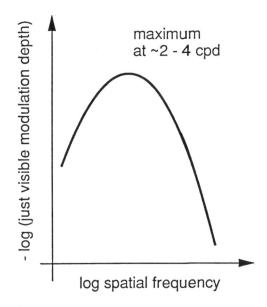

Figure 15.1

Typical spatial contrast sensitivity function (CSF) of the human visual system. The curve is misleading for image communication applications, since the low-frequency drop-off appears to be as important as the high-frequency drop-off. (from [18].)

- When extended to the two-dimensional spatial frequency plane, the high-frequency branch covers a proportionally larger area than the low-frequency branch.

To illustrate this with numbers, let us consider the spectrum of a television signal that contains frequency components up to 20 cpd both horizontally and vertically. With a peak of the spatial CSF at 4 cpd, less than 4 percent of the entire two-dimensional frequency range is covered by the low-frequency drop-off of the CSF. In an image communication system, we should hide noise at high spatial frequencies. Hiding noise at low spatial frequencies is usually not worth the effort.

To transform the spatial-frequency response of the human visual system into the coordinate system of the video signal, we have to assume a certain viewing distance. Viewing distances of 4 times screen height or 6 times screen height are recommended by the CCIR for subjective tests with broadcast television signals [45]. In practice, the viewing distance is determined, for example, by the size of people's living rooms and television sets, and practical systems have to work well for a variety of viewing distances.

Note that the spatial CSF as shown in figure 15.1 is applicable only for frozen noise, as it appears, for example,

A

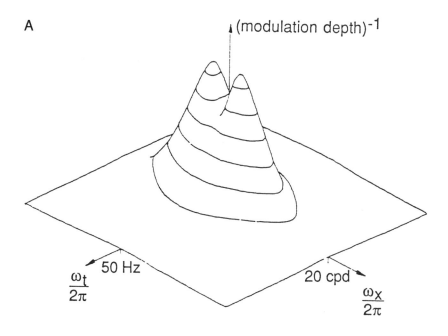

B

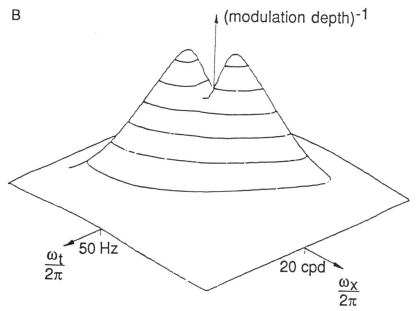

Figure 15.2
Spatiotemporal frequency response of the human visual system.
(A) The eye fixates the screen. (B) Assuming a smooth-pursuit eye
movement, velocity 2 deg/sec; (C) assuming a smooth-pursuit eye
movement, velocity 8 deg/sec. ω_x is spatial frequency, ω_t is temporal
frequency. (from [18].)

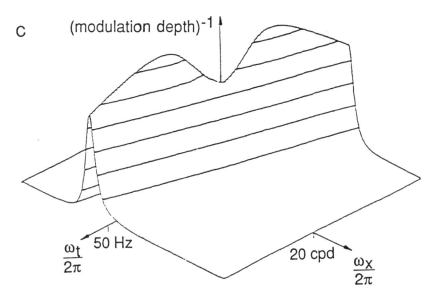

C   (modulation depth)$^{-1}$

$\frac{\omega_t}{2\pi}$ 50 Hz   20 cpd $\frac{\omega_x}{2\pi}$

Figure 15.2 (continued)

in printed material. With video sequences we usually observe dynamic noise with a broad temporal spectrum. The spatiotemporal CSF was measured first by Robson [30] in the 1960s, and later by Kelly [21] over a wider range of conditions. A model fit to Robson's data is shown in figure 15.2(A) [12]. The spatiotemporal CSF is separable at high spatial and temporal frequencies but nonseparable at low frequencies.

The Importance of Eye Movement

The shape of the CSF in figure 15.2(A) seems to imply that less spatial resolution is required when the picture contents move. In fact, various sampling or coding schemes for moving video signals have been proposed to take advantage of the shape of the spatiotemporal CSF, for example by omitting spatial and temporal high-frequency components altogether [19, 24, 33, 34, 37, 38, 40].

A simple experiment that we carried out some years ago shows that motion-dependent blur cannot be tolerated if impairments are supposed to be below the visibility threshold. Motion was generated by artificially panning a still picture at three different speeds (0, 2, and 10 deg/sec). The picture contents were blurred by a one-dimensional horizontal Gaussian filter. The visibility threshold for just-not-visible blur was then measured in subjective tests. Surprisingly, blur visibility is not significantly affected by the motion speed. Even for very rapid motion, the visibility threshold is hardly higher than for a still picture. Subjects follow the picture contents by smooth-pursuit eye movements and compensate its motion [13, 29, 44].

Smooth-pursuit eye movements give rise to a Doppler effect. If translation of the eye relative to the screen is assumed, the frequency response of the human visual system can be easily transformed into the screen coordinate system using

$$\omega_x = \omega_x^*$$
$$\omega_y = \omega_y^*$$
$$\omega_t = \omega_t^* - \omega_x^* \cdot v_x - \omega_y^* \cdot v_y,$$

where ω_x and ω_y are the horizontal and vertical frequency, respectively, and ω_t is the temporal frequency in the screen coordinate system [11–13, 39]; ω_x^*, ω_y^*, and ω_t^* are the corresponding quantities in the eye coordinate system; and (v_x, v_y) is the eye velocity. Using this coordinate transformation, we plotted the spatiotemporal CSF [figure 15.2(A)] for smooth-pursuit eye movements of $v_x = 2$ deg/sec and $v_x = 8$ deg/sec [Figure 15.2(B) and (C)]. The effective spatiotemporal frequency response of the human visual system is dramatically altered by eye movements. Through eye movements we can perceive very high temporal frequencies at high spatial frequencies. According to Tonge [39] temporal frequencies on the screen up to 1000 Hz can be perceived. This effect does not contradict the flicker fusion effect that, depending on the brightness

A

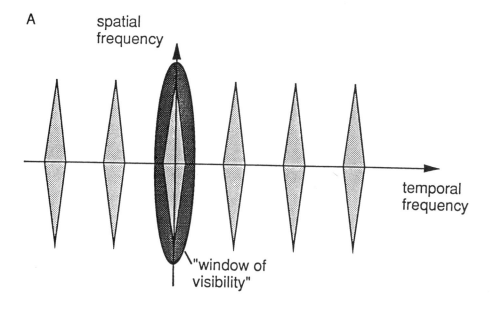

spatial
frequency

temporal
frequency

"window of
visibility"

B

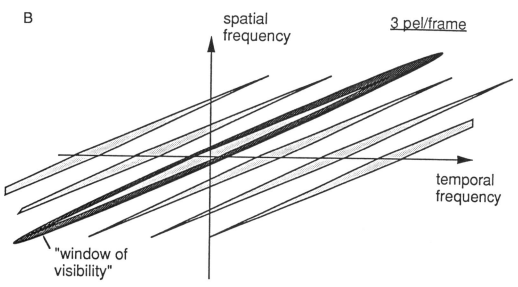

spatial
frequency

3 pel/frame

temporal
frequency

"window of
visibility"

Figure 15.3
(A) Spectrum of a temporally sampled still image. Temporal sampling produces replications of the baseband. The pass-band region of the spatiotemporal frequency response of the human visual system is shown as a "window of visibility," that suppresses spectral replications. (B) Spectrum of a temporally sampled image. The image contents is assumed to be moving at a velocity of 3 pel/frame. A smooth-pursuit eye movement compensates the motion and shears the window of visibility to match the image base band. (from [18].)

level, occurs at a temporal frequency below 80 Hz [20]. Flicker fusion is measured for $\omega_x = \omega_y = 0$.

Smooth-pursuit eye movements have important consequences for the temporal bandwidth of display devices for moving images. Television phospors, for example, do not get away with a bandwidth of a few 10s of Hz, as figure 15.2(A) would suggest. They need to display the full range up to 1000 Hz to avoid visible blur of fast motion.

Temporal Sampling

Temporal sampling of the video signal produces replications of the baseband at higher temporal frequencies. This is shown for a velocity $v = 0$ in figure 15.3(A) and for $v = 3$ pel/frame of the picture contents in figure 15.3(B). The spatiotemporal frequency response of the human visual system defines a "window of visibility" in spatiotemporal frequency space [42]. If the eye tracks the image contents, it fully passes the baseband of the signal and suppresses all temporal replications [11–13, 39]. Thus the human visual system acts as a motion-compensated interpolation filter [figure 15.3(B)]. It is sometimes argued that temporal aliasing sets in at a velocity of 1 pel/frame. This argument is valid only if a single pel is considered by itself. In spatiotemporal frequency space, there is no spectral overlap even at higher motion speeds. The baseband can be recovered as long as the image contents can be tracked.

The preceding argument assumes that there is only one motion that can be tracked. Video sequences usually contain several motions of different magnitude and direction. These motions usually occur in different parts of the image, and tracking of the image contents can be assumed locally in fovea but not over the entire visual field. At a spatial discontinuity of the optical flow field, or if *transparent motion* (i.e., two distinct motions at the same position in the image) occurs, only one motion can be compensated by smooth-pursuit eye movements.

For several applications multidimensional filtering of the video signal that involves time as one dimension is desirable. Deinterlacing and frame rate conversion require temporal interpolation [11]. Recursive temporal filters can be used for noise reduction. Because of smooth-pursuit eye movements, any type of temporal filtering has to be carried out with motion compensation to avoid visible blur of the picture contents. On the other hand, compensation is required only for motion that can be tracked by the human visual system. A detailed theoretical analysis that includes imperfections of human visual motion tracking for accelerated motion is presented in chapter 8. Further insight is provided in chapter 12. Not enough is known yet about the limits of motion compensation by smooth-pursuit eye movements, and little effort has been made to incorporate these limits into technical motion compensated filters.

Noise-Shaping DPCM

As an example throughout this chapter we consider a simple differential pulse code modulation (DPCM) system. Figure 15.4 shows the block diagram of a DPCM system. At the coder the difference e between the input video signal S and the prediction signal $\hat{S}$ is quantized and transmitted. At the decoder, $\hat{S}$ is added to the quantized prediction error e' to produce a reconstructed signal S'. Because both coder and decoder require exactly the same prediction values $\hat{S}$, the coder also computes the reconstructed signal S', and the prediction is based on previously transmitted values of S'. The coder in figure 15.4 contains an additional noise feedback of the quantization error q through a filter $H(\omega_x, \omega_y, \omega_t)$. Without such a noise feedback, that is, $H(\omega_x, \omega_y, \omega_t) = 0$, the DPCM system will produce a flat reconstruction noise spectrum, at least if the quantizer is relatively fine. With noise feedback the power spectral density of the reconstruction error $r = S - S'$ will be shaped according to

$$\Phi_{rr}(\omega_x, \omega_y, \omega_t) = \Phi_{qq}(\omega_x, \omega_y, \omega_t) \cdot |1 - H(\omega_x, \omega_y, \omega_t)|^2,$$

where Φ_{qq} is the (flat) power spectral density of the quantization error q[10] [14]. To optimize $H(\omega_x, \omega_y, \omega_t)$, frequency-weighted mean-squared error is an appropriate distortion measure. By varying $H(\omega_x, \omega_y, \omega_t)$ we change only the spectral shape of the reconstruction error. We do not trade off quality, for example, between textured regions, flat areas, and edges in the image, which would require a more elaborate measure. The linear effects described in preceding paragraphs provide a sufficient model for human visual perception, if our goal is noise shaping.

Frequency-weighted mean-squared error based on CSF data [figure 15.2(a)] was used to predict the gains by noise shaping in an adaptive intrainterframe DPCM system for a transmission rate of about 30 Mbit/sec [14]. The luminance signal Y was sampled at 10.125 MHz, and one-dimensional noise shaping was used along the scan line.

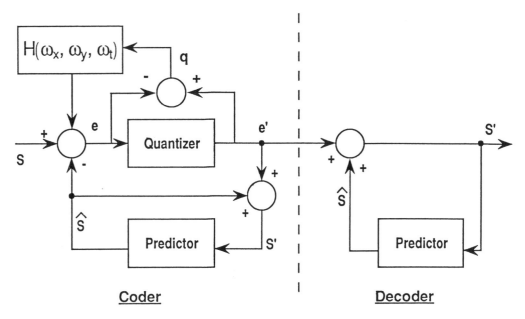

Coder   **Decoder**

Figure 15.4
DPCM coder and decoder with additional quantization noise
feedback. (from [18].)

Table 15.1
Noise Shaping Gains for an Adaptive Intrainterframe DPCM
Coder [15]

Signal	Direction of Noise Feedback	Theoretical Gain	Subjective Tests
Y	Horizontal	3.0 dB	3.0 dB
R-Y	Vertical	2.2 dB	2.3 dB
B-Y	Vertical	4.4 dB	4.4 dB

Sampling frequencies were 10.125 MHz/3.375 MHz/3.375 MHz for
Y/R-Y/B-Y. Viewing conditions CCIR 500, viewing distance 6 times
screen height.

The color difference signals $R - Y$ and $B - Y$ were sampled at 3.375 MHz, and one-dimensional noise shaping in the vertical direction was used. Viewing conditions corresponded to CCIR Rec. 500 [45] with a viewing distances of 4 times and 6 times screen height. As shown in table 15.1, theoretical gains are almost identical with those that can be measured in subjective tests. For this system, gains by two-dimensional noise shaping over one-dimensional noise shaping are very small due to line interlace. Temporal noise shaping could theoretically yield significant additional gains, if the eye would fixate the screen. However, in practice, eye movements always occur, and temporal high-frequency noise becomes more visible (figure 15.2).

Local Subthreshold Summation

In the previous section we used frequency-weighted mean-squared error as a distortion measure. If we are interested only in noise shaping, this distortion measure is satisfactory. However, with almost any coding scheme, reconstruction errors are distributed unevenly over the image. Some regions are easy to code, and errors are small, whereas some other regions are hard to code, and the error magnitude is larger. When designing a coder, we will somehow distribute reconstruction errors in the image. A global measure like mean-squared error cannot appropriately predict how errors will add up to a visible distortion. Errors that are far apart in space or time will probably exceed the visibility threshold independently, whereas neighboring errors will somehow interact.

Basic Experiments

A basic psychovisual experiment suitable for exploring subthreshold summation is shown in figure 15.5 [12]. A narrow strip of dynamic white noise on a gray background is shown to the test subjects. The variance of just-not-visible noise is measured as a function of the bar width BW. The results in figure 15.6 show that the visibility threshold for narrow noise bars is much higher than for wider bars. The threshold variance for $BW \rightarrow \infty$ does not

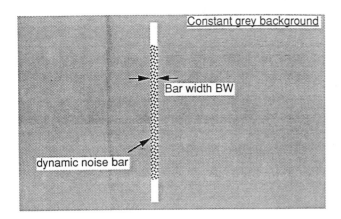

Figure 15.5
Basic psychovisual experiment to measure spatial subthreshold summation. A bar of dynamic white noise is shown on a constant gray background. Tick marks above and below the bar help the subjects to find the stimulus at visibility threshold. (from [18].)

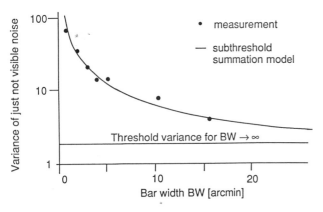

Figure 15.6
Visibility threshold versus noise bar width of the experiment shown in figure 15.5. The curve was produced using the model shown in Figure 15.8. (from [18].)

drop to zero, as one would expect for a global measure. Rather, the results in figure 15.6 suggest a local subthreshold summation.

A similar experiment can be carried out for temporal subthreshold summation [12, 22]. Instead of varying the area covered by noise, we vary its duration. Figure 15.7 shows results for flashes of dynamic white noise that fills the entire screen. Short noise flashes are less visible, but beyond a duration of 500 ms, there is practically no change in visibility threshold. Temporal subthreshold summation is also discussed by Watson in [41].

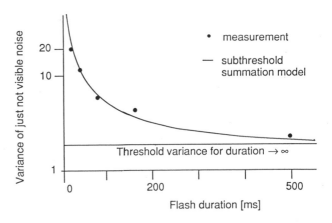

Figure 15.7
Visibility threshold versus duration of a noise flash. The curve was produced using the model shown in Figure 15.8. (from [18].)

A Local Mean-Squared-Error Measure

The results in figures 15.6 and 15.7 can be explained by the simple model shown in figure 15.8 [12]. Noise amplitude is first squared and then convolved with a temporal and a spatial impulse response. A leaky temporal integrator with a time constant $\tau = 230$ ms and an isotropic spatial Gaussian filter with a spread constant $\tau = 13$ arcmin provide a good fit to the measured data. Rather than global mean-squared error, this model calculates local mean-squared error as a function of space and time. The final image sequence after thresholding indicates where and when errors may be visible. Such a model also explains why it is hard to point out exactly where and when just-visible errors occur. The resolution of the local mean-squared-error signal is low compared with the resolution of a video signal.

When optimizing an image coder, it is useful to look at a *potential visibility histogram* as shown in figure 15.9 [12]. The local mean-squared error computed according to figure 15.8 indicates potential visibility of the coding error. If potential visibility never exceeds the threshold, distortions will not be visible anywhere in the picture. Two example histograms of not-visible errors are shown in figure 15.9. If the coder is not well adapted to the properties of human vision, potential visibility will often be far below threshold, and bits can be saved by representing the image less accurately in the corresponding regions. If the coder exploits the properties of human vision well, the potential visibility histogram peak just below the visibility

Measurement and Prediction of Visual Quality

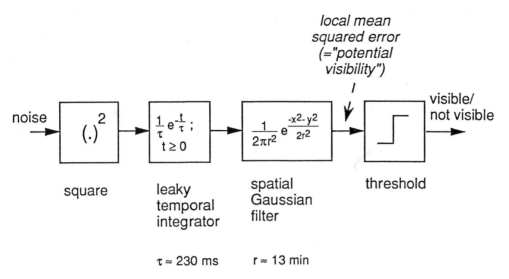

Figure 15.8
Local mean-squared-error model of subthreshold summation. (from [18].)

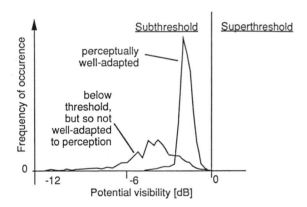

Figure 15.9
Potential visibility histograms. For a perceptually well-adapted coder, the histogram will be peaked just below visibility threshold. (from [18].)

threshold. A perceptually optimized coding scheme keeps errors just below the visibility threshold everywhere in the picture.

DPCM Masking Functions without Masking

Let us apply the local mean-squared-error model (figure 15.8) to the problem of optimizing the quantizer of a DPCM system (figure 15.4). To simplify discussion, we ignore noise shaping and set $H(\omega_x, \omega_y, \omega_t) = 0$.

Image-coding engineers have long known that larger quantization errors can be tolerated for large prediction error magnitudes $|e|$. Because large prediction errors occur

at edges, this finding has been explained as a result of edge masking [23, 25, 28, 32], as, for example, investigated by Fiorentini [5–7]. For several DPCM systems, envelopes of the quantization error characteristic

$$q(e) = e'(e) - e$$

have been determined in subjective tests for just-not-visible distortions. A typical result measured by Pirsch is shown in figure 15.10 [28]. If the maximum allowable quantization error magnitude has been determined for each prediction error e, it is straightforward to construct an optimum nonuniform quantizer by drawing a zigzag curve under the envelope [35, 36]. Note that $q = 0$ at the representative levels of the quantizer, and that $|q|$ is maximum at its decision thresholds. The envelope of the quantization error characteristic that yields just-not-visible distortions is commonly called *masking* function to emphasize its psychovisual significance [23, 25, 28, 32, 43].

When a nonuniform quantizer is used in a DPCM system, stronger noise typically shows up in narrow strips along edges ("edge busyness") [28]. From figure 15.6 we conclude that much larger error amplitudes are admissible within these strips than in flat regions, simply because of the spatial extent of the noise pattern. In [14] we used the local mean-squared error-model (figure 15.8) to derive the shape of the quantization error envelope $M(|e|)$ for just-not-visible errors at edges. The reader is referred to [14] for mathematical details, but we present the basic argument here.

Assume that errors become visible if the local mean-squared quantization error exceeds a threshold. Further

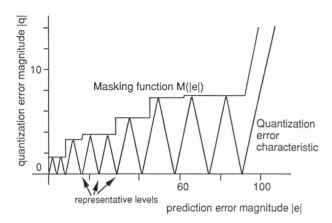

Figure 15.10
Masking function for an adaptive intrainterframe DPCM measured by Pirsch [28]. A piecewise constant envelope of the quantization error characteristic is varied in subjective tests. (from [18].)

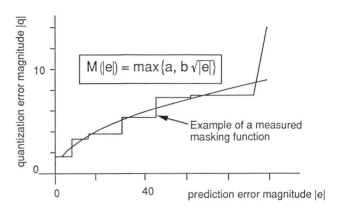

Figure 15.11
Comparison between a masking function measured in subjective tests (figure 15.10) and the masking function derived from a subthreshold summation model. (from [18].)

assume that an image consists of flat areas of perfectly constant luminance and of straight edges. A prototypical edge has an orientation, a width, and a slope. The quantization error envelope has to be determined such that edges of the least favorable orientation do not produce visible errors. The slope of the edge determines the magnitude of the prediction error (and of the quantization error via the masking function) that can occur. For a given slope, the width of the edge is limited, since the product of width and slope cannot exceed the amplitude range of the video signal. Because noise at edges and in the adjacent flat areas is summed up in the local mean-squared-error measure, there is a trade-off between quantization noise in the flat areas and at edges. If the noise in flat areas is already at the visibility threshold, no additional quantization at edges is admissible. The corresponding DPCM quantizer is uniform and has many representative levels. However, if the quantization noise in flat areas is below the visibility threshold, coarser quantization at edges is allowed. If an edge is steep, the quantization noise strip is narrow, and the quantization error magnitude may be large without exceeding the local mean-squared-error threshold.

The mathematical analysis of the mean-squared-error trade-off between flat areas and edges of different slopes leads to the *b-quantizer* with an envelope function

$$M(|e|) = \max(a, b\sqrt{|e|}),$$

where a and b are parameters that depend on the parameters of human vision and on the predictor used. The

square-root characteristic nicely corresponds to the shape of masking functions measured in subjective tests, as shown for example in figure 15.11. Note that we have derived a "masking function" from a subthreshold summation argument, but without any masking effects. We shall show a masking function that incorporates edge masking in a later section.

Isotropic Intraframe Prediction

In an intraframe DPCM system the choice of prediction coefficients influences the admissible coarseness of the quantizer. It was first reported in [27] that a predictor with only positive coefficients results in a coarser quantizer for just-not-visible errors than a statistically optimized predictor that minimizes mean-squared prediction error. This result can be explained by an argument similar to the one used in the previous section. A statistically optimized predictor tends to be extremely anisotropic. Figure 15.12 shows local mean-squared prediction error at edges of various orientation [8, 9]. The statistically optimized predictor predicts horizontal and vertical edges very well, but fails at diagonals. Diagonal edges are less frequent in most pictures, and they contribute little to global mean-squared error. However, for a coded picture to be indistinguishable from the original, quantization errors have to be below the visibility threshold everywhere in the picture, including at diagonal edges.

The coarsest quantizer for just-not-visible distortion results when we make the predictor as isotropic as possible [8, 27]. In figure 15.12 we also show the performance

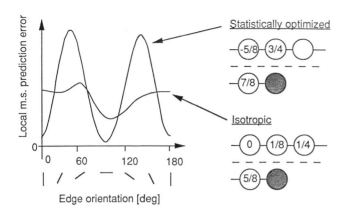

Figure 15.12
Local mean-squared-error performance of two intraframe predictors at an ideal edge. The arrangement of neighboring previously transmitted pels used for prediction and the prediction coefficients are shown on the right. Sampling frequency was 10.125 MHz in a 625-line television system with 2:1 line interlace. (from [18].)

of another predictor that was obtained by minimizing the local mean-squared prediction error at edges of most unfavorable orientation. Compared with the statistically optimized predictor, horizontal and vertical edges are predicted worse, but diagonals are significantly improved. The coefficients of the isotropic predictor are all positive. From a perceptual point of view, the isotropic predictor is superior to the statistically optimized predictor.

It is difficult to design an isotropic intraframe DPCM coder, since pels have to be encoded in scan-line order, and the predictor may use only previously encoded pels in the "causal neighborhood." Other schemes, for example, transform coding [26] or Laplacian pyramids [1] do not require the pels to be encoded in a certain order and thus more naturally avoid a strong preference of some edge orientations over others.

Masking at Luminance Edges

The visibility of noise depends on the background pattern upon which the noise is superimposed, because of non-linearities in the human visual system. We say that the background pattern "masks" the noise, since one usually thinks of the effect that noise becomes less visible. However, we should keep in mind that noise can also become more visible through the background pattern. In this section we discuss masking at luminance edges.

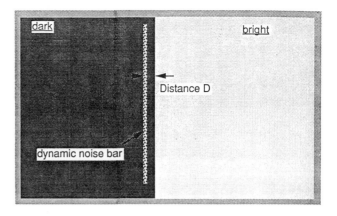

Figure 15.13
Basic experiment to measure masking at a luminance edge. (from [18].)

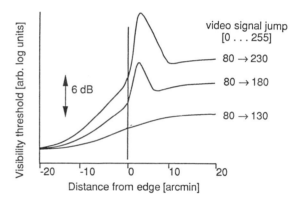

Figure 15.14
Masking at an edge as it can be measured with the experiment outlined in figure 15.13. The curves are fits of the w-model [12, 15–17] to psychovisual measurements. Viewing conditions correspond to CCIR 500 [45]. (from [18].)

Basic Experiment

Masking at luminance edges can be measured as shown in figure 15.13. We superimpose a narrow bar of dynamic noise at a distance D from a luminance discontinuity and measure its threshold of visibility. Visibility threshold as a function of distance from the edge is shown in figure 15.14 for three different edge contrasts. The curves in figure 15.14 have been fitted to the results of psychovisual tests using the "w-model" developed by the author [12, 15–17]. Similar curves were first measured by Fiorentini [5–7]. As a manifestation of Weber's law, the visibility threshold is higher on a bright background than on a dark background [3]. For low edge contrast, the visibility thres-

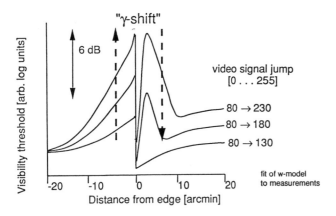

Figure 15.15
Masking curves of figure 15.14 transformed in the video signal domain. The nonlinear γ-characteristic of the display device results in the γ-shift. (from [18].)

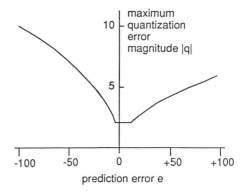

Figure 15.16
Asymmetrical masking function derived with a model that takes into account masking and subthreshold summation. The result corresponds to Schäfer's results obtained in subjective tests [31]. (from [18].)

hold changes monotonically across the edge. For higher edge contrast, there is a characteristic peak on the bright side of the edge. This peak corresponds to the bright Mach band due to lateral inhibition in the retina [3] and has been explained as a saturation effect [12, 15−17].

The γ-Shift

In figure 15.14 visibility threshold was plotted in units of physical luminance on the screen, as it would be measured for example in cd/m^2. This physical luminance is non-linearly related to the amplitude of the luminance signal through the γ-characteristic of the display [25]. To transform the masking curves in figure 15.14 into the domain of the video signal we have to incorporate the slope of the γ-characteristic [12, 16]. The slope of the γ-characteristic is different on the dark and the bright sides of the edge, and the two parts of the curve are shifted relative to each other (figure 15.15). We refer to this effect as the γ-shift. Far away from the edge, the γ-characteristic roughly compensates for Weber's law. At the edge, the visibility threshold curves are neccessarily discontinuous. For a low-contrast edge, the visibility threshold is lowered on the bright side of the edge. In this case, noise is "unmasked" by the edge. Only for high-contrast edges is the visibility threshold elevated on the bright side of the edge. Masking on the dark side of the edge is more reliable. In psycho-visually optimized image communication systems, more errors should be hidden on the dark sides of edges.

Asymmetric Masking Functions

We showed earlier that the shape of DPCM "masking functions" can be explained without employing edge masking. Let us now incorporate masking at edges and revisit masking functions. With DPCM, positive prediction errors usually occur at the bright side of an edge, whereas negative prediction errors occur at the dark side of the edge. Because masking is more pronounced on the dark side of the edge, coarser quantization is possible. We have used natural test pictures and the w-model of masking in conjunction with the subthreshold summation model (figure 15.8) in computer simulations to obtain the asymmetrical masking function shown in figure 15.16 [12]. Without exceeding the visibility threshold, the amplitude of quantization errors can be almost twice as large for negative prediction errors as for positive prediction errors. A very similar result has been obtained by Schäfer in subjective measurements of an asymmetrical masking function [31]. Asymmetrical quantizer characteristics also make sense in other coding schemes, such as the Laplacian pyramid [1], where positive amplitudes in the bandpass images occur at the bright side of an edge, and negative values on the dark side of an edge.

Conclusions

We have reviewed a number of psychovisual phenomena that are of fundamental importance in the design and evaluation of image communication systems.

We discussed linear effects in the first part of the chapter. The spatiotemporal frequency response of the human visual system has a band-pass characteristic due to lateral inhibition in the human retina. Noise should be hidden at high spatial frequencies, but this is less effective at low spatial frequencies. Smooth-pursuit eye movements have to be taken into account when applying the spatiotemporal frequency response of the human visual system. Because the eye acts as a motion-compensating filter, high temporal frequency components can be perceived. Thus it is not justified to blur moving image contents. We showed how spatial noise shaping can be incorporated into a DPCM coder advantageously, both for the luminance and for the chrominance signals.

We also looked at subthreshold error integration. Experimental results were presented that suggest a local rather than a global mean-squared-error measure. Potential visibility histograms were proposed as a tool to evaluate the psychovisual quality of impaired images. Clearly, perceptually optimized coding schemes distribute the error in the image as evenly as possible. Looking at the "masking function" of DPCM coders, we found that these do not neccessarily reflect the masking effect at edges, as has been commonly claimed. Rather, the shape of the masking function can be derived from a local mean-squared-error measure in conjunction with an edge image model. Similar arguments led to the insight that isotropic image coding schemes are to be preferred over anisotropic schemes. Isotropic predictors for intraframe DPCM were presented as an example.

Finally, we considered masking at edges as an important nonlinear psychovisual effect. The nonlinear γ-characteristic of the display device has to be taken into account, resulting in a γ-shift of the masking curves. Interestingly, noise may become more visible on the bright side of an edge, particularly for low-contrast edges. Masking at the dark side of an edge is more reliable, and thus this is where quantization errors should be hidden. In a DPCM coder this effect can be exploited by coarser quantization of negative prediction errors.

For brevity this chapter had to omit numerous psychovisual phenomena, such as color perception, that are nevertheless significant for image communication systems. Multichannel models of human vision have attracted a lot of interest recently, and they may have potential for capturing masking effects that lead to further compression without visible impairments.

The search for a universal objective measure of image quality will fascinate researchers for a number of years to come. Until this search has come to a successful end, we will have to include a subjective evaluation of image quality in the design of image communication systems. Partial models, like the ones presented in this chapter, can nevertheless help us to understand and exploit properties of the human visual system.

References

[1] P. J. Burt and E. H. Adelson (1983). The Laplacian pyramid as a compact image code. *IEEE Trans. on Communications* COM-31:(4) 532–540.

[2] F. W. Campbell and R. W. Gubisch (1966). Optical quality of the human eye. *Journal of Physiology* 186:558–578.

[3] T. N. Cornsweet (1970). *Visual Perception*. New York: Academic Press.

[4] R. Forchheimer and T. Kronander (1989). Image coding: From waveforms to animation. *IEEE Trans. on Acoustics, Speech, and Signal Processing* 37(12):2008–2023.

[5] A. Fiorentini, M. Jeanne, and G. Toraldo di Francia (1955). Measurements of differential threshold in the presence of a spatial illumination gradient. *Atti. Fond. G. Ronchi* 10:371–379.

[6] A. Fiorentini and M. T. Zoli (1966). Detection of a target superimposed to a step pattern of illumination. *Atti. Fond. G. Ronchi* 21:338–356.

[7] A. Fiorentini and M. T. Zoli (1967). Detection of a target superimposed to a step pattern of illumination. II, Effects of a just-perceptible illumination step. *Atti. Fond. G. Ronchi* 22:207–217.

[8] B. Girod (1983). Prädiktoroptimierung unter Berücksichtigung multiplikativen Quantisierungs-rauschens. *Kleinheubacher Berichte, Band 27*, ed. Fernmeldetechnisches Zentralamt, 393–403.

[9] B. Girod (1984). Isotropic intraframe prediction. *Proc. of the International Picture Coding Symposium*, Rennes.

[10] B. Girod (1984). Reconstruction noise shaping in the context of predictive TV signal coding. In *Links for the Future: Proc. of the IEEE International Conference on Communications*, Amsterdam, 711–717.

[11] B. Girod, R. Thoma, (1985). Motion compensating field interpolation from interlaced and non-interlaced grids. 2nd International Technical Symposium on Optical and Electro-Optical Applied Science and Engineering, *Proc. SPIE Conf. B 594: Image Coding*, Cannes, France, 186–193.

[12] B. Girod (1988). Ein Modell der menschlichen visuellen Wahrnehmung zur Irrelevanzreduktion von Fernsehluminanzsignalen. VDI-Verlag, Düsseldorf: VDI-Fortschritt-Berichte, Reihe 10, Nr. 84. In German.

[13] B. Girod (1988). Eye movements and coding of video sequences. *SPIE* vol. 1001, *Visual Communications and Image Processing '88*: 398–405.

[14] B. Girod, H. Almer, L. Bengtsson, B. Christensson, P. Weiss (1988). A subjective evaluation of noise shaping quantization for adaptive intrainterframe DPCM coding of color television signals. *IEEE Trans. on Communications* 36(3): 332–346.

[15] B. Girod (1988). Spatial and Temporal Masking by Saturation in the Human Fovea. First Annual Meeting of the International Neural Network Society, September 1988.

[16] B. Girod (1989). The information theoretical significance of spatial and temporal masking in video signals. *SPIE/SPSE Symposium on Electronic Imaging, Conf. on Human Vision, Visual Processing and Digital Display*, Los Angeles, Calif.

[17] B. Girod (1989). Perceptual Gains for Coding of Moving Images without Visible Impairments. Optical Society of America Topical Meeting on Applied Vision, San Francisco.

[18] B. Girod (1992). Psychovisual aspects of image communication. *Signal Processing* 28: 239–251.

[19] G. Karlsson and M. Vetterli (1987). Subband coding of video signals for packet switched networks. In *Proc. Visual Communications and Image Processing II, SPIE* 845: 446–456.

[20] D. H. Kelly (1971). Theory of flicker and transient responses. I, Uniform fields. *Journal Optical Society of America* 61(4): 537–546.

[21] D. H. Kelly (1972). Adaptation effects on spatio-temporal sine-wave thresholds. *Vision Research* 12: 89–101.

[22] J. J. Koenderink and A. J. van Doorn (1978). Detectability of power fluctuations of temporal visual noise. *Vision Research* 18: 191–195.

[23] J. O. Limb and C. B. Rubinstein (1978). On the design of quantizers for DPCM coders: A functional relationship between visibility, probability and masking. *IEEE Trans. on Communications* COM-26(5): 573–578.

[24] A. B. Lippman and W. Butera (1989). Coding image sequences for interactive retrieval. *Communications of the ACM* 32(7): 852–860.

[25] A. N. Netravali and B. Prasada (1977). Adaptive quantization of picture signals using spatial masking. *Proc. of the IEEE* 65(4): 536–548.

[26] A. N. Netravali and B. G. Haskell (1988). *Digital Pictures: Representation and Compression*. New York, London: Plenum Press.

[27] P. Pirsch (1980). A new predictor for DPCM coding of TV signals. In *Proc. International Conf. on Communications* (ICC 80), Seattle, Wash., 31.2.1–32.2.5.

[28] P. Pirsch (1981). Design of DPCM quantizers for video signals using subjective tests. *IEEE Trans. on Communications* COM-29(7): 990–1000.

[29] D. A. Robinson (1965). The mechanics of human smooth pursuit eye movement. *Journal of Physiology* (London) 180: 569–591.

[30] J. G. Robson (1966). Spatial and temporal contrast sensitivity functions of the visual system. *Journal of the Optical Society of America A* 56: 1141–1142.

[31] R. Schäfer (1980). Irrelevanz in Fernsehbildern. Final report no. TK 0075. Federal Ministry of Science and Technology, Germany. In German.

[32] R. Schäfer (1983). Design of adaptive and nonadaptive quantizers using subjective criteria. *Signal Processing* 5(4): 333–345.

[33] W. F. Schreiber and A. B . Lippman (1989). Reliable transmission of EDTV/HDTV signals in low-quality analog channels. *SMPTE Journal* 98: 5–13.

[34] W. F. Schreiber et. al., (1989). A compatible high-definition television system using the noise-margin method of hiding enhancement information. *SMPTE Journal* 98: 873–879.

[35] D. J. Sharma and A. N. Netravali (1977). Design of quantizers for DPCM coding of picture signals. *IEEE Trans. on Communications* COM-25(11): 1267–1274.

[36] D. K. Sharma (1978). Design of absolutely optimal quantizers for a wide class of distortion measures. *IEEE Trans. on Information Theory* IT-24: 693–702.

[37] G. J. Tonge (1982). Three-dimensional filters for television sampling. *IBA Report* no. 117/82, June.

[38] G. J. Tonge (1984). The television scanning process. *SMPTE Journal* 657–666.

[39] G. J. Tonge (1986). Time-sampled motion portrayal. In *Proc. Second International Conference on Image Processing and its Applications*. London: IEE Conf. Publications.

[40] A. B. Watson (1990). Perceptual-components architecture for digital video. *Journal of the Optical Society of America A* 7(10): 1943–1954.

[41] A. B. Watson (1979). Probability summation over time. *Vision Research* 19: 515–522.

[42] A. B. Watson, A. J. Ahumada, and J. Farell (1986). Window of visibility: Psychophysical theory of fidelity in time-sampled visual motion displays. *Journal of the Optical Society of America A* 3(3): 300–307.

[43] A. B. Watson (1987). Efficiency of an image code based on human vision. *Journal of the Optical Society of America A* 4(12): 2401–2417.

[44] G. Westheimer (1954). Eye movement responses to horizontally moving stimulus. *Arch. Ophthalmology* 52: 932–941.

[45] CCIR (1982). Method for the subjective assessment of the quality of television pictures. CCIR Rec. 500-2.

Index